PROCEEDINGS OF NATO
ADVANCED STUDY INSTITUTE
MENAGGIO, ITALY

The first NATO Advanced Study Institute on Artificial Intelligence and Heuristic Programming was held at Menaggio, Italy, in August 1970. The meeting was sponsored by the Scientific Affairs Division of NATO.

Artificial Intelligence
and Heuristic Programming

EDITORS : N.V.FINDLER : BERNARD MELTZER

American Elsevier Publishing Company, Inc.
New York   1971

Published in the United States by

AMERICAN ELSEVIER PUBLISHING COMPANY INC.

52 Vanderbilt Avenue

New York, New York 10017

International Standard Book Number 0-444-19597-1

Library of Congress

Catalog Card Number 71-164036

Preface

This volume consists of a series of articles based on the lectures given at the First Advanced Study Institute on Artificial Intelligence and Heuristic Programming, held at the Grand Hotel Victoria, Menaggio, Italy, from 3 to 15 August 1970.

The coverage was exceptionally wide in many senses: the topics ranged from extremely abstract accounts of parts of the field to concrete implementations and experiments; the material presented ranged from the tutorial type dealing with well-established results to accounts of research on the frontiers of our knowledge; and the participants, lecturers and students alike, were not only from many scientific disciplines, but also from many countries on both sides of the Atlantic.

This rich mixture resulted in exceptionally lively and illuminating discussions, both in the lecture room and, usually to the small hours of the morning, in the open-air *ristorantes* overlooking the lovely Lago di Como. New intellectual channels were opened up between different subjects, for example, the semantics of logic and the analysis of pictures. Alas, much of this – since it was not recorded – will have to be passed on by word of mouth; but there is little doubt that their effect will be seminal.

We wish to thank the Scientific Affairs Division of NATO for its generous funding and support of the enterprise; gratitude having been defined as 'a lively anticipation of favours to come', we may hope that this Institute will turn out to be the first of a series.

Our thanks are due also to the management of the Grand Hotel Victoria, and to Miss M. van den Berge for her indispensable services as secretary of the Institute.

N. V. FINDLER
B. MELTZER
Menaggio – Lago di Como
August 1970

Contents

THEOREM PROVING

Building deduction machines   3
   J.A.ROBINSON

Prolegomena to a theory of efficiency of proof procedures   15
   B.MELTZER

PROBLEM-ORIENTED LANGUAGES

Problem-solving compilers   37
   E.W.ELCOCK

A survey of seven projects using the same language   51
   N.V.FINDLER

PROBLEM SOLVING

Heuristic search : concepts and methods   81
   E.SANDEWALL

Formation and execution of plans by machine   101
   D.MICHIE

A general game-playing program   125
   J.PITRAT

INTEGRATED SYSTEMS

The frame problem in problem-solving systems   159
   B.RAPHAEL

NATURAL LANGUAGE AND PICTURE PROCESSING

Jigsaw heuristics and a language learning model   173
   R.K.LINDSAY

Natural language for instructional communication   191
   R.F.SIMMONS

Making computers understand natural language   199
   J.PALME

Picture-descriptions   245
   M.CLOWES

COGNITIVE STUDIES

Cognitive learning processes: An explication   261
   M.KOCHEN

Computer simulation of verbal learning and concept formation
(abstract only)   319
   L.W.GREGG

List of Contributors   320

Index   321

Theorem Proving

Building Deduction Machines

J.A.ROBINSON

In a *deduction problem*, it is to be determined whether a given *assumption A* logically implies a given *conclusion C*. A positive solution consists of showing that C follows from A; a negative solution, of showing that C does *not* follow from A.

We write: $A \rightarrow C$ for: C follows from A. And we will write: (A, C) for: the problem of determining whether $A \rightarrow C$.

A deduction machine is one which solves deduction problems. In order to build a deduction machine we must specify:

(1) the *input language*, in which the assumptions and conclusions are to be expressed;

(2) the *output language*, in which the solutions are to be formulated;

(3) the *deduction algorithm*, which for each problem computes the output from the input.

The deduction machine is then essentially any suitable computing device, programmed so as to execute the deduction algorithm.

DEFINITION OF 'FOLLOWS FROM'

No matter what language we are dealing with, the notion of logical consequence is essentially the same. There is a set of possible *interpretations* of the language, and, relative to each interpretation, each expression of the language *denotes* a particular object. As the interpretation varies, so, in general, does the object denoted by a given expression. In particular, the *sentences* of the language denote truth values (*true* or *false*), and a given sentence will in general denote *true* (that is, be true) in some interpretations and *false* in others. The details will of course depend on the language, but the broad picture is always along these lines.

Within this framework, what it means for one sentence C to 'follow logically from' another sentence A is simply that *there is no interpretation under which A is true and C is false*, within the class of interpretations which are being considered.

This being the definition of 'follows from', the problem of *detecting* whether $A \rightarrow C$ is simply a matter of detecting whether, within the class of all interpretations, there is one under which A is true and C is false.

4) *Theorem Proving*

So, viewed in this general way, a deduction problem is a *search* problem, the search space being the set of all interpretations.

A very simple illustration of this general idea is given by the language of *boolean forms*. A boolean form, or formula of the propositional calculus, is either a *boolean variable* p, q, r, and so on, or else is constructed from other boolean forms by one of several methods of construction: it may be, for example, the *negation* of a form A; the *conjunction* of a set of forms $A_1, \ldots, A_n$; the *conditional* $A \supset B$ of two forms A, B; and so on. The class of all interpretations in this case is simply the class of all *assignments of truth values* to the variables. Relative to each assignment, each form takes on a truth value, in the obvious way. And now we can say that one form C follows from another form A just in case there is no assignment in which A comes out true while C comes out false.

In this case, all deduction problems are computably solvable, by, for example, the method of truth tables. But even here, the search space is infinite (assuming, as is usual, that the language contains infinitely many variables); and the deduction algorithm depends on the fact that the search space can be structured in a suitably finitary fashion so that each problem involves only a finite amount of work.

In the general case, one cannot expect so easy a deduction algorithm. Indeed, the theorem of Church (1936) states that for all sufficiently rich languages there does not exist any deduction algorithm, if by this we mean an algorithm which solves *all* deduction problems for the language. However, there is a useful category of languages (which includes the so-called first-order predicate calculus) for which there exist algorithms which solve all *positively* solvable deduction problems. These algorithms will, in other words, detect the *presence* of the relation 'follows from' between two sentences of the language, but not, in general, its *absence*.

These 'semi-decision procedures' have the abstract character of a 'generate and test' computation. There is a sequence $D_1, D_2, \ldots$, in general infinite, of *candidate solutions*, which can be effectively generated. These are usually pieces of text in the output language, and when interpreted as meaningful items of discourse they read as tracts of deductive reasoning. Then there is an effective *criterion of correctness* which can be applied to each candidate solution in turn at the time it is generated, by virtue of which it can be computationally decided whether that candidate solution is in fact a solution. The deduction algorithm is simply the program which calls in the generator and the tester alternately until the tester detects a solution, if indeed a solution is ever generated in the time available.

These generalities apply, *mutatis mutandis*, to all tractable cases. Languages which do not even have a semi-decision procedure can scarcely be said to be 'mechanizable' at all. Of course one can still mechanically conduct searches of their semantic spaces, in some sense; but there is no longer any satisfactory theory of such searching, and one must presumably fall back on 'heuristic' rationalizations to justify one's design of the computation and one's expectations about its performance.

It is remarkable that in all of the semi-decision procedures of the generate-and-test variety there is essential use made of a certain 'compactness' phenomenon related to the growth of finitary tree structures. This phenomenon has come to be associated with the name of König (König 1926).

A *finitary* tree is one in which *no node has more than a finite number of immediate successors*. (It may well be that, throughout the tree, there is no upper bound on the number of immediate successors which a node might have, that is, it may be possible to find a node in the tree which has more than N immediate successors, where N is any number chosen in advance; even so, the tree is still finitary provided no one node has an actual infinity of immediate successors.)

The König phenomenon can be expressed in a variety of ways, one of which is the following: *if each branch of a finitary tree T eventually terminates, then T contains only finitely many nodes*.

The significance of the König phenomenon for deduction algorithms is that they frequently take the form of the construction of a finitary tree, about which it can be shown that *if* the input to the algorithm is a positively solvable problem *then* every branch of the tree must eventually terminate. Because of the König phenomenon, this then means that if the algorithm is applied to a positively solvable problem it will eventually halt. Since it can also be shown that for negatively solvable problems some branch of the tree must continue to grow indefinitely without ever terminating, this yields the complete justification of the claim that the process is a semi-decision procedure.

The finitary tree constructed by the algorithm can be viewed, intuitively, as the trace of a search of the whole semantic space (the set of all interpretations of the language concerned) by means of a series of successively finer and finer partitions of it into more and more (but always finitely many) subspaces. The search moves from one stage to the next by splitting up one of the current subspaces into finitely many parts; and the process is governed globally by a plan which guarantees that, for any point p in the space, there is at least one sequence of parts $P_1, P_2, \ldots$, taken from successive stages of the search which 'converges to p', in the sense that, first,

$$P_1 \supseteq P_2 \supseteq \ldots \quad \supseteq P_j \supseteq \ldots$$

and, second, for *any* set Q such that p is in Q, there is a number k such that $Q \supseteq P_k$.

At each stage of the search the finitely many subspaces of the current partition are each examined to determine *whether a possible counterexample might lie in that subspace*. (A counterexample for a problem (A, C) is an interpretation under which A is true and C false.) If it is found that *no* counterexample could lie in a particular subspace, that subspace is 'dead' and *is removed from the search*. Only 'live' subspaces are carried forward to the next stage, one of them being split as explained above.

This intuitive account is very general, and will take on its full significance only when superposed on a number of typical deduction algorithms, whose particular details might otherwise be confusing and apparently arbitrary.

It is accordingly proposed to consider next, in some detail, an actual deduction algorithm, which happens to embody most of the modern ideas and techniques which are at present in active use.

SIMPLE FIRST-ORDER LANGUAGES

A simple first-order language is determined by its *vocabulary*. A vocabulary is a set of symbols, each of which is classified as either a *variable*, a *function symbol*, or a *relation symbol*. Function symbols and relation symbols are also each assigned a non-negative integer as their *degree*.

For each vocabulary V the following sets of expressions are defined: *terms V, atoms V, clauses V*. The definitions are:

(1) each variable in V is in *terms V*;

(2) if f is a function symbol of degree n in V, and if $t_1, \ldots, t_n$ are all in *terms V*, then

$$f(t_1, \ldots, t_n)$$

is also in *terms V*;

(3) if R is a relation symbol of degree n in V, and if $t_1, \ldots, t_n$ are all in *terms V*, then

$$R(t_1, \ldots, t_n)$$

is in *atoms V*;

(4) if C is a finite set whose elements are all of the form $[A, W]$, where A is in *atoms V* and W is a truth value (that is, either *true* or *false*) then C is in *clauses V*.

(We often write a clause $\{[A_1, W_1], \ldots, [A_n, W_n]\}$ as $\left\{ \begin{matrix} u_1 & & u_n \\ A_1, & \ldots, & A_n \end{matrix} \right\}$, where u_j is a blank if $W_j = true$, and is a horizontal line if $W_j = false$. We also often omit the surrounding braces.)

SUBSTITUTIONS; INSTANCES; VARIANTS

A *substitution* is an operation

$$\theta = \{t_1/x_1, \ldots, t_n/x_n\}$$

performable on an expression to yield another expression. It is carried out by replacing each occurrence of x_j by an occurrence of t_j. The x_j are all variables, and the t_j are all terms. We write

$$E\theta$$

for the result of performing θ upon the expression E. E may be a term, an atom, or a clause. We say that $E\theta$ is an *instance* of E.

If two clauses P, Q are each instances of the other, then we say P is a *variant* of Q, and Q is a *variant* of P. For example, the following clauses are mutual variants:

$$P = \{R(x, y), \bar{K}(y, z), \bar{M}(z)\}$$
$$Q = \{R(u, x), \bar{K}(x, y), \bar{M}(y)\}$$

Since $\quad P = Q\{x/u, y/x, z/y\}$

and $\quad Q = P\{u/x, x/y, y/z\}$.

SEMANTICS FOR SIMPLE FIRST-ORDER LANGUAGES

If V is a vocabulary, then an *interpretation of V* is a mapping of the set *atoms V* into the set $\{true, false\}$. The intuitive idea behind this definition is that each term is taken to be an individual object; each function symbol f is taken to denote the function which yields (the term) $f(t_1, \ldots, t_n)$ when applied to the terms $t_1, \ldots, t_n$; and each relation symbol R is taken to denote the relation which, when applied to the terms $t_1, \ldots, t_n$, yields as value the truth value on to which the atom $R(t_1, \ldots, t_n)$ is mapped by the interpretation.

If H is an interpretation of V and C is in *clauses V* then we say that:

(1) C is *true in H* iff $HA = W$ for at least one $[A, W]$ in C;

(2) C is *always true in H* iff every instance of C over *terms V* is true in H.

The idea here is that each clause is interpreted as the universally quantified disjunction of its components, each component $[A, W]$ being interpreted as the *assertion* or *denial* of the atomic sentence A according as W is *true* or W is *false*. It can be seen from the definitions that the empty clause (written: $\square$) is always false in every interpretation.

SIMPLE DEDUCTION PROBLEMS

A simple deduction problem is given by a finite set K of clauses over some vocabulary V. The problem is to determine whether there exists an interpretation of V in which each clause in K is always true – or, what is the same, whether there is an interpretation of V in which each clause in K^* is true. By K^* we mean: the set of all *instances* of clauses in K.

It is quite straightforward (cf. Davis and Putnam 1960) to transform a deduction problem (A, C), given in the usual first-order predicate calculus, into an equivalent simple deduction problem K. The relationship between (A, C) and K is such that:

$$A \to C \text{ iff } K \text{ is unsatisfiable}$$

where: K is unsatisfiable *means* there is no interpretation in which each clause in K^* is true.

CONTRADICTIONS

We say that a (finite or infinite) set K of clauses is a *contradiction*, or is *contradictory*, iff there is no interpretation in which each clause in K is true. Note carefully the difference between K being a contradiction and K being unsatisfiable. Obviously we have

> K contradictory *implies* K unsatisfiable but not, in general, the converse.

When K is finite, it is *decidable* by computation whether or not K is contradictory. However, if K is infinite, the most we can say is that it is *semi-decidable* whether or not K is contradictory: that is, we can give an algorithm which will detect the *presence* of contradictoriness in K, but not necessarily its *absence*.

This is precisely how the König phenomenon enters into the theory of simple deduction problems. For it is an easy matter to show, by appeal to the König phenomenon, for all infinite sets K of clauses, that:

> *if K is contradictory then some finite subset of K is contradictory.*

On this last proposition rests all the theory of simple deduction problems. For to show that $A \to C$, one first obtains the equivalent K, and then systematically tests the finite subsets of K^* for contradictoriness; or performs some equivalent process such as is about to be described.

UNIFICATION

Efficient exploitation of the compactness phenomenon in simple first-order languages now depends heavily on a technique of computation which has come to be known as *unification*.

The *input* to a unification computation consists of
(1) a finite set P of expressions, each of which is either an atom or a term;
(2) a partition Q of P.

The objective of the computation is to determine whether or not there exists a substitution θ (and, if so, to construct one) which *unifies* Q in the sense that:

$$\text{if } X \underset{Q}{\equiv} Y \text{ then } X\theta = Y\theta$$

The unification computation is discussed in great detail in a number of readily available references (for example, Robinson 1965), and in particular is the subject of a paper being published simultaneously with these Proceedings, as part of the Sixth Edinburgh Machine Intelligence Workshop (Robinson 1971). Accordingly, no further details will be given here. We shall continue our discussion with the assumption that 'unifying substitutions' can always be quickly computed, given the partition to be unified, provided that the partition *is* unifiable; and that its lack of unifiability can be quickly detected, if the contrary is the case. This assumption is fully justified by the references cited.

LATENT CONTRADICTIONS

We have seen that it is decidable whether a finite set K of clauses is a contradiction, but only semidecidable whether it is unsatisfiable. There is an important intermediate property between contradictoriness and unsatisfiability, which is much 'closer' to unsatisfiability, and yet is still decidable. This is the property of being a *latent contradiction*.

We say that a set K of clauses is a *latent contradiction* iff there is a substitution θ such that $K\theta$ is a contradiction.

When K is finite, it is decidable whether K is a latent contradiction because one need only consider the various partitions Q of the set P of all atoms which appear in clauses of K, *modulo* which K is a contradiction. By

$$K \text{ is contradictory modulo } Q$$

we mean that for every interpretation H which satisfies

if $X \underset{Q}{\equiv} Y$ then $HX = HY$

for all atoms X, Y in P, at least one clause in K is false in H.

Such partitions are called *deadly* partitions for K.

If any of the deadly partitions for K is also unifiable, with θ as unifying substitution, then it is easy to see that $K\theta$ is contradictory. While if, for some θ, $K\theta$ is contradictory, then the partition Q defined by

$$X \underset{Q}{\equiv} Y \text{ iff } X\theta = Y\theta$$

for all X, Y in P is clearly unifiable and deadly.

Thus *it is a finite computation to decide whether K is a latent contradiction, and if so, to compute a θ such that $K\theta$ is an actual contradiction.*

It is an open question how *efficient* the latent contradiction detector can be made. This is a very good research topic in combinatorial computing.

ELABORATIONS

Given the capability of detecting latent contradictions, we now consider the

B

problem of detecting by computation the unsatisfiability of a finite set K of clauses.

A set M of clauses will be called an *elaboration* of K if it consists of finitely many clauses, each one of which is a variant of some clause in K, and no two of which have any variables in common.

It is an easy consequence of our earlier definitions and results that:

> K *is unsatisfiable*
>
> *iff*
>
> *some elaboration of K*
> *is a latent contradiction.*

We can classify the elaborations of K by the number of variants they contain of each clause in K. Suppose $K = \{K_1, \ldots, K_n\}$; then the vector $\alpha = (\alpha_1, \ldots \alpha_n)$ whose jth component is the number α_j of variants of the clause K_j which are in the elaboration M will be called the *extent* of M. If α is the extent of M, and β of N, we write $\alpha \leqslant \beta$ to mean that $\alpha_j \leqslant \beta_j$ for $j = 1, \ldots, n$. Two elaborations with the same extent are equivalent, for our purposes, since either *both* of them, or *neither* of them, will be latent contradictions.

The various extents correspond to the integral lattice points of the principal orthant of an n-dimensional euclidean space, a correspondence which may assist the imagination in studying the question of searching the 'elaboration space' of a set of clauses.

From the definition of a contradiction, it is clear that if the elaboration M is a latent contradiction then every elaboration N such that

> *extent of M* $\leqslant$ *extent of N*

will also be a latent contradiction.

The overall computation thus takes the form of a search through the space of extent-vectors, armed with the decision algorithm which, on being given the extent-vector α as input, will determine whether an elaboration of extent α (of the set of clauses under examination) is a latent contradiction. It is an important and interesting open problem to find how best to organize this search. One particular train of ideas about it leads to the notion of *resolution*.

RESOLUTION

The resolution method (Robinson 1965) seeks to show that a finite set K of clauses is unsatisfiable by adding further clauses to K, according to a principle to be explained in a moment, until at last it is possible to add, in accordance with that principle, the *empty* clause.

The principle is this: *to a set S of clauses one may add a clause C, provided that C is a resolvent of two clauses in S.*

One says that C is a *resolvent* of clauses A and B when the following is true:

(1) A includes a nonempty subset P, and B includes a nonempty subset N, of the respective forms:

$$P = \{[A_1, true], \ldots, [A_p, true]\}$$
$$N = \{[B_1, false], \ldots, [B_q, false]\};$$

(2) The set $\{A_1, \ldots, A_p, B_1, \ldots, B_q\}$ is unifiable (that is, the partition Q in which it is the only part, is unifiable);

(3) C is $(A - P)\theta \cup (B - N)\theta$, where θ is the substitution computed by the unification algorithm for the input Q;

(4) A and B have no variables in common.

(By extension, C is said to be a resolvent of A' and B', whenever A' and B' are, respectively, variants of A and B, and C is a resolvent of A and B.)

One also speaks of *deducing* clauses by resolution. Indeed, if C is a resolvent of A and B then C is in fact a logical consequence of A and B.

The key properties of resolution are:

(1) a finite set of clauses has only finitely many different resolvents, up to within variants;

(2) a set K of clauses is unsatisfiable iff the empty clause is deducible from K by resolution.

It is possible to devise various constraints on the principle of adding resolvents to a set of clauses, whereby fewer of the resolvents are eligible for such addition, without sacrificing the second (or, of course, the first) of these two key properties. For example, the clause A can be required to contain *no* pairs $[L, W]$ in which W is *false*.

A deduction algorithm involving resolution then consists essentially of a method for deciding, given a set S of clauses, which one from among the resolvents *eligible* for addition to S should be *selected* for addition to S, and of a main routine which iterates this decision until the empty clause becomes eligible for addition.

There has been considerable effort devoted, in the last several years, to the design of good deduction algorithms using resolution (cf. Kowalski 1969). It would probably be worth while to devote a comparable effort to developing efficient techniques for detecting latent contradictions, using other notions. While it may be the case that resolution is in some sense the most efficient framework for discovering latent contradictions, it is not at present possible to give a proof of this, or even to give a satisfactory explanation of what is meant by it. The question of *efficiency* in deduction machines remains a most elusive one: how to define it, in the first place, and how to get it, in the second place, are two important open problems. Perhaps there are phenomena, as yet unknown, which put barriers of an intrinsic theoretical kind across the path towards really efficient deduction machines. The theory of computational complexity, still in its infancy, may have something eventually to say about this, but at present affords no enlightenment.

Very little is known about building deduction machines for languages other than first-order languages, beyond the generalities outlined at the beginning of this paper. Work is at present in progress (Robinson 1969) to investigate the language of *simple type theory* (or 'predicate calculus of order omega') and also the type-free language, based on the ideas of application and abstraction, which has come to be known as the *lambda-calculus*. The problems which arise are in part those which have been studied for several generations already within the field of mathematical logic; but there are also problems of a more purely computational character. For instance it suffices, in most cases, for a logician's purposes, to show that a procedure 'eventually' terminates after 'only' finitely much computing – that is, to show that an upper bound *exists* to the amount of work necessary for whatever the task under consideration may be. But for the 'epistemological engineer' this is not good enough. He needs to have information about the *size* of the upper bound, and he needs to be able to devise ways of performing the task which consume far less resources than those required by the often drastically inefficient processes which are all that are needed for existence proofs. Moreover the epistemological engineer is vitally interested in *lower* bounds on the amount of work required to carry out the tasks under consideration, since it is with these that he must compare the amounts of work actually expended by his machines, in order to measure their efficiency.

BIBLIOGRAPHY

Church, A. (1936)   A note on the *entscheidungs* problem. *J. symbolic Logic*, **1**, 40–1, 101–2.

Davis, M. & Putnam, H. (1960) A computing procedure for quantification theory. *J. Ass. comput. Mach.*, **7**, 201–15.

Guard, J., *et al.* (1969) Semi-automated mathematics. *J. Ass. comput. Mach.*, **16**, 49–62.

Henkin, L. (1950) Completeness in the theory of types. *J. symbolic Logic*, **15**, 81–91.

Herbrand, J. (1930) Researches into the theory of demonstration. (Chapter 5, translated from the original French, of Herbrand's PhD thesis.) In: *From Frege to Godel: a source book in mathematical logic* (ed. van Heijenoort, J.). Cambridge, Mass: Harvard University Press, 1967.

König, D. (1926) Sur les correspondences multivoques des ensembles. *Fundamenta Mathematicae*, **8**, 114–34.

Kowalski, R. (1969)   Search strategies for theorem proving. *Machine Intelligence 5*, pp. 181–201 (eds Meltzer, B. & Michie, D.). Edinburgh: Edinburgh University Press.

Prawitz, D. (1960)   An improved proof procedure. *Theoria*, **26**, 102–39.

Robinson, J. A. (1963)   Theorem proving on the computer. *J. Ass. comput. Mach.*, **10**, 163–74.

Robinson, J. A. (1965)   A machine-oriented logic based on the resolution principle. *J. Ass. comput. Mach.*, **12**, 23–41.

Robinson, J. A. (1969)   Mechanizing higher order logic. *Machine Intelligence 4*, pp. 151–70 (eds Meltzer B. & Michie, D.). Edinburgh: Edinburgh University Press.

Robinson, J. A. (1971) Computational logic: the unification computation. *Machine Intelligence 6*, pp. 63–72 (eds Meltzer B. & Michie, D.). Edinburgh: Edinburgh University Press.

Smullyan, R. M. (1968) *First order logic*. Berlin: Springer-Verlag.

Prolegomena to a Theory of Efficiency of Proof Procedures

B.MELTZER

INTRODUCTION

The key question in the development of automatic proof procedures is efficiency, but it is rather surprising how little serious discussion and analysis of it there has been in the now quite voluminous literature of the subject. It is true that lip service is paid to its importance, when sometimes a new inference system or a new 'strategy' is proposed and recommended for its greater 'efficiency' or 'power'; but the evidence for the claim seldom will stand up to even cursory examination, being based on perhaps one or two examples and then often confusing the simplicity of a proof with the ease of finding it. In this field there has also been a great deal of discussion of the relative merits of 'complete' or 'incomplete' or 'heuristic' procedures, often without too clear notions of what these are and certainly seldom with any serious consideration of how their different characteristics affect their effectiveness in finding proofs.

This state of affairs is understandable, since questions of this kind are by no means easy to handle in a fruitful way. It may need to be tackled from a number of points of view before the best is found. In the lectures I shall present an approach due to Dr R. Kowalski. The presentation is based on his recently completed thesis, and its fruitfulness appears to be confirmed by work by him and Mr D. Kuehner on the design of a proof procedure, which has taken place since the work reported in the thesis. Fuller accounts of all these matters will be published elsewhere.

ILLUSTRATIVE EXAMPLES

Consider the following 'toy' problem: From the three axioms

1. $P(a, b)$
2. $(x)(Ez)(y)[P(x, y) \supset P(z, y)]$
3. $(x)(y)[P(x, y) \supset Q(y)]$

deduce $Q(b)$.

An *informal* proof is obvious. From (3) infer the special instance

$$P(a, b) \supset Q(b)$$

and then $Q(b)$ follows from (1). The irrelevance of (2) is immediately obvious, and, in fact, one could hardly conceive of a more efficient proof.

The *formal* methods used or proposed for automatic theorem-proving generally transform the problem into a different representation, one in which the desired conclusion is not deduced but its negation refuted (*reductio ad absurdum*), and all sentences are in the standard form of *clauses*. The problem now is to show the unsatisfiability of the following set of clauses:

1. $P(a, b)$
2. $\bar{P}(x, y) \, P(f(x), y)$
3. $\bar{P}(x, y) \, Q(y)$
4. $\bar{Q}(b)$

The method of *unifiable partitions*, described in Professor Robinson's lectures at the Institute, would examine the possible unifiable partitions of all the atoms in these clauses (plus renamed replicas of them, in the general case), and would in particular discover that the following partition with the indicated substitutions

$$\{P(a, b) \text{ from } (1), P(x, y) \text{ from } (3)\} \quad \text{subst: } \{a/x, b/y\}$$
$$\{Q(y) \text{ from } (3), Q(b) \text{ from } (4)\} \quad \text{subst: } \{b/y\}$$
$$\{P(x, y) \text{ from } (2)\} \quad \text{subst: null}$$
$$\{P(f(x), y) \text{ from } (2)\} \quad \text{subst: null}$$

yields the following Boolean set, which can be shown by some algorithm (for example, truth-tables) to be contradictory:

$$P(a, b)$$
$$\bar{P}(x, y) \, P(f(x), y)$$
$$\bar{P}(a, b) \, Q(b)$$
$$\bar{Q}(b)$$

Clearly, in this form, the method is highly inefficient, and this would become even more striking if the proof had required the use of more replicas of the input clauses.

The formal methods currently used in automatic theorem-provers, while based on the use of unifying substitutions, do not effect partitions, but implement *inference systems*.

Unrestricted resolution, applied to our example yields the following proof:

5. $P(f(a), b)$
6. $\bar{P}(x, y) \, P(f(f(x)), y)$ } Level 1
7. $Q(b)$
8. $\bar{P}(x, y) \, Q(y)$
9. $\bar{P}(x, b)$

17. $\square$ } Level 2

If we look upon the input set of clauses as being of level 0, their possible resolvents make up the set of level 1, all resolvents which can be formed using at least one clause of level 1 make up the set of level 2, and so on. This generation of clauses level by level is referred to as 'level saturation'. Here (where not all the level 2 clauses are exhibited), a large number of irrelevant and redundant clauses are generated before the first empty one. Note the strategy's failure to notice, after generation of clause (7), that a contradiction, by resolution with (4), was available.

In the hope of generating less irrelevant clauses, many *refinements* of resolution have been proposed and programmed, most of them retaining the former's apparently attractive characteristic of logical completeness. Two examples follow.

The set-of-support refinement is suggested by the intuition that we are not really interested in drawing large numbers of logical inferences from the input set but only in proving a particular theorem – in this case $Q(b)$. In particular, resolvents which derive only from the axioms of the theory would possibly be irrelevant. Accordingly, in this procedure, only such resolvents are produced whose ancestry contains the negation of the theorem to be proved. In our toy example this is clause (4), $\overline{Q}(b)$, and the proof, using level saturation, reads:

5. $\overline{P}(x, b)$ Level 1
6. $\square$ Level 2

which is highly efficient.

Another refinement of resolution is P_1-*deduction*, in which a resolution is carried out only if one of the parents consists entirely of un-negated atoms. With level saturation this gives the following proof:

5. $P(f(a), b)$ $\left.\right\}$ Level 1
6. $Q(b)$

7. $P(f(f(a)), b)$ $\left.\right\}$ Level 2
8. $Q(b)$
9. $\square$

This proof reveals two kinds of inefficiency: the irrelevance of the clauses (5) and (7), and the redundancy of clause (8).

It is clear that the performance of these inference systems on the given example could alter if the generation of sentences followed some scheme other than 'level saturation'. This scheme is essentially what is usually referred to as a 'breadth-first' search strategy; one might also use 'depth-first' methods. The method above, which has been implemented in a number of theorem-proving programmes, is the 'two-pointer' scheme, which is used in some examples referred to later and works as follows: Let $C_1 C_2 \ldots \ldots C_i \ldots C_j \ldots$

be the 'trace' of the search, that is, the sequence of clauses in the order in which they are generated, an initial subsequence of it being the input set. Two pointers, A and B, point to the next two clauses whose resolution is to be attempted – any resulting resolvents being added to the end of the sequence. Both pointers start at C_1, thereafter A moves one step to the right at a time, after each of which B goes back to C_1, and moves progressively step by step to the right until it reaches A.

THE NOTION OF A PROOF PROCEDURE

The considerations developed in this paper will be about proof procedures of the inference type, and therefore not immediately applicable to those of 'semantic' type, such as the method of truth-tables or the method of unifiable partitions which was one of those illustrated in the previous section. But the ideas behind the treatment of efficiency here are probably sufficiently general to be amenable to application to such procedures too.

A *proof procedure P* consists of two parts: an inference system and a search strategy. We write

$$P = (I, \Sigma)$$

where I denotes an *inference system*, Σ a *search strategy*.

The inference system I may be, for instance, a set of axioms and a set of inference rules. It may have no axioms but be a function of a set of input sentences. Most of our considerations will be applicable to general inference systems, but to fix ideas we shall often refer to systems of the latter kind. Denote the set of input sentences by S_0 – in modern theorem-provers these will usually be clauses. So we write

$$I = I(S_0)$$

For a given inference system the set of inference rules determines a *search space* S^*, namely, all sentences in the language which are derivable by the rules, whether ultimately from axioms or from S_0. Derivations constructible by means of the rules are said to be *admissible* for I.

The search strategy Σ is an algorithm for generating derivations admissible for I in order eventually to generate a proof of a theorem. Σ induces an ordering of occurrences of sentences from S^*.

One must carefully distinguish an admissible derivation of a sentence C from the sequence of sentences generated by Σ before obtaining a first proof of C. Such an admissible derivation contains only sentences necessary for the proof of C. (Examples of search strategies currently used are level saturation, Wos and Robinson's unit preference and Kowalski's diagonal search.)

Proof procedures $P = (I, \Sigma)$ can often be analyzed in more than one way into an inference system and a search strategy. For example, the method of set-of-support introduced by Wos and Robinson can be looked upon either as a restricted inference rule determining a restricted search space, or as unrestricted resolution with a restricted search strategy. The former seems more natural.

THE DIFFERENT NOTIONS OF COMPLETENESS

The above analysis shows there are three quite different notions of completeness, one for inference systems, one for search strategies, and one for proof procedures, which are often confused by workers in artificial intelligence.

The completeness of an *inference system* is a purely logical notion. An inference system I is deduction-complete *for a set of sentences S*, if whenever S_0 logically implies $C \in S$, there is a derivation of C from S_0 which is admissible for I. Usually S is the set of all sentences constructible in the language of I. The inference systems used in most contemporary theorem-provers are not deduction-complete, but often have the property of refutation-completeness. An inference system I is refutation-complete if whenever S_0 logically implies a contradiction there is an admissible derivation of an effectively recognizable contradiction.

A *search strategy* Σ is complete for an inference system I, if Σ will eventually generate all derivations admissible for I. This is a purely combinatorial notion. It is obvious that Σ may be complete or incomplete independently of whether I is complete.

A *proof procedure* $P = (I(S_0), \Sigma)$ is deduction-complete *for a set of sentences S*, if whenever S_0 implies a sentence $C \in S$ then Σ eventually generates an admissible derivation of C. A similar definition applies to refutation-completeness.

Note that a proof procedure P can be complete even when Σ is incomplete for the inference system; this is illustrated by the example, previously given, of unrestricted resolution with Σ incorporating set-of-support restrictions. On the other hand, if P is complete, the inference system I must be too.

Note also that a proof procedure incomplete for S may be complete for some decidable proper subset of S. In fact, any effective proof procedure will always be complete for some set of sentences.

The original completeness proofs published in the literature for unrestricted, hyper-, clash, and AM-clash resolution were stated for proof procedures, where Σ could be interpreted as complete level saturation search. But the original proofs for set-of-support, merging, and linear resolution were stated for inference systems I.

Kowalski in his thesis takes the view that in the preferred analysis of a proof procedure $P = (I, \Sigma)$, I should incorporate the 'logical' and Σ the 'heuristic' restrictions, although it is not obvious how to define this distinction. So, for example, in the case already mentioned of set-of-support resolution, one would incorporate the set-of-support restrictions in I and thereby make it feasible for Σ to be complete, which would not have been possible if I had been unrestricted resolution.

COMPLEXITY AND DIFFICULTY OF PROOFS

When people engage in attempts to prove mathematical theorems there is no definite correlation between the simplicity or complexity of the proof found and the ease or difficulty of finding it. It may require a lot of effort, along fruitless paths, to find a transparently simple proof, and on the other hand a long but straightforward combinatorial demonstration may require relatively little effort because of the absence of errant by-paths.

There are various ways one might think of for measuring the *complexity* of informal proof, such as: number of sentences used, number of distinct occurrences of symbols used, or a weighted combination of these two. Similar measures could be used for machine proofs, though in resolution procedures it has been customary to use 'level' or, in other words, the length of the longest branch of the proof tree; the latter can be a highly unrealistic measure since it puts a premium on 'bushy' proof-trees. However, one condition that should clearly be insisted on in any measure of complexity is that any sub-derivation of a derivation should have a complexity less than or equal to that of the derivation itself.

Difficulty should be measured by the total effort, in some sense, needed to obtain a first proof, including work done on unsuccessful attempts. For informal proofs one might think of measures of the following kind: total time, total number of sentences, or total number of symbols constructed before obtaining a first proof; similarly for machine proofs, though number of sentences is a better measure than total time, since it enables comparisons to be made between informal and formal theorem-provers independent of computer implementation.

EFFICIENCY OF PROOF PROCEDURES

If numbers of sentences are used as measures for difficulty and complexity one may be inclined to define efficiency to be the following ratio: number of sentences in first proof, divided by number of sentences generated in finding that proof. But this does not really capture the notion of the efficiency of the *proof procedure* as distinct from the search strategy. For even if this ratio equals unity for some theorem, the proof itself may be so complex that the difficulty (numbers of sentences generated) is much greater than what can be achieved by informal methods.

Of two proof procedures, one P_1 must be accounted more efficient than another P_2 when the number of sentences generated before a first proof is less for it. It is reasonable to postulate some informal proof method $P*$ which is to be the 'ideal' for comparisons of efficiency; it may be assumed that $P*$ is never less efficient than any formal method P, for in particular $P*$ can be assumed to be intelligent enough to be capable of employing the methods of P.

If then we were to demand of a proof procedure P that for a set of sentences S its formal difficulties are to coincide with the informal difficulties, this might be interpreted in one of the following ways:

For all theorems in S

(a) difficulties for P and $P*$ are equal;

(b) the difficulties are to differ at most by some given ϵ; or

(c) the average difference in difficulty $\leqslant \epsilon$.

It is true that in general these tests are not effective, and also that $P*$ is not an absolute standard of efficiency but relative to variable standards of human performance. But the value of these notions depends upon their utility for founding a theory of efficiency.

Given a proof procedure $P = (I, \Sigma)$, one can immediately point to some of the important factors affecting its efficiency. For example, if the inference system I admits – for a given theorem – no proofs containing fewer than n sentences then n is a lower bound on the difficulty of proving the theorem by means of P; thus an earlier proof may have been possible if I had been less restrictive. On the other hand, a less restrictive I may increase the numbers and kinds of redundant and irrelevant derivations admitted by I, so increasing difficulties. Some of these factors will be discussed below.

As well as proof procedures P, search strategies Σ admit the notion of efficiency (though inference systems I do not). A search strategy Σ_1 is more efficient than Σ_2, when Σ_1 generates fewer derivations than does Σ_2 before completion of first proof.

$P = (I, \Sigma)$ can be hopelessly inefficient even when Σ is most efficient for I, as in the example of an inordinately complex proof cited at the beginning of this section. On the other hand, while efficient search strategies cannot guarantee efficient proof procedures, the latter can be rendered intolerably inefficient by employing an inefficient Σ; for example, Σ might be incomplete, generating a potentially infinite set of irrelevant derivations; or, Σ might be complete but delay generation of the first proof beyond some tolerance limit.

Is there then any general requirement that should be imposed on search strategies? Dr Kowalski in his thesis has proposed and used the following one:

'Search strategies should attempt to generate simpler before more complex proofs.'

The main justification for this principle is that it has enabled some progress to be made in the theory of efficiency and its applications. But one may also argue in its favour that, within constraints imposed by logical considerations, mathematicians, all else being equal, seek to find simpler before more complicated proofs. Another, probably less cogent, consideration is the following: since in general the inference systems I used in automatic proof will not be deduction-complete, it is inevitable that simple proofs will often be inadmissible; this handicap is to some extent mitigated by employing search strategies with the above property.

The distinction that has been developed here between proof procedures and search strategies should help to resolve some of the long-standing controversy about whether one should use 'complete' or 'heuristic' methods. For it gives rise to a division of labour between (a) logical studies of inference systems, and (b) studies of the operational research and AI type of search strategies. The latter would include the use of learning, analogy, induction, and other heuristic techniques.

DELETION RULES IN RESOLUTION PROCEDURES

We apply some of the notions developed to a discussion of certain inference-related rules like deletion of variants or, more generally, subsumed clauses in resolution procedures.

These rules can be defined only in the context of search strategies. For, one cannot operationally specify the requirement that subsumed clauses do not occur within a refutation D of an initial set of clauses S_0, without referring to the subsuming clauses which themselves need not occur either in D or S_0.

Both the completeness and efficiency of deleting subsumed clauses depend upon the sequence in which the search strategy generates resolvents. A deletion rule R for a proof procedure P is complete *relative to P*, if P employing R generates a proof of a theorem whenever P, without R, generates a proof of the same theorem. Below are two examples showing, within the context of a particular search strategy, how completeness in one case and efficiency in the other may be adversely affected by the form of the deletion rule.

In the context of the 'two-pointer' search strategy described at the end of the second section, suppose we have the following deletion rule: Let C_r occur before the just generated C_s in the trace ($r < s$), and let a subsumption relation hold between them. If C_r properly subsumes C_s, delete C_s; if C_s properly subsumes C_r, delete C_r; and if they both subsume each other (the improper case), delete C_r. Then it is easily seen that the following unsatisfiable set of four clauses of the 'toy' example of the second section:

1. $P(a, b)$
2. $\bar{P}(x, y) \, P(f(x), y)$
3. $\bar{P}(x, y) \, Q(y)$
4. $\bar{Q}(b)$

cannot be refuted by P_1-resolution (which is complete) with this search strategy and deletion rule, for the next clauses in the trace are:

5. $P(f(a), b)$
6. $Q(b)$ deleted
7. $P(f(f(a)), b)$
8. $Q(b)$ deleted
9. $P(f(f(f(a))), b)$
10. $Q(b)$

and so on. Every other clause from (6) onwards is $\{Q(b)\}$, but in due course gets deleted before it has a chance of being resolved with (4) to generate the refutation.

If however the deletion rule is modified so that in the improper case, that is, when C_r and C_s mutually subsume each other, it is C_s that is deleted and not C_r, then the refutation goes through. *This* deletion rule Kowalski terms *simple deletion* and in fact shows for most resolution systems I and strategies Σ, it is complete.

But simple deletion, though it may be complete, may delay proof and contribute to inefficiency. Consider the following unsatisfiable set of five clauses:

1. $G(y) \, P(y)$
2. $\bar{G}(f(x))$
3. $P(f(a))$
4. $\bar{P}(f(b)) \, P(a)$
5. $\bar{P}(f(a))$.

If ordinary binary resolution is used, with the two-pointer search strategy and *no* deletion rule, the following clauses will be generated and no more:

6. $P(f(x))$
7. $G(f(b)) \, P(a)$
8. $G(f(a))$
9. $\square$
10. $P(a)$
11. $\square$
12. $P(a)$
13. $\square$

If now simple deletion is used, (3) will be deleted, (9) will not be generated, and the first generation of the empty clause will occur only at (11), thus delaying refutation.

Kowalski gives instructive examples and some general theorems on relative completeness and efficiency of deleting tautologies and variants as well as subsumed clauses.

REDUNDANT AND IRRELEVANT INFERENCES

Pure redundancy occurs when a proof procedure generates distinct derivations of the same sentence C before the first proof. But other kinds are also possible, for example – in some resolution contexts – when derivations of C^1 and C occur with C^1 subsuming C.

An irrelevant derivation is one which for reasons other than redundancy is not necessary for construction of the proof. There is of course a close connection between these two phenomena. If a redundant sentence is eliminated, this generally means also elimination of many irrelevant derivations in which this clause would otherwise have participated.

A good deal of the early progress in automatic theorem-proving can be interpreted as the elimination of certain kinds of redundancies. The representation of logical formulae as *sets* of Skolemized clauses, which themselves are *sets* of literals, at one stroke gets rid of possible redundancies caused in other systems by explicit rules (or axioms) governing, for example,

double negation
commutativity of disjunction and conjunction
associativity of disjunction and conjunction
idempotency of disjunction
renaming of bound variables
vacuous quantifiers
interchanging adjacent quantifiers of same type
use of existential quantifiers.

The next most significant advance was Prawitz's procedure for restricting instantiation of matrix clauses over the Herbrand universe. This improved efficiency by eliminating redundancies without complicating proofs. And in Robinson's resolution procedure the unification algorithm eliminates redundancy by omitting infinitely many ground derivations lifted by single general derivations.

Kowalski in his thesis has obtained some firm results on redundancy and irrelevant derivations, often related to results on proof complexity, for various procedures such as unit preference, marked factoring, decomposed hyper-resolution, M-clashes, and so on. Generally speaking, redundant and irrelevant derivations may be eliminated either by prohibition as in some of these procedures, or by specific deletion rules of the kind discussed in the previous section. But an inference system which cuts out many redundant and irrelevant derivations may still not be made efficient thereby, *if* the effect is to generate proofs of great formal complexity. To discuss this question, it is useful to use the notion of a *refinement*.

An inference system I^1 is a *refinement* of an inference system I, when
$$S^{1*} \subset S^*,$$
that is, the search space of I^1 is properly contained in that of I. For example, set-of-support resolution is a refinement of unrestricted binary resolution.

It can then be seen that if I^1 is a refinement of I, (I^1, Σ) may be less efficient than (I, Σ) if I^1 does not admit the first proof obtained by Σ which is admissible for I. So, under the assumption that Σ generates simpler before more complex proofs, $P^1 = (I^1, \Sigma)$ is more efficient than $P = (I, \Sigma)$ when I^1 admits the simplest proof admitted by I; for in that case those derivations generated by P 'outside' P^1 are irrelevancies and redundancies not admitted by I^1.

But (I^1, Σ) can be more efficient than (I, Σ) *even* when I^1 eliminates simplest proofs. For example, suppose Σ is a level saturation strategy and we assume for simplicity that the proof procedure stops at completion of a level. Let $d(N)$ be the number of sentences generated by (I, Σ) up to and including level N, and d^1 the corresponding function for (I^1, Σ). Then if the former's first proof occurs at level N, while the latter's occurs only at a level $N^1 > N$, the latter will be more efficient if only $d^1(N^1) < d(N)$. It is interesting that estimates of
$$r(N) = \frac{d^1(N)}{d(N)}$$
can sometimes be made by comparing derivations admissible for I and I^1. And bounds on the difference between N and N^1 (as a function of S_0) can often be extracted from completeness proofs for I^1 relative to I.

The situation as regards refinements can be summed up as follows: If I^1 refines I and Σ generates simpler before more complex proofs then the greater the number of derivations eliminated and the simpler the proofs admitted by I^1, the more efficient is (I^1, Σ) than (I, Σ). Refinements often over-complicate proofs, while their reverse, extensions, often introduce too many irrelevancies and redundancies. The latter problem is especially acute for inference systems employing higher-order logic or first-order logic with axiom schemata. Gould's negative results show for example that there is no algorithm for eliminating in higher-order logic the kind of irrelevancies eliminated by the unification algorithm in first-order logic. Darlington's '*f*-matching' is an attempt to do something like this for axiom schemata in first-order logic.

THE NOTION OF POWER OF AN INFERENCE SYSTEM

This notion, which has often been used in discussion of proof procedures, may be quantified as follows: I is more powerful than I^1 when the simplest proof admitted by I is simpler than the simplest proof admitted by I^1 for the same theorem. That this notion is not of great significance is evidenced by the fact that among resolution systems unrestricted resolution is the most powerful (though not uniquely so). In fact, in general, an inference system I is never less powerful than another I^1 if I extends I^1. Gödel's results on the reduction of lengths of proofs due to extending one's logic by one order may be a pointer to interesting applications in the future.

IMPROVEMENT OF EFFICIENCY

If one accepts the general principle, proposed above, that difficulties of formally generated first proofs should tend towards those of informally obtained first proofs, one may propose the following guidelines for design of efficient proof procedures $P = (I, \Sigma)$:

(1) Complexities of first proofs should also approximate those of informal proofs.

(2) I should restrict as much as possible admissibility of both redundant derivations and derivations irrelevant to a simplest proof.

(3) Σ should generate simpler before more complex proofs.

(4) Σ should generate derivations in a selective order determined by intelligent estimates of their relevance to a simplest proof.

It will be noticed that no requirements on completeness, whether of inference system or of search strategy, are listed above. The relevance of such requirements to attaining efficiency will be discussed in the next section.

It is desirable that formal complexities of proofs should approximate – they are unlikely to be less than – those of informally obtained first proofs of the same theorems, otherwise difficulties will also tend to be much larger.

The requirement (2) above suggests research into the construction of refinements of inference systems designed to eliminate as many redundancies as possible while still retaining simplest proofs – one would aim at methods of recognizing redundancies before rather than after their generation.

The requirement (4) highlights the need to simulate intelligent informal methods of finding proofs. In this connection, Kowalski has formalized the theorem-proving problem in a way which generalizes the path-finding problem for graphs, and so made available methods using heuristic estimates of costs of goal attainment like those studied by Hart-Nilsson-Raphael and Pohl.

Since informally obtained first proofs of theorems are often, and probably usually, more complex than later proofs, the first proof generated by an ideally efficient (I, Σ) is likely to be more complex than the simplest proof theoretically possible for a given theorem. This suggests the possibility of improving efficiency by appropriate choice of refinements. It also suggests looking for schemes to obtain simplest proofs of theorems after generating the more complex *and more efficiently obtained* first proofs admissible for refinements. One such method, for resolution type procedures, is the following: Suppose I^1 is a refinement of I, and (I^1, Σ) is more efficient than (I, Σ). Let D^1 and D be the simplest respective refutations, so that D^1 is more complex than D. Now although D^1 may not lift a ground refutation it is easy to construct both a ground refutation D_0 and a modification (which Kowalski terms a 'contraction') D_1 of D^1, which is a refutation of S_0 and lifts D_0. If S_0^1 is the set of initial (ground) clauses of D_0, Σ applied to $I(S_0^1)$ will generate a simplest refutation D_2 of S_0^1. If D_2 be now 'lifted' to the general level, a refutation D_3 will be produced which is simpler than D^1, and either identical with or of a complexity equivalent to that of D.

COMPLETENESS, INCOMPLETENESS, AND EFFICIENCY

Completeness and efficiency are always to be evaluated relative to the set of sentences S within which a proof procedure P is expected to prove theorems. If we denote by S^* the set of all sentences, we assume that S and S^*-S can be effectively distinguished from each other. It may be noted again that there is always some subset of S^* for which P is complete, but this subset need not be recursive.

All P, whether complete or incomplete, are limited in practice by the amount of effort available for generating a proof of a given theorem. So if P fails to find a proof, there are three possibilities:

(1) Theorem is not valid.

(2) Theorem is valid but cannot be proved with effort available.

(3) Theorem is valid but unprovable by P even with *unlimited* effort.

So complete and incomplete procedures differ only as regards (3).

Referring again to the principle that for efficient P formal difficulties should tend towards informal difficulties of first proofs of theorems, we note that *this can be evaluated independently of P's completeness or incompleteness*. So when a best (most efficient) proof procedure fails to obtain a proof of a given theorem within given limitations of effort available, it may be inferred that the theorem is too difficult to be proved by any good proof procedure within the same limitations. Thus an incomplete P^1 can be superior to a complete P. P may fail to prove even with considerable but not unlimited effort theorems which can be proved informally with less difficulty. Or, P^1 may because of its incompleteness be incapable of proving only informally difficult theorems, which are in any case too difficult to be proved by any efficient proof procedure within the bounds of effort available.

What matters for efficiency is not the number of times an incomplete procedure P^1 fails to prove theorems which are theoretically unprovable for it, *but* the number of times it fails to prove theorems informally provable with less effort than that it has unsuccessfully expended. A complete or an incomplete P fails to be satisfactory only when it fails to prove with a given bounded amount of effort a theorem which is informally provable with comparable effort.

In the literature, inference systems and proof procedures have been proposed which were conjectured to be complete: for example, Wos and Robinson's paramodulation without functional reflexivity, and Darlington's f-matching. The longer these are conjectured, but not proved, to be complete, the less significant for efficiency is the possibility of their incompleteness. Their increased suitability is due not only to the increased likelihood of their completeness, but *mainly* to the likelihood that only informally difficult theorems are formally unprovable for them – since the simpler possible counter-examples that would have been tried by workers in the field have failed! These then are likely to be good candidates for automatic theorem-proving.

An absolute preference for incomplete procedures could only rationally be based on their being able to eliminate a greater number of irrelevant derivations. And this, when successful, they sometimes can do, as is exemplified by the fact that decision and semi-decision procedures for sets of sentences $S \subset S^*$ can sometimes be more efficient than procedures complete for S^*. This also accounts to a significant degree for the effectiveness of resolution, since it is not deduction-complete.

But the disadvantage of incomplete proof procedures is that usually little or no information is available concerning the extent or character of their incompleteness. For example, no such information is available for Guard's programs. One would certainly ask of such programs that only very few if any easy theorems should be unprovable. Norton's program for problems in group theory fails to satisfy this requirement.

An advantage of complete proof procedures is that because of their better understood structure one can often, by analysis, determine properties of their global behaviour. For example, completeness proofs for refinements I^1 of inference systems I provide information about the comparative efficiencies of proof procedures (I, Σ) and (I^1, Σ). Thus, when the completeness proof of I^1 relative to I proceeds by transforming proofs D admissible for I into proofs D^1 admissible for I^1 – then one can compare the complexities of D and D^1, and hence go on by the method indicated in a previous section to compare efficiencies. Limited information can also sometimes be extracted from completeness proofs employing semantic arguments (for example, semantic trees). One finds a relation between the complexity of a resolution proof and the complexity of a certain kind of semantic argument for establishing the same theorem.

We go on to consider the question of the desirability of completeness or incompleteness for *search strategies*; and we shall assume as before that in a proof procedure $P = (I, \Sigma)$ the 'logical' restrictions have been incorporated in I rather than Σ.

The usual argument for employing incomplete Σ is on the basis of human behaviour. One points to the high degree of selectivity mathematicians show in exploring possibilities for proving theorems. This might suggest that informal search strategies must almost certainly be incomplete. But it is unlikely that an intelligent prover of theorems would eliminate on *purely heuristic grounds* a logically possible subproof of a given theorem. The apparent contradiction can be resolved as follows: One should interpret selectivity *positively*, as employing highly discriminating but not incomplete heuristics for *ordering* logically possible subproofs with respect to their expected relevance to a proof – instead of negatively as eliminating beyond reconsideration possible but unlikely subproofs of the alleged theorem. So for example, in resolution procedures, deleting clauses with nesting of function symbols deeper than some bound is a negative approach; but giving preference, between two clauses of otherwise equal merit, to the one with less functional nesting is the preferable thing to do. (This yields an improvement of Kowalski's diagonal search.) Or, as another example, Wos and Robinson's unit selection heuristic is a negative one, whereas diagonal search employing length of clause as heuristic function is a positive one.

Thus complete search strategies employing positive criteria for discrimination, since they simulate intelligent human search methods more faithfully than incomplete ones, are more likely to further the goals of automatic theorem-proving.

LITERATURE

Dr Kowalski's thesis is: 'Studies in the completeness and efficiency of theorem-proving by resolution', University of Edinburgh, 1970.

For newcomers to the subject of automatic theorem-proving, there is appended a rather comprehensive list of references taken from the thesis. The following selection of them may be of help in connection with the specific examples and instances used in the lectures to illustrate general considerations:

Complete inference systems and proof procedures
Andrews (1968); Davis (1963); Kowalski & Hayes (1969); Kowalski (1970a); Loveland (1970); Prawitz (1960); Robinson (1965a); Robinson (1965b); Robinson (1967b); Slagle (1967); Wos, Carson & Robinson (1964); Wos, Robinson & Carson (1965).

Incomplete inference systems and proof procedures
Darlington (1968); Gould (1966); Guard, Oglesby, Bennet & Settle (1969); Norton (1966); Robinson & Wos (1969); Robinson (1969).

Search strategies
Hart, Nilsson & Raphael (1968); Kowalski (1970b); Loveland (1970); Sandewall (1969).

Power of inference systems
Gödel (1936).

APPENDIX: NOTE ON THE 'IDEAL' PROOF PROCEDURE P*
In a discussion following one of the lectures, Professor Robinson suggested that it might be possible to give greater precision to the notion of an 'ideal' proof procedure $P*$. A pointer in this direction is an unpublished result (attributed to Rabin) to the effect that no procedure for generating Herbrand instances can be perfect, that is, can be guaranteed never to yield irrelevant instances. This suggests that an 'objectively' defined, and non-trivial, best $P*$ might be feasible, at least within restriction to a given class of proof procedures and, perhaps, a given class of theorems.

BIBLIOGRAPHY

Allen, J. & Luckham, D. (1970)   An interactive theorem-proving program. *Machine Intelligence 5*, pp. 321–36 (eds Meltzer, B. & Michie, D.). Edinburgh: Edinburgh University Press.

Andrews, P. B. (1968)   Resolution with merging. *J. Ass. comput. Mach.*, **15**, 367–81.

Brown, T. C. (1968)   *Resolution with covering strategies and equality theory.* California: California Institute of Technology (1968).

Chang, C. L. (1969)   *Renamable paramodulation for automatic theorem-proving with equality.* Bethseda, Maryland: National Institute of Health.

Darlington, J. L. (1968)   Automatic theorem-proving with equality substitutions and mathematical induction. *Machine Intelligence 3*, pp. 113–27 (ed Michie, D.). Edinburgh: Edinburgh University Press.

Darlington, J. L. (1969) Theorem-proving and information retrieval. *Machine Intelligence 4*, pp. 173–81 (eds Meltzer, B. & Michie, D.). Edinburgh: Edinburgh University Press.

Davis, M. (1963) Eliminating the irrelevant from mechanical proofs. *Proc. Symposia in applied Mathematics*, **15**, 15–30. American Mathematical Society.

Doran, J. & Michie, D. (1966) Experiments with the graph traverser program. *Proc. Roy. Soc. (A)*, **294**, 235–59.

Gelernter, H. (1959) Realization of a geometry theorem-proving machine. *Proceedings of the IFIP Congress 1959*, pp. 273–82.

Gilmore, P. C. (1960) A proof method for quantification theory. *IBM J. Res. & Dev.*, **4**, 28–35.

Gödel, K. (1936) Über die Länge von Beweisen. *Ergebnisse eines math. Koll.*, **7**, 23–4.

Gould, W. E. (1966) A matching procedure for ω-order logic. *Scientific Report No. 4, AFCRL 66–781*, Applied Logic Corporation, Princeton, New Jersey.

Green, C. C. (1969) The application of theorem-proving to question-answering systems. *Ph.D. thesis*. Stanford University, Stanford, California. Also *Stanford Artificial Intelligence Project Memo* AI–76.

Guard, J. R., Oglesby, F. C., Bennet, J. H. & Settle, L. G. (1969) Semi-automated mathematics. *J. Ass. comput. Mach.*, **16**, 49–62.

Hart, T. P. (1965) A useful algebraic property of Robinson's unification algorithm. *Artificial Intelligence Project Memo 91*, Project MAC, MIT, Cambridge, Massachusetts.

Hart, P. E., Nilsson, N. & Raphael, B. (1968) A formal basis for the heuristic determination of minimum cost paths. *I.E.E.E. Trans. sys. Sci. & Cyber. SSC–4*, pp. 100–7.

Kleene, S. C. (1967) *Mathematical Logic*. New York: John Wiley & Sons.

Kowalski, R. A. (1968) Panel discussion: Formal systems and non-numerical problem solving by computers. *Fourth Systems Symposium*. Case Western Reserve University, Cleveland, Ohio.

Kowalski, R. A. & Hayes, P. J. (1969) Semantic trees in automatic theorem-proving. *Machine Intelligence 4*, pp. 87–101 (eds Meltzer, B. & Michie, D.). Edinburgh: Edinburgh University Press.

Kowalski, R. A. (1970a) The case for using equality axioms in automatic demonstration. *Symposium on Automatic Demonstration, Lecture Notes in Mathematics 125*, pp. 112–27. Berlin and New York: Springer-Verlag.

Kowalski, R. A. (1970b) Search strategies for theorem-proving. *Machine Intelligence 5*, pp. 181–201 (eds Meltzer, B. & Michie, D.). Edinburgh: Edinburgh University Press.

Loveland, D. W. (1968) Mechanical theorem-proving by model elimination. *J. Ass. comput. Mach.*, **15**, 236–51.

Loveland, D. W. (1970) A linear format for resolution. *Symposium on Automatic Demonstration, Lecture Notes in Mathematics 125*, pp. 147–63. Berlin and New York: Springer-Verlag.

Luckham, D. (1970)   Refinement theorems in resolution theory. *Symposium on Automatic Demonstration, Lecture Notes in Mathematics 125*, pp. 163–91. Berlin and New York: Springer-Verlag.

Meltzer, B. (1966)   Theorem-proving for computers: some results on resolution and renaming. *Comput. J.*, **8**, 341–3.

Meltzer, B. (1968)   Some notes on resolution strategies. *Machine Intelligence 3*, pp. 71–5 (ed Michie, D.). Edinburgh: Edinburgh University Press.

Meltzer, B. (1970)   Power amplification for theorem-provers. *Machine Intelligence 5*, pp. 165–79 (eds Meltzer, B. & Michie, D.). Edinburgh: Edinburgh University Press.

Morris, J.B. (1969)   E-resolution: extension of resolution to include the equality relation. *Proceedings of the International Joint Conference on Artificial Intelligence*, Washington, D C, pp. 287–94.

Nerode, A. & Smullyan, R.M. (1962)   *Review of:* Beth, E.W., The foundations of mathematics, a study in the philosophy of science. *J. symb. Logic*, **27**, 73–5.

Nilsson, N.J. (1968)   Searching problem-solving and game-playing trees for minimal cost solutions. *IFIP Congress Reprints*, H, pp. 125–30.

Norton, M.N. (1966)   ADEPT – a heuristic program for proving theorems of group theory. *Ph.D. thesis.* MIT, Cambridge, Massachusetts.

Pohl, I. (1969)   Bi-directional and heuristic search in path problems. *Ph.D. thesis.* Stanford University, Stanford, California. Also *SLAC Report* No. 104 (1969).

Pohl, I. (1970)   First results on the effect of error in heuristic search. *Machine Intelligence 5*, pp. 219–36 (eds Meltzer, B. & Michie, D.). Edinburgh: Edinburgh University Press.

Prawitz, D. (1960)   An improved proof procedure. *Theoria*, **26**, 102–39.

Prawitz, D. (1969)   Advances and problems in mechanical proof procedures. *Machine Intelligence 4*, pp. 59–71 (eds Meltzer, B. & Michie, D.). Edinburgh: Edinburgh University Press.

Raphael, B. (1969)   Some results about proof by resolution. *SIGART Newsletter* No. 14, pp. 22–5.

Robinson, G.A. & Wos, L. (1969)   Completeness of paramodulation. (Abstract.) *J. symb. Logic*, **34**, 160.

Robinson, G.A. & Wos, L. (1969)   Paramodulation and theorem-proving in first-order theories with equality. *Machine Intelligence 4*, pp. 135–50 (eds Meltzer, B. & Michie, D.). Edinburgh: Edinburgh University Press.

Robinson, J.A. (1965a)   A machine-oriented logic based on the resolution principle. *J. Ass. comput. Mach.*, **12**, 23–41.

Robinson, J.A. (1965b)   Automatic deduction with hyper-resolution. *Int. J. comput. Math.*, **1**, 227–34.

Robinson, J.A. (1967a)   Heuristic and complete processes in the mechanization of theorem-proving. *Sys. & comput. Sci.*, 116–24. Toronto: University of Toronto Press.

Robinson, J.A. (1967b)   A review of automatic theorem-proving. *Proc. Symp. App. Math.*, **19**, 1–18.

Robinson, J.A. (1968a)   The generalised resolution principle. *Machine Intelligence 3*, pp. 77–94 (ed. Michie, D.). Edinburgh: Edinburgh University Press.

Robinson, J. A. (1968b)   New directions in mechanical theorem-proving. *Proceedings of the IFIP Congress 1968*, pp. 206–10. (Invited papers.)

Robinson, J. A. (1969)   Mechanizing higher-order logic. *Machine Intelligence 4*, pp. 151–70 (eds Meltzer, B. & Michie, D.). Edinburgh: Edinburgh University Press.

Robinson, J. A. (1970)   Theoretical approaches to non-numerical problem solving. *Lecture Notes in Operations Research and Mathematical Systems, No. 28*, pp. 20 (eds. Banerji, R. & Mesarovic, M. D.) Berlin & New York: Springer-Verlag.

Sandewall, E. (1969)   Concepts and methods for heuristic search. *Proceedings of the International Joint Conference on Artificial Intelligence*. Washington, D C (7–9 May 1969), pp. 199–218.

Sibert E. E. (1969)   A machine-oriented logic incorporating the equality relation. *Machine Intelligence 4* pp. 103–33 (eds Meltzer, B. & Michie, D.). Edinburgh: Edinburgh University Press.

Slagle, J. R. (1963)   A heuristic program that solves symbolic integration problems in freshman calculus. *Computers and Thought* (eds Feigenbaum, E. & Feldman, J.). New York: McGraw-Hill.

Slagle, J. R. (1965)   A proposed preference strategy using sufficiency-resolution for answering questions. *Lawrence Radiation Laboratories Memo.* UCRL – 14361.

Slagle, J. R. (1967)   Automatic theorem-proving with renamable and semantic resolution. *J. Ass. comput. Mach.*, **14,** 687–97.

Slagle, J. R., Chang, C. L. & Lee, R. C. T. (1969)   Completeness theorems for semantic resolution in consequence finding. *Proceedings of the International Joint Conference on Artificial Intelligence*. Washington, D C (7–9 May 1969), pp. 281–5.

Wos, L., Carson, D. F. & Robinson, G. A. (1964)   The unit preference strategy in theorem-proving. *Proc. AFIPS 1964 Fall. J. comput. Conf.*, **26,** 616–21.

Wos, L., Robinson, G. A. & Carson, D. F. (1965) Efficiency and completeness of the set of support strategy in theorem-proving. *J. Ass. comput. Mach.*, **12,** 536–41.

Wos, L., Robinson, G. A., Carson, D. F. & Shalla, L. (1967)   The concept of demodulation in theorem-proving. *J. Ass. comput. Mach.*, **14,** 698–709.

Wos, L. & Robinson, G. A. (1969)   Maximal model theorem. (Abstract.) *J. sym. Logic*, **34,** 159–60.

Problem-oriented Languages

Problem-solving Compilers

E.W.ELCOCK

INTRODUCTION

This paper is concerned with programming languages which are mainly declarative in content in that much less information is given than is usual about the order in which individual operations are to be carried out.

The title of the paper reflects the fact that compilers for such languages must transform declarative statements about data into algorithms for the construction of data satisfying all the declarative statements made about them.

The paper introduces two languages, ABSYS and ABSET, both the work of the Computer Research Group in Aberdeen, and comments briefly on some other work in this area.

There are various motives for preferring program in the form of unordered declarative statements as opposed to ordered imperative statements. First, in many problems concerned with complex but well-structured data, it is advantageous and certainly nearer to informal mathematical practice to be able simply to assert things about the structure of data, instead of being constrained to sequences of imperative statements to construct particular data. Secondly, transformations are more easily carried out on such a program: this is important for compilation itself where, in the process of translation into machine code, we are concerned with transformations into equivalent algorithms and where an ultimate objective might be an appropriate choice of representations.

ABSYS: AN INFORMAL ACCOUNT

ABSYS (standing for ABerdeen SYstem) is a working, on-line incremental compiler for assertions. It was completed in 1968 and reported in part in Foster and Elcock (1969). Some of the following material is taken directly from this paper.

Assertions: the AND connective. The basic statements are not instructions to do something as in ALGOL, but assertions about the data. An individual assertion asserts a relation about data objects. Thus

$$x = y$$

asserts x and y satisfy an equality relation with the sense of 'substitutable for' and with the expected properties of reflexivity, transitivity, and so on. In the same spirit, the arithmetic operators have their usual properties so that, for example, the assertions $a=b+1$, $a=1+b$, $1+b=a$, and so on, are equivalent.

A written program consists of assertions. The individual assertions of a program have an implicit (not written) **'and'** connective with properties similar to its logical counterpart. The system acts to construct data satisfying the conjunction of assertions: for example, the trivial program

$$x=y \quad y=2$$

would make both x and y the datum 2. If the conjunction of assertions of a program is found to be unsatisfiable then the program terminates unsuccessfully. Thus the program $x=y$ $x=2$ $3=y$ would terminate with an indication that the assertions are unsatisfiable since no data x, y can be constructed to satisfy what has been asserted about x, y, 2, and 3.

Data directed control. A written assertional program places no explicit constraints on the order in which particular operations are performed. However the on-line system is incremental in that, as assertions are accepted by the system, whatever processing can be done on the basis of data already present, is done.

This lack of concern with control is sufficiently novel in programming systems to be worth elaborating by means of a trivial example of list processing. Consider the following constructions in a conventional list processing language with assignment:

(1) the constructor: $z \leftarrow cons$ (x, y) which the programmer must ensure is only processed when x and y have the desired values and the current value of z is no longer needed;

(2) the selector operations *hd* and *tl:* similar comments to (1);

(3) a test such as *equal* $(x, hd\,(z))$: similar comments to (2).

In ABSYS

$$z=[x \& y] \quad (\text{'\&' is infix } cons)$$

simply *asserts* that z is a list whose head is x and whose tail is y. Whether the assertion acts to construct z, or to select x and y, or to test whether x, y, and z satisfy the asserted relation, depends solely on the data environment at the time the assertion is processed. A less trivial example: the assignment statement

$$z2 \leftarrow cons(cons(hd(z1), cons(hd(tl(z1)), nil)), cons(cons(hd(z1),$$
$$cons(hd(tl(z1))), nil), nil))$$

expresses only one facet of the ABSYS assertions

$$z1 = [a, [b, c]]$$
$$z2 = [[a, b], [a, c]]$$

which assert a simple relation over the lists $z1$ and $z2$.

Functions. A lambda construction allows the assertion of functions other than primitive functions of the system. Lambda expressions are sufficiently well known for the ABSYS implementation to be discussed only briefly and by example.

The assertion

$$f' = \textbf{lambda } x, y => z \ll x = [z \& q'] \, y = [z \& r'] \gg$$

introduces a new function such that

$$f(m, n) = b$$

is equivalent to

$$\ll m = [b \& q'] \, n = [b \& r'] \gg$$

that is, an assertion that m and n are lists with the same first item b. The primes serve to introduce new identifiers, the textual scope of which is delimited by $\ll$ and $\gg$ brackets.

Note. There are no restrictions on the sorts of the parameters of a function: for example, a function may take functions as its arguments and return a function as its result. For example,

$$comb' = \textbf{lambda } f, g => r \ll r = \textbf{lambda } x \ll f(g(x)) \gg \gg$$

Partial applications of functions. Functions may be introduced by partial application of other functions. Thus

$$g' = f'(1)$$
$$f = \textbf{lambda } x, y => z \ll z = x + y \gg$$

asserts that g is the function $\textbf{lambda } y => z \ll z = 1 \mid y \gg$. Although this is a trivial example, partial application is, as we shall see later, a very powerful mechanism.

The OR connective: assertion of alternatives. Alternatives can be asserted by the construction

$$\{a1 \textbf{ or } a2\}$$

where $a1$ and $a2$ are conjunctions of assertions. The assertional (implicit) **and** and **or** distribute so that, for example,

$$a1 \{a2 \textbf{ or } a3\} \, a4$$

is equivalent to

$$\{a1 \, a2 \, a4 \textbf{ or } a1 \, a3 \, a4\}$$

The system attempts to construct distinct data to satisfy each conjunction of assertions, each conjunction in effect constituting a separate (parallel) computational branch of the total program.

By distribution, a total program could be transformed into a normal form of a disjunction of conjunctions of elementary assertions. In this normal form the conjunctions in effect constitute parallel non-interacting programs. ABSYS distributes the **and** and **or** connectives in a way which attempts to minimize duplication of processing. The computational branch associated with a particular conjunction terminates when unsatisfiability is detected. An example: First a preliminary assertion:

$$in' = \textbf{lambda } m, s \textbf{ key } s$$
$$\ll s = p' \& q'$$
$$\{m = p \textbf{ or } in(m, q)\} \gg$$

The **key** statement indicates that data which must be determined before evaluation of the function body. Since there is no explicit ordering of processing, it is possible that, without the **key** statement, a call of *in* might give rise to a further recursive call of *in* in the **or** assertion before processing the assertion $s = p' \& q'$ and so lead to processing which does not terminate. The **key** statement prevents this by making s a critical datum: the recursive call $in(m, q)$ is now not processed until after the assertion $s = p' \& q'$ which either determines a q or is unsatisfiable and gives termination. The function *in* is such that, for example, the assertion

$$in(x', [1, 2, 3])$$

is equivalent to asserting

$$\{x' = 1 \textbf{ or } x = 2 \textbf{ or } x = 3\}$$

If in addition we were now to assert

$$in(x, [2, 3, 4])$$

equivalent to

$$\{x = 2 \textbf{ or } x = 3 \textbf{ or } x = 4\}$$

distribution would lead to nine computational branches being explored of which all but two would terminate unsatisfiable, leaving two live branches in one of which x was the datum 2 and in one of which x was the datum 3.

The set constructor. There is a primitive relation **set**: it takes as parameters a prototype set element and an assertion and produces as its result the set of prototype elements satisfying the assertion (cf. $s = (x/p)$). The assertion is typically explicitly or implicitly (by distribution) a disjunction of conjunctions of elementary assertions. The set constructor initiates the parallel computations associated with the disjunction. Some of these terminate because of unsatisfiability. The result set is obtained by extracting the datum corresponding to the prototype set element from each of the surviving terminal computational branches.

A set is represented by a list but the ordering of elements in the list is not defined by the constructor.

An example:

$$t' = \mathbf{set}(x, \ll x = [x1', x2', x3']$$
$$in(1, x) \quad in(2, x) \quad in(3, x) \gg)$$

asserts that t is the set of list-triples of permutations of the integers 1, 2, 3: that is, the set of elements [1, 2, 3], [2, 3, 1], [3, 1, 2], [1, 3, 2], [2, 1, 3], [3, 2, 1].

Negation. If a is an assertion then

$$\mathbf{not} \ll a \gg$$

is satisfiable if a is unsatisfiable and vice versa. It distributes with respect to **or** and the implicit **and** in the expected way: **not** acts like a degenerate **or** in that it initiates an independent computational branch but one in which the criteria for termination are reversed.

Examples:

$$setdiff' = \mathbf{lambda} \; s1, s2 \Longrightarrow \mathbf{key} \; s1, s2$$
$$\ll s = \mathbf{set}(x', \ll in(x, s1)$$
$$\mathbf{not} \ll in(x, s2) \gg \gg) \gg$$

$$distinct' = \mathbf{lambda} \; l \; \mathbf{key} \; l$$
$$\ll \{ null(l) \; \mathbf{or}$$
$$l = p' \& q' \quad \mathbf{not} \; (\ll in(p, q) \gg)$$
$$distinct(q) \} \gg$$

$distinct(l)$ asserts that no two elements of the list l are equal.

A final simple example: the set of 3×3 magic squares.

$$magic\text{-}squares' = \mathbf{set}(ms',$$
$$\ll i9' = [1, 2, 3, 4, 5, 6, 7, 8, 9]$$
$$ms = [x11', x12', \ldots, x33']$$
$$in(x11, i9)$$

.

.

.

$$in(x33, i9)$$
$$distinct(ms)$$
$$x11 + x12 + x13 = 15$$

.

.

.

$$x31 + x22 + x13 = 15 \gg)$$

A more efficient (but still naive) version which reduces the number of interpretations examined is obtained by recognizing that the *in* assertions together with the assertion *distinct(ms)* are simply asserting *ms* to be a

D

permutation of the numbers 1 to 9. Using a similar construction to that for the set t above we can therefore write:

$$magic\text{-}squares' = \mathbf{set}(ms',$$
$$\ll ms = [x11', x12', \ldots, x33']$$
$$in(1, ms) \quad in(2, ms) \ldots . in(9, ms)$$
$$x11 + x12 + x13 = 15$$
$$.$$
$$.$$
$$.$$
$$x31 + x22 + x13 = 15 \gg)$$

It is of course also possible to write less naive versions which embody information obtained from preliminary reasoning about the problem: that is, that the centre square must be 5; the corner squares even; and the face squares odd.

AN ILLUSTRATION OF THE USE OF ABSYS IN THE CONTEXT OF A NON-TRIVIAL PROBLEM

The following problem is a brain-teaser taken from a well-known British Sunday newspaper.

The six members of the committee voted to elect a chairman:

(1) Each member cast one vote and each received one vote.

(2) Nobody voted for himself.

(3) Nobody voted for the man who voted for him.

(4) Nobody voted for the man who voted for the man who voted for him.

They were secretive but truthful about how the votes were cast. Only three of them spoke.

(5) Dale: Either Baker voted for Elton, or I voted for Adams, or Forrest voted for me.

(6) Forrest: Either Elton voted for me, or Baker voted for Dale, or Adams voted for Clark.

(7) Clark: Either I voted for Elton, or Dale voted for Baker, or Forrest voted for me.

Each man was indicating that one, and only one, of the possibilities he mentioned was correct.

Protocol for problem statement: choice of representations, functions etc. I am going to use the identifiers a to f for the names of the committee members. The relevant assertions in ABSYS are:

$$a' = \text{'}adams' \quad b' = \text{'}bake'r \text{ etc.}$$

where '*adams*' is a quoted identifier.

The relation *vf* (*voted for*) is from c to c where c is the committee set, and in fact the problem could be stated by direct use of some representation of the Cartesian product set $c \times c$.

However a little thought shows that the first four constraints of the problem imply that for any committee of 6 members (our case), any possible voting relation meeting these constraints can be represented by a simple circular list in which each committee member appears once and once only, that is, a list of the form

$$l' = [a, d, c, b, f, e \& l]$$

with the interpretation that x immediately proceeds y in the list is equivalent to $vf(x, y)$. This representation and its associated interpretation of themselves capture the first four constraints.

Instead of using a circular list, it is more convenient (for example, for the definition of vf in the interpretation) simply to repeat the first member of the list as in:

$$l1' = [a, d, c, b, f, e, a]$$

Let us represent the expression x voted-for y by a list-pair $[x, y]$.

Using these representations and their associated interpretation, we can now introduce a function to assert an expression 'x voted-for y' in the context of a voting relation:

$$v' = \textbf{lambda } vr', e' \textbf{ key } vr$$
$$\ll e = [x', y'] \quad vr = p' \& q'$$
$$\{p = x \quad q = y \& r' \quad \textbf{or } v(q, e)\} \gg$$

Thus $v(l, p)$ asserts that p is a list-pair $[a, b]$ say, and that a immediately precedes b in the list l: that is, in our interpretation $v(l, p)$ asserts that a voted for b is consistent with the voting relation l. Consider now the statements made by Dale, Forrest, and Clark. Each is made up of three primitive statements one and only one of which is true. Let us represent such a statement by a list-triple each member of which, remembering our previous representation of 'voted-for', is a list pair. Thus:

$$dstat' = [[b, e], [d, a], [f, d]]$$
$$fstat' = [[e, f], [b, d], [a, c]]$$
$$cstat' = [[c, e], [d, b], [f, c]]$$

With this representation and its associated interpretation we can now introduce a function to assert a statement (of this general form) in the context of a voting relation:

$$g' = \textbf{lambda } stat', vr' \textbf{ key } stat, vr$$
$$\ll stat = [s1', s2', s3'] \quad v1' = v(vr)$$
$$\{v1(s1) \quad \textbf{not} \ll v1(s2) \gg \quad \textbf{not} \ll v1(s3) \gg$$
$$\textbf{or} \quad v1(s2) \quad \textbf{not} \ll v1(s1) \gg \quad \textbf{not} \ll v1(s3) \gg$$

    or $v1(s3)$ **not** $\ll v1(s1)\gg$ **not** $\ll v1(s2)\gg\}\gg$

where the function $v1$ is the previously introduced function v partially applied to its first argument $(v1(s)=v(vr,s))$.

Note that the order of the formal parameters of g has been chosen so that g may be partially applied to a statement giving rise to a unary function with domain a voting relation: for example, $g(dstat)$ is a function which when applied to a voting relation asserts the whole of Dale's statement in the context of the voting relation. This will be useful later.

We now introduce the *set* of possible voting relations meeting the first four constraints: that is, in our chosen representation, the set of permutations of lists of the form *l*1 with fixed first member (say a): let us call this set *candidate set* (cs).

This is done by the ABSYS **set** statement:

$$cs' = \mathbf{set}(x', \ll x=[a, x1', x2', x3', x4', x5', a]$$
$$in(b, x)\ \ in(c, x)\ \ in(d, x)\ \ in(e, x)\ \ in(f, x)\gg)$$

similar to that in the example asserting the permutation set t in the section on 'The set constructor'.

We now want to restrict the set cs by the assertions corresponding to the statements made by Dale, Forrest, and Clark. Restriction of a set by a function which *makes an assertion about* the set members is the library function

$$restrict' = \mathbf{lambda}\ f',\ s' => rs'\ \mathbf{key}\ f, s$$
$$\ll rs = \mathbf{set}(m', \ll in(m, s)\ \ f(m)\gg)\gg$$

We can now assert the answer set (that is, the set of voting relations meeting *all* constraints) to be:

$$ans' = restrict(g(dstat), restrict(g(fstat),$$
$$restrict(g(cstat), cs)))$$

The complete program for asserting that *ans* is the set of voting relations meeting all the given constraints could now read:

$$a' = `adams'\ \ b' = `baker'\ \ c' = `clark'$$
$$d' = `dale'\ \ e' = `elton'\ \ f' = `forrest'$$
$$cs' = \mathbf{set}\ (vr', \ll vr=[a, x1', x2', x3', x4', x5', a]$$
$$in(b, vr)\ \ in(c, vr)\ \ in(d, vr)$$
$$in(e, vr)\ \ in(f, vr)\gg)$$
$$dstat' = [[b, e], [d, a], [f, d]]$$
$$fstat' = [[e, f], [b, d], [a, c]]$$
$$cstat' = [[c, e], [d, b], [f, c]]$$
$$v' = \mathbf{lambda}\ vr',\ e'\ \mathbf{key}\ vr$$
$$\ll e=[x', y']\ \ vr=p'\&q'$$
$$\{p=x\ \ q=y\&r'\ \ \mathbf{or}\ v(q, e)\}\gg$$

$$g' = \textbf{lambda } stat', vr' \textbf{ key } stat, vr$$
$$\ll stat = [s1', s2', s3']\quad v1' = v(vr)$$
$$\{v1(s1)\quad \textbf{not} \ll v1(s2) \gg\quad \textbf{not} \ll v1(s3) \gg$$
$$\textbf{or } v1(s2)\quad \textbf{not} \ll v1(s1) \gg\quad \textbf{not} \ll v1(s3) \gg$$
$$\textbf{or } v1(s3)\quad \textbf{not} \ll v1(s1) \gg\quad \textbf{not} \ll v1(s2) \gg\} \gg$$

$$ans' = restrict(g(dstat), restrict(g(fstat), restrict(g(cstat), cs)))$$

$$ans \ldots$$

$$[\;[`adams', `elton', `forrest', `dale', `baker', `clark', `adams']\;]$$

The final line

$$ans \ldots$$

is a request for printout of the set which in this case turns out to have only one member.

COMMENTS ON ABSYS AND RELATED LANGUAGES

It is interesting to comment briefly on recent papers by Nevins (1970) and Fikes (1970). These also present languages which explore the problems of construction of data to satisfy given constraints. Both languages are, however, non-interactive.

It should be emphasized that in what follows I am concerned only with the expressive power of language concepts and not with the mechanisms of the compiler problem-solving underlying their use. Both Nevins' and Fikes' papers are interesting from this point of view and the reader is referred to them for details.

Nevins, starting with a rather different motivation from our own, has extended IPL-V to provide a language which has many similarities with ABSYS. Although the language is less general than ABSYS (for example, it has no functional capability), like ABSYS the extension provides a declarative system with a single equality relation (again essentially by list pattern matching) and with a similar treatment of propositional connectives to ABSYS. There are no set constructions in the language but instead a construction **find** $x, p(x)$ with the meaning 'find an x satisfying the formula p'. This operates like the ABSYS set construction but terminating with the first valid interpretation found.

Nevins makes some provision for program guidance of the generation of interpretations by the use of what he calls 'critical' formulae. These can be designated by the programmer and act to interrupt any particular (depth first) generation process in favour of some other.

Fikes' system is rather different. The language, REF, has a very simple imperative component with assignment, conditional jumps for loops, and a computed goto, but with no block structure, function capability, or general set constructions. The constraint satisfaction features are contained in select, condition, and exclusion statements, which can be used in a REF procedure. The statement **select**(n, m) is used to assign an arbitrary integer in the range [n, m]; the condition statement asserts that a Boolean expression must be true, and the exclusion statement asserts that its arguments have different values. Using these statements it is possible to write a procedure which specifies its result in terms of a space of candidate results and a selection criterion.

The procedure may consist entirely of select and condition statements. Thus, the REF procedure for the 3×3 magic square given in Fikes (1970) is:

> **begin**;
> **set vector** m **to select** (1, 9), **select** (1, 9), **select** (1, 9), **select** (1, 9),
> **select** (1, 9), **select** (1, 9), **select** (1, 9), **select** (1, 9), **select** (1, 9);
> **condition** $m[1] + m[2] + m[3] = 15$;
> .
> .
> .
> **condition** $m[3] + m[5] + m[7] = 15$;
> **condition excl** ($m[1], m[2], \ldots, m[9]$);
> **end**;

superficially very similar to the simpler of the two ABSYS constructions, with **select** acting like *in*. The similarity is somewhat misleading however simply because the set of values of the components of M happen to be the set of integers 1 to 9, the only kind of set capable of being handled by the current select statement of REF. It does not, for example, seem possible in REF to parallel the second ABSYS construction for magic squares. It is also worth noting that the REF procedure returns a single magic square not the set of magic squares as in the ABSYS construction (the word *set* in the REF procedure is to be interpreted as a verb!).

The imperative part of REF gives the programmer some control over the order in which constraint statements are processed by the REF interpreter and hence provides some control of the first stage search process carried out by the REF interpreter. However its main function might be thought of as compensating for the weakness of the declarative part of the language – this last statement reflecting a personal view of the goals of programming style!

It is interesting to compare from this point of view a 'mixed' REF procedure with an ABSYS construction to solve a problem of crypt-addition considered by Fikes (1970). The problem is to find transformation(s) from letters to decimal digits which make true the summation

SEND

+MORE

MONEY.

No digit may be assigned to more than one letter, and leading zeros are not allowed in the numbers formed by the addends and the sum.

Although, as pointed out by Fikes, '. . . it is possible to state the verifying conditions for this problem as a single equation

$$1000s + 100e \times \ldots = \ldots 10e + y'$$

the procedures to be written will use the column addition process exploited by most humans when solving such problems.

The REF procedure given by Fikes is:

    begin;

        set vector $a1$ **to** x, s, e, n, d;

        set vector $a2$ **to** x, m, o, r, e;

        set vector *sum* **to** m, o, n, e, y;

        set vector l **to** d, n, e, s, r, o, m, y;

        for $i \rightarrow 8$ **do to** $l1$;

    $l1$: **set** $<l[<i>]>$ **to select** $(0, 9)$;

        condition excl $(<l[1]>, <l[2]>, <l[3]>, \ldots, <l[8]>)$;

        condition $\sim(<m>=0) \wedge \sim(<s>=0)$;

        set $<carry>$ **to** 0;

        for $j \rightarrow 4$ **do to** $l2$;

        set $<i>$ **to** $6 + - <j>$;

        if $<a1[<i>]> + <a2[<i>]> + <carry> < 10$ **then** $l3$;

        condition $<a1[<i>]> + <a2[<i>]> + <carry>$

                $= 10 + <sum[<i>]>$;

        set $<carry>$ **to** 1;

        goto $l2$;

    $l3$: **condition** $<a1[<i>]> + <a2[<i>]> + <carry>$

                $= <sum[<i>]>$;

        set $<carry>$ **to** 0;

    $l2$: ;

        condition $<m> = <carry>$;

        end;

A comparable ABSYS construction is:

    encodings' = **set** $(l'$,

    $\ll l = [d', n', e', s', r', o', m', y']$

    $d + e = x1'$ $\{x1 = y$ *carry*$1' = 0$ **or** $x1 = y + 10$ *carry*$1 = 1\}$

$n + r + carry1 = x2'$ $\{x2 = e$ $carry2' = 0$ **or** $x2 = e + 10$ $carry2 = 1\}$

$e + o + carry2 = x3'$ $\{x3 = n$ $carry3' = 0$ **or** $x3 = n + 10$ $carry3 = 1\}$

$s + m + carry3 = x4'$ $\{x4 = o$ $m = 0$ **or** $x4 = o + 10$ $m = 1\}$

$l = subset(8, [0, 1, 2, 3, 4, 5, 6, 7, 8, 9])$

not $\ll s = 0 \gg$ **not** $\ll m = 0 \gg$

    $\gg)$

where *subset* is a library function such that $l = subset(8, [0, 1, 2, 3, 4, 5, 6, 7, 8, 9])$ asserts the disjunction of the set of assertions each of which asserts l a distinct subset of size 8 of the set of integers 0 to 9. This assertion could of course be replaced by a lengthier compound assertion using *in*.

In fact, one would probably not write the above construction since it is clear that the inclusion of the possibility of m being zero in the fourth of the addition with carry statements is silly. Since leading zeros are not allowed m must be 1 when it is clear that s must be 8 or 9 and o must be zero. A construction using this information is:

$encodings' = \textbf{set}(l',$

$\ll l = [d', n', e', s', r', o', m', y']$

$d + e = x1'$ $\{x1 = y$ $carry1' = 0$ **or** $x1 = y + 10$ $carry1 = 1\}$

$n + r + carry1 = x2'$ $\{x2 = e$ $carry2' = 0$ **or** $x2 = e + 10$ $carry2 = 1\}$

$e + carry2 = x3'$ $\{x3 = n$ $carry3' = 0$ **or** $x3 = n + 10$ $carry3 = 1\}$

$m = 1$ $o = 0$

$\{s = 9$ $carry3 = 0$ $[d, n, e, r, y] = subset(5, [2, 3, 4, 5, 6, 7, 8])$

or $s = 8$ $carry3 = 1$ $[d, n, e, r, y] = subset(5, [2, 3, 4, 5, 6, 7, 9])\}$

    $\gg)$

DEVELOPMENTS SINCE ABSYS

At the stage of development of ABSYS reached in the informal account above, it was clear that further development would mean extending the language so that it should be possible to influence the problem-solving behaviour (that is, the details of the generation process of the parallel computations or interpretations), for example, by being able to give additional problem domain dependent information which could be utilized by the sequencer. Such extensions would need further primitives, syntactic constructions, and, possibly, more sophisticated sequencers. To do this conveniently (that is, without recourse to low level code) would mean a treatment, in the language, of assignment, reference, and storage allocation.

We were also aware of certain deficiencies in that part of ABSYS which had already been implemented. These included a particular choice of implementation of the **and** and **or** connectives and **not** which, among other things, made distribution inflexible and inhibited good design of set operations. A related deficiency was the fact that ABSYS used a single equality relation (essentially a generalized list pattern-matching process). This creates difficulties in, for example, the introduction of new sorts. Thus, it is not possible to represent an integer fraction by a list-pair and have the standard equality relation between fractions because, although with such a representation [2,4] and [6, 12] are equal as fractions, they are not equal as lists. Although this kind of difficulty can be overcome to some extent at the cost of less elegant representations and programming, we decided for this and other reasons that a single equality relation was unacceptable.

At the same Workshop, *Machine Intelligence 4*, at which the ideas of ABSYS were presented, Robinson (1969) gave a paper on the mechanization of higher-order logic. We must acknowledge the influence of this paper on our subsequent work. Whilst encouraging us by similarities between the idea of semantic partitions and the treatment of parallel computations in ABSYS, it confirmed our dissatisfaction with the consequences of our particular implementation of propositional connectives and equality in ABSYS and was a contributory stimulus to our re-examination of the primitive notions of ABSYS.

We decided that, rather than extend ABSYS in the ways already mentioned, a fundamental redesign was appropriate. The result of this redesign is a language we have called ABSET (the name because important primitive concepts of the language are founded on the elementary theory of sets). ABSET contains within it the possibility of ABSYS-like constructions but one is not committed to them. In designing ABSET we have rather focused our attention on certain fundamental problems raised by our work on ABSYS: the elementary notions of value, equality, representation and sorts, the distinction between ordering of decisions and an order of evaluation, and, not least, the manipulation of partly evaluated program.

The current state of our work on ABSET has been reported recently at the Sixth Machine Intelligence Workshop held in Edinburgh in July 1970 (Elcock *et al.* 1971).

ACKNOWLEDGEMENT

The material presented here is, in the main, derived from the collaborative effort of the Computer Research Group in Aberdeen as reported in the two papers referred to in the text. They should not however be held jointly responsible for all views expressed. A version of the voting plan problem was presented by P.M.D. Gray at a joint meeting with the Department of Machine Intelligence and Perception of the University of Edinburgh, Easter 1969.

The work reported in this paper is sponsored by the Science Research Council.

REFERENCES

Elcock, E. W., Foster, J. M., Gray, P. M. D., McGregor, J. J., & Murray, A. M. (1971) ABSET, a programming language based on sets; motivation and examples. *Machine Intelligence 6* pp. 467–92 (eds Meltzer, B. & Michie, D.). Edinburgh: Edinburgh University Press.

Fikes, R. E. (1970) REF–ARF: a system for solving problems stated as procedures. *Art. Int.*, **1**, 27–120.

Foster, J. M. & Elcock, E. W. (1969) ABSYS 1: an incremental compiler for assertions; an introduction. *Machine Intelligence 4*, pp. 423–9 (eds Meltzer, B. & Michie, D.). Edinburgh: Edinburgh University Press.

Nevins, A. J. (1970) A programming language with automatic goal generation and selection. *J. Ass. comput. Mach.*, **17**, 216–30.

Robinson, J. A. (1969) Mechanizing higher-order logic. *Machine Intelligence 4*, pp. 151–70 (eds Meltzer, B. & Michie, D.). Edinburgh: Edinburgh University Press.

A Survey of Seven Projects Using the Same Language

N.V.FINDLER

INTRODUCTION

In general, the selection of a computer language to solve a particular problem is based on pragmatic grounds. One would like to use a language the information structures and processes of which are 'reasonably similar' (homomorphic?) to those of the physical entity under study. The so-called symbol manipulating languages, for example, have proved to be valuable tools because of the flexibility and ease with which they can handle the structures of cognition, natural language, algebra, music, and so on.

Another criterion of the selection is that the language should not be restricted in applicability to a small range of problems. One would not like to learn a new language, so to speak, for every task. Further, it would be a welcome phenomenon if the language to be used is a familiar one in its basic syntax and semantics.

We have designed and implemented an Associative Memory, Parallel Processing Language, AMPPL-II, that seems to satisfy the above criteria. It is an extension of the Symmetric List Processor, SLIP (Weizenbaum 1963). We have recently reported on it (Findler and McKinzie 1969a, Findler 1970), and also a book will soon be published (Findler, Pfaltz and Bernstein 1971) that incorporates, besides this, three other related computer languages. These are all embedded in FORTRAN IV. It means that, apart from a small number of routines that are coded in assembly language, all the operations are represented by FORTRAN subprograms. This fact has obvious implications with regard to (1) learning and using the language, and (2) transporting it from one type of machine to another. One must also note that the powerful input/output, diagnostic and arithmetic facilities of FORTRAN represent such a bonus that they can be appreciated only by those who have used other processing languages, such as IPL-V or LISP.

AMPPL-II is actually a by-product of some long-term research effort at simulating human cognition. It has, however, been found that its range of applicability is rather wide, embracing both numerical and non-numerical areas. In the following, we demonstrate the above statement by describing seven projects that are being programmed in the FORTRAN-SLIP-AMPPL package. Although these projects have not yet reached completion they should provide some insight into the objectives and techniques of research in Artificial Intelligence.

A QUESTION-ANSWERING SYSTEM CONCERNING KINSHIP RELATIONS

We have recently reported on an IPL-V program that could generate and query kinship structures (Findler and McKinzie 1969b). The idea was to build complex, inter-related data structures from the simplest possible information source, in this instance from birth and marriage cards. Various types of questions could then be answered by retrieving information of the data structure. We can, for example, (1) print out a family tree between given limits; (2) specify a complex chain of relations originating from a particular individual and find the names of the persons that satisfy the relation criteria along the chain; (3) find the names of the people only at the end of this traversal operation; (4) verify whether a given chain of relations in fact connects two given individuals; (5) list all possible chains of relations between two given individuals.

The program was such that data source cards and inquiry cards could be freely intermixed. In fact, it was possible to generate a partial kinship structure, make enquiries about it, and then to continue to generate the structure within the same computer run. Pseudo-members were automatically substituted in case of missing links.

The program was tried out by using as data source the first fifteen chapters of Robert Graves: *The Greek Myths, Volume I.* The incestuous and polygamous ties between the divine participants has proved to be a challenging but successful test environment.

New developments in AMPPL-II enable us to construct an even more powerful system. In order to describe it, we must briefly discuss the problem of definitions. Wiley R. McKinzie and I are engaged on this project, and Rowan Snyder was also associated with it for a while.

Let us first consider the following formula, analogous to algebraic functions which defines a Relation (REL) between an Object (OBJ) and a Value (VAL):

$$\mathrm{REL(OBJ)} = \mathrm{VAL}$$

The first entity, REL, is always symbolic; the other two, OBJ and VAL, can be either symbolic or numeric, simultaneously or separately. [Examples are: COLOR(APPLE) = RED, NUMBER(BOYS) = 14.] Regardless of which type, a further classification is possible as to whether an entity is a single item or one of different kinds of lists. The first kind of list simply contains various equivalent names of the same item. (One can think of synonyms within the given context.) This is called the Equivalence List. The second kind of list bears the name of a number of subunits any processing on which is always uniform. An example of this is the students of a class, who always have the same teacher, always stay in the same classroom, and so on. Distinguishing processes, such as grading of individual exams, are not to be carried out on the elements of so designated lists. Finally, the third kind of list has distinct and, in some respect, independent elements. An example of this is the pieces of furniture in a certain room if one would like to, say, paint them in different colors.

We have stated before that items on the Equivalence List can be considered as context-dependent synonyms. As a logical extension of this idea, names of various types of sublists may also appear on an Equivalence List. Here we discuss only two of these.

(1) Let us define Reverse Relation, REVREL.

$$\text{If REL1(OBJ)} = \text{VAL} \quad \text{and}$$
$$\text{REVREL(REL1)} = \text{REL2} \quad \text{then}$$
$$\text{REL2(VAL)} = \text{OBJ}$$

Note also that

$$\text{REVREL(REVREL(REL1))} = \text{REL1}.$$

Examples are shown in table 1.

TABLE 1. Relations and reverse relations

REL	REVREL
husband of	wife of
parent of	child of
spouse of	spouse of
greater than	less than
above	below
inside	outside
left of	right of
superset of	subset of
similar to	similar to

(2) The second type of sublist of the Equivalence List refers to a more general concept, to the Defined Entity. It is constructed of Primitive Entities, possibly other Defined Entities, and connecting operators. The operators are listed in table 2. Only the last one needs special mention before examples

clarify the meaning of all of them. The left hand side operand of ↓ is considered to be in Teutonic genitive (the possessive case denoted with an apostrophe and the letter 's'). The possessed item is the right hand side operand. Let us also define a special entity SELF in order to be able to exclude self-referencing in unwanted cases. The symbol ⇒ (programmer's notation: .DEF.) is to mean 'defined as'.

TABLE 2. Various operators for defined entities

Symbolic notation	Type	Representing	Programmer's notation
¬		Boolean NOT	.NOT.
←		reverse	.REV.
<		less than	.LT.
≤		less than or equal to	.LE.
>	unary	greater than	.GT.
≥		greater than or equal to	.GE.
Max		maximum	.MAX.
Min		minimum	.MIN.
=		equivalent or synonymous	.EQ.
∧		Boolean AND	.AND.
∨	binary	Boolean OR	.OR.
↓		concatenated	.CON.

Examples follow.

(1) PARENT ⇒ FATHER ∨ MOTHER

that is, a parent is defined a father or mother;

(2) CHILD ⇒ ← PARENT

that is, the child is defined as the reverse of the parent;

(3) GRANDFATHER ⇒ (FATHER ∨ MOTHER) ↓ FATHER

that is, the grandfather is defined as the father's or mother's father;

(4) HUSBAND ⇒ SPOUSE ∨ ¬WIFE

that is, the husband is defined as a spouse but (and) not wife;

(5) BROTHER ⇒ ((MOTHER ∧ FATHER) ↓ SON) ∧ ¬SELF

that is, the brother is defined as the mother's and father's son but (and) not self; if we wish to include half-brothers as well, we can put

BROTHER ⇒ ((MOTHER ∨ FATHER) ↓ SON) ∧ ¬SELF

that is, the mother's *or* father's son but (and) not self.

(6) If *V* is a scalar describing quality, we can say

$$\text{GOOD} \Rightarrow >V1$$
$$\text{BAD} \Rightarrow <V2$$
$$\text{BEST} \Rightarrow \text{Max } V$$
$$\text{WORST} \Rightarrow \text{Min } V$$

(7) If L is a scalar describing persons' height, we can define

$$\text{TALL} \Rightarrow >L1$$
$$\text{SHORT} \Rightarrow <L2$$
$$\text{MEDIUM BUILT} \Rightarrow \leqslant L1 \wedge \geqslant L2$$

(8) $\text{GRANDFATHER} \Rightarrow = \text{GRANDPA} \wedge = \text{GRANDAD}$,

that is, the grandfather is synonymous with grandpa and grandad.

There are altogether seven basic questions a retrieval system for relations can answer. These are as follows:

(a) Is a particular relation, between a given object and value, true?

(b) What is (are) the value(s) belonging to a given relation-object pair, if any? $\text{REL(OBJ)} = ?$

(c) What is (are) the object(s) belonging to a given relation-value pair, if any? $\text{REL}(?) = \text{VAL}$

(d) What is (are) the relation(s) that connect(s) a given object-value pair, if any? $?(\text{OBJ}) = \text{VAL}$

(e) What relation-object pair(s) belong(s) to a given value, if any?

$$?(?) = \text{VAL}$$

(f) What relation-value pair(s) belong(s) to a given object, if any?

$$?(\text{OBJ}) = ?$$

(g) Finally, what object-value pair(s) belong(s) to a given relation, if any? $\text{REL}(?) = ?$

The answers are obtainable by using one simple instruction in every case.

Another high-level retrieval process can be accomplished by the function

$$\text{FIND(A, B, C)}$$

After its execution, the value of FIND is equal to the name of a list containing all xs for which it is true that

$$\text{A}:\text{B} = \text{C}:\text{X}$$

The sign ':' may be verbally interpreted as 'is related to'. It is assumed that there are at least two Relation Descriptors in one of the following six forms:

$$\begin{bmatrix} \text{Q(A)} = \text{B} \\ \text{Q(C)} = \text{X} \end{bmatrix}, \text{ or } \begin{bmatrix} \text{A(Q)} = \text{B} \\ \text{C(Q)} = \text{X} \end{bmatrix}, \text{ or } \begin{bmatrix} \text{A(B)} = \text{Q} \\ \text{C(X)} = \text{Q} \end{bmatrix}, \text{ or }$$

$$\begin{bmatrix} \text{Q(B)} = \text{A} \\ \text{Q(X)} = \text{C} \end{bmatrix}, \text{ or } \begin{bmatrix} \text{B(Q)} = \text{A} \\ \text{X(Q)} = \text{C} \end{bmatrix}, \text{ or } \begin{bmatrix} \text{B(A)} = \text{Q} \\ \text{X(C)} = \text{Q} \end{bmatrix}.$$

Here, Q is an entity common to the two (or more) Relation Descriptors both in content and in position (same type of entity). Further, the type of the entities A and C, and also B and X are identical. (This refers to REL, OBJ, or VAL, and to whether symbolic or numerical.) The following two examples should make this whole idea clear:

(1) Suppose in the Simulated Associative Memory (SAM), we have Relation Descriptor words standing for

> .   .   .   .
> .   .   .   .
> .   .   .   .

PATERNAL UNCLE (JIM) = WILLIAM

> .   .   .   .
> .   .   .   .
> .   .   .   .

PATERNAL UNCLE (TONY) = MARTIN, DONALD

> .   .   .   .
> .   .   .   .
> .   .   .   .

If

A = JIM,
B = WILLIAM,
C = TONY,

the resulting X will be the list containing MARTIN and DONALD since JIM's relation to WILLIAM is the same as that of TONY's to MARTIN and DONALD – they are the paternal uncles of the people in question (Q = PATERNAL UNCLE).

(2) Let SAM now contain

> .   .   .   .
> .   .   .   .
> .   .   .   .

UNCLES OF (JACK) = {JOE, BILL, PETER}

> .   .   .   .
> .   .   .   .
> .   .   .   .

AUNTS OF (JACK) = {MARY, CARON}

> .   .   .   .
> .   .   .   .
> .   .   .   .

If A = UNCLES OF,
B = {JOE, BILL, PETER},
C = AUNTS OF,

the resulting x will be the list with {MARY, CARON} since {JOE, BILL, PETER} are the uncles of the same person (Q = JACK) whose aunts are {MARY, CARON}.

It is quite easy to see how compound kinship relations can be defined and the relevant members retrieved by using the above described facilities. The evolving program is rather complex.

An interesting application of and extension to the program will be made in conjunction with a social anthropologist, Woodraw W. Denham, who at present is collecting data on kinship relations among the members of the Australian aboriginal tribe *Alyawara*.

ON THE PROBLEMS OF TIME, RETRIEVAL OF TEMPORAL RELATIONS, CAUSALITY, AND CO-EXISTENCE

In the interpretation of scientific data, working hypotheses are formed that are based on *prima facie* relations between patterns of events. The discovery of causality calls for testing these working hypotheses under a wide variety of conditions. The logic of the concept of causality requires that the researcher should, first of all, sort out predecessor-successor relations. It seems obvious that when huge masses of time-relevant data are to be analyzed, the computer should come to the scientist's aid in this non-trivial task. Yet, the passage of time, one of the most salient of human experiences, has received relatively little study in question-answering programs. The time variable is at the heart of practically all physical, biological, and psychological events. It is, therefore, the fundamental coordinate of every process-descriptive model. A graduate student, David Chen, and I are engaged on a project, which is aimed at this problem.

We are not concerned with stochastic phenomena in this work. The blurring effect of probability distributions is replaced by the following paradigm:

$$\text{Event } E_i \text{ has } \begin{bmatrix} \text{relevant} \\ \text{irrelevant} \end{bmatrix} \begin{bmatrix} \text{starting time} \\ \text{duration} \\ \text{finishing time} \end{bmatrix}.$$

One can find meaningful examples of all six possible cases. Furthermore, partial chronological data can be given in the 'irrelevant' case by saying that

$$\text{Event } E_i \text{ occurred } \begin{bmatrix} \text{fully} \\ \text{partially} \end{bmatrix} \begin{bmatrix} \text{before} \\ \text{during} \\ \text{after} \end{bmatrix} \text{ event } E_j.$$

Here, the 'partially during' combination is not sensible. The distinction between relevancy and irrelevancy is indeed useful since chronological data in real life are often incompletely specified because of lack of information, measurement errors, conflicting data sources, and so on.

E

One has to make important decisions in connection with a question-answering system whose data base is time-dependent events. These decisions are with reference to the following:

(1) *Input mode.* The simplest and least error-prone method should be used. The translation into data structure should be relatively easy.

(2) *Internal representation.* Updating and search processes should be straightforward. Inconsistencies and lack of information in the input data must be found easily and completely for reporting back to the user. There can be designed redundancy but only as much as to make the overall system, including information structures *and* processes, quasi-optimum.

(3) *Data manipulation.* As discussed above, this issue must be considered in conjunction with the internal representation.

(4) *Direct and inferred retrieval techniques.* One must aim at obtaining only valid and all valid answers. This should comprise 'raw' data from the source information and implicit data generated by logical inferences. We want to deduce the possibility of complex causal relations, to prove or disprove hypotheses about compound co-existence relations, and so on.

A detailed discussion of the above is beyond the scope of the present paper. We shall sketch only a few points that may be of general interest.

We have defined *point events* that take place momentarily and *duration events* that have distinct starting and finishing times. For example, 'to wake up' is a point event (although many of us may disagree with this statement) and its effect, 'to be awake' is lasting. Point events are usually, but not necessarily contiguously, followed by duration events that are their effects.

In order to be realistic about simultaneity, we have assumed a quantized time scale. Further, we have considered the time coordinate unbounded in both directions. Absolute and relative specification of time points may be given. In the latter case, partial restrictions can also be included in the input phase. A time point may be antecedent of, equitemporal or circa-equitemporal with another time point. An axiomatic logical calculus can be established to describe the rules of deduction.

Finally, we list a few simple questions that should be answered by the system:

(1) Can the start of event E_i cause event E_j?

(2) Does event E_i co-exist with event E_j? (Co-existence meaning partial or complete overlap.)

(3) Can the completion of event E_i cause event E_j?

(4) Is event E_i longer than event E_j?

(5) How many and which events are such that:

(a) Their start may cause event E_i?

(b) They may co-exist with event E_i?

(c) Their completion may cause event E_i?

(d) Their duration is longer than that of event E_i?

(6) Are there sequences of events (only consecutive, only contiguous, or also overlapping) that lead to event E_i, and, if so, how many and which ones? (NB: chain of causally connected events.)

(7) Let us generalize the concept of co-existence: The formula

$$\{E_x\} := \{E_i\} \oplus \{E_j\} \oplus \neg \{E_k\}$$

defines a set of events $\{E_x\}$ as being a subset of events $\{E_i\}$ that co-exist (partial or complete overlap) with events in set $\{E_j\}$ but which must not co-exist with events in set $\{E_k\}$.

If the sets $\{E_i\}$, $\{E_j\}$, and $\{E_k\}$ are given, how many and which events form set $\{E_x\}$?

(8) From among a set of events $\{E_i\}$, which event lasts shortest and longest?

(9) From among a set of events $\{E_i\}$, which event starts or finishes earliest or latest?

(10) From among a set of events $\{E_i\}$, which event lasts closest to a given time interval?

(11) We can restrict the causal relationship between two events, E_i and E_j, by saying that E_j must start or finish at least t_{ij} time units after E_i starts.

Suppose a matrix of this kind of restrictions is given for a set of events, we can ask a question similar to (6):

Are there sequences of events that can form a chain of potentially causal links leading to a given event and, if so, how many and which ones?

The subject matter of this project is closely related to the problems of the Critical Path Method and PERT, although the primary context has been the interpretation of experimental data in physics or chemistry.

STUDIES ON THE BEHAVIOR OF AN ORGANISM

IN A HOSTILE ENVIRONMENT

We have recently reported on a simulation project concerning a self-preserving and learning organism (Findler and McKinzie 1969c). The organism had a major goal, survival, and various subgoals, such as optimization of its state of health, maximization of pleasure, minimization of pain, exploration and control of its environment, and so on. It perceived a set of stimuli and emitted a set of responses the quality of which improved with experience. The latter was achieved by means of some rudimentary rote and associative learning of patterns.

A graduate student, A. E. C. Allan, and I are engaged on a model that goes well beyond the above outlined project. The block diagram of figure 1 illustrates the organism and its interface with the outside environment.

The *environment* is represented by a set of functions {g} the ith of which is expressed as

$$g_i = g_i \left[\{g(t-1)\}, \{a(t-1)\}, r, t\right].$$

where $\{g(t-1)\}$ is the set of stimulus functions at time $(t-1)$ – that is, the time scale is quantized; $\{a(t-1)\}$ is another set of functions representing the actions of the organism at time $(t-1)$; r is a location vector in the environment space; and t is time.

The *perceptors* work, to some extent, in parallel. Danger and high intensity signals, however, suppress parallelism. Also, a sudden problem of importance, such as the appearance of an item blocking some action of the organism, may reduce the overall attention and focus certain perceptors towards the item in question.

The *'filtering'* effect may somewhat distort and reduce the amount of incoming information. It has a stochastic and a deterministic component. The latter expresses the facts that, for example, visual stimuli follow the inverse-square-distance law, audio stimuli the inverse-cube-distance law, and so on. Special attention may enhance the resolution in perception. Scanning and localized attention co-occur to some degree and may increase in importance at each other's expense.

The *short-term memory* has a limited capacity. *Forgetting* in it is quasi-deliberate. It is controlled by the *importance selector* mechanism that transfers items to the *long-term memory* or pushes them out into the ocean of forgetting. The importance selector mechanism searches the long-term memory before it makes a decision. The contents of the two types of memory are data (descriptive information), values (observed and believed goals) and programs (prescriptive information).

The *effectors* are controlled partly by the short-term memory, mostly for quick-response and relatively unimportant actions, partly by the long-term memory for complex, planned actions and instinctive or much-practiced behavior.

The *planning* and *abstracting* are interactive long-term memory processes. The planning process may construct a tentative behavioral structure in two different ways. It can chart a traversal path on the 'action tree' (a concept similar to the well-known 'game tree' entity), which had been explored before, or it may build the action tree and chart a 'promising path' on it, relying on the principle of similarity to past experiences. In most cases, the combination of these two actions has to be followed.

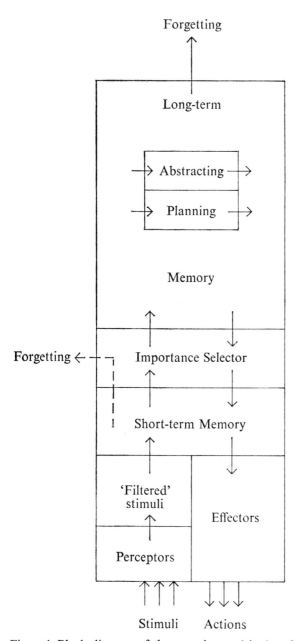

Figure 1. Block diagram of the organism and its interface with the environment.

The abstracting process makes inductive and deductive inferences. It generalizes by ignoring unimportant details. Abstracting relies heavily on rote and associative learning processes.

Forgetting from the long-term memory is spontaneous and uncontrollable. The strength of associative links between items becomes lower and lower with time. Below a certain threshold value, access via that particular link will be impossible. On the other hand, successful usage of the access linkage would reinforce the association.

Finally, the *actions* of the organism take place in two distinct ways:

(1) The organism can use its effectors in order: (a) to move itself from one place to another at a 'terrain'-dependent speed. The speed is a function of the difficulty of and the organism's familiarity with the terrain. (For example, the exploratory mode requires more cautious behavior.) This, of course, costs energy and energy can be recuperated only at certain locations. The objective of moving is twofold: either to go to a 'recharge-repair' station (*see* below) or to explore. The drive to explore (with qualifications and restrictions) is built into the organism. (b) To move certain objects, below a given size, from one place to another (for example, obstructing items). This again costs energy. Planning must tell the organism to evade or remove an object. (c) To subject itself to a concentrated 'recharge-repair' process. It excludes all other activity except the receiving of danger signals from the environment.

(2) The other type of action of the organism affects its internal environment. On the basis of experience, it may rearrange its subgoals that, in general, form the basis of the decision-making processes. Namely, instead of a single evaluation function, the organism has an ordered set of subgoals. These are arranged in a hierarchy of subordination and co-ordination. Changes in the hierarchy are affected through learning.

Within a given time interval, the organism cannot perform more than one of the following things:

(a) take one action through its effectors;
(b) make an observation about the outside environment;
(c) contemplate, that is, evaluate a subgoal, plan, abstract, decide, and so on.

Finally, it is worth noting that numerical and symbolic data, algorithmic and heuristic processes, descriptors with partial and full information are mixed throughout the whole project, which is at a middle stage of development.

COMPUTER SIMULATION OF SOLVING CROSSWORD PUZZLES
BY HUMANS

Studies on human problem-solving have been in the focus of Artificial Intelligence research since the beginning of work in this area. The very fact that the problems to be dealt with are ill-structured and ill-defined renders them highly challenging.

The interdisciplinary nature of Computer Science becomes obvious with this project – Linguistics, Psychology, and the Humanities all would contribute to a successful model. A graduate student, Wiley R. McKinzie, and I are engaged in this work.

There can be two basically different approaches. We could aim at programming the 'world's best crossword-puzzle solver' or we could direct our interest towards how humans do this task, and learn about it and learn from it. We have adopted the more modest second objective, which is still extremely challenging.

Our technique can be formulated as follows: we solve, say, half a dozen crossword puzzles (CWP) and set up a complex information structure in which the clue words and the solution words appear, all embedded in a reasonably large superset of words. The words or, rather, concepts are tied together by associative linkages. We shall call this whole entity the *cognitive map*. Let us define a *plane* in the cognitive map, being the locus of concepts held together by some common property. Such are, for example, agriculture, Latin America, music, and so on. Some of the information appears on lists, with pointers to one or several planes, since this is the natural thing to do. For instance, if the clue asks for a New York City bank, people who do not live in that city have to search a shorter or longer list of banks in their mind while New Yorkers may get some additional mnemonic aid by imagining going along certain streets and rediscovering bank buildings there. Similarly, if you do not know the alphabetically arranged list of the fifty states in the USA, you would do well by reconstructing mentally the map and enumerate the states therefrom.

One must bear in mind that there are two, not necessarily identical, cognitive maps one deals with. One of these is that of the creator of the CWP and the other one is that of the problem solver. For example, we often find clue words unsatisfactory or misleading – an instance of different cognitive maps.

The associative linkages represent various types of ties. At the lowest level, synonyms are connected. (Note that there are no 'perfect' synonyms, they may be equivalent in one, some, or most, but hardly ever all, contexts.

Consider, for example, *rich, well-to-do, wealthy, opulent,* and *affluent.*)
Antonyms belong to this category, as well. They are simply negated synonyms.
Note that in our interpretation, not only single words but whole logical
units, possibly comprising several words, appear at the nodes of the cognitive
map. Homonyms, that is, particular word forms that have multiple meanings,
must also be noted here.

The next higher level of linkage connects concepts or words frequently
used together. For example, *pile* and *sand, sand* and *castle, castle* and *home,*
home and *garden,* and so on, is a one-dimensional section of an indefinitely
long chain of this type.

We may have a linkage that stands for some logical tie. For example,
brick, mortar, timber, roofing slate, glass, and so on, are all connected in a
logical way. Pointers to superset and subset units also belong to this category.

There can be some wild associations, such as the ones used by poets or
even wilder. The examples *sunshine* and *smile, lips* and *strawberries,* may
give an idea of what we mean here.

The cognitive map must also contain circumscriptions or explanations of
concepts modified by one or more other words. It may, therefore, contain
whole phrases. The description of the nodes of the cognitive map is completed by its syntactic information, such as which part of speech the entity
is, how its singular and plural (noun, pronoun), cases (pronoun), tenses
(verb), adverb (adjective), and so on are formed.

It is important to emphasize that the cognitive map so constructed is not
'preprocessed', or 'tailor-made' for one or several CWPs. It models a section
of a human cognitive map. The latter, however, is a dynamic entity – it may
change gradually as a consequence of certain learning processes.

There are noticeable inter-personal differences at two levels of CWP
solving. These are intriguing problems, indeed, and we describe them in the
following.

The first activity is related to finding a particular answer word. It is
accomplished by a complex interplay of a search in the cognitive map
(semantic scan), on one hand, and of a pattern-matching process, on the
other. The pattern matching is a multi-level phenomenon. The first, simplest
and immediate-response, test considers only whether a word is short (say,
less than five letters) or long. The second stage counts the number of letters
in a word and rejects unsatisfactory candidates. As more and more letters
become known from intersecting word solutions, the pattern matching will
consist of elaborate masking and comparing operations.

The semantic scan and the pattern matching processes occur alternatively, sometimes quasi-simultaneously. Often, short lists of potentially acceptable answer words are formed by the semantic scan, and are then further scrutinized by the current template. We conjecture here that a learning process tends to steer the human CWP solver towards an optimum sequencing technique. Namely, it seems evident that unduly frequent pattern-matching, particularly in the early stages of the solution, could prove inhibitory in the overall search. (Although, in the extreme, the exclusive application of the proverbial British Museum algorithm could also arrive at the solution of the CWP. This technique consists of an exhaustive search of words tested, in our case, with regard only to their acceptability in the template.) On the other hand, a much too rare resort to pattern matching can be wasteful and may lead to dead ends.

A very important technique must also be mentioned here. Well-versed users of a language have developed a powerful feel for the morphemes and frequent groupings of letters in that language. They intuitively follow an information theoretic approach when they fill in gaps of missing letters, even in unknown words. We also intend to incorporate this idea in our model by using, in the qualitative sense, tables of frequencies of occurrence of digrams, trigrams, and so on, and a list of morphemes, prefixes and suffixes.

A high-level learning process in the computer program is envisaged, which would simulate the human tendency to arrive at an 'optimum balance' among the above discussed three methods. This optimum, if any, assumedly depends on the CWP at hand and on the problem-solver's capabilities, such as his associative and pattern-matching faculties, his active and passive vocabulary, and so on.

The other source of divergence between individuals is of strategical import. Briefly, it amounts to how long one should try using the combination of the semantic scanning, pattern matching, and information theoretic guessing for a particular word. Also, when one abandons a word and interrupts the search for it, what is next to do? Should one look for intersecting words and how many times should one change from 'across' to 'down' from 'down' to 'across' or go on 'systematically' through all 'across' clues, then through all 'down' clues?

The hierarchy of priorities must be quite flexible and problem-dependent for a good problem-solver. How do we simulate this behavioral component? The number of questions one can ask is practically unlimited: How do we simulate the sudden help provided by pattern matching? Is, perhaps, a part of the list constructed by the semantic scan below the level of consciousness? What is the relative level of importance of the letters already found at different positions of an unknown answer word? How does the probability of finding the answer per unit time vary with time? What are the relative contributions of the three solution techniques?

Humans have the excellent capability of approximate sorting and resorting items by a variety of simple and complex criteria. How can we simulate that?

We often find ourselves in a dead end in our problem-solving processes. The computer would do that even more so. Suppose the clue word is 'First Woman'. The answer is obviously 'Eve'. However, the program may go in the wrong direction by retrieving the synonym of 'Woman', 'Lady'. Of course, the 'First Lady' is the President's wife, and we might get 'Pat Nixon' that luckily does not satisfy the pattern-matching condition, it is longer than three letters.

We are currently working with CWPs for adults. We have also studied some children's puzzles rather briefly. It seems plausible that the solution processes would be somewhat different for the latter. Not only is the vocabulary more restricted but the answers are 'closer to the surface', there is much less 'plane jumping', the puns (a very tough nut for us) are easier, and so on.

As can be seen, this project is developing into a true marriage of algorithmic and heuristic processes. The amount of knowledge one can supply to the program is really unlimited. Learning can take place in a variety of different ways. We have mentioned two before. Other modes are with reference to learning new words and new associations.

The project is at a relatively early stage of development. We conclude by saying that no construct may be rich enough to model language other than language itself.

AN INFORMATION-RETRIEVAL SYSTEM BASED ON NOISEFREE AND NOISY DIAGRAMS

In the last decade, interest has been increasing both in question-answering systems and in logic concerning geometrical objects. The reader is referred to the survey papers on the first topic (Kasher 1967, Simmons 1969) and to Evans (1964) and Kochen (1969) with regard to the second one.

A graduate student, Rudolf Meyer, and I are engaged in developing a system that accepts data, and answers questions about noisefree and noise-disturbed two-dimensional objects. At present, the set of objects consists of circles, squares, rectangles and triangles (isosceles, equilateral, and so on).

The input specifies their type and position in a coordinate system, and nothing more. This is stored in an appropriate data structure. Questions, to be described below, are translated into a logical format and interpreted. A search is then performed for all correct answers, which are finally translated back into English for output.

Let us first see the six major types of *questions* one can ask in the *noisefree* case:

$$(1) \text{ Is } n_i \begin{bmatrix} \text{completely} \\ \text{partially} \\ \text{tangentially} \\ \text{immediately} \end{bmatrix} \begin{bmatrix} \text{above} \\ \text{below} \\ \text{to the right of} \\ \text{to the left of} \\ \text{inside of} \end{bmatrix} n_k ?$$

Here n_i and n_k are identification labels assigned by the user. Any combination of the members in the first bracket ('adverbs') and in the second one ('positionals') forms a legitimate question, except 'immediately' cannot be followed by 'inside of'. That is, there are 19 different questions of type 1.

$$(2) \text{ Which } \begin{bmatrix} \text{figure} \\ \text{circle} \\ \text{triangle} \\ \text{square} \\ \text{rectangle} \end{bmatrix} \text{ extends most to the } \begin{bmatrix} \text{right} \\ \text{left} \\ \text{top} \\ \text{bottom} \end{bmatrix} ?$$

Now all 20 possible combinations of the members in the first bracket ('objects') and in the second ('directions') are legitimate questions. Horizontal and vertical tangents of the objects define their limits in the sense of the question.

$$(3) \text{ Which } \begin{bmatrix} \text{figure} \\ \text{circle} \\ \text{triangle} \\ \text{square} \\ \text{rectangle} \end{bmatrix} \text{ is } \begin{bmatrix} \text{completely} \\ \text{partially} \\ \text{tangentially} \\ \text{immediately} \end{bmatrix} \begin{bmatrix} \text{above} \\ \text{below} \\ \text{to the right of} \\ \text{to the left of} \\ \text{inside of} \end{bmatrix} \text{which} \begin{bmatrix} \text{figure} \\ \text{circle} \\ \text{triangle} \\ \text{square} \\ \text{rectangle} \end{bmatrix} ?$$

Here again the only combination not permitted is 'immediately' followed by 'inside of'. This leaves 475 different questions of type 3. 'Partially inside of' means partially overlapping.

$$(4) \text{ Which is the } \begin{bmatrix} \text{largest} \\ \text{smallest} \end{bmatrix} \begin{bmatrix} \text{figure} \\ \text{circle} \\ \text{triangle} \\ \text{square} \\ \text{rectangle} \end{bmatrix} ?$$

All 10 combinations of the members in the first bracket ('adjectives') and in the second are legitimate.

(5) How many $\begin{bmatrix} \text{figures} \\ \text{circles} \\ \text{triangles} \\ \text{squares} \\ \text{rectangles} \end{bmatrix}$ are there in the diagram?

There are 5 possible questions of type 5.

(6) Is n_i $\begin{bmatrix} \text{larger than} \\ \text{smaller than} \\ \text{of the same size as} \\ \text{similar to} \end{bmatrix}$ n_k?

The first three of the four 'comparatives' refer to area size, the last one to geometrical similarity.

The *answers* to be given in the respective six cases are as complete as possible:

(1) $\begin{bmatrix} \text{circle} \\ \text{rectangle} \\ \text{square} \\ \text{triangle} \end{bmatrix}$ n_i is $\begin{bmatrix} \text{completely} \\ \text{partially} \\ \text{tangentially} \\ \text{immediately} \end{bmatrix}$ $\begin{bmatrix} \text{above} \\ \text{below} \\ \text{to the right of} \\ \text{to the left of} \\ \text{inside of} \end{bmatrix}$ $\begin{bmatrix} \text{circle} \\ \text{rectangle} \\ \text{square} \\ \text{triangle} \end{bmatrix}$ n_k.

Further, if the two objects are not situated 'immediately', the objects in between the two, if any, and their identification label will also be given. With all 'partially' answers, a distinction will be made between intersection and non-intersection.

(2) $\begin{bmatrix} \text{figure} \\ \text{circle} \\ \text{triangle} \\ \text{square} \\ \text{rectangle} \end{bmatrix}$ n_i extends most to the $\begin{bmatrix} \text{right} \\ \text{left} \\ \text{top} \\ \text{bottom} \end{bmatrix}$.

More than one object may appear in the answer.

(3) $\begin{bmatrix} \text{circle} \\ \text{triangle} \\ \text{square} \\ \text{rectangle} \end{bmatrix}$ n_i is $\begin{bmatrix} \text{completely} \\ \text{partially} \\ \text{tangentially} \\ \text{immediately} \end{bmatrix}$ $\begin{bmatrix} \text{above} \\ \text{below} \\ \text{to the right of} \\ \text{to the left of} \\ \text{inside of} \end{bmatrix}$ $\begin{bmatrix} \text{circle} \\ \text{triangle} \\ \text{square} \\ \text{rectangle} \end{bmatrix}$ n_k.

Here again there can be several answers. Additional information, similarly to answer (1), may be given.

$$(4) \begin{bmatrix} \text{figure} \\ \text{circle} \\ \text{triangle} \\ \text{square} \\ \text{rectangle} \end{bmatrix} n_i \text{ is the } \begin{bmatrix} \text{largest} \\ \text{smallest} \end{bmatrix} \text{ with area equal to } \ldots$$

Several objects may satisfy the above criterion.

$$(5) \text{ There are} \ldots \begin{bmatrix} \text{figures} \\ \text{circles} \\ \text{triangles} \\ \text{squares} \\ \text{rectangles} \end{bmatrix} \text{ in the diagram.}$$

$$(6)\, n_i \text{ is } \begin{bmatrix} \text{larger than} \\ \text{smaller than} \\ \text{of the same size as} \\ \text{similar to} \end{bmatrix} n_k.$$

If the answer is 'same', the type and the area of the object will also be given. 'Similar to' makes sense with triangles and rectangles only.

One can ask for all relations between two objects, all object pairs for which a relation is true, distances between the centers of gravity of two objects, and so on.

The second phase of the project consists of establishing a set of simple *commands that move objects* by translation, rotation, symmetric reflection with regard to a given axis, scale-true changes in size, and various distortions.

Thirdly, *noise* is introduced in the diagram by different methods. Techniques are to be studied that reduce the effect of the noise. A metric of the noise space is to be defined. We shall look for the boundaries in the noise domain within which the right answers are still given to the questions discussed above.

Programming has been started in this project.

STUDIES ON DECISION MAKING USING THE GAME OF POKER

After some dormant period following an initial study (Findler 1961), a project on human decision-making under uncertainty and risk was restarted. A postdoctoral fellow, Heinz Klein, a graduate student, William Gould, and I have been engaged in this work. Two more students, Alexander Kowal and John Menig, have recently joined us. Also, we must acknowledge the contribution by a whole class of students whose term projects are being made use of in this study.

The main task of present-day research in heuristic programming is to identify human decision-making techniques by means of empirical investigations, to formulate these as explicatory hypotheses and then to express them precisely as computer programs. For a critical survey of such programs, *see* Klein (1970). The theories so obtained are tested in three stages, as expounded by Newell and Simon in several well-known papers. [*See*, for example, Newell and Simon (1961).]

The first, and simplest, test considers only whether the simulation program can accomplish the same task, such as prove a theorem, make a legal (and hopefully) good move in chess, and so on. This is a 'sufficiency' test showing that the mechanisms incorporated in the model are sufficient for solving some problems.

The second test stage checks whether the methods used by the program and by the human subject were qualitively the same. This, of course, is a much stronger proof but it can cover only a certain range of behavior.

The last, and most exacting, test consists of a detailed, step-by-step comparison between the protocol of the think-aloud process and the trace of the computer program. A reasonable conformity indicates a 'good' theory whereas the lack of it warrants modifications in the program.

The above expresses our goal – we have wanted to study how humans make decisions on the basis of imperfect information, and to form a theory of it in terms of a running program. This is in accordance with the main problem of modern psychology: How to fit a 'voluntaristic' choice into a deterministic science. A successful model of decision making would be of obvious value to the social scientist, psychologist, military strategist, and so on. Draw-poker was selected as the environment for decision making, a game rich enough and well known in many parts of the world. The variables that affect a decision are relatively small in number and can be easily identified. This renders our objective of creating a rigorous model, which can be made both descriptive and normative, reasonable. In the following, we describe some problems which have arisen in the project.

If pay-off is measured in money, poker is a zero-sum game. Yet, experience shows that some people win, others lose consistently. Two explanations offer themselves for this phenomenon:

(a) The utility *v.* money function is non-linear and varies from individual to individual. Pay-off is measured in utility and since the financial resources of the players are different and, also, people play for the 'fun of it', so they tend to deviate from a normative strategy based on money.

(b) Some players make wrong decisions consistently because of insufficient experience, inferior memory, and computational ability, and/or pathological fondness of risk, as compared to others.

For lack of sound evidence supporting the first explanation, we have assumed that the sole objective of the game is to maximize monetary gains and the reasons listed under (b) must hold.

In spite of this simplification and the exclusion of explicit or implicit cooperation between players, poker seems to share many important features with 'real life' problems. Such are:

(1) In order to evaluate alternative courses of action, the players have to assume (a) a likely 'state of nature' based on subjective probabilities, (b) plausible (not necessarily rational) actions by the other participants.

(2) A player can *manipulate information* by (a) buying some information representing the others' situation, (b) giving away some information misleading other players about his own situation.

The decisions themselves are based on the information held, real or imagined, on the players' subgoals with values attached to them, and on the processes that operate on all these. Multi-stage decision making, as in poker, requires tactical and strategical considerations. Tactical considerations refer to momentary and short-term goals (within a bidding cycle, within a game) whereas the strategical ones apply to the whole period of competition among the same participants (an evening of play). The style of resource management is a visible projection of a player's strategy. This is in obvious analogy with the policy decisions in commercial enterprises and in political campaigns.

The *total information* available to a player consists of

(a) the value of his hand;

(b) his betting behavior in the current and past games (his expected 'image' with other players);

(c) the opponent's betting behavior in the current and past games;

(d) the number of cards drawn by the player and the opponents.

We envisage and have, in fact, planned a learning process that builds up players' 'image' on the basis of their game-playing behavior.

We can characterize players' information by using the usual distinction made depending on the *a priori* knowledge of probability distribution functions. It can, therefore, be

(a) *certain* (own hand, opponents' bets, and so on);

(b) *risky* (expected distribution of hands, chances of being high before and after draw, chances of improving hand by the draw);

(c) *uncertain* (the future behavior of the opponents in betting and drawing).

It is beyond the scope of this paper to compare in detail a game of perfect information, such as chess, and poker, a game of imperfect information, from the behavioral point of view. Briefly, chess derives its challenge solely from the computational complexity involved whereas in poker the challenge comes from inferences to be made in relying on past events and current probabilities, and from the ill-structured task of optimum long-term money management. While bluffing has no or very little role in chess, it is a major, multifaceted component of playing poker. Beginners, for example, do not usually realize that under-representing a strong hand ('sandbagging') is as important as over-representing a weak one. No consistent behavior must become apparent, either.

Bluffing has two objectives: a direct monetary one in the short run, whether bluffing is associated with a strong or weak hand, and another one, to keep the communication channel noisy in the long run. Even from this simple description of bluffing, one can see the contours of a complex optimization procedure.

There are basically two, not completely disjoint, approaches to learn about human decision-making in poker and to derive an optimum strategy for it. First, we could build an abstract mathematical model. It has to be empirically meaningful, that is, the relations between its symbols and functional dependencies, on one hand, and human behavior in actual play, on the other, must be realistic and easily identifiable. The model should cover all aspects of behavior that are relevant to the play.

The other approach is to try to find out what information-processing mechanisms are at work, what distinguishes a mediocre or poor player from an excellent one. We can then build a symbol-manipulating model with a rather rigorous explicatory and predictive power. By systematic modifications of the model, one could hopefully arrive at a set of mechanisms and memory structures that is optimum although it may not represent any real-life player. It is also of special interest to compare the characteristics of the optimum strategy so obtained with the recommendations found in the vast literature on poker.

The first approach, in its extremity, has never been accomplished because the presently available tools of the theory of games are not sufficiently rich for the complexity of poker. However, these models are valuable inasmuch as they pinpoint certain problems and give a sound idea of the restrictions in their assumptions. They also help organize a conceptual framework for other types of investigation. We note here that even if the abstract mathematical approach could handle all aspects of poker, the derived optimum strategy is likely to be such that the data processing and memory requirements prescribed would exceed human capabilities.

Our technique does incorporate certain computational aspects of the first approach but basically follows the second one. An executive routine was first constructed to perform the banker's role and to do various housekeeping duties. Accordingly, it

shuffles and deals cards,

calls players for opening bets,

takes bets,

calls for draw cards,

carries out the showdown.

It also posts certain public information, such as the state of the game (opening, betting before draw, draw, opening after draw, betting after draw, evaluation), the general betting sequence (the betting history of each player in the current game), the size of the pot, and so on.

This executive routine accepts up to eight sets of heuristic rules (= eight players) covering all possible states of the game and expressed in the form of a decision tree. Or else, it can generate decision trees and thereby create opponents for a single set of rules to be tried out. The so-generated decision trees are based on a series of Monte Carlo calculations carried out earlier. On the basis of these calculations, we were able to arrive at a certain flexible way of partioning the problem space and discover effective but simple rules of betting and drawing for each subspace. It turned out that not all variables are relevant ('active') in every stage of the game. This is important from the human player's standpoint since psychological evidence indicates that man seldom attends to more than a rather limited number of features of his environment at a time. (Of course, 'good' decision makers are concerned with the most important features.)

Students in a course were to program various heuristic rules to be found in the literature on poker, by relying on their experience and imagination. These rules were built into the main framework and submitted to analysis. The analysis can be shortened and the statistical results can be made more significant by using various short-cuts. Such are:

(a) The hands dealt are reproduced for different players in subsequent games, similarly to the practice in bridge tournaments;

(b) In addition to considering the final financial status of each player after a series of games, we form for them two probability distribution functions, namely, the loss/game and win/game distributions. Obviously, for a good player, the modal value of the first would be in the low value region (close to that of the ante) since he must realize very soon that he cannot win. The

F

opposite is true for his win/game distribution – when he wins, he makes sure that the opponents are carried as far as possible in the betting process.

We are, therefore, planning to compare the vital statistics of these two curves, representing each strategy, versus the same representing the average of the strategies of other players. Not only would this method yield a reliable ranking, but also we could pick the best features of every strategy, combine them, and arrive at a quasi-optimum machine player.

Besides the last-mentioned process, various other types of high-level learning have been considered and planned. Let us discuss here only two, very briefly.

We could develop a 'Bayesean' player who keep on readjusting his strategy by comparing the actual outcomes of events with the ones he previously expected. To formulate it in a less 'partisan' manner: How is 'rationality' adopted and what changes does it undergo in the decision maker? The conjecture is that rationality is inborn but the value scale becomes adjusted continually.

Sophisticated players capture the characteristics of their opponents' strategies fairly soon and adapt their own strategy accordingly. They also tend to make sure that no consistent 'image' can be formed of them by the opponents. Or else, they deliberately reveal a false image, which fact can be made use of subsequently. It is a difficult and challenging task to simulate these aspects of the game.

The system design part is completed and programming has reached a rather advanced stage with this project.

A SELF-REPAIRING PROGRAMMING SYSTEM

The living brain is known for its tremendous survival ability. Not only can one stay alive after serious brain lesions but, also, very often the initial impairment of functioning gradually disappears to some extent. This effect is largely due to the redundant and statistically-distributed logic in the gray matter.

Computer hardware and software designers have taken the course of action diametrically opposite to the above. Mainly for reasons of economy, practically no system incorporates redundancy in a sophisticated manner. Error detection and correction are limited to comparatively very simple techniques. The malfunctioning of a component or a routine, if and when detected, must result in the termination of operation.

Let us now imagine a self-contained computer travelling on an artificial satellite. It is exposed to the potentially detrimental effects of colliding with tiny meteorites, cosmic radiation of various kinds, and so on. It is vital for the mission of the satellite that the functioning of the computer should be 'sufficiently' reliable. By 'sufficiently' we mean that even if the computations become interrupted, and programs and data are garbled temporarily, the operations may resume, and the impairment caused should gradually disappear.

A graduate student, Michael Kessler, and I are engaged on a project that aims at this ultimate goal. We are at a very early stage of work, consequently the following ideas are rather tentative as yet.

We wish to present a task to the system in a highly abstract and concise manner. When we first formulate a problem, any problem in fact, it has to be in an extremely detailed manner. Think of a child whom you want to send the first time to the neighborhood supermarket to buy a pound of sugar. If he has never been there with you before, you explain to him the whole process step by step, how to get to the supermarket, where to find the sugar, how and where to pay the cashier, how to get help if needed, and so on, and so forth. However, when you send him the second time (and he has a reasonable level of intelligence) to buy some different item, say, a pound of butter, all you have to tell him is to do exactly the same things as before except for the location of dairy products, which is two rows to the left of the shelves where sugar is found.

In other words, when you give instructions to, when you teach an intelligent person, you build for him (or, better, teach him how to build) flexible subroutines to which you can refer in subsequent interactions. A sort of program library develops in the evolving mind – *experience* is gained.

This is roughly our objective, to teach a system in a gradually higher and higher mode of communication. The abstract description of the task can generate code for a program that performs the task. Suppose there is a store of Program Building Blocks (PBB) which can be small open and closed subroutines, individual instructions, and other program segments. Each of these PBBs is assigned a generalized label, which may bear the statistical 'strength' of linkages to other PBBs and some crude taxonomic description regarding its area of applicability. When a task is presented to the system, a search process is set up to establish temporary linkages between PBBs, and a simple, largely unmodifiable executive routine calls the program so constructed.

The idea is to store multiple copies of the abstract task description. So, if some damage occurs to a program part or to some of the task descriptions, it will be noticed and the code will be regenerated. We are not concerned with the engineering problem of detecting damage. Also, hardware failure is restricted to the computer memory.

Let us now sketch a simple example of this approach. Suppose the task is to test two list structures for equality. This in fact is a very common activity, paraphrased in a multitude of different ways, in our everyday life.

The abstract task description would consist of the definitions of

(1) a list structure,

(2) systematic traversing of a list structure,

(3) comparing atomic symbols,

(4) dichotomic (yes-no) answers.

The first and the last are static descriptions, the second and the third are dynamic, process descriptions. The first definition refers to two lower levels, to lists and to symbols – it is therefore a hierarchical definition. So is the second definition because it must refer to horizontal sequencing, descending and ascending. Both of the first two definitions are recursive in nature. Finally, the last definition will be used at two different levels, at the level of symbol comparisons and at the level of program output. For epistemological reasons, it is advantageous to use recursive definitions and definitions that can be used at several levels.

We have to discuss yet how data are stored and how they can survive lesions of varying severity. We have intended to model stored information in terms of a cognitive map, similar in nature to that in the project on cross-word-puzzle solving. Damage is represented by cutting off access routes between entities. A gradual improvement in the retrieval capability of the system takes place when roundabout associations are discovered and detours are short cut.

ACKNOWLEDGEMENT

The work reported here has been supported by the National Science Foundation, Grant *GJ-658*.

REFERENCES

Evans, T. G. (1964) A heuristic program to solve geometry – analogy problems. *Proc. AFIPS 1964 SJCC*, **25,** 327–38. Baltimore: Spartan Books.

Findler, N. V. (1961) Computer model of gambling and bluffing. *IRE Trans. on Electronic Computers*, *EC–10*, pp. 97–8.

Findler, N. V. (1970) On the role of exact and non-exact associative memories in human and machine information processing. *Computer and Information Sciences*, Vol. 2 (ed. Tou, J. T.). New York: Academic Press.

Findler, N. V. & McKinzie, W. R. (1969a) On a new tool in Artificial Intelligence research. *Proc. Int. Conf. on Artificial Intelligence*, pp. 259–70, Washington, DC.

Findler, N. V. & McKinzie, W. R. (1969b) On a computer program that generates and queries kinship structures. *Behav. Sci.*, **14**, 334–43.

Findler, N. V. & McKinzie, W. R. (1969c) Computer simulation of a self-preserving and learning organism. *Bull. Math. Biophys.*, **31**, 247–53.

Findler, N.V., Pfaltz, J. L. & Bernstein, H. J. (1971) *Four High Level Extensions of FORTRAN IV: SLIP, AMPPL-II, TREETRAN and SYMBOLANG* (to be published by Spartan Books).

Kasher, A. (1967) Data-retrieval by computer: A critical survey. *The Growth of Knowledge* (ed. Kochen, M.). New York: Wiley.

Klein, H. (1970) *Heuristische Entscheidungsmodelle*. Wiesbaden: Gabler.

Kochen, M. (1969) Automatic question-answering of English-like questions about simple diagrams. *J. Ass. comput. Mach.*, **16**, 26–48.

Newell, A. & Simon, H.A. (1961) Computer simulation of human thinking. *Science*, **134**, 2011–17.

Simmons, R. F. (1969) Natural language question-answering systems: 1969. *Comm. Ass. comput. Mach.*, **13**, 15–30.

Weizenbaum, J. (1963) Symmetric list processor. *J. Ass. comput. Mach.*, **6**, 524–44.

Problem Solving

Heuristic Search : Concepts and Methods

E.J.SANDEWALL

INTRODUCTION

Of three lectures on this topic, the first one was used to discuss the general concept of 'heuristic', and that special case which has been mostly studied, viz. tree search. In the second lecture, the 'representation problem' of phrasing various practical problems in the tree search representation was discussed with a number of actual examples. In the third lecture, some theorems and experimental results about the efficiency of various methods were described. Some of the results were later used by Drs Michie and Palme in their lectures.

On page 98, there is a list of some well-known heuristic programs. Although a few names may be missing, the list should be sufficiently complete to prove one thing: the interest in heuristics has increased sharply during the last few years.

Two approaches have been competing. In his report on SIN, Moses (1967) characterizes them as emphasizing *generality* and *expertise*, respectively. In the generality approach, one tries to write a general program which can solve all kinds of problems, provided only that (adequately phrased) information about the particular 'problem environment' of each problem is provided. The 'General Problem Solver' (sic!) (Newell and Simon 1961), DEDUCOM (Stagle 1965a), and the Graph Traverser (Doran & Michie 1966) are examples of this approach.

In the approach that stresses expertise, one concentrates instead on writing a good program for solving problems in one given problem environment. SIN itself is a typical example of that approach, as are game-playing programs [Samuel (1959), Greenblatt, Eastlake and Crocker (1967)], and some programs which, according to rumour, are being used for industrial purposes.

The advantages and disadvantages of each approach are obvious: generality has to be paid for by a decrease in program efficiency. An advantage with the generality approach is that one single heuristic method can quickly be put to use in a variety of problem domains.

It would seem, however, that methods which have been developed in one 'expertise' program *can* be carried over to another problem environment and another program. The only problem is to pull out the abstract heuristic methods from the program descriptions, which are often quite technical and detailed.

One example of this will suffice. The SIN program contains an important heuristic, which Moses describes as follows: 'The Edge heuristic is based on the Liouville theory of integration. In this theory it is shown that if a function is integrable in closed form, then the form of the integral can be deduced up to certain coefficients. A program which employs the Edge heuristic, called EDGE, uses a simple analysis to guess at the form of the integral and then it attempts to obtain the coefficients' (Moses 1967, p. 8). The Edge heuristic is further described on seventeen pages in chapter 5 (Moses 1967).

Unfortunately, the author fails to formulate this important heuristic method in abstract terms. Such an abstract formulation could, for example, run as follows:

> The purpose of the integration program is to start from a given, initial object, and to apply the right operators (from a given set of operators) in the right order, until the given object has been transformed into a given target set (that is, the set of all expressions where the integral sign(s) have been eliminated). The Edge heuristic relies on information which is local to this particular problem environment, and which makes it possible to say, during the search of the solution tree, where in the target set we will eventually land. The EDGE program utilizes this information to get a better estimate of the remaining 'distance' to the target set from each node.

With such a description, it becomes clear that the same heuristic may well be applicable to other problem environments, in other expertise-oriented programs.

Abstract method descriptions, as outlined here, cannot of course serve as substitutes for conventional ones. A concrete description, like the one Moses has given for SIN, will always be needed by the user of the program, or the researcher who attempts to improve on previous work. By contrast, the abstract description is useful for the man who wants to carry over methods to other problem environments, and (of course) for the theoretician who, some time in the future, will attempt to build a mathematical theory of heuristics.

The moral is, therefore, that we need an abstract frame of reference, a set of concepts for describing and analyzing heuristic methods. Such concepts would help in the dissemination of know-how; they would also make it possible to compare the efficiency of various methods and programs, expertise-oriented as well as generality-oriented.

In this report, we shall attempt to set up such a 'frame of reference'. In the following section, we formulate a general 'transformation problem', and discuss some of its cases. In the subsequent two sections, various commonly used heuristic techniques are formulated and discussed. Our stock of concepts is tested in the final sections, where abstract descriptions of some well-known programs and heuristic methods are given.

HEURISTIC SEARCH: RULES OF THE GAME

The problem environments for heuristic search methods always include a set P of *objects* and a set Q of *operators* on these objects. The following problem has often been studied, [*see* for instance Newell *et al.* (1960) *and* Doran (1967)], and has sometimes been referred to as *the* problem-solving problem:

> *Basic transformation problem.* Given an *initial set* $R \subseteq P$, a *target set* $M \subseteq P$, determine r in R and $q_1, q_2, \ldots q_k$ in Q such that
>
> $$q_k(q_{k-1}(\ldots q_2(q_1(r)) \ldots))$$
>
> exists and is a member of the target set M. We call this a transformation problem *from R to M*.

A method for solving basic transformation problems is called a *heuristic search method* if it searches the tree(s) of all possible operator applications, and the order, in which the nodes of this tree are inspected, is governed in some ways by properties of the nodes which have already been created. Heuristic methods require, therefore, that the objects in P are known as symbolic expressions or otherwise have a non-trivial information content. They cannot simply be non-informative tokens of the form 'p_i'.

The following variations on the basic transformation problem occur frequently:

Operators with several outputs. The problem specification is changed as follows. Application of an operator can return a set of objects, rather than a single object. In the transformation process, each output of the operator must then be transformed into the target set.

Example: In analytic integration, the target set M consists of the set of all formulae where the integration sign does not occur. The rule

$$\int A + B dt = \int A dt + \int B dt$$

can be used as an operator q defined by

$$q(\int A + B dt) = \{\int A dt, \int B dt\}$$

In other words, q tells us to integrate $A + B$ by integrating A and B separately. (The final task of joining together the solutions to those two integration problems with a $+$ sign is a trivial matter.)

Operators with several inputs. The problem specification is changed as follows. Initially, each member of R is considered *available*. At each cycle of the solution process, one selects one operator q_j^i which requires i arguments, and i available objects

$$p_1, p_2, \ldots p_i.$$

If $q_j^i(p_1, p_2, \ldots p_i)$ is defined, it is included among the available objects. *Problem:* find some available object which is also a member of M.

Example: This variation frequently occurs in 'forward' logical inference, for instance, in the resolution logic environment.

It has been common practice in heuristic research to consider the cases of several inputs or several outputs as trivial extensions of the one-input/one-output case. For example, the General Problem Solver is formulated in terms of one input operator, and then immediately applied to a problem environment where a two-input operator (Modus Ponens in forward proof) is essential. Similarly, Slagle's group have attempted to use their MULTIPLE program [which is designed for one-input, multiple-output operators, *see* Slagle & Bursky (1968)] to the resolution logic environment, where the most important operator has two inputs and one output.

The fact that an operator requires several inputs can be 'hidden' in various ways. In the case of Modus Ponens, which takes A and $A \supset B$ as inputs, one can say that the operator 'essentially' takes $A \supset B$ as input, so that the merit of an $A \supset B$ formula determines whether the operator shall be applied or not. If the system decides to apply Modus Ponens to a formula $A \supset B$, it checks whether the formula A is available. If it is not, the output is 'failure'. Another, and more general, way of hiding multiple inputs is to consider the set of all available objects as a 'higher level' object. Similarly, the operators are re-defined to accept one higher level object as input, and to emit an incremented object as output.

The disadvantage of all such tricks is that important information gets lost to the system. For example, with the introduction of 'higher level' objects and operators, one will have

$$q(q'(p)) = q'(q(p))$$

(except when $q'(p) - p$ is essential for the application of q, or $q(p) - p$ is essential for the application of q'). It is hard to make traditional tree-search routines 'aware' of such commutativity. In our opinion, one should instead face the fact that some operators take multiple inputs, and study them separately.

Thus the failure to recognize multiple-input operators has led to inefficient programs. It has also led to a regrettable lack of communication: techniques which have been designed for handling multiple-input operators (such as the various 'strategies' for the resolution method) have not been recognized as heuristic methods. People seem to think that they are technical details for handling resolution, whereas in fact they are examples of quite general heuristic principles. One can make a parallel with the 'Edge' heuristic discussed above: general principles have gone unnoticed for lack of abstract concepts to phrase them in.

As a first step to remedy this situation, let us introduce separate names for the various kinds of operators. The terms in table 1 are believed to be illustrative.

TABLE 1

number of inputs	number of outputs	name
one	one	perporator
one	multiple	diporator
multiple	one	conporator
multiple	multiple	fociporator

Our second step will be to illustrate these general concepts and principles by re-interpreting some current heuristic methods (including the unit preference strategy in resolution [*see* Wos *et al.* (1964)]). This is done in later sections.

Some other complications which may occur in the basic transformation problem are:

Operators with or-connected outputs. One often encounters operators which, like diporators, yield a set of objects as outputs, but which merely require that *one* of the outputs is to be transformed to the target set. Such or-connections may occur

(a) intrinsically, for instance 'in order to prove $A \lor B$, prove A or prove B';

(b) because the operator is ambiguous, for example, in resolution logic, where the resolution operator takes two clauses as input and gives one clause as output. Each of the two clauses is a set of literals, and the operator 'annihilates' (in a certain sense) two literals, one from each input. The operator has one output for each combination of literals in the two inputs, and is therefore ambiguous;

(c) because the operator requires a parameter, which may or may not be in the set of objects. For example, in order to prove B in conventional predicate calculus, it is sufficient to prove A and $A \supset B$, where A is arbitrary.

(In example (b), we assume forward proof, and in (a) and (c), backward proof.) We shall refer to all operators which yield or-connected outputs as *ambiguous*. Thus (a) exemplifies an ambiguous perporator, (b) an ambiguous conporator, and (c) an ambiguous diporator.

Still another complication is

Operators with restricted domain. That is, a domain which is a proper subset of the set *P*. Some possible ways of dealing with this complication are discussed in the next section.

Example. In integration, the partial integration operator is not always applicable.

A final complication is

No back-up. In typical problem-solving, application of an operator is never irrevocable: we are always permitted to back up in the solution tree and try some other operator on a previously used object. In some situations [for example, the Edinburgh studies of heuristic automata (Doran 1969)], one encounters similar problems where back-up is not permitted. The transformation problem then boils down to the problem of selecting the best operator at each step.

Sometimes, as for instance in planning, a back-up problem can be transformed to a no-back-up problem, or vice versa. We therefore consider both kinds as variants of the same basic problem.

Summing up, transformation problems can be characterized by a few features, as follows:

(1) What kinds of operators? (per-, con-, di-, foci-porators)

(2) Are operators ambiguous?

(3) Are there restrictions to the domain of operators?

(4) Is back-up permitted?

APPROACHES TO HEURISTIC SEARCH

In this section, we shall attempt to classify and name some methods of heuristic search. Our classification will be put to use in the next few sections, where some previously published methods for heuristic search are reviewed.

In each cycle of the heuristic search process, the program should select one operator to use, and one object (or set of objects) to use it on. Object selection seems to be performed in most cases by one of the following two methods:

(a1) *Labyrinthic methods* proceed down the search tree, and have an explicit mechanism for deciding direction in the tree. This mechanism tells the program 'this is a good branch, go in the same direction', or 'this is a bad branch, back up – – steps and select another branch'.

(a2) *Best bud methods* use an evaluation function which assigns a priority or *merit* to each growth direction (bud) in the tree. At each cycle, the program takes a global look at all the buds, selects the best one, sprouts it, and iterates the cycle. In the new cycle, the best bud from last cycle is no longer a candidate, but it has yielded several new buds. All other buds from last cycle are candidates anew. Back-up occurs automatically if the new buds are unable to compete with the stand-by buds from last cycle.

Methods (a1) and (a2) have been formulated for *perporators*. It is easy to extend them to *diporators*. For *conporators*, it is sometimes a good idea to select one input to the operator according to a labyrinthic or best-bud method, and then to select 'best companions' to the selected first input. We consider this the generalization of (a1) and (a2) to multiple-input operators. A third method category for them would be

(a3) *Best bud bundle methods*, which use an evaluation function that assigns a priority to each combination ('bundle') of 'buds', and selects the best one in each step.

GPS and SIN use labyrinthic methods, whereas SAINT, the Graph Traverser, MULTIPLE, and PPS [*see* Sandewall (1968)] use best-bud methods. The unit preference heuristic (strategy) in resolution is an example of a best bud bundle method.

Another (and at least in principle, independent) basis of classification is how the program selects the operator in each cycle. The following methods have often been used in practice:

(b1) *Object(s) first, one operator afterwards method:* First select the most promising object(s) to work upon, according to a labyrinthic or best-bud method. After that, find a good operator to apply to it (them).

(b2) *Exhaustive method:* Select object(s) as in (b1) and apply all operators to it.

(b3) *Object(s) first, a few operators afterwards method:* A compromise between (b1) and (b2): a few (but not all) operators are selected and applied to the object(s).

(b4) *Object and operator together method:* Consider all possible object-operator combinations and select one of them, using a priority function (This is, in other words, a best-bud method, where each object-operator combination is considered as a 'bud').

The MULTIPLE program and the Graph Traverser are examples of (b2), GPS and SAINT are examples of (b3), whereas unit preference and PPS are examples of (b4).

In methods (b2) and (b3), object selection in one cycle is effectively a choice of operator in the previous cycle. Therefore, they can be considered as special cases of (b1), with a very careful and time-consuming method for operator selection.

The four cases above are clearly not exhaustive, as it is in principle quite possible to run an operator first, object afterward method. Also, labyrinthic instead of best-bud selection of operators is possible (one would keep using the same operator until a 'back-up' or 'change operator' criterion is satisfied). However, these possibilities are probably useless for practical problems.

If the number of operators is very large, or if some operators are ambiguous with a large number of alternatives, then it is not possible to search through all possible cases. This excludes (b2) and (b4) methods. One must first select the proper object(s), and then use a function which selects one or a few operators (and ways of applying them, if ambiguous). Usually, this function recognizes features in the given object, features which determine what operators may be suitable.

In many practical problem environments, one encounters operators which are defined only on a subset of the set P of objects. This restriction has been dealt with in at least two ways, which provides us with a classification in still another dimension:

(c1) *Consider as failure.* If we have heuristically selected an object and an operator, and it turns out that the object is not in the domain of the operator, then give up this branch and try something else.

(c2) *Solve sub-problem.* Let M' be the domain of the operator. Solve the transformation problem from the given object to M', and apply the given operator to the result. Formally, we extend the definition of our operators, so that $q(p) = q(p_1)$, where p_1 is the (possibly ambiguous!) solution to the transformation problem from p to the domain of q.

SAINT uses a type (c1) method, whereas GPS and PPS use type (c2) methods.

In conclusion, we have pointed out three features of heuristic methods which can be used to classify and characterize them:

(a) Mode of object selection.

(b) Mode of operator selection.

(c) Way of handling restricted domains for operators.

SOME FREQUENT TECHNIQUES IN HEURISTICS

In this section, we shall discuss the use of 'merit orderings', plans, and feature vectors ('images') in heuristic methods.

Use of merit orderings. Definitionwise, best-bud methods require that there exists a way of selecting the 'best' one from a set of buds. In all best-bud type methods known to the author, this selection is based on an (explicit or implicit) partial ordering $>$ on the set P of objects. Some maximal bud

according to $>$ (that is, some bud $b*$ such that no other bud satisfies $b>b*$)
is then selected as 'best bud', and is sprouted.

In some, but not in all, cases, the *merit ordering* $>$ is implemented as an
explicit *merit assignment function e*, that is, a mapping from P to the set of
real numbers. $>$ is then defined in an obvious manner by

$$p_1>p_2 \equiv e(p_1)>e(p_2)$$

The problem of finding a suitable merit ordering for a given problem
environment is of course crucial. Often, it is thought about as an *estimate of
distance*. One attempts to define a function d, where $d(p_1, p_2)$ is a rough estimate of the work (the number of operator applications) required to transform
p_1 into p_2. Similarly, one attempts to compute

$$D(p, B) = \min_{b \in B} d(p, b)$$

for reasonable sets B. The merit function e is then defined, for example, as

$$e(p) = -D(p, M).$$

The use of merit orderings is not restricted to best-bud methods. In labyrinthic methods, the criterion for abandoning a path and trying another may
be that $q(p)<p$ by some merit ordering. GPS utilizes just this. [The name
'General Problem Solver' has sometimes been criticized as being too un-
informative. It is natural to call a heuristic method *goal-directed* if its merit
function is defined by D. The variant of GPS described in Newell and Simon
(1961) can then be characterized as a goal-directed perporator search method.]

At first sight, the idea of using a merit ordering has much appeal, although
on closer scrutiny this turns out to be less than obvious. It all depends on
what kind of economy we desire.

Suppose we are solving a transformation problem for perporators, and
that we have already searched part of the tree. Then which of the following
quantities do we want to minimize in our next step?

(d1) *The number of steps* (that is, operator applications) in the 'solution
path' from the initial set R to the target set M?

(d2) The *remaining number of steps* in the 'solution path' from the selected
bud to a member of the target set M?

(d3) The (remaining) *number of steps, including steps that are performed in
blind alleys* (that is, the total number of arcs in the solution tree the way it
looks when we have reached M)?

(d4) The quantity mentioned in (d3), except that if a path is trodden,
abandoned through back-up, and then resumed, the steps which are trodden
several times shall be counted as multiple steps?

If the path to the solution of the transformation problem is to be used as a

G

plan for a more expensive activity in another environment, then (d1) is of course the correct criterion. On the other hand, if we are interested in a member of *M*, rather than in the path to this member (for example, if we are searching for a solution to an integration problem), then (d3) or (d4) would be the correct quantity to minimize. (d3) should be used if the entire search tree is stored in memory, and (d4) should be used if the search tree is stored implicitly on the push-down-list, so that abandoned paths are garbage-collected and all work there has to be re-performed.

If criterion (d1), (d3), or (d4) is to be used, then the 'merit' of a bud is not simply a function of that bud and the target set, but instead a function of the whole 'stump' of the solution tree that has been searched up to now. For example, if the criterion (d3) is used, then the remaining work from a bud is affected if there exists some other bud which has almost as much merit, and which in the future may attract the problem-solver's attention for blind-alley work. It follows that the idea of a merit ordering is sound only if we want to use criterion (d2) – and this is exactly the criterion for which we did not find any obvious application.

Although theoretically shaky, the use of merit orderings seems to be the only technique available today. If criteria (d3) or (d4) are relevant (which is usually the case), then the use of a distance estimate as a merit function is even more questionable. But again, the distance estimate seems to be the only technique we have.

Use of plans. Let *P*, *Q*, *R*, and *M* define a transformation problem for which a solution is known, and let *P'*, $Q' = Q$, *R'*, and *M'* define a transformation problem which is to be solved. Assume also that there exists some mapping *h* which maps *P'* onto *P*, *R'* onto *R*, etc. in such a way that if *p* and $q(p)$ are steps in the known solution, and if $p = h(p')$, then $q(p) = h(q(p'))$. In other words, the function *h* maps solutions in *P'* onto solutions in *P*. Then we can clearly find a solution in *P'* by just re-tracing the solution in *P*.* The solution in *P* will be referred to as a *plan* for the solution in *P'*.

This ideal situation probably never exists, except when *h* is the identity function. However, it may be the case that the requirement $q(p') = h(q(p))$ *often* (though not always) holds. Then it can still be a good strategy to try to follow the plan. If it does not work, we have to resort to another plan, or to the object-operator selection methods mentioned above. (In other words, use

*To ensure that we have a solution, we must assume that *only* members of *M'* are mapped into *M*, that is,

$$h(p') \in M \supset p' \in M'$$

Moreover, it is essential that *R'* is mapped onto (rather than into) *R*, and that *M'* is mapped onto *M*.

of plans may be considered as yet another method, (b5), of operator selection.)

Plans can be generated in several ways, for example, by memorization of previous, successful solutions (Doran's heuristic automaton), by human advice, or by 'look-ahead': solution of an analogous problem in an auxiliary problem space [as in the PLANNER system (Hewitt 1967) and the PPS].

When the problem environment is predicate calculus, the 'abstraction function' h can, for instance, be selected so as to throw away everything except the variables in the formulas [planning GPS: *see* Newell (1964)] or to throw away everything except the boolean connectives (PLANNER).

A third technique is

Use of images. By an image, we mean an item which expresses some, but not all, the information of an object in the set P. The image may be, for example, a vector of features in the object, or (in the case of a LISP-type formula), the top-level structure of the object, with lower level sub-expressions being replaced by asterisks. Although they rarely talk about it in abstract terms, many creators of heuristic programs do in fact use such images.

Images are used for several purposes, including:

(1) as a basis for merit functions (a numerical value is assigned to each feature, and merit is computed as a weighted average of the feature values) or distance functions (computed as a weighted average of 'distance' between features);

(2) as objects in an auxiliary problem space used for planning;

(3) in methods of type (b3), for the selection of operators that should be applied to a given object.

Examples: (1) game-playing programs and (with certain modifications) Doran's heuristic automaton; (2) planning GPS, PLANNER, PPS; (3) GPS.

In this section, we have described and classified general heuristic techniques, and given references from each technique to actual programs which utilize it. In the next two sections, we shall build an inverse system of references. Each section will review one heuristic program in terms of the classification and concepts above.

HEURISTICS IN THE SAINT PROGRAM

In the earlier sections, some aspects of heuristic programs have been discussed. As an exercise in the use of these concepts, we shall now give a description of Slagle's program SAINT. We wish to demonstrate that, with the concepts that have been introduced, the description can be more abstract and involve less programming details than before.

Problem environment. The set P of objects consists of all formulae built from real numbers, variables, various arithmetic functions (addition, subtraction, multiplication, power function, logarithmic, trigonometric, and inverse trigonometric functions), and one functional: the integration operator. The target set M consists of all objects which do not contain the integration operator. The initial set R consists of one single object, which is given to the program on each occasion of use.

The set Q consists of 44 operators. All are perporators, except for one diporator, the formula for the integral of a sum. Some of the perporators (for example, the substitution operator) are ambiguous and governed by a parameter. Most operators have a restricted domain.

Discussion of heuristic method. It is natural to sort the operators in Q into the following disjoint categories:

(a) Standard forms (26 operators). These are perporators whose output is always in the target set M (if the input contains only one occurrence of the integral operator). An example of such a perporator is

$$\int c^v dv = c^v / \ln c$$

Remark: the possibility of singling out those operators which land in the target set is particular for this problem environment, and does not occur in, for example, logical inference.

(b) Algorithm-like transformations (8 operators). These are operators which, if applicable, are usually appropriate. The diporator is one of them.

(c) Heuristic transformations (10 operators). These are operators which may or may not be appropriate. Substitution is one of them.

Let us call these sets $Q1$, $Q2$, and $Q3$, respectively, and define:

$P1 =$ the set of all objects in P which are in the domain of some operator in $Q1$;

$P2 =$ the set of all objects in $P - P1$ which are in the domain of some operator in $Q2$;

$P3 = P - P1 - P2$.

Objects in $P1$ have a solution just around the corner, and should of course be given top priority. For objects in $P2$, we know which operator should be applied (it turns out that there is never more than one), so such objects are given higher priority than objects in $P3$. For objects in $P3$, several operators may be applicable, so a heuristic search has to be performed.

Each object p stands for an expression built with functions. The 'maximum depth' of this expression is significant for the following reasons: (1) the members of $P1$ (usually) have small maximum depth; (2) operators often perform only a small change (one or a few units) on the maximum depth of their input. Under such conditions, it is reasonable to use the depth of an expression as a gross measure of its 'distance' to the target set, and (therefore?) to use it as a merit function.

With this background, the heuristic method used by SAINT can be outlined.

Images. The SAINT program uses images (feature vectors) with eleven components. Maximum depth of expression is one of them. Images are used for three purposes:

(a) selection of best bud (only maximum depth component used);
(b) selection of appropriate operators for a given object in $P3$;
(c) selection of parameters for ambiguous operators.

Handling of restricted domain. If a selected operator is not applicable to a selected object, SAINT just gives up. It does not try to solve a sub-problem.

Object and operator selection. Abstractly speaking, the SAINT program uses an 'object first, a few operators afterwards' selection system, where objects are selected with a best bud method based on a merit ordering. However, there are certain complications to this simple scheme.

The following merit ordering is used:

$p > p'$ **iff** p is a member of $P1$ and p' is not,
     or p is a member of $P2$, and p' is a member of $P3$,
     or   both p and p' are members of $P3$, but p has less maximum depth than p' has.

At each step, SAINT selects some maximal bud in the search tree according to this partial order, and applies suitable operators to it. The operators are selected according to table 2. In $P2$, only one operator is usually applicable;

TABLE 2.

if object is in	then select operator(s) from
$P1$	$Q1$
$P2$	$Q2$
$P3$	$Q3$

in $P3$, the object's image determines which operators shall be selected. Notice in particular that if object is in $P2$, then an operator from $Q3$ is never selected, even if the object is in its domain. The reason is that an object in $P2$ can be transformed one or more steps by operators in $Q2$, and then the desired operator in $Q3$ can be applied to the result. This is sufficient (and is in fact a good pruning technique), since operators in $Q2$ effect only trivial modifications on the objects.

Programming. Since only one operator is applied to objects in $P1$ and $P2$, these objects and operators can be given a separate and 'algorithmic' treatment. The heuristic search need only cover objects in *P3* and operators in *Q3*.

Like most heuristic programs, SAINT maintains a bud list, that is, a list of objects to which no operator has yet been applied. This list contains members of *P3* ordered according to (the merit order) $>$.

Somewhat idealized, the cycle in the SAINT program runs as follows:
(1) Take the first object on the bud list. (This is a maximum bud in *P3*.)
(2) Select suitable operators for this object. Apply them. The set of results is called *P''*.
(3) For each member of *P''*, check if some member of *Q1* or *Q2* is applicable. If so, apply it. If it was a member of *Q1*, terminate. Otherwise, include the result in *P''* and perform (3) on it again.
(4) Let P^+ be the modified *P''* after all *Q1* or *Q2* operators have been applied. By hypothesis, $P^+ \subset P3$. Merge P^+ into the bud list according to $>$.
The cycling starts in step 3 with the bud list empty, and with *P''* = the given, initial object ('the given integration problem').

Remarks. This description of the SAINT program is based on a rather short summary of the work on SAINT (Slagle 1963), rather than the full thesis. There may therefore be mistakes in details of our description. However, let us repeat that the intention in this section was to demonstrate how exactly the same material may be described in completely different terms when it is to be used for another purpose.

To facilitate comparison, let us finally give a short dictionary (table 3) that translates between Slagle's terminology and ours.

TABLE 3

Slagle	here
heuristic goal list	bud list
(temporary) goal list	P'', P^+
character	image
characteristic	feature

THE UNIT PREFERENCE HEURISTIC IN RESOLUTION

The purpose of this section is the same as that of the last section, that is, to demonstrate the usefulness of abstract heuristic concepts. In addition, we shall try to show that the so-called strategies used in resolution are in fact heuristic methods, and amenable to the same treatment as other such methods. [Feigenbaum (1968) argues a similar standpoint.] Therefore, we have chosen to deal with the unit preference strategy for resolution.

Problem environment. Each object in the set *P* is a set of *literals*, a literal being a symbolic expression (**not** (R_i...)) or (R_i...). The target set *M* has one member: the null set (that is, the set of no literals). The initial set *R* consists of a relatively small number of objects and is given to the program on each occasion of its use.

Notice that in this case, *R* is given as input to the program, and *M* is fixed. In the case of SAINT, we had the opposite situation.

The set *Q* consists of a two-input conporator ('resolution') and a perporator ('factoring'). Both have a restricted domain, and both are ambiguous. The ambiguities are moderate: the number of alternatives is finite and so small that all can be tried.

Images. Unit preference uses images for object-operator selection. The image of an object is an integer, viz. the number of literals in the object. Operators can be extended to images in the following manner: if the inputs to the resolution operator have images *j* and *k*, then the output (if it exists) has image $j+k-2$. Similarly, if the input to the factoring operator has image *j*, then the output, if it exists, has $j-1$ as image. [It may accidentally happen that the image of the output is less than (but never greater than) $j+k-2$ or $j-1$. Such accidents are rare and do not affect the heuristics.]

Discussion of heuristic method. Since the target object has image zero, and the operators effect a relatively small change on images, it is reasonable to take the image of an object as a crude estimate of its merit in the search towards the target, with small images having a higher merit. Therefore, operations which decrease the image can be expected to bring us closer to a solution. This gives us a preference for factoring, and for resolution when one input has image 1.

A trivial strategy would be to reduce the image to zero through successive factorings. However, we run into problems with the restricted domains of the operators: factoring when the image of the input is 1 (that is, the last step) is never possible, and in all reasonable problems we would fail long before that.

Resolution when the partner's image is 1 ('unit resolution') seems to be a better strategy, and is what our heuristics prefers as first choice. When it cannot be had, we perform other resolutions or factoring for a couple of steps, in the hope of achieving unit resolution later.

Handling of restricted domain. If a desired operator is not applicable, the unit preference method just gives up.

Object and operator selection. Unit preference utilizes a best bud bundle method, where a suitable operator and its input(s) are selected together. The system makes implicit use of a merit ordering $>$ defined on $I \cup I^2$ as in table 4.

TABLE 4

numerical relationship ($<$ means 'less than')		merit ordering ($>$ means 'better than')	
$j < m$	$\rightarrow$	$\{1, j\} > \{1, m\}$	(1)
$k \neq 1,\ m \neq 1$	$\rightarrow$	$\{1, j\} > \{k, m\}$	(2)
$k \neq 1$	$\rightarrow$	$\{1, j\} > k$	(3)
if i, j, k, m all are $\neq 1$, we have:			
$i + j < k + m$ or			
$i + j = k + m,\ \min(i, j) < \min(k, m)$	$\rightarrow$	$\{i, j\} > \{k, m\}$	(4)
$i + j \leqslant k$	$\rightarrow$	$\{i, j\} > k$	(5)
$k < i + j$	$\rightarrow$	$k > \{i, j\}$	(6)

For example, we have:
$$\{1, 2\} > \{1, 4\} > 2 > 3 > \{2, 2\} > 4 > \{3, 2\} > 7 > \{6, 2\} > \{5, 3\} > \{4, 4\} > 8 > \ldots$$
The relation $>$ is extended to $P \cup P^2$ in the obvious way.

In each cycle, unit preference uses $>$ to select one maximal object or object-pair and applies the correct operator (factoring in the case of an object, resolution in the case of an object-pair) to it. In case of ambiguity, all alternatives are treated with the same priority. If operator application in some alternative is successful, and the output has higher priority than the input (and, therefore, higher priority than the other alternatives processed together with this one), then the higher priority is honoured immediately.

Programming. Although our reference says little about the actual program that performs the unit preference heuristics, the following are some suggestions for such a program.

The program utilizes lists $L_1, L_2, \ldots L_j, \ldots$, where L_j contains all generated objects with image j, together with the following information for each object:
(1) Has factoring been attempted on this object?
(2) If factoring is ambiguous, for which cases has it been attempted?
(3) With what other objects has resolution been attempted?
(4) If resolution is ambiguous, for which cases has it been attempted?
The answers to these questions can be represented as follows:
(1) for each list L_j, where $j \leqslant 2$, a pointer indicates how far down the list factoring has proceeded;
(2) for the pointed-at element of each list L_j, the attempted alternatives are

listed (for all other alternatives of L_j, either none or all alternatives have been attempted);

and similarly, for each object p_{jm} on each list L_j,

(3) for each list L_k, where $k \leqslant j$, a pointer indicates how far down L_k resolution with p_{jm} has been attempted;

(4) for the pointed-at element of each list L_k, the attempted alternatives are listed.

With these conventions, programming is straightforward.

Remark. The images used by the unit preference method have a noteworthy property: the image of the output of an operator is a function of the image(s) of the input(s), if the operator is applicable; but the image does not contain enough information to determine applicability. This 'semi-deterministic' property has otherwise been characteristic of planning methods, notably planning GPS, and PLANNER. As a result of some current work, we believe that semi-deterministic images have interesting theoretical properties.

Pruning criteria. The unit preference heuristics should only be used in combination with various pruning criteria, such as:

(1) Restriction on search depth. The depth of an object is the number of resolutions that were required to construct it. Objects of depth $\geqslant k_0$ (where k_0 is a fixed parameter) are rejected.

(2) Set of support strategy. A subset T of R is singled out as 'essential initial objects', and nodes, all of whose ancestors are in $R - T$, are given zero merit.

(3) Rejection by pattern. Objects p which conform to certain patterns [for example, contain two literals of the form A and (NOT A)] are rejected.

We have now made a distinction between *heuristics* (that is, rules which govern the order in which the solution tree is searched) and *pruning criteria* (which are extreme cases of heuristic rules since they cut off some 'branches' altogether). In the resolution literature, both heuristics and pruning criteria are called *strategies*.

Pruning criteria can formally be treated as further restrictions on the domains of operators. The first two pruning criteria above can (alternatively) be implemented by using images $<j, d, s>$, defined as follows:

If p is a member of the initial set R, p's image is $<j, d, s>$, where

j is the number of literals in p;

d is zero;

s is the truth-value of: $p \in T$

If p was derived through resolution, and the images of the inputs were $<j_1, d_1, s_1>$ and $<j_2, d_2, s_2>$, then the image of p is $<j, d, s>$, where:

$j = j_1 + j_2 - 2$ (the number of literals in p)

$$d = \max(d_1, d_2) + 1$$
$$s = s_1 \vee s_2$$

Finally, if p was derived through factoring, and the image of the input was $<j, d, s>$, then the image of the output is $<j-1, d, s>$.

When the partial order $>$ is extended to triples $<j, d, s>$ and pairs of such triples, the following items are considered as zeroes (i.e. $<$ all other items) and therefore rejected:

$$<j, d, s> \qquad\qquad \text{when } (d > k_0) \textbf{ or not } s$$
$$\{<j_1, d_1, s_1>, <j_2, d_2, s_2>\} \text{ when } (d_1 > k_0) \textbf{ or } (d_2 > k_0) \textbf{ or not}$$
$$(s_1 \vee s_2)$$

With these exceptions, the order $>$ treats $<j, d, s>$ like j, and $\{<j_1, d_1, s_1>, <j_2, d_2, s_2>\}$ like $\{j_1, j_2\}$.

Notice that if we ignore the accidents mentioned on page 95, both operators are semi-deterministic on these extended images.

Modification: the fewest-component preference heuristic. Slagle has proposed to streamline the unit preference heuristics into a fewest-component preference method. The idea is to change the definition of the merit order so that the special preference for pairs $\{1, j\}$ is dropped. The details are: in the definition of $>$ in table 4, drop rules (1) through (3), and use rules (4) through (6) even if some of $i, j, k,$ or m equals 1. For the redefined $>$, we have, for example:

$$\{1, 1\} > 2 > \{1, 2\} > 3 > \{1, 3\} > \{2, 2\} > 4 > \ldots$$

CONCLUSION

We have defined a number of concepts which are useful for the compact and abstract definition of heuristic methods. For illustration, these concepts have been applied to two well-known methods. Examples of their compactness can be found on pages 97 (set of support strategy) and 98 (fewest-component preference heuristics). We have argued that abstract descriptions of a similar kind will be useful as complements to conventional descriptions of heuristic programs and methods.

INDEX OF HEURISTIC METHODS AND PROGRAMS

Arrow method   (Hart, Nilsson and Raphael 1968),
    (Nilsson 1968)

DEDUCOM   (Slagle 1965a)

Fewest-component preference heuristic (Slagle 1965b)

GPS (General Problem Solver) (Newell *et al.* 1960), (Newell and
    Simon 1961)

Graph Traverser   (Doran and Michie 1966), (Doran
    1968)

Heuristic automaton	(Doran 1969)
Logic theory machine	(Stefferud 1963), (Millstein 1964)
MULTIPLE	(Slagle and Bursky 1968)
PLANNER	(Hewitt 1967)
Planning GPS	(Newell *et al.* 1960), (Newell 1964)
PPS (Planning Problem Solver)	(Sandewall 1968)
SAINT	(Slagle 1963)
SIN	(Moses 1967)
Unit preference heuristic	(Wos *et al.* 1964)

ACKNOWLEDGEMENT

This paper is a slightly updated version of a paper which was printed in *Proceedings of the International Joint Conference on Artificial Intelligence* (editors Donald E. Walker and Lewis M. Norton), Bedford, 1969.

BIBLIOGRAPHY

Doran, J. E. & Michie, D. (1966)   Experiments with the Graph Traverser program. *Proc. Roy. Soc., A*, **294**, 235–59.

Doran, J. E. (1968)   New developments of the Graph Traverser, *Machine Intelligence 2*, pp. 119–35 (eds Dale, E. & Michie, D.). Edinburgh: Edinburgh University Press.

Doran, J. E. (1969)   Planning and generalisation in an automaton/environment system. *Machine Intelligence 4*, pp. 433–54 (eds Meltzer, B. & Michie, D.). Edinburgh: Edinburgh University Press.

Feigenbaum, E. (1968)   Artificial Intelligence: Themes in the Second Decade. *Proc. IFIP Congress 1968*. (Invited papers.) Edinburgh.

Greenblatt, R. E., Eastlake, D. E. & Crocker, S. (1967)   The Greenblatt Chess program. *Proc. Fall J. comput. Conf.*, **31**, 801–10.

Hart, P. E., Nilsson, N. J. & Raphael, B. (1968)   A formal basis for the heuristic determination of minimum cost paths. *IEEE. Trans on Sys. Sci. & Cyb. SSC–4*, 100–7.

Hewitt, C. (1967)   PLANNER, a language for proving theorems in robots. *AI Project Memo 137*, project MAC, Cambridge, Mass: MIT.

Millstein, R. (1964)   The logic theorist in LISP. *Memo VCRL–70037*. California: Lawrence Radiation Laboratory.

Moses, J. (1967)   Symbolic Integration. *PhD Thesis*, MIT *Math. Dept.*, Cambridge, Massachusetts.

Newell, A. *et al.* (1960)   Report on a general problem-solving program. *Proc. IFIP Congress 1959*, p. 256.

Newell, A. & Simon, H. (1961)   GPS, a program that simulates human thought. Reprinted in: *Computers and Thought* (eds Feigenbaum, E. & Feldman, J.). New York: McGraw-Hill.

Newell, A. (1964)   The possibility of planning languages in man-computer communication. *Communication Processes 63*.

Nilsson, N. J. (1968)   Searching problem-solving and game-playing trees for minimal cost solutions. *Proc. IFIP Congress 1968*, H, pp. 125–30.

Samuel, A. L. (1959)   Some studies in machine lecturing using the game of checkers. Reprinted in: *Computers and Thought* (eds Feigenbaum, E. & Feldman, J.). New York: McGraw-Hill.

Sandewall, E. J. (1968)   A planning problem solver based on look-ahead in stochastic game trees. *Computer Science Report 13*, Uppsala University.

Slagle, V. R. (1963)   A heuristic program that solves symbolic integration problems in freshman calculus. Reprinted in: *Computers and Thought* (eds Feigenbaum, E. & Feldman, J.). New York: McGraw-Hill.

Slagle, J. R. (1965a)   Experiments with a deductive question-answering program. *Comm. Assoc. comput. Mach.*, **8**, 792.

Slagle, J. R. (1965b)   A proposed preference strategy using sufficiency-resolution for answering questions. *Memo UCRL–14361*. California: Lawrence Radiation Laboratory.

Slagle, J. R. & Bursky, P. N. (1968)   Experiments with a multi-purpose, theorem-proving program. *J. Assoc. comput. Mach.*, **15**, 85–99.

Stefferud, E. (1963)   The logic theory machine: a model heuristic program. *Memo* R M –3731–cc. Santa Monica: RAND Corporation.

Wos, L., Carson, D. & Robinson, G. (1964)   The unit preference strategy in theorem-proving. *Proc. Fall joint computer conf.*, **26**, 616–21. Baltimore: Spartan.

Formation and Execution of Plans by Machine

D.MICHIE

INTRODUCTION

Let us consider some definitions of artificial intelligence:

(1) B. Raphael, at this meeting, has suggested that AI is a collective name for problems which we do not yet know how to solve properly by computer. As soon as convincing success is attained in any particular domain, that domain is transferred by tacit consent into an appropriate established category of computer science – information retrieval, adaptive control theory, computational linguistics, optical character recognition, and so on, as the case may be. The only merit of which I am aware for this point of view is that it enables the worker in AI to claim as his exclusive professional territory the entire field of research in computer science, since *research* is by definition limited to those domains in which convincing success has not yet been attained. I am not sure how universally this would be accepted by computer men as a merit.

(2) N.J. Nilsson (1971), in the first sentence of his excellent book 'Problem-solving methods in Artificial Intelligence', defines the goal of work in AI as being 'to build machines that perform tasks normally requiring human intelligence'. On this definition the development of weather-prediction programs by computational meteorologists would be classified as AI.

We will reject both these definitions, which in their different ways look at problems and programs *from the outside*, and instead attempt a formulation *from the inside*. We ask not 'What does the program do?' but 'How does it do it?'. There will of course be machine tasks of such complexity that they cannot, in any practical sense, be mastered at all except by AI methods. But I am running ahead of my theme and will reserve examples of such tasks for a later stage.

The definition of AI which I wish to put forward lays emphasis on the nature of the processes which are implemented, in particular the *building of models* and the *formation of plans*. The questions which I would ask about a program are the following:

(1) Does the program utilize a model of its task environment? The essence

of a model in this sense is that it has predictive power: that is, it is possible to compute from the model the likely consequences, in terms of new inputs, of specified alternative outputs.

(2) Does the program use its model to form plans of action to be executed in the task environment?

(3) Do these plans include directed sampling of the task environment so as to guide execution along conditional branches of the plan?

(4) Can the program re-formulate a plan when execution leads to states of the environment which were not predicted in the model?

(5) Can the program utilize the record of failures and successes of past plans to revise and extend the model inductively?

If the answers to all these questions are affirmative, then the program undoubtedly represents an exercise in artificial intelligence. If only some are affirmative then it is a partial exercise in AI; study is concentrated on one or more vital *components* of intelligent behaviour, for example, theorem-proving routines such as those described here by J.A.Robinson, or packages for heuristic search, rote-learning, concept-formation, and so forth. If the answers are all negative then we are probably dealing with an exercise in conventional data-processing, industrial automation, numerical analysis, pattern recognition, or the like. Such programs may be *clever*, often to a superhuman degree, without prompting the word 'intelligent' as a description of their operations.

A merit of the definition advanced here is that it is clear-cut. It also corresponds fairly well to the ways in which we use the words 'intelligent' and 'clever' to differentiate among various information-processing accomplishments, whether in the world of adult humans, of children, of animals or of machines. We say 'How clever!' as we watch the spider spin her web. Suppose that at an early stage of her work we destroy a few bridges here and there and let her continue to run her inherited program. When we see the consequences – the germ of her supreme construction systematically converted to a shapeless tangle of threads – we say 'How unintelligent!'. Likewise for the target-seeking missile, the industrial robot, the programs for controlling city traffic, for monitoring the motions of the stock exchange, for computing the orbits of earth satellites, for critical path analysis of large projects, for handling air-line reservations, for modelling the national economy; all these are self-evidently clever in the extreme. But we would be less likely to use the word 'intelligent' to describe them than when speaking about the accomplishments of a two-year-old child.

A possible demerit of our definition is that it omits work which may have a more profound impact on the artificial intelligence field than any developments from within the field, in particular innovations in

(a) the theory of computation, for example current advances being made by Dana Scott (1970);

(b) software instrumentation for AI work, in the form of special programming systems, such as the ABSET language described at this conference by E. W. Elcock.

There are parallels here with astronomy, where the development of the field was critically dependent on

(a) the foundations of physics laid by Newton;

(b) the invention and development of the telescope by Lippershey (popularly, but erroneously, ascribed to Galileo).

Perhaps, then, there is no demerit in my definition after all; we do *not* classify Newton's contribution as 'astronomy', and we are happy to leave Lippershey's on the borderline, rating him an 'astronomer' to the extent that he used the instrument of his invention to make observations on the heavenly bodies. If the computation theorists and the designers of AI-oriented compiler systems are content with these analogies and classifications then so am I.

PLANS AND PATHS

The formation of a plan by machine will be discussed in the context of problem-solving. We are not interested in random plans. We demand some notion of states of the machine's environment which constitute *problems* for it, and of other states of the environment which can be accepted as *solutions* to these problems. The machine's task is to construct a specification for a chain of actions leading from a given problem state to a solution state.

We will thus be concerned largely with *path* problems: an *initial state* must be transformed by *a sequence of operations* into a state satisfying a *goal condition*. Let us consider some set of states and operations as constituting a *model* of an external world, with the correspondences shown in table 1.

TABLE 1

states of the model	situations in the world
operations on the model	actions in the world
definitions of the operations over the states	physical laws of the world

We later discuss automatic procedures for finding paths in such models as having relevance to the formation of plans by a robot. For the moment we shall confine ourselves to problems of path-finding *in the model*, which we denote by the pair (X, Γ'). X is a set of states and Γ' a set of unary operations, $\Gamma'_i : X \to X$. Observe that this representation formally defines a *coloured directed graph*, the colours corresponding to the different members, $\Gamma'_1, \Gamma'_2, \Gamma'_3,$ ..., of Γ'.

The coloured directed graph is thus the common representation to which we shall refer problem-solving of the type considered here. 'Representation' is intended in a sense similar to that of Amarel (1968). The terms, 'representation' and 'models', will be used interchangeably. A sequence of representations $(X^{(1)}, \Gamma'^{(1)}), (X^{(2)}, \Gamma'^{(2)}), \ldots (X^{(k)}, \Gamma'^{(k)})$ can be envisaged for a given problem such that for each n, $0 \leqslant n < k$, $(X^{(n+1)}, \Gamma'^{(n+1)})$ is a homomorphic image of $(X^{(n)}, \Gamma'^{(n)})$, usually regarded as being a 'better' representation and typically having a smaller X and/or Γ'. Systematic procedures for transforming from one representation to another are of central importance. The intelligent solver first strives for a representation which so reduces the problem space as to trivialize the task of searching it. Only when no further reduction can be achieved does he embark on processes of search. The 'representation problem' is again mentioned towards the end of this paper. The sections which follow are concerned solely with how to make the best of a given representation, treated as fixed.

Stages of solving a path problem. Solving a path problem by computer can be analyzed into the following stages:

(1) devise an appropriate representation of the problem;

(2) devise a strategy appropriate to that representation;

(3) translate the representation and the strategy into program;

(4) run the program.

In the early days only stage (4) was mechanized. High-level languages have extended the machine's sway to (3). The user now has the option, by expressing (1) and (2) in a sufficiently powerful language, of handing over responsibility for stage (3) to the compiler. It would be nice if mechanization could be pushed further. To do this in any degree for stage (1) is perhaps too much to hope for, but approaches to stage (2) have been under investigation for many years and are collectively known as 'heuristic search'.

The heuristic search philosophy says: Let us restrict attention to some class of problems for which a single standard representation can be devised, appropriate to all problems in the class. Let us then devise a standard strategy for dealing with this common representation, and translate once and for all the representation and associated strategy into a program and put it in the library. This leaves only stage (1) to the user, and even so in watered down form. For each new problem that he wishes to attack he must write an 'application package' to map the elements of his chosen representation on to corresponding elements of the standard representation.

The *standard representation* adopted for heuristic search is the directed graph, of which the nodes represent discrete states and the arcs represent the generation of possible successor states of a given state. Together with the set X, the function for generating successor sets, $\Gamma : X \rightarrow 2^X$, defines the problem graph. It does so in a way which limits its utility as a basis for problem-representation as compared with the coloured graph representation (X, Γ') mentioned earlier. It is, however, the basis of search algorithms considered by Moore (1959), Doran and Michie (1966), Hart, Nilsson and Raphael (1968) and Pohl (1970a). The (X, Γ') model, on the other hand, has been used for the algorithms of Newell and Simon (1961), Dijkstra (1959), Michie (1967a), Doran (1968) and Michie and Ross (1970). Heuristic search is the design of effective graph-searching procedures which utilize features of intermediate problem states, either to decide which state to transform next, or which transformation to apply next, or both.

Let us go over the four stages given earlier, with the use of a heuristic search routine in mind.

(1) Devise a representation of the problem in graph form and express it as an 'application package'.

(2) Supply heuristic aids for the search strategy: e.g., a function for evaluating problem states, or for selecting operations, or both.

(3) Compile the 'application' and 'heuristic' packages, and load the search routine.

(4) Run.

The saving consists in the lightening of the user's task under (1) and (2). In place of constructing a representation *de novo* he is given a framework, and in place of a fully-fledged strategy he is asked only for hints, as it were. If he has none to offer, most heuristic search routines are capable of being run under default settings, giving the effect of exhaustive 'breadth-first' search. This will find a solution, if one exists, albeit expensively.

GRAPH-SEARCHING ALGORITHMS

The use of graphs as models for problems goes back to the earliest days of graph theory. Their use as models of game-playing (of which problem-solving can be regarded as a specialization) was developed by von Neumann and Morgenstern (1944) and first used as the basis of a game-playing computer program by Strachey (1952). The basic principles have been lucidly expounded by Davies (1950), who considers among other things the *one-person* game, or 'puzzle'; this defines the class of problem which can be mapped on to a graph in the manner exploited in heuristic search. The first use of this representation as the basis of a computer program, the 'General Problem Solver' (GPS) was

H

made by Newell, Shaw and Simon (1957). Their formulation can be expressed as in table 2. It may on occasion be convenient to depart from this clean segregation of terminology, and speak, for example, of operations and operators interchangeably.

TABLE 2

Problem	Graph
Given: an initial state a desired property defined on states a repertoire of operations,	Given: a node of a connected graph a set of nodes, satisfying a goal predicate a set of unary operators generating the arcs of the graph,
Find: a sequence of operations which will transform the initial state into a desirable state.	Find: a sequence of operator applications which will generate a path from the initial node to a goal node.

GPS. The GPS approach will be outlined rather briefly, as it does not lie on the main line of developments to be reviewed here, which can more naturally be derived from early work by Moore (1957). The main features of GPS are:

(1) For each state a vector of *differences* is calculated, that is, properties in respect of which differences from the desired state(s) exist.

(2) There is an *operator-difference table* which records the user's ideas concerning the usefulness of individual operators for reducing the various differences.

(3) The table is used to select an operator to apply to the current state, with the object of reducing one of the differences.

(4) If the operator proves applicable to the given state it is applied, and a new current state thereby produced. Otherwise, a new problem ('sub-goal') is set up in which the desired state is defined as one to which the given operator *is* applicable. GPS effects the new search by calling itself recursively.

(5) The foregoing procedure is iterated until a goal state is located, or the search abandoned.

The rationale of GPS can be questioned at two points: (1) there is an implicit assumption that properties on which the differences are calculated enjoy sufficient mutual independence ensuring that while one difference is being decreased others are not thereby increased; and (2) if an operator is inapplicable to a given state it would seem at least as rational to try another operator on that state rather than embark recursively on a whole new search. As yet, GPS has not demonstrated convincing advantages for the latter course. The matter is discussed in an important paper by Ernst (1969). A case study in which GPS was applied to eleven different problems has been published by Ernst and Newell (1969).

Moore's algorithm for shortest paths. To introduce the problem of finding a shortest path, we define a directed graph G as (X, E) where:

X is the set of nodes;

E is a set of arcs $\{(x_i, x_j) \mid x_i, x_j \in X\}$;

$\Gamma: X \rightarrow 2^X$ gives the set of immediate successors of any node $x \in X$ to which it is applied, and can be defined: $\lambda x \{y \mid (x, y) \in E\}$.

To find the shortest path from a starting node x_0 to one satisfying a goal predicate P, Moore proposed the procedure now widely familiar as 'breadth-first' search, which can be described as follows:

(1) Label x_0 with the integer 0.

(2) Define 'apply Γ to x_i' to mean 'generate the set $\Gamma(x_i)$, delete from it any repetition of a node produced by a previous application of Γ, attach to each remaining member the label associated with x_i incremented by 1 and a pointer leading back to x_i'.

(3) Of the set of labelled nodes which as yet have no pointers to them, apply Γ to that with the lowest-valued label; in case of ties, choose arbitrarily.

(4) Iterate step (3) until a node satisfying P is produced.

The label of the goal node gives the length of the minimal path, and this path can be reconstructed by retracing the sequence of pointers from the goal node back to the root node.

Dijkstra's algorithm for minimal cost paths. Now consider the case where the arcs are of variable length. A minimal-length path over such a graph corresponds to a minimal-cost solution of the problem which the graph represents, if the length of an arc is taken to represent the cost associated with the corresponding operation. To deal with this idea we re-interpret Γ in terms of the operators $\Gamma'_1, \Gamma'_2, \ldots \Gamma'_m$ where m is the number of operators in the complete set, and add to X an additional node called $x_{undefined}$ which is by convention the successor obtained by applying an operator 'inapplicable' under the rules of the problem to the given state. Moreover, $\Gamma'_i(x_{undefined}) = x_{undefined}$ for all i.

We shall now express Dijkstra's algorithm, using this notation, by re-writing step (2) of Moore's algorithm as follows:

(2) Define 'apply Γ to x_i' to mean 'generate the set $\bigcup_{j=1}^{m} \Gamma'_j(x_i)$'. To each node in this set attach the label associated with x_i incremented by the cost

of the corresponding Γ', and a pointer leading back to x_i.

For any node which as a result now has two labels, delete the one of higher value and the corresponding pointer.

Doran and Michie's algorithm for low-cost searches. The search algorithms described so far express the idea that what matters is the cost associated with the final solution path and that the cost of conducting the search itself can be disregarded. This would be appropriate, for example, if the design of an optimal route for road traffic offered economies on a scale of millions of pounds while the cost of computing the corresponding search by such a near-exhaustive procedure was measured in thousands. In other cases, however, the converse can apply, and the all-important consideration then becomes to construct a path, not necessarily optimal, at as little cost as possible.

For problems of this type Doran and Michie (1966) introduced the idea, familiar in earlier game-playing studies (*see* Samuel 1960), of guiding the search by an *evaluation function.* They re-interpreted this in the graph-searching context as an *estimator of distance* to the goal node along the minimal path. Instead of choosing for the next application of Γ the node with least distance from the start, as in Moore's and Dijkstra's algorithms, their Graph Traverser algorithm chooses the one with least *estimated distance* to the goal. The resultant economies of search effort can be large, depending on how good an evaluation function is available, that is, how well the distance estimator correlates with the actual distances to the goal. At the same time the guarantee of finding a minimal path is lost.

Hart, Nilsson and Raphael's algorithm. The next logical step, to combine the two criteria in some way, was proposed by Hart, Nilsson and Raphael (1968), who suggested the use of an evaluation function $f(x)$ defined as $g(x)+h(x)$ where g measures the distance from the start and h estimates the remaining distance to the goal. Further, they were able to establish a condition under which optimality in respect of final path length can be conserved. The condition states that $h(x) \leqslant h_p(x)$ everywhere, where h_p measures the actual distance to the goal. This result applies to the Dijkstra-type situation as well as to the case where all arcs have unit costs.

Pohl (1970a, b) has introduced an adjustable parameter ω, and defines $f(x)$ as $(1 - \omega)g(x)+\omega h(x)$, thus enabling one to consider, in a given case, various departures from the above-stated boundary condition in either direction. Among the results proved by Pohl, the following are of particular interest:

(1) Although setting $\omega = 0$ minimizes the path cost, setting $\omega = 1$ does not necessarily minimize the search cost. Unfortunately this has only been proved for the case where the graph is an infinite tree, and for the case where

$h = \dfrac{1}{1 + h_p}$ over an infinite graph.

(2) If $\omega < 1$ then the search of an infinite graph is bound to find the goal. The argument depends on the idea that even the highest-valued node with $g(x) = 1$, having $f(x) = M$ say, must be expanded before any node at a distance such that $(1 - \omega)g(x) > M$. This argument can be applied inductively to all nodes with $g = 2, 3, 4, \ldots$ to show that exhaustive search must eventually take place up to any stated distance from the start.

Searching a coloured graph: $GT2$, $GT3$ and $GT4$. Extensions of the Graph Traverser algorithm were incorporated in versions known as GT2, GT3 and GT4 by Doran (1968), Marsh (1969), and Michie and Ross (1970). They will be described here in the form found in GT4.

Partial development. Instead of applying *all* the operators when a node is chosen for development (expansion) GT4 applies one only on each occasion (*see* Lin 1965, Michie 1967a). The problem representation is thus (X, Γ'), corresponding to a coloured graph. A counter is associated with each node of the search tree, and this counter is incremented each time the *develop* routine is applied to the node. The counter thus holds the index number of the next operator in the repertoire to be applied. When this number exceeds the size of the repertoire the node is marked as fully developed.

When the branching ratio of the problem graph is high, the saving of computational cost introduced by this form of the algorithm is correspondingly great. It is therefore worth bringing up to date some of the original formulations so as to extend them to the 'partial development' version of heuristic search, as follows:

(1) A formal description of GT4 is given in Michie and Ross's paper.

(2) Doran and Michie's original measures of various parameters of search efficiency need to be redefined thus: $P^* =$ length of minimal path, $P =$ length of path found, $D =$ number of nodes generated during the search. Then $P^*/P =$ path efficiency, $P/D =$ penetrance and $P^*/D =$ total search efficiency. All these measures attain the value 1 when evaluation function and operator-selection function are both optimal. Note that:

$$\text{total search efficiency} = \text{path efficiency} \times \text{penetrance}.$$

(3) The Hart-Nilsson-Raphael theorem, put forward for the search algorithm A^* which uses full development, extends to algorithms of the GT4 type. Let us depict the main control loop as in figure 1.

We model our proof on Nilsson's (1971) proof of the admissibility of A^* and show that GT4 cannot terminate with a non-optimal solution path $(P > P^*)$. Let x_g be a goal node and let g_P measure the distance of a node

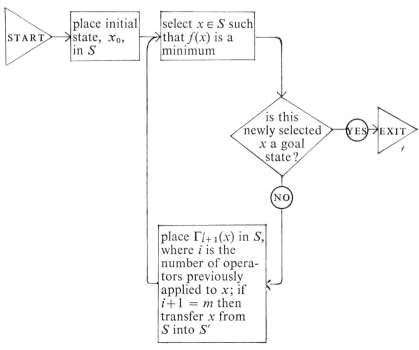

Figure 1. Diagrammatic outline of a form of the GT 4 algorithm to which the Hart–Nilsson–Raphael result can be extended (*see* text). $S \cup S'$ is the set of states already generated, including the initial state. S' is the set of states marked as fully developed.

from the root of a search tree along a minimal path. The proof proceeds by contradiction.

Assume that the search terminates with:

$$P > P^*. \tag{1}$$

Immediately before termination x_g is selected, and at this moment:

$$x_g \text{ must be a node in } S \text{ with minimum value of } f. \tag{2}$$

But $f(x_g) = g(x_g) + h(x_g) = P + h(x_g)$; therefore:

$$f(x_g) \geqslant P. \tag{3}$$

Clearly a minimal path to a goal does exist, and at least one of its nodes in $S \cup S'$ is in S: if they were all in S' then a complete minimal path would have been found, in contradiction to (1).

Let $x \in S$ be on a minimal path.

$$f(x) = g(x) + h(x) = g_P(x) + h(x) \leqslant g_P(x) + h_P(x).$$

Therefore $f(x) \leqslant P^* < P$, which contradicts (2) and (3) above.

(4) The proof of Pohl's theorem that for $\omega < 1$ a search must find a goal if one exists is clearly also valid for GT4. As sketched earlier, we can always find

a distance M, from the start, such that all nodes at distance 1 must be developed before any at distance $M+1$.

Denote by N^1 the set of nodes $\{n_1^1, n_2^1, n_3^1, \ldots\}$ at distance 1 from the start and define $f_{max}(N^1)$ as $\max(\{f(n_1^1), f(n_2^1), \ldots\})$, and h_{max} similarly. We have $f_{max}(N^1) = (1 - \omega) + \omega h_{max}(N^1)$. We find the required value of M by setting $(1 - \omega)(M + 1) > f_{max}(N^1)$, from which

$$M > \frac{\omega}{1 - \omega} h_{max}(N^1).$$

The argument can be extended to exhaust the sets N^1, N^2, N^3, ...

'Learning' features of G T4. Michie and Ross investigated two ways in which a heuristic search program might dynamically monitor and improve its own performance during exploration of a problem domain, namely

(1) optimization of the parameters of its own evaluation function, and

(2) re-ordering of the operators in its repertoire so as to promote earlier selection of those for which evidence of usefulness has been collected.

Both methods were shown to operate successfully under experimental trial. An interesting feature of scheme (1) was the use of a standard procedure [Hooke and Jeeves' (1961) 'pattern search'] for numerical function optimization disguised in such a way that G T4 was able to enter the optimization mode by calling itself recursively.

We now turn to the relevance of heuristic search to the formation of plans.

AUTOMATIC GENERATION OF PLANS

We consider:

(1) How to make a plan when both the input state and the effects of the available operators are fully specified. This is *simple planning*.

(2) How to make a plan when not all the above conditions are fulfilled. This is *complex planning*.

(3) How to incorporate the *execution* of plans formed under either regime into an integrated system of planning and action.

A notable excursion into this territory has been Green's (1969) demonstration of a complete system of resolution theorem-proving as a means of generating plans. A description of the initial situation, of the goal situation, and of the effects of the available actions is given in the form of a set of axioms in first-order logic; the resolution procedure is then called to prove the conjecture that *there exists a situation satisfying the goal description*. As a side-effect of a successful proof, a plan is produced for successively transforming the initial into the goal situation.

An extremely clear summary of this approach is given in chapter 7 of Nilsson (1971), who discusses its relationship to heuristic search methods.

Nilsson also points out certain difficulties attendant on Green's approach (*see also* B. Raphael in this volume): we shall not elaborate on these here, but merely cite them as motivation for exploring a little further the concepts of heuristic search. In particular we want to see if they can be extended, or buttressed by outside aids, so as to meet some at least of the requirements of complex planning. In doing so we follow closely in the footsteps of J. E. Doran (1969, 1970). Indeed the subsequent discussion is to a considerable degree an attempt to re-express in a more functional form design ideas on which Doran has already reported.

Simple plan-formation. The formation of *simple plans* can be accomplished by heuristic search alone. The final 'plan' incorporates a path, interpreted as a sequence of actions leading from the initial situation to the goal situation. It is useful to consider the relationship of plans, in the sense discussed here, to computer programs – a program is in a certain sense a *plan of computation.* If we do this we can see rather clearly why the plans produced by heuristic search in the manner described earlier constitute a limited class, and why a simple lookahead over states and actions is not powerful enough to generate plans beyond a very special class of situation. These plans are all of the form 'do a_1; **then do** a_2; **then do** a_3; . . .'. They thus correspond to programs with assignment statements but no tests, and hence no conditional jumps. What is the class of problem for which a program of this restricted form is adequate? The answer is that the problem must be a puzzle, that is, *a one-person game with perfect information, without chance moves and with a uniquely specified initial state.* The key notion is that of *complete specification.* By completely specifying the input state and the effects of all the permitted actions we contrive that every intermediate state of the problem can in principle be computed explicitly by lookahead. Since the essence of a conditional is to ask a question about the current state: 'does it possess such and such a property?', and since complete specification answers all such questions in advance, we can see why it is that for puzzles, and only for puzzles, a solution path can be adequately defined by an algorithm without conditionals.

We call such a plan a *simple goal algorithm,* and represent it as the result of applying a plan-constructor function, *consplan,* say, in a domain X of which a subset Y is specified as constituting a set of goal states. Thus for all $x \in X$, *consplan* $(x, Y) \equiv P$ such that $P(x) \in Y$. P is formed by function composition of a sequence of operators selected from the repertoire Γ'. As before, we include in X a state $x_{undefined}$ which is by convention the result of applying an operator to a state to which it would otherwise be inapplicable. Further, $\Gamma'_i(x_{undefined}) = x_{undefined}$ for all i.

A POP-2 function for applying a sequence or *path* formed from such operators is the following:

> **function** *run x path;*
> *loop:* **if** *null (path)* **then** *x* **exit;**
> *apply (x, hd(path))→x;*
> *tl(path)→path;*
> **goto** *loop*
> **end;**

Notice the distinction between the *path* (operator sequence) and the *special plan* (simple algorithm) which actually applies the sequence. We can produce the second from the first by the POP-2 device of *partial application*, thus

> *run (% path1 %)→plan1; run (% path2 %)→plan2; and so on.*

Application of the resulting plans to their proper arguments in X, thus *print (plan1(x1))*, will produce a member of Y as output.

Automatic construction of special plans is done by *consplan* through iterative application of a function *strategy:* $X→\Gamma'$. *strategy* is implemented precisely as a heuristic search routine, for example by partial application of GT4 to all but the first (that is, the state identifier) of its parameters. *consplan* can be written in POP-2 as follows:

> **function** *consplan x goalset;*
> **vars** *path gammadash; nil→path;*
> *loop:* **if** *member(x, goalset)* **then** *run(% path %)* **exit;**
> *strategy(x)→gammadash;*
> *path <> [% gammadash %]→path;*
> *gammadash(x)→x;*
> **goto** *loop*
> **end;**

Note that *consplan(x, Y) = P* and that P is a *simple* goal algorithm, that is, it can be viewed as a special plan for transforming one particular $x \in X$ into a goal state. *consplan* produces a separate plan, P_i, for every separate x_i.

Now consider a T such that for all $x \in X$, $T(x) \in Y$. Such a T is a *complex goal algorithm*, that is, a 'general plan' for the whole domain X. A valid, though inefficient, implementation of T is given by the POP-2 function:

> **function** *transform x; apply (x, consplan(x, Y))* **end;**

This implementation is in *heuristic search form*. The action of *transform* is to call the heuristic search routine embedded in *strategy* to construct and run a special plan. Can we specify a function, *condense* say, which will convert this into a *good* implementation of T, that is, an implementation in *algorithmic form* without redundant branching?

Memo functions. In order to show how a *condense* function may be constructed, we shall conduct a brief digression on the subject of the 'memo' function (Michie 1967b, Popplestone 1967). Since full documentation of successive forms of the device is already available, this digression will be confined chiefly to the main features of the current implementation 'LIB FULL MEMO-FNS' in the Edinburgh Multi-POP library (Marsh 1970, 1971). The present account, however, incorporates certain features not explicitly provided for in the library package.

The basic notion is to give the programmer a facility for attaching to any POP-2 function a private memory, or 'rote', and for using the rote for the storage and look-up of the results of previous calls of the function. Thus at any given stage the rote contains information about a sample of the total function space. This sample may take the form simply of a table of argument-result pairs, but in the new version of memo functions such a representation is regarded as a special case of a more general form. The general form does indeed consist of a table of pairs, but the pairs are of argument-result *sets* not of argument-result instances.

An *argument set* is represented as a triple (*xpred, poslist, neglist*). *xpred* is a predicate over *x*, *poslist* is an exception list of elements known to be members of the set but which test *false* on *xpred*, while *neglist* is an exception list the members of which test *true* on *xpred* but are known *not* to be members of the set.

Membership of an argument set is tested by:

    function *xmember x;*
    if *listmember*(*x, poslist*) **then** *true*
    elseif *listmember*(*x, neglist*) **then** *false*
    else *xpred*(*x*) **close**
    end;

For a given application one or more of these three categories may be vacuous: if for example a numerical function is memo-ized and is known to be continuous monotonic then predicates can define intervals, and all exception lists left empty. *Result sets* are represented by canonical representatives: for instance, a real number by a rounded decimal numeral.

Evaluation of a memo function involves an initial search of the argument column of the rote table. If this search succeeds, evaluation takes place by look-up, followed immediately by exit (we omit here details concerned with 'refreshing' and 'forgetting').

If the primary search fails, the function is evaluated by calculation, the result is converted to canonical form, and a second search is conducted, this time *on the result column*. If this fails, then a new 'argument-set, result-set' entry is constructed and added to the rote. If, however, the 'result search' succeeds in finding a match in the result column, then a new member has been discovered for the corresponding argument-set, not included in the current argument-set description (it *must* be a member because it gives the same canonical value of *y* as the already proved members of the set). The description is therefore up-dated by adding the new member to *poslist*. If the generalizer can then remove it, and any others in *poslist*, by a safe extension of *xpred*, then it does so. The process is sketched in figure 2.

Complex plan-formation: the 'condense' function. With this preamble we assert that the *automatic formation of complex plans* requires a procedure consisting of:

(1) a search routine;
(2) a rote-memory routine; and
(3) a generalization routine.

The design and implementation of (1) and (2) are well understood; indeed, they have the status of standard library functions. Any planner synthesized from these building blocks need therefore be no worse than its generalization routine. In other words, there exists a decomposition of the problem of plan-formation which trivializes all but the generalization component. A recipe for re-composition of a complex planner from the building blocks will now be given.

The *'condense'* function needed for conversion of *T* from heuristic search form into algorithmic form is achieved by memo-izing the heuristic search routine, *strategy*, along lines similar to those explored in Marsh (1970). After this, the desired conversion to algorithmic form occurs automatically in a stepwise fashion through successive applications of *T*. In POP-2:

> **function** *condense xset transform;*
>
> *newmemo*(*strategy, rotesize, strategyarity, xmember, ymatch, rote-*
> > > *update, canon*)→*strategy;*
>
> *applist*(*xset, transform*);
> *transform*
> **end;**

The second appearance of the identifier '*transform*' leaves the condensed version on the stack as the result; it is not of course a call of the function.

Running *condense* with *xset* = *X* results in total conversion of *T* into *extensional algorithmic form*, that is, into a state-action table. In the next section we shall use a toy problem as a worked example.

Substitution of a 'generalize' function as an actual parameter in the *roteup-*

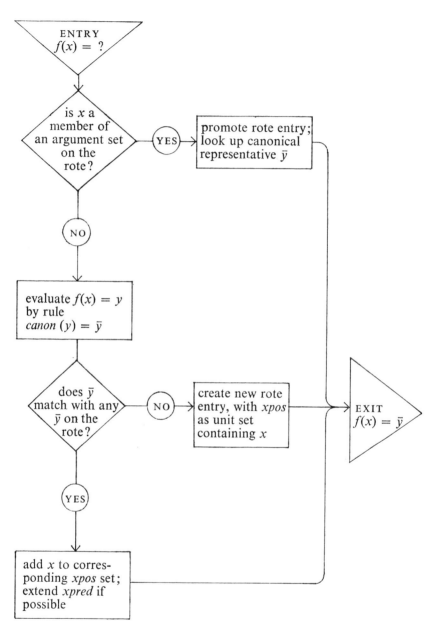

Figure 2. Outline diagram of the generalized memo function.

date place of *newmemo* results in conversion of *T* into *intensional algorithmic form*, that is, into a predicate-action table. Such a table is essentially a form of 'decision table' [*see* King (1967) for a review] and is formally equivalent to a computer program of conventional test-and-loop type.

The mechanization of inductive generalization is a problem of depth and difficulty which, in the opinion of some, will dominate work in AI in the 1970s. Useful beginnings have been made, as in the recent work of Plotkin (1970, 1971). Consequently generalizers are becoming available which, when called by the search-plus-memory system described, can play a part in the automatic formation of complex plans.

Self-optimization of the 'strategy' function. As remarked earlier, it is possible for a heuristic search routine to modify its own mode of execution by accumulating information about the problem domain. New information can be used to 'tune' the heuristic function, *h*, or to change the preference ordering of operators. Inductive reorganization of the strategy table by a generalizer is a further example. In these cases there is not one single function corresponding to the POP-2 function *strategy*, but a sequence $S_0, S_1, S_2 \ldots S_k$, and correspondingly $T_0, T_1, T_2, \ldots T_k$ for the *transform* function. S_k and T_k correspond to the ultimate 'steady state' condition supervening when *strategy* has been applied to every member of X and hence has had its entire extension fixed in rote form (a state that can only be attained if *rotesize* $\geqslant$ size of X). Thus the output of *condense* is not only a different algorithm from the input but also represents a different function.

This is a convenient point at which to introduce a further form of self-optimization which can be introduced into *strategy* with a marked increase of power. Turning back to the flow-chart of figure 1, consider the box 'place $\Gamma'_{i+1}(x)$ in $S \ldots$'. This corresponds to a call of the *develop* function of GT4, and specifies that the next operator in the set Γ' be applied to x. A small change in the definition of *develop* causes the rote of *strategy* to be first searched at this point. If the search is successful then the result of the search, instead of Γ'_{i+1}, is applied to x and x is marked as fully developed. In consequence successive calls of *strategy* result in less and less tree-like modes of evaluation as more and more of the lookahead is conducted in non-branching 'bamboo' form. In particular, whenever special plans have in the past been constructed by *consplan* these are fully exploited in the heuristic search. The effect of this is to make the planning process proceed in increasingly large and more 'purposive' units, analogous to the use of subroutines, or G. A. Miller's 'chunks'.

Chunking is further potentiated, and another category of self-optimization is added, if macro-operators, compounded pairwise from existing members of Γ', are automatically added to the repertoire. The criterion of compounding is statistical co-occurrence in past successful paths, so that the new additions may be termed 'useful clichés'. Since operators eligible for compounding can include macro-operators produced by previous compounding, useful clichés may grow to any length. This feature is not implemented in GT4, but a similar mechanism has been used by Callaway and Notley (1969) to good effect.

A toy problem. Consider the following trivial puzzle: there is an algebra of elements $\{1, 2, 3, \ldots 30, undefined\}$ with unary operators

> d, meaning 'multiply by 2',
>
> e, meaning 'subtract 11',
>
> s, meaning 'subtract 7'.

If the result of an operation gives a number lying outside the range 1–30, then the result is *undefined*, as also is the result of applying any operator to *undefined*.

We now ask for a plan to transform, say, 1 into 20. By breadth-first lookahead we get the tree shown in figure 3, as grown during a call of *consplan*. We now call *condense*([1, 2, 3 . . . 30], *transform*)→*transform*;

After *transform*(1) has been executed, the *strategy* rote looks like this (compare with figure 3):

> [[LAMBDA X; FALSE END] [1   2   4   8   5   10] []] D
>
> [[LAMBDA X; FALSE END] [16] []] E

It could be said to present a condensation of the information of figure 3. After exit from *condense*, 29 calls later, the rote looks like this (elements of lists have been re-ordered here for tidiness):

> [[LAMBDA X; FALSE END] [1 2 3 4 5 6 7 8 10 14] []] D
>
> [[LAMBDA X; FALSE END] [16   18   21   25] []] S
>
> [[LAMBDA X; FALSE END] [9 11 12 13 15 17 19 22 23 24 26 27 28
>
> 29 30] []] E

This last corresponds to a program for solving the '20 puzzle' in extensional algorithmic form. A generalizer might convert the above rote into something like:

> [[LAMBDA X; X < 9 END] [10   14] []] D
>
> [[LAMBDA X; FALSE END] [16   18   21   25] []] S
>
> [[LAMBDA X; TRUE END] [][]] E

corresponding to the sort of routine which a human programmer might write, for instance:

> **function** *strategy x;*

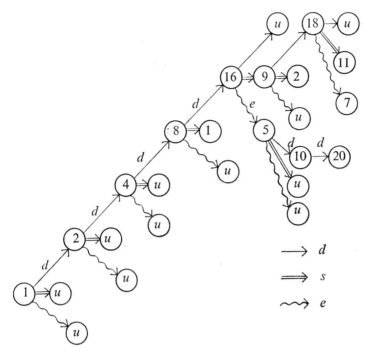

Figure 3. Breadth-first search of a closure defined by 31 elements $\{1, 2, 3, \ldots,$ 30, *undefined*$\}$ and operators d ('double'), s ('sevenoff') and e ('elevenoff'), taking '1' as the initial node of the search tree. The final path, to which labels have been attached in the diagram, is (d, d, d, d, e, d, d).

> **if** $x < 9$ **or** $x = 10$ **or** $x = 14$ **then** d
> **elseif** $x = 16$ **or** $x = 18$ **or** $x = 21$ **or** $x = 25$ **then** s
> **else** e **close**
> **end**;

The same algorithm is depicted as a 'strategy tree' in figure 4. The process of plan-formation, as considered here, can be thought of as the *extraction of a strategy tree from a problem graph*.

THE REPRESENTATION PROBLEM

Reference has been made to the stepwise modification of the function through the sequence $T_0, T_1, T_2, \ldots, T_k$, effected by various self-optimizing features of *strategy*, the POP-2 implementation of S. *strategy* acts on a representation, (X, Γ'). Do any of the above modifications alter (X, Γ')? Is (X, Γ') changed as a result of memo-izing *strategy*, splitting it into a rule part and a rote part? (1) Optimization of the *parameters of h* does not affect (X, Γ'), but only the order in which the rule part of *strategy* selects states from X for development. (2) Optimization of the *ordering of operators* within Γ' likewise does not

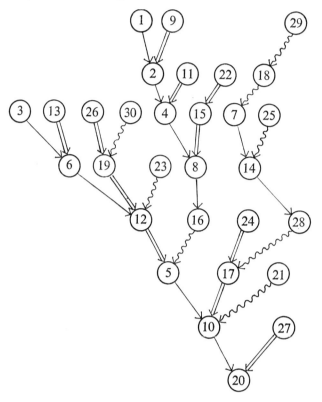

Figure 4. Tree representation of the *strategy* function expressed algorithmically in the text.

affect (X, Γ'), but only the order in which the rule part of *strategy* selects operators from Γ'.

(3) Formation of *useful clichés* does affect (X, Γ'); Γ' is enlarged in a way which enables the size of the effective search space to be reduced.

(4) *Memo-ization of strategy* has a profound effect, not in changing (X, Γ'), but in superseding it by degrees. By pairing members of X, each with a specified member of Γ', a situation is attained in the limit (in T_k) in which the *problem graph* is replaced by a *strategy tree*, as shown in figure 4. The work of searching the graph is replaced by the lighter task of determining the set-membership of the members of X lying on the solution path.

To describe this process as a change of representation of the problem would be misleading. It is not related in any obvious way to the transformation from a problem space to an 'image space' discussed by others (Minsky 1963, Amarel 1968). It should rather be seen as a gradual *replacement* of a representation by a solution.

PLAN-FORMATION BY ROBOTS

Discussion so far has been restricted to operations conducted *in the model*, and the plans generated by the various procedures have all taken the form of algorithms for converting an initial state of the model into a goal state of the model. Can we run these algorithms so as to bring about consequences in the outside world? How do we extract the actions from the plan? Clearly the operators chained together in the plan are not *themselves* actions in the required sense, since they act on *descriptions* of the world and produce new *descriptions*. Actions act on the world itself. They *can* however be converted into the required actions by a transfer function mapping the unary operators into nullary actions. These are parameterless routines which operate the external devices of the robot, which in turn engage with the external world.

Denoting the transfer function by '*actof*', the required effect is obtained by rewriting the function *run* as follows:

> **function** *run x path;* **vars** *laststate newstate nextop;*
> *loop:* **if** *null* (*path*) **then** [%*"done"*, *newstate* %] **exit;**
> *hd* (*path*)→*nextop; x*→*laststate;*
> *nextop*(*x*)→*x;*
> *apply* (*actof*(*nextop*));
> *constate* (*laststate, observe*())→*newstate;*
> **if** *disagree* (*x, newstate*) **then** [%*"failed"*, *newstate* %] **exit;**
> *tl* (*path*)→*path;*
> **goto** *loop*
> **end;**

'*observe*' inputs data from the outside world through sensors, such as TV cameras. '*constate*' takes a state of the model and the input data and constructs a new state of the model. '*disagree*' provides feedback: it compares two states of the model (one obtained by simulation and one by observation) and if they disagree beyond a permitted tolerance, exit occurs to the top-level calling function, *transform*. The latter can be extended recursively, as follows, so as to re-initiate plan-formation when a 'fail' exit occurs:

> **function** *transform x;* **vars** *result;*
> *apply* (*x, consplan* (*x, y*))→*result;*
> **if** *hd* (*result*) = *"done"* **then** *hd* (*tl* (*result*))
> **else** *transform* (*tl* (*result*)) **close**
> **end;**

The purpose of this section has been to extend the earlier scheme in a natural fashion to cover the more general case where plans are formed in the model but *executed in the world*. Justification can be derived from the practical

I

difficulties which current approaches based on resolution theorem-proving are encountering (*see* Raphael 1971). Trial of the new formulations and routines using actual robot hardware lies in the future.

WHY USE ROBOTS FOR STUDIES OF PLAN-FORMATION?

The major argument for attempting to implement intelligent problem-solving abilities in real-world task environments is that AI is difficult and challenging enough without seeking to make it more so. Hence any approach which gratuitously adds to this difficulty the further requirement of expertise in some application field unrelated to AI should be embarked on with circumspection. The point is illustrated in table 3, where two categories of domain for AI work are contrasted. In the right-hand column four domains are listed which have the inviting feature that the research worker can derive a 'flying start' from his life-long familiarity with the task environment. The last two involve typical robot studies, on which the discussion of plan-formation in this paper is intended to have a bearing.

TABLE 3. Examples of problem domains belonging to two contrasted categories. To mechanize in either category requires a particular domain-independent expertise – that is, in AI – together with domain-specific expertise. In domains of the left-hand category, expertise is possessed only by specialists, but in the right-hand category domain-specific expertise is possessed in high degree by all normal adults.

Domains requiring expert knowledge	Domains in which everyone is an expert
Chess	Recognizing faces
Mass spectroscopy	Learning a language
Industrial control	'Hand-eye' problems
Medical diagnosis	Exploring a terrain

ACKNOWLEDGMENTS

I am indebted to my colleague Robert Ross for his able assistance in getting this paper into final form, and for spotting a number of errors. I also wish to thank J. A. Robinson, who read the paper in manuscript, for many helpful comments and criticism. The work is part of a study in machine simulation of learning, cognition and perception supported financially by the Science Research Council.

BIBLIOGRAPHY

Amarel, S. (1968) On representations of problems of reasoning about actions. *Machine Intelligence 3*, pp. 131–71 (ed Michie, D.). Edinburgh: Edinburgh University Press.

Callaway, J. & Notley, M.G. (1969) The discrimination Graph Traverser. *Technical Report No 2027*, Computing Research Division, International Computers Limited.

Davies, D.(1950) A theory of chess and noughts and crosses. *Science News*, pp. 40–64. London: Penguin Books Ltd.

Dijkstra, E. (1959) A note on two problems in connection with graphs. *Numerische Mathematik*, **1**, 269–71.

Doran, J.E. & Michie, D. (1966) Experiments with the Graph Traverser program. *Proc. Roy. Soc., A*, **294**, 235–59.

Doran, J.E. (1968) New developments of the Graph Traverser. *Machine Intelligence 2*, pp. 119–35 (eds Dale, E. & Michie, D.). Edinburgh: Edinburgh University Press.

Doran, J.E. (1969) Planning and generalization in an automaton/environment system. *Machine Intelligence 4*, pp. 435–54 (eds Meltzer, B. & Michie, D.). Edinburgh: Edinburgh University Press.

Doran, J.E. (1970) Planning and robots. *Machine Intelligence 5*, pp. 519–32 (eds Meltzer, B. & Michie, D.). Edinburgh: Edinburgh University Press.

Ernst, G. (1969) Sufficient conditions for the success of GPS. *J. Ass. comput. Mach.*, **16**, 517–33.

Ernst, G. & Newell, A. (1969). *GPS: A Case Study in Generality and Problem Solving*. New York and London: Academic Press.

Green, C.C. (1969). Theorem-proving by resolution as a basis for question-answering systems. *Machine Intelligence 4*, pp. 183–205 (eds Meltzer, B. & Michie, D.). Edinburgh: Edinburgh University Press.

Hart, P., Nilsson, N. & Raphael, B. (1968) A formal basis for the heuristic determination of minimum cost paths. *IEEE Trans. on sys. Sci. and Cybernetics*, *SSC*–4, 100–7.

Hooke, R. & Jeeves, T.A. (1961) 'Direct search' solution of numerical and statistical problems. *J. Ass. comput. Mach.*, **8**, 212–29.

King, P.J.H. (1967) Decision tables. *Comput. J.*, **10**, 135–42.

Lin, S. (1965) Computer solution of the travelling salesman problem. *Bell Sys. Tech. J.* 2245–69.

Marsh, D.L. (1969) LIB GRAPH TRAVERSER. *Multi-POP Program Library Documentation*. Edinburgh: Department of Machine Intelligence and Perception, University of Edinburgh.

Marsh, D. (1970) Memo functions, the Graph Traverser and a simple control situation. *Machine Intelligence 5*, pp. 281–300 (eds Meltzer, B. & Michie, D.). Edin. U.P.

Marsh, D. (1971) LIB FULL MEMOFNS. *Multi-POP Program Library Documentation*. Edinburgh: Department of Machine Intelligence and Perception, University of Edinburgh.

Michie, D. (1967a) Strategy-building with the Graph Traverser. *Machine Intelligence 1*, pp. 135–52 (eds Collins, N.L. & Michie, D.). Edinburgh U.P.

Michie, D. (1967b) Memo functions: a language feature with 'rote-learning' properties. *Research Memorandum MIP–R–9*. Edinburgh: Department of Machine Intelligence and Perception, University of Edinburgh.

Michie, D. (1968) Memo functions and machine learning. *Nature*, **218**, 19–22.

Michie, D. & Ross, R. (1970) Experiments with the adaptive Graph Traverser. *Machine Intelligence 5*, pp. 301–18 (eds Meltzer, B. & Michie, D.). Edinburgh: Edinburgh University Press.

Minsky, M. (1963) Steps toward artificial intelligence, *in: Computers and Thought*, pp. 406–50 (eds Feigenbaum, E.A. & Feldman, J.). New York: McGraw-Hill.

Moore, E. (1957) The shortest path through a maze. *Proc. int. Symp. on the theory of switching*, *II*, p. 285. Cambridge, Mass.: Harvard University Press.

Newell, A., Shaw, J.C. & Simon, H.A. (1957) Preliminary description of general problem solving program – 1 (GPS–1). *CIP Working Paper 7*. Pittsburgh: Carnegie Institute of Technology.

Newell, A. & Simon, H.A. (1961) GPS, a program that simulates human thought. *Lernende Automaten* (ed. Billing, H.), p. 109. *Reprinted in: Computers and Thought* (eds. Feigenbaum, E.A. & Feldman, J.). New York: McGraw-Hill (1963).

Nilsson, N.J. (1971) *Problem-Solving Methods in Artificial Intelligence*. New York: McGraw-Hill (in press).

Plotkin, G.D. (1970). A note on inductive generalisation. *Machine Intelligence 5*, pp. 153–63 (eds Meltzer, B. & Michie, D.). Edinburgh: Edinburgh University Press.

Plotkin, G.D. (1971). A further note on inductive generalisation. *Machine Intelligence 6*, pp. 101–24 (eds Meltzer, B. & Michie, D.). Edinburgh: Edinburgh University Press.

Pohl, I. (1970a) First results in the effect of error in heuristic search. *Machine Intelligence 5*, pp. 219–36 (eds Meltzer, B. & Michie, D.). Edinburgh: Edinburgh University Press.

Pohl, I. (1970b) Heuristic search viewed as path finding in a graph. *Memo RC2770* (revised). IBM Thomas J.Watson Research Center.

Popplestone, R.J. (1967) Memo functions and the POP–2 language. *Research Memorandum MIP–R–30*. Edinburgh: Department of Machine Intelligence and Perception, University of Edinburgh.

Raphael, B. (1971) The frame problem in problem-solving systems. *Artificial Intelligence and Heuristic Programming*, pp. 159–69 (eds Findler, N.V. & Meltzer, B.). Edinburgh: Edinburgh University Press.

Samuel, A.L. (1960) Programming computers to play games, *in: Advances in Computers 1*, pp. 165–92 (ed Alt, F.). New York & London: Academic Press.

Scott, D. (1971) Outline of a mathematical theory of computation. *Proceedings of the Princeton Engineering Conference* (in press).

Strachey, C. (1952). Logical or non-mathematical programmes. *Proc. Ass. comput. Mach. Meeting*, p. 46. Toronto.

Von Neumann, J. & Morgenstern, O. (1944) *Theory of Games and Economic Behaviour*. Princeton: Princeton University Press.

A General Game-Playing Program

J. PITRAT

INTRODUCTION
A general game-playing program must know the rules of the particular playing game. These rules are:
(1) an algorithm indicating the winning state;
(2) an algorithm enumerating legal moves. A move gives a set of changes from the present situation.
There are two means of giving these rules:
(1) We can write a subroutine which recognizes if we have won and another which enumerates legal moves. Such a subroutine is a black box giving to the calling program the answer: 'you win' or 'you do not win', or the list of legal moves. But it cannot know what is in that subroutine.
(2) We can also define a language in which we describe the rules of a game. The program investigates the rules written with this language and finds some indications to improve its play.

With this method the program can find the different possible kinds of moves; for instance the possibilities of pawn promotion at chess. It can find also that, at chess, pawns always move forward; that in all cases, except capture *en passant*, the capturing piece goes to the square of the captured piece; that we can castle at most once, and so on.

With the first description of the rules, we observe some of these facts, but we cannot be sure that they are laws. We can wait a long time before observing a promotion at chess. It does not occur very often in a play, although this possibility has a great importance for the players' strategy.

We have already seen that with the second method of description, the program can find some important characteristics of the game before the first play. Another aspect of the second method is that it is more convenient to write the rules in a special language than in a general programming language.

LANGUAGE USED TO DESCRIBE THE RULES OF A GAME
We choose the second method. The language is suitable to describe games on a rectangular board. But it can describe other games. It has some limitations and cannot describe any game, even on a board.

My aim is not to define the language accurately, but to give a quick idea of it.

The initial board is read at the beginning of each play. It is not described by the rules.

Variables. They are a sequence of alphanumeric characters. They have two characteristics.

(1) Their value may be an integer or a pair of integers. In the second case, the value of the variable can represent a square of the board. The value of the first element of the pair is the abscissa of the square, the value of the second, the ordinate. We can use the operations + and − with the variables.

If v is (3, 2) and HP is (0, 1) the value of 'v + HP' is (3, 3). We can multiply a variable by an integer. If k is 2, (k * v) is (6, 4).

We can apply four functions to these variables, the value of the functions being an integer.

(a) OCCUPY(V) – 3 values are possible: empty, friend, enemy.

(b) NATURE(V) – The value of the function is the type of the piece which occupies the square v. The function is undefined if the square is empty. At chess, there may be six values: *King, Queen, Rook, Bishop, Knight, Pawn.* For some games, like go-moku, only one value is possible.

(c) ABSCISSA(V) – Its value is the first coordinate of square v.

(d) ORDINATE(V) – Its value is the second coordinate.

The program finds the type of the variables with the context. There are no constants, but the values of a variable may be defined at the beginning.

(2) Variables have another characteristic, but only in the case where their value is given initially. Some have only one initial value (an integer or a pair of integers), others have two initial values: one of these values is for the first player, the other for the second player. These variables are useful for describing the rules for the two players with only one algorithm. For instance the value of FRIEND is 1 for the first player and 2 for the second. The value of CHP is (0, 1) for the first player and (0, −1) for the second. This is very useful to describe the pawn moves at chess: we add CHP to the value of the pawn square. We obtain the value of a square where the pawn can go if it is empty.

It is also useful to introduce the variable KA whose values are (6, 1) for the first player and (6, 8) for the second, and KB: (7, 1) or (7, 8). If we want to see if short castling is possible, we must check that OCCUPY(KA) and OCCUPY(KB) have the value EMPTY.

Statements. Each statement may begin by a label. When the label is optional, it is placed between parentheses in the description of the statement. We do not describe statements in BNF., but we give the general form of each statement.

(1) ARITHMETIC.

(*Label*). ARITHMETIC $*\left\{\begin{array}{l} variable \\ pseudo\ function \end{array}\right\} = arithmetic\ expression.$

The operators may be: $+$, $-$, $*$ in the arithmetic expression. We may also use the four functions. Their value is an integer or a pair of integers. The variable of the first statement must be of the same type as the result of the arithmetic expression.

A pseudo function may be:

ABSCISSA(V)

ORDINATE(V)

where V is a variable, its value is a pair of integers.

In that case the value of the arithmetic expression must be an integer. The effect of the statement is to give the value of the expression to the first or the second element of the pair V.

After execution of an arithmetic statement, the following statement is executed.

(2) Unconditional GO TO.

. GO TO $*$ L.

The next statement to be executed is the statement labelled L.

(3) Computed GO TO.

(*Label*) . CPTD GO TO $*$ *arithmetic expression* $= I_1$, L_1 . I_2, L_2 . . .

I_n, L_n.

I_j are variables, L_j are labels. We compute the arithmetic expression. If its value is I_k, the next statement to be executed is the statement labelled L_k.

For example:

. CPTD GO TO $*$ NATURE(SQ) $=$ KING, TA . QUEEN, TB . ROOK,

TC . BISHOP, TD . KNIGHT, TE . PAWN, TF.

If the square SQ is occupied by a bishop, the next statement will be the statement labelled TD.

(4) IF.

(*Label*) . IF $*$ *arithmetic expression* 1 *relation arithmetic expression* 2.

L1, L2.

L1 and L2 are labels. The relation may be: $=$, $\neq$, $>$, $\geqslant$, $<$, $\leqslant$. The arithmetic expressions are computed. If the relation is true, the next statement is L1, if false, L2.

(5) END.

It indicates the static end of the algorithm: it is the last statement.

(6) FINISHED.

      (*Label*) . FINISHED *

It indicates the dynamical end of the algorithm. The execution stops if we go to this statement.

(7) SCANNING.

      L1 . SCANNING * V . L2.

v is a variable; its value is a pair of integers.

We define an auxiliary label by concatenation of the letter x with the symbols of L1. We represent concatenation by ‖. If L1 is AB, x‖L1 is XAB. We can call this new label elsewhere in the algorithm.

The result of this statement is given by figure 1.

With this statement we may scan the board. A call to L1 initializes the scanning, and the first value of v is (1, 1). At each call to x‖L1, we give

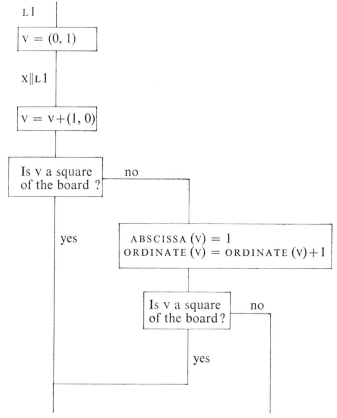

  The next statement to execute   The next statement
    is the following one.   is L2.

Figure 1. Flowchart of the scanning statement

to v the value of the next square. When the scanning is completed, we go
to L2.

(8) LOOP.

$$\text{L1 . LOOP} * \text{V1} = \text{V2 . I}_1, \text{I}_2, \ldots \text{I}_N . \text{L2}. \qquad\qquad N > 0$$

V1, V2, I$_1$, I$_2$, ... I$_N$ are variables. Their value is a pair of integers.

We define two auxiliary labels: X‖L1 and Z‖L1 and two auxiliary variables:
W‖L1 and Y‖L1. We can use these labels and these variables in the algorithm.
Their meaning and the result of the statement is given by figure 2.

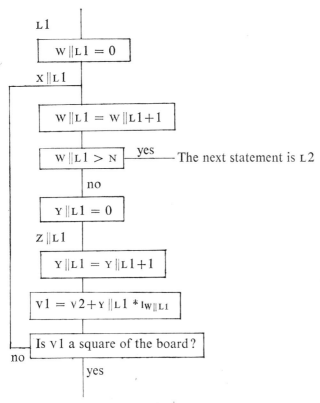

The next statement to execute is the following one.

Figure 2. Flowchart of the loop statement

If we transfer to L1, we initialize the loop, and we give to V1 the value
of V2 plus the value of I$_1$. If we transfer to Z‖L1, we add once more the
same increment I$_j$: we make one step more in the same direction. If we are
off the board, we add to V2 the next increment I$_{j+1}$.

If we transfer to X‖L1, we add to V2 the next increment. We make one step in a new direction. If we have used the N increments, the next statement is L2.

The value of W∥L1 shows which increment has to be used and the value of Y∥L1 how many steps we have taken in one direction.

(9) RESULT.

> (*Label*). RESULT * *Nature of the result.*

The nature of the result may be:

> *victory*
>
> *no victory*
>
> *draw*
>
> *loss*
>
> . . .

This statement is used one or several times in the algorithm indicating the winning state: No victory is not necessarily a loss: that is, we have not yet won, but we do not lose.

Then, we execute the next statement.

(10) MOVE.

> (*Label*). MOVE * *Submove* 1 *Submove* 2 . . . *Submove* N   N > 0

There are five kinds of submoves.

V, V1, V2 are variables, their value is a pair of integers, P is a variable, its value is an integer.

(1) TRAVEL, V1, V2. The piece in square V1 goes to square V2. If V1 is empty or if V2 is not empty, there is an error.

(2) CAPTURE, V. The piece in square V is captured. If there is not an enemy piece in V, there is an error.

(3) PUT, P, V. The player puts a piece of type P in square V. If V is not empty, there is an error.

(4) PROMOTION, P, V. The friendly piece in square V gets a new type P. If there is not a friendly piece in V, there is an error.

(5) INDIC, M, P. It is often necessary to use 'indicatifs' to describe the game when the knowledge of the board is not sufficient. For instance, in chess, if we want to castle or to capture *en passant*, we introduce three indicatifs:

(1) PASSANT Its value is 0 after a move, except when a pawn has been moved forward two squares. In that case the value of PASSANT is the abscissa of the pawn.

(2) CAS1 and CAS2 for short and long castling. Each indicatif has two values, one for each player. For a player the value of CAS1 is 0 if short castling is still possible, because there has been no move of the King or of the Rook in column 8. If not, its value is 1.

We have the possibility of changing their value in playing a move. If we move our King, we indicate in the MOVE statement that the values of CAS1 and CAS2 will be 1. We use the submoves: INDIC, CAS1, ONE. INDIC, CAS2, ONE. which give to the indicatifs CAS1 and CAS2 the value of the variable ONE which has been defined at the beginning as 1.

We shall give a part of the algorithm enumerating legal moves at chess, with some comments.

A . SCANNING * V . M.

M is the label of the first statement of the part of the algorithm which examines if castling is possible. If we were playing a variety of chess where there is no castling, we would write the statement: M . FINISHED *

. IF * OCCUPY(V) = FRIEND . B, XA .

If there is not a friendly piece in square v, we look at the following square.

B . CPTD GO TO * NATURE(V) = KING, CK . QUEEN, CQ . ROOK,

CR . BISHOP, CB . KNIGHT, CN . PAWN, CP .

We give the algorithm only for two cases: Queen and Knight.

CQ . LOOP * W = V . HP, HN, VP, VN, BP1, BP2, BN1, BN2 . XA.

We have a Queen in square v. The value of HP is $(0, 1)$, HN: $(0, -1)$. VP: $(1, 0)$ . . . BN2: $(-1, -1)$. When we know the moves of the Queen in the eight directions, we look at the following square.

. CPTD GO TO * OCCUPY(W) = EMPTY, E . FRIEND, XCQ.

ENEMY, F .

If there is a friendly piece in square w, we try the following direction.

E . MOVE * TRAVEL, V, W.

. GO TO * ZCQ.

The square w is empty. We go further in the same direction.

F . MOVE * CAPTURE, W . TRAVEL, V, W.

When we execute a move statement, we output the submoves with the actual value of its variables. In other words, if v is $(2, 2)$ and w is $(7, 7)$, we output:

CAPTURE$(7, 7)$. TRAVEL, $(2, 2)$, $(7, 7)$.

. GO TO * XCQ.

There is an enemy piece in w. We cannot go further in this direction. We try the next direction.

CN . LOOP * Y = V . OT, OMT, MOT, MOMT, TO, TMO, MTO, MTMO . XA.

We have a Knight in square v. The value of OT is $(1, 2)$, OMT: $(1, -2)$, MOT: $(-1, 2)$ . . . MTMO: $(-2, -1)$.

. CPTD GO TO * OCCUPY(Y) = EMPTY, H . FRIEND, XCN . ENEMY, I.

If there is a friendly piece in square Y, there is no move.

H . MOVE * TRAVEL, V, Y.

. GO TO *XCN.

I . MOVE *CAPTURE, Y . MOVE, V, Y.

. GO TO *XCN.

. . .

We describe the moves of King (CK), Rook (CR), Bishop (CB), Pawn (CP) and castling (M).

. END.

For chess, the difficulty of the algorithm is in the description of castling and of the pawn moves.

Conclusion. There are several ways of improving this language.

(1) It would be convenient to take the moves as values of a new type of variables and use statements to modify these variables. For instance, if Q and R are such variables, we could write:

Q = R + *submove.*

This is useful if we do not know at one time all the submoves of a move – for instance at checkers when we capture several Pawns.

(2) It would be useful to describe the connections between one move and the others – for instance, if the existence of a friendly move follows from the existence of enemy moves. In chess we cannot castle if there is an enemy move capturing our King. I gave this possibility to the language. I do not describe it here because it is not essential.

(3) It would be convenient to have subscript variables. If we could use them, we could describe the moves of any rider like Queen, Rook, Bishop . . . with one subroutine, and with another the moves of any jumper like Knight, King . . .

Remark. I first wrote an interpreter for the language, then a compiler. With the second solution, the execution is approximately 20 times faster. As we shall see later, it is more sophisticated than an ordinary compiler, it is more than a simple translator.

NECESSARY CONDITIONS FOR A MOVE TO OCCUR

Introduction. The algorithm enumerating legal moves shows, for each move, how this move modifies the board. For example, if the move has only one submove: TRAVEL, (3, 2), (4, 4)., then there are two changes on the board after this move:

(3, 2) becomes empty

(4, 4) is occupied by the piece which was in (3, 2).

This information is necessary for playing the move. But it is not sufficient if we want to have an efficient game playing program. The program must know why this move exists. For example, if there is an enemy move Q which is dangerous because some conditions $c_1, c_2, \ldots c_n$ are true on the board, and if the program knows these conditions, it chooses only from the moves which change at least one of these conditions. In the same way, it is useful to know that some interesting move would appear if there were some change on the board.

The knowledge of these necessary conditions for a move to occur is important, but it is not given by the algorithm. The program must find them in studying the algorithm.

Construction of the flowchart. The program constructs the flowchart of the algorithm. ARITHMETIC, MOVE and RESULT statements have one successor. The IF statement has two and COMPUTED GO TO has $N > 0$. We replace SCANNING and LOOP statements by the equivalent flowchart.

Unconditional GO TO and END statements disappear: they are a consequence of the linear description of the algorithm.

We gather in one statement all the FINISHED statements of the algorithm.

Principle of the method that finds the conditions. Suppose that we have the flowchart of figure 3, '*a*' being the condition of an IF statement, for instance:

OCCUPY(BR) = EMPTY.

Here BR is a variable, its value is a square; B, C, D are move statements.

If we execute the IF statement, we are sure to execute the move statement D, whatever '*a*' is: true or false. So, for the move described by D, the condition '*a*' is not necessary. But it is necessary that '*a*' be true if we want to execute statement B. If the value of BR is $(5, 4)$, it is necessary that $(5, 4)$ be empty. It is one of the necessary conditions for the move described by B. In the same way, it is necessary that '*a*' be false if we want to execute C.

We can see the method used: in a first step, which will be made once when we read the algorithm, we determine the 'conjugué' of each transfer

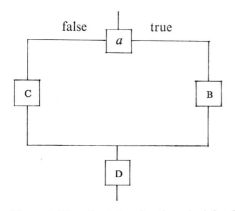

Figure 3. Flowchart showing the principle of the method that finds the conditions

statement: IF and COMPUTED GO TO. The 'conjugué' of the statement s is the first statement that we are sure to execute if we execute s, whatever path we take after s.

In a second step, when we execute the algorithm, at each transfer statement we store the condition used with the name of the conjugué. We erase this condition when we execute the conjugué. At each move statement, we output the conditions stored at this moment: these are the necessary conditions for the move to occur.

We shall develop these two points.

Determination of conjugués. The 'conjugué' of a transfer statement s (IF, COMPUTED GO TO) is the first statement T which we are sure to execute if we execute s, whatever path we take after s. There is always a conjugué: we have only one dynamical end, and we are sure to execute it if we have a correctly written algorithm.

We determine the conjugué for each transfer statement once after reading the algorithm. This search does not use the values of the variables and is the only function of the flowchart. This is done in two steps.

First step. We look for a path from the transfer statement s to the dynamical end of the algorithm. We get this path by looking at all the branches of the transfer statements encountered, till we obtain the dynamical end. When we arrive at a transfer statement, we develop one branch and we put the other unexplored branches in a push-down.

To avoid loops, we put a mark on the transfer statements already explored. If we find a statement with a mark, we stop developing this branch and we take another unexplored branch in the push-down.

We are sure to get such a path, because from any point of an algorithm, there is always one possibility, at least, to go to the end. If not, there is a programming error in the algorithm.

By this process we have a succession of statements (not all transfer statements):

$$s, s_1, s_2, \ldots s_n.$$

the last statement s_n being the dynamical end. s_{i+1} is one of the possible successors of s_i. There may be several paths between s and the dynamical end, but this is not important, we only want to get one of them.

Second step. The 'conjugué' is on every path between s and the dynamical end, it is one of the statements of the path found by us: it is one of the s_i, $i = 1, \ldots n$. The conjugué of the statement s is the first s_i that we are sure to execute after s.

So we consider all the s_i, beginning with s_1 until we get the conjugué. We want to see if s_i belongs to all the paths issued from s. If such is the case, s_i is the conjugué:

We are sure to execute this statement after s.

It is the first statement with this property, because this property does not hold for $s_1, s_2, \ldots s_{i-1}$.

To find if all the paths issued from s run through s_i, we put at the beginning a mark on s_i, and we use the same method as in the first step: we try to go from s to the dynamical end, but in this case we cannot cross s_i which has a mark and is taken as already explored. If we can find a path, s_i is not the conjugué: a path exists where we do not execute s_i. We resume the procedure with s_{i+1}. But if there is no path, s_i is the conjugué: in every path from s to the dynamical end we execute s_i and it is the first statement with this property.

By this method, we associate with each transfer statement another statement (not always a transfer statement) called its 'conjugué'. The conjugué may be the dynamical end.

This is done only once, after reading the rules of a game. For example, in the chess algorithm, we see by this method that the conjugué of the computed GOTO following CQ is XCQ. This is trivial: if OCCUPY(W) is *enemy*, we go to F, then to XCQ. If it is *empty*, we go to E then to ZCQ, then to XCQ or to the preceding COMPUTED GOTO seen above (we replaced the loop by the equivalent flowchart). If it is *friend* we go to XCQ.

How to find the conditions. When, during the execution of an algorithm, we meet a COMPUTED GO TO or an IF statement, we put the condition associated with this statement in a push-down, with the name of the conjugué of the statement. In the condition we put the value of the variables. For example, if the condition of an IF statement is OCCUPY(BR)=EMPTY and if the value of BR is $(4, 5)$ when we execute this statement, we put in the push-down:

OCCUPY$(4, 5)$=EMPTY.

if the condition is true. If the condition is false, for instance if $(4, 5)$ is *friend*, we put:

OCCUPY$(4, 5)$=FRIEND.

When we execute a new statement s (not only a transfer statement) we see if it is the conjugué of conditions in the push-down (they are necessarily at the top). If such is the case, we erase these conditions. They are no longer necessary: we execute the statement s and the following one even if these conditions are false. As the statement may be the conjugué of several transfer statements, we can erase several conditions at the same time.

When we meet a result statement or a move statement, we output the conditions in the push-down with the description of the result or of the move. Thus we get the necessary conditions for this move or for this result.

For example: If we are at chess and we have:

White Rook in (3, 1)

White Bishop in (1, 2)

Black Knight in (4, 5).

The move: 'Bishop captures Knight' has with this method the conditions:

OCCUPY(1, 2) = FRIEND

NATURE(1, 2) = BISHOP

OCCUPY(2, 3) = EMPTY

OCCUPY(3, 4) = EMPTY

OCCUPY(4, 5) = ENEMY.

This move changes two squares:

OCCUPY(4, 5) becomes FRIEND

NATURE(4, 5) becomes BISHOP

OCCUPY(1, 2) becomes EMPTY.

The move: 'Rook goes to (1, 1)' has the conditions:

OCCUPY(3, 1) = FRIEND

NATURE(3, 1) = ROOK

OCCUPY(2, 1) = EMPTY

OCCUPY(1, 1) = EMPTY.

The changes are:

OCCUPY(3, 1) becomes EMPTY

OCCUPY(1, 1) becomes FRIEND

NATURE(1, 1) becomes ROOK.

Actually we do not write all the conditions in the push-down. We are interested only in the conditions which can be changed when we play a move. The value of a loop counter has no interest, the player can do nothing with it. Also we only keep conditions which specify the occupation or the nature of a square or the value of an indicatif. When we (or the opponent) play, we can change these conditions and destroy the move or the result.

Remark. This method is simple, but there are some cases where we have difficulties.

(1) The algorithm is not well written; some transfer statements are not necessary. In that case the program can consider as necessary some conditions which are not. It is difficult to write a program which gives a better algorithm! This error is not frequent and it is not very important to have more conditions than necessary.

(2) There is another case where the method fails, and where we forget conditions, which is more unpleasant. This case occurs when the value of a variable is not the same if we take different paths and if this variable is used in a transfer statement. The value of the variable stores the result of a preceding condition.

For example, let us consider figure 4. '*a*' is a condition. The second test: '$A = 0$' is equivalent to testing whether '*a*' is true. With our method we say that after statement s the condition '*a*' is no longer necessary. So we miss a condition.

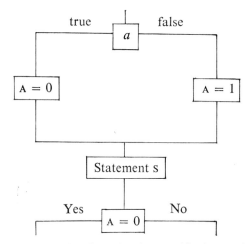

Figure 4. Flowchart showing an objection to the preceding method

But we can improve the method, and remove this difficulty. We associate with each variable a list of conditions, by the following method:
(a) initially this list is empty;
(b) when we define the value of a variable (by an arithmetic statement) we put in the associated list the conditions in the push-down and the conditions of the lists of the variables used to define the new value. We put each condition only once. But we erase the conditions associated with this variable before the statement.

At each transfer statement we add to the push-down the conditions which are in the lists associated with the variables used in the statement. The conjugué associated with all these conditions is the conjugué of the transfer statement.

In the example given above, when we execute the ARITHMETIC statement '$A = 0$' we associate '*a true*' which is in the push-down at this time. Statement s erases '*a true*' from the push-down. But when we test '$A = 0$', we put in the

K

push-down (if A has not been defined again) the conditions associated with the variable A: we will have again the condition '*a true*'.

With this method we do not miss conditions, but we often have unnecessary conditions.

I have not written this new program, because the case of a variable which memorizes the result of a transfer statement does not occur in the games studied. There are not many ARITHMETIC statements in the algorithms, and generally their result is quickly used.

*Modifications.** It is important to see what moves could exist if there were one or several changes on the board. We could perform this change and execute the algorithm again. But this method wastes computer time. And we often do not know what modifications it is interesting to examine. So, I prefer to generate the 'moves which could be possible' at the same time as legal moves. We must improve the preceding method.

Let '*a*' be the condition of a transfer statement s. Suppose that this condition bears on the occupation or the nature of a square. In a first step we execute the algorithm normally: the next statement will be the statement designated by the real value of the condition '*a*'. But we keep:

the value of the variables;

the conjugué of the transfer statement s;

the other statements issuing from the transfer statement s;

the values taken by the condition '*a*' to get these other statements.

For example, suppose s is:

AB . CPTD GO TO * OCCUPY(BR) = FRIEND, BC . ENEMY,

BD . EMPTY, BE.

Suppose that the value of BR is $(3, 2)$ and that there is an enemy man in $(3, 2)$. We put in the push-down the condition: 'OCCUPY$(3, 2)$ = ENEMY' and we execute BD. But we also store that if: 'OCCUPY$(3, 2)$ = FRIEND' we must go to BC and if 'OCCUPY$(3, 2)$ = EMPTY' we must go to BE.

When the normal execution is completed, we restore these situations. We put in the push-down the conditions not fulfilled, with a special indication, and we execute the algorithm until we are at the conjugué of the transfer statement s. The following statements have already been executed during the normal execution. If we meet a move or a result statement, we output the push-down with indication of the conditions not fulfilled.

If, during such an execution, we meet a new transfer statement, we can carry out the same process again. We can generate moves which require *n*

---

*This word is better than forcing, used in Pitrat (1968), which is confusing.

modifications on the board. We can stop this process if $n > N$, N being an important parameter of the program.

With this method we have the moves which would exist if there were one or several modifications on the board. It is not necessary to execute all the algorithm for each modification.

Example. In a game of chess there is a friendly Rook in $(8, 5)$, a friendly Bishop in $(7, 4)$, an enemy Bishop in $(8, 6)$, an enemy Queen in $(8, 7)$ and an enemy King in $(8, 8)$. Among the moves with modifications, we shall get:

Rook in $(8, 5)$ *captures* $(8, 7)$.

Conditions: friendly Rook in $(8, 5)$

   $(8, 6)$ becomes empty

   $(8, 7)$ enemy.

The second condition is not fulfilled.

Rook in $(8, 5)$ *captures* $(8, 8)$.

Conditions: friendly Rook in $(8, 5)$

   $(8, 6)$ becomes empty

   $(8, 7)$ becomes empty.

   $(8, 8)$ enemy.

The second and the third conditions are not fulfilled.

Bishop in $(7, 4)$ *captures* $(8, 5)$.

Conditions: friendly Bishop in $(7, 4)$

   enemy in $(8, 5)$.

The second condition is not fulfilled.

Example. In a game of Go moku, $(6, 5)$, $(6, 6)$ and $(6, 8)$ are empty, and there is a friendly piece in $(6, 7)$ and $(6, 9)$. The program will see that there is a possibility of winning with three modifications:

   $(6, 5)$ becomes FRIEND

   $(6, 6)$ becomes FRIEND

   $(6, 7)$ is FRIEND

   $(6, 8)$ becomes FRIEND

   $(6, 9)$ is FRIEND.

The program applies this process only to transfer statements of which the condition is on the occupation or the nature of a square, or the value of an indicatif: a move can change such conditions and we can hope that the move would become legal.

Applications. It is very useful to know what are the necessary conditions for a move to exist and the moves which could exist if there were some modifications. I used this in positional playing, and I am writing a general game-playing program which is able to learn combinations. I shall give one application to the search for a win.

THE SEARCH FOR A WIN

Introduction. In some games like chess, tic-tac-toe, Go moku . . . we are very often near winning. If the opponent did not play to avoid this threat, we should win. The reason is that there are only a few conditions to realize or to destroy which prevent us from winning. We can expect to win with a small number of moves.

In other games, like checkers, there is no danger of an immediate loss during a great part of the play. This danger occurs only at the end. In these games, we may be sure from the beginning that we will lose; for instance, if the opponent has twelve men and we have only eight. But there will be generally many moves before he will win.

The following method is possible for any game, but it is, in practice, useful only for the first class of games.

Blockade and threat. In any case we can always try to see if we can win whatever the opponent plays. We expand the tree of the moves and we see if there is a sequence of moves which leads to a winning state for all the opponent's replies.

But generally the expansion of the tree is so large that it is not practically possible, except for games where there is always a small number of legal moves. However it is sometimes possible when we manage to reduce drastically the number of the opponent's replies. There are two methods for this: (1) *Blockade* and (2) *Threat*.

(1) *Blockade*

We try to decrease the number of the opponent's legal moves. This is useful in games with a high number of moves when, for some reason, this number can decrease – for example, if one must play a capture when there is such a move. If we play a move which creates a capture for the opponent, he will have only one legal move. This is interesting if this move is bad for him.

We can also create situations where all the opponent's possible moves are bad for him. We use the obligation of playing, and the opponent has only a few moves to play, because the others have bad consequences for him. In many games a player must play when it is his turn.

Example. Tic-tac-toe (*see* figure 5). If we play: man in (3, 3) goes to (2, 3) this move is not dangerous. But the opponent must play. He must move the center pawn and he will lose.

This situation is infrequent in chess (we can see some in plays by Nim-

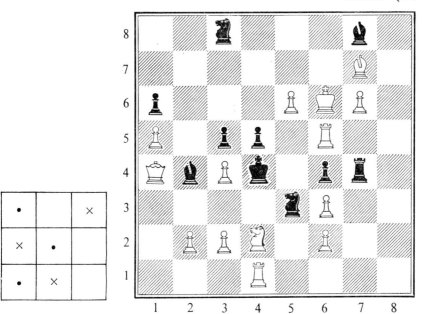

Figure 5. Blockade in
tic‑tac‑toe

Figure 6. Blockade in chess

zovich), but very frequent in chess problems, where situations are specially constructed.

Example. [H. d'Ogly *v* Bernard given in Le Lionnais and Maget (1967)].
The situation is shown in figure 6:
Mate in two moves. The key move is: Queen in (1, 4) goes to (1, 1). It does not threaten a mate in one move. But Black must play, and each move creates a possibility of mate.

For instance:

Rook   in (7,4) goes to (8,4) is followed by: King in (6,6) goes to (7,5)
Knight in (5,3) moves   is followed by: Rook in (6,5) captures (4,5)
Bishop in (2,4) captures (4,2) is followed by: Pawn in (2,2) goes to (2,3)
Bishop in (7,8) goes to (8,7) is followed by: King in (6,6) goes to (6,7).
There are 25 legal moves for Black, and each of them is bad. Such a situation rarely occurs in a real game!

(2) *Threat*

A threat is a move such that, if we could play again, we would be sure to win, whatever the opponent does. In a simpler case, we have a winning move if we could play again. For instance a check at chess: such a move creates a winning move: a move capturing the opponent's King. In Go moku, if we have pieces in (6, 1), (6, 2), (6, 3) and if (6, 4), (6, 5) are empty, if we put a piece in $(6, 4)$ we threaten to play in $(6, 5)$. If the opponent does not put a piece here, we win. We call such a threat an *immediate* threat. There are some threats which are not immediate threats: we are sure to win if we could play again, but we do not win immediately.

Example. In Go moku, if we have: friendly piece in $(6, 5)$ and $(6, 6)$; $(6, 3)$, $(6, 4)$, $(6, 7)$, $(6, 8)$ empty. Then the move: 'put a piece in $(6, 4)$' is a threat. If we could play again, we put a piece in $(6, 7)$. If the opponent puts a piece in $(6, 3)$, we put one in $(6, 8)$ and we also win. We are sure to win, but after two moves.

In chess there are also non-immediate threats. But generally moves threatening mate are checks. In chess problems, the key move must not be a check. So it is often a non-immediate threat. The opponent must destroy this

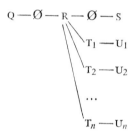

Figure 7. Description of a threat

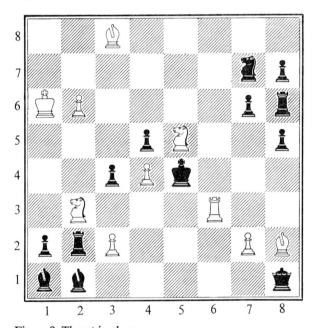

Figure 8. Threat in chess

threat. If Q is a threat to win in two moves, we have the situation shown in figure 7 (Ø indicates an opponent's no move).

If the opponent does not play after the key move Q, we should play R. If he does not play again, we play the winning move S. So the opponent tries to destroy S with the moves $T_1, T_2, \ldots T_n$. But for each of them, there is a winning move U_i.

But the opponent can play the move X after Q. He will try to destroy the threat. He can do several things:

(a) destroy R with move X. After X, R is no longer legal.

(b) counter R. R is still a legal move after X, but if we play R, we lose before we could play the winning move S. In chess, for instance, X can pin the piece moved by R. If we move this piece to give a check, the opponent captures our King.

(c) create a new reply T_{n+1}, with no winning move U_{n+1} after it.

(d) destroy one of the U_i.

(e) X is an immediate threat. It creates the winning move Y for the opponent. If we play R, he will play Y before S.

Let us give an example [Hartong given in Le Lionnais and Maget (1967)]: *see* figure 8: Two mover.

Q is: Knight in (5, 5) captures (3, 4)

R is: Knight in (3, 4) goes to (4, 6)

S is: Knight in (4, 6) captures (5, 4)

T_1: King captures (4, 4) U_1: Knight in (2, 3) captures King
T_2: King goes to (4, 3) U_2: Rook in (6, 3) captures King
T_3: King goes to (5, 3) U_3: Rook in (6, 3) captures King
T_4: King captures (6, 3) U_4: Pawn in (7, 2) captures King
T_5: King goes to (6, 4) U_5: Rook in (6, 3) captures King
T_6: King goes to (6, 5) U_6: Rook in (6, 3) captures King
T_7: King goes to (5, 5) U_7: Pawn in (4, 4) captures King.

Some opponent's possibilities after Q are:

(1) Knight in (7, 7) goes to (5, 8). He will have a new T_i: 'Knight in (5, 8) captures Knight in (4, 6)' without U_i.

(2) Pawn in (7, 6) goes to (7, 5). He creates a T_i: 'Rook in (8, 6) captures Knight in (4, 6)' without U_i.

(3) Queen in (8, 1) captures (8, 2). He creates a T_i: 'Queen in (8, 2) captures Knight in (4, 6)' without U_i.

(4) Queen in (8, 1) goes to (6, 1). The Knight in (3, 4) is pinned. If we play R, the opponent captures our King with his Queen.

(5) Pawn in (4, 5) captures Knight in (3, 4). The opponent destroys R.

(6) Rook in (2, 2) captures (2, 3). This move destroys u_1. T_1 is possible after R. . . .

This is only a study of the key move threat and of the possibilities of escape for the opponent. This is not a study of two movers which, for each opponent's reply, give a new winning move.

We see that if a move threatens to win in many moves, the opponent will have many possibilities of destroying this threat, so we do not limit the number of his moves very much; on the other hand, if there is an immediate threat, he can only destroy the winning move, and generally there are not many moves which do it. For this reason, immediate threats (like a check in chess) are very useful. In chess we find other threats, but not very often. But in Go moku, moves threatening to win in two moves occur very frequently. In that case the opponent can destroy the dangerous moves by playing in the squares where we want to play and destroying R or s, or he can play an immediate threat that we must destroy, because, if not, he would win before us.

The search for a win with immediate threats. We shall consider only immediate threats. We neglect blockade, but it is not very important because such cases are infrequent. We neglect also non-immediate threats, and this is a more serious limitation of the program. In some games, like Go moku, such threats are very frequent. The method which I shall describe can be complicated for such threats.

The method sees whether we can win with a succession of checks in chess, and with patterns where there are already three of the five necessary men in Go moku.

When we try to find a possibility of winning, there are two problems:
(a) Finding threatening moves and the opponent's replies.
(b) Pruning and developing the *and/or* tree.

We shall study these two points, but deal quickly with the second, which is well known.

How the program finds threatening moves and opponent's replies

(1) *Finding immediate threats.* We want to find a couple of moves of the player: Q — R such that, if we play Q, then R is a winning move. So the first thing to do is to execute the algorithm indicating how to win. There are two cases:

(a) the algorithm indicates that we do not win, and that p conditions: c_1, c_2, . . . c_p, are necessary for this no-winning situation. These p conditions prevent us winning, and we shall try to destroy them. We have this case in chess: $p = 1$; one condition prevents us winning: there is an enemy man in the square s, if the opponent's King is in square s.

(b) the algorithm indicates that there is a win with p modifications. Let $m_1, m_2, \ldots m_p$ be the conditions which must be fulfilled and $d_1, d_2, \ldots d_r$ the existing necessary conditions. We must fulfil the m_i without destroying the d_j.

We do not examine the case where one move Q can destroy (fulfil) the p conditions. It is a winning move, we play it and there is no problem. Also we do not examine the case where more than two moves are necessary: there is not an immediate threat.

If there is an immediate threat, there are four basic possibilities.

(a) $p = 1$: only one condition has to be destroyed (fulfilled). Let this condition be on square s. But no move can do it, we must have an intermediate state for square s. Q changes s at this state and then after R we have the desired condition destroyed.

I know no game where this occurs, but it is theoretically possible. Suppose that we are playing a game where the moves are those of chess, but where we win if square (5, 8) becomes empty. Suppose that there is an enemy piece in (5, 8). We cannot win with one move. We must play at least two moves: the first move Q will capture the piece in (5, 8) and the second move R will move our piece out of (5, 8). The reason is that no friendly move can change: square s = enemy, into the state: square s = empty. We must pass by the intermediate state: square s = friendly.

(b) We must fulfil one or several conditions. The legal move Q fulfils all these conditions, but it destroys some conditions which are necessary and were already fulfilled. We must play R for correcting the bad effect of Q.

Example. In tic-tac-toe, *see* figure 9.

There is a possibility of winning with one modification. Two conditions are already fulfilled: (1, 3) and (3, 3) friendly, but (2, 3) must become friendly. Move Q: (3, 3) goes to (2, 3) fulfilling this condition. But it destroys the

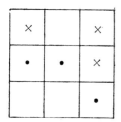

Figure 9. Second kind of threat in tic-tac-toe

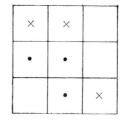

Figure 10. Third kind of threat in tic-tac-toe

condition: (3, 3) friendly, which was fulfilled. So we must play R: (3, 2) goes to (3, 3) and we correct the effect of Q.

(c) One or several conditions must be fulfilled (destroyed), but no move can do this. Q will create a situation where such a move exists; after Q there will be a winning move R which was not legal before playing Q. We are always in this case at chess. R is a move capturing the opponent's King: Q is a move creating R: a check.

We have also this case in tic-tac-toe, in figure 10. There is a winning state with one modification: (3, 3) becomes friendly. Q is: (3, 1) goes to (3, 2) and creates R: (3, 2) goes to (3, 3).

Two methods enable us to find such couples.

(1) For each friendly move Q, we generate all the friendly moves R_i created by Q. The number of R_i is smaller than the number of legal moves. We play Q, then R_i and we examine if we have won.

(2) We generate the moves R_i which fulfil (destroy) the necessary winning (non-winning) conditions. There is no legal move of this type, but we generate the moves which could exist if there were some modifications on the board. Then, for each R_i, we generate the moves Q_{ij} which give changes such that R_i becomes legal.

I choose the second method which is more directed toward the winning state. It is more interesting if there are many legal moves.

(d) Q fulfils (destroys) some conditions and R the others. In that case we can swap Q and R. We have two couples:

Q followed by R

R followed by Q.

Example. In Go moku: friendly piece in (6, 1), (6, 2) and (6, 4); (6, 3) and (6, 5) empty. There are two conditions to fulfil: (6, 3) and (6, 5) become occupied by a friendly piece. Q is: put a piece in (6, 3) and R is: put a piece in (6, 5).

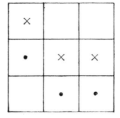

Figure 11. Fourth kind of threat in tic–tac–toe

Figure 12. Reply to a threat in tic–tac–toe

Example. In tic-tac-toe, figure 11. Q is: $(2, 2)$ goes to $(2, 3)$; R is: $(3, 2)$ goes to $(3, 3)$.

In chess we never have this case: there is only one condition which prevents us from winning. But in fairy chess we can have this case. If each player has two Kings and if to win we must capture these two Kings, we can have:

Q: move capturing the first King

R: move capturing the second King.

There can be combinations of the four basic situations: Q fulfils some conditions, but destroys one condition already fulfilled. R reinstates this condition and fulfils the others. This is a combination of cases (b) and (c).

In all the cases we have some couples of friendly moves: Q — R such that if we could play anew after Q, we should win in playing R. We are not obliged to generate all the moves, but only the moves which destroy or fulfil a well-defined condition.

(2) *Finding the opponent's replies.* If we play move Q, the opponent can try two things if he does not want to lose:

(a) If there is a winning move for him, he plays this move and wins before we can play R. If such is the case, we eliminate the couple Q — R.

Example. Tic-tac-toe, figure 12.

Q is: $(2, 2)$ goes to $(2, 3)$

R is: $(3, 2)$ goes to $(3, 3)$.

But, after Q, the opponent plays: $(1, 2)$ goes to $(1, 1)$ and wins. So we eliminate Q.

In the same manner, a piece which is pinned at chess in front of our King cannot make a check.

(b) The opponent has no winning move. He must destroy R if he does not want to lose. For this, he must destroy, at least, one of the necessary conditions for R to occur.

For each necessary condition of R, we enumerate the opponent's moves which destroy it. If there is a condition:

friendly piece in square K;

The opponent will try to capture it.

enemy piece in square K;

The opponent will try to move it.

square K empty;

The opponent will try to put a piece here.

If an opponent's move destroys several conditions of R, we consider it only once.

Example. R is: friendly Bishop in $(7, 7)$ captures enemy King in $(8, 8)$. There are two conditions: friendly Bishop in $(7, 7)$ and: enemy in $(8, 8)$. The move: enemy King captures Bishop – destroys these two conditions. But we keep it only once.

In chess, the move R captures the enemy King. The conditions of R are:
friendly piece in a
enemy in b (square of the King)
squares $c_1, c_2, \ldots c_n$ empty (n may be 0).
If there is a check, the opponent must destroy one of these conditions:
capture the piece which gives a check
move his King
put one of his pieces in a square c_i (if $n \neq 0$).
In each case the program finds this property, well-known to chess players.

In fairy chess, this theorem is not always true. Suppose that there is a check by a Grasshopper [the Grasshopper moves in the same directions as a Queen, but a man (white or black) must be on his line; the Grasshopper can go to the square immediately behind this man (called *sautoir*), if this square is empty or occupied by an enemy man. (*See* Le Lionnais and Maget 1967)] and that the sautoir is an enemy piece in square d. The conditions of the move R: Grasshopper captures King are of the same nature as in chess, except the condition: enemy piece in square d. The opponent can destroy the threat by taking his piece out from d.

With this method, for each threatening move Q, we have the replies: T_1, $T_2, \ldots T_n$. After each T_i we must verify that there is not another winning move R'. If such is the case, we delete T_i.

Example. Friendly Rook in $(6, 8)$. Enemy King in $(8, 8)$. $(7, 8)$ empty.

R is: Rook captures King in $(8, 8)$.

T_1: King in $(8, 8)$ goes to $(7, 8)$, destroys two conditions of R:
$(8, 8)$ enemy and $(7, 7)$ empty. But, after T_1, there is a winning move R': Rook captures King in $(7, 8)$. We delete T_1.

If after doing this $n = 0$, we shall win in playing Q, because the opponent can destroy R only by creating a new winning move. In chess we say in that case that there is checkmate after Q.

Remark. Multiple attacks. We can have the move Q several times as first member of a couple $Q - R$. We can win if we play Q then R_1 *or* if we play Q then $R_2 \ldots$ *or* if we play Q then R_n. If we play Q, the opponent must destroy R_1 and $R_2 \ldots$ and R_n. This situation is very interesting because it is difficult to destroy n moves with only one move, and this decreases drastically the number of opponent's replies.

We could write a special procedure for this case. But it is difficult; the

opponent has two possibilities. Let us take the case of a double threat: $n = 2$.
(a) The opponent destroys one condition common to R_1 and R_2, if there are such conditions. This is always the case in chess; in a double check there is always one condition common to R_1 and R_2: enemy piece in square A (if the enemy King is in A). The opponent destroys the two threats in destroying this condition. It is well known: if there is a double check, the opponent must move his King.
(b) There is a move which destroys one condition of R_1 and one different condition of R_2. We can see that this case never occurs in orthodox chess, but we can find such cases in fairy chess.

Example. Friendly Grasshopper in $(6, 8)$. Enemy Bishop in $(7, 8)$. Enemy King in $(8, 8)$. Friendly Rook in $(8, 5)$. $(8, 6)$ and $(8, 7)$ empty.

R_1 is: Grasshopper captures King.

       Conditions: $(6, 8)$ friendly Grasshopper

                         $(7, 8)$ enemy

                         $(8, 8)$ enemy.

R_2 is: Rook captures King.

       Conditions: $(8, 5)$ friendly Rook

                         $(8, 6)$ empty

                         $(8, 7)$ empty

                         $(8, 8)$ enemy.

The enemy move: Bishop goes to $(8, 7)$, destroys these two moves. It destroys the condition; $(7, 8)$ enemy, of R_1 and the condition; $(8, 7)$, empty of R_2. In this case the opponent is not obliged to move his King.

    But it is difficult to write such a program for multiple threats. It is more convenient, when we have several couples $(Q - R)$ with the same Q, to consider only the first and to eliminate the others. The program will try to destroy R_1 with T_1 or T_2 . . . or T_p. If the move T_i does not also destroy the other winning moves R_j, T_i is eliminated: We verify always after each T_i that there is no winning move. As multiple threats are not very frequent, this method does not waste much computer time and is easy to implement.

    Finally, we have the threatening moves and for each one, the possible opponent's replies. We give in figure 13 an example of the result of this method. We are playing chess.

First step · List of couples $Q - R$ of friendly moves, R being a winning move. In chess we are always in the third case, Q creates R.

 (1) Knight in $(4, 5)$ captures $(6, 6)$ – Knight in $(6, 6)$ captures King

 (2) Knight in $(4, 5)$ captures $(6, 6)$ – Queen in $(2, 3)$ captures King

 (3) Knight in $(4, 5)$ goes to $(5, 7)$ – Knight in $(5, 7)$ captures King

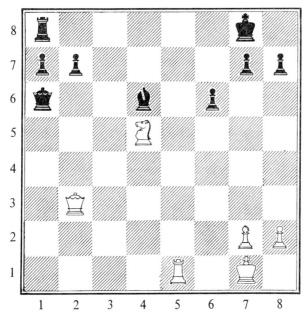

Figure 13. Threatening moves in a chess position

 (4) Knight in (4, 5) goes to (5, 7) – Queen in (2, 3) captures King
 (5) Knight in (4, 5) goes to (6, 4) – Queen in (2, 3) captures King
 (6) Knight in (4, 5) goes to (5, 3) – Queen in (2, 3) captures King
 (7) Knight in (4, 5) goes to (3, 3) – Queen in (2, 3) captures King
 (8) Knight in (4, 5) goes to (2, 4) – Queen in (2, 3) captures King
 (9) Knight in (4, 5) goes to (2, 6) – Queen in (2, 3) captures King
(10) Knight in (4, 5) goes to (3, 7) – Queen in (2, 3) captures King
(11) Rook in (5, 1) goes to (5, 8) – Rook in (5, 8) captures King.

There are two double checks. We eliminate, as we have said above, couples (2) and (4).

Second step · For each threatening move Q, we try to find the opponent's replies. We show this for three moves Q.

(a) *Couple* 1. The conditions of R are:

 (6, 6) White Knight
 (7, 8) Black.

Enemy moves destroying the first condition:

 (1) Pawn in (7, 7) captures Knight.

The second condition:

 (2) King goes to (8, 8)
 (3) King goes to (6, 8)

(4) King goes to (6, 7).

But after move (1) there is a winning move: Queen in (2, 3) captures King in (7, 8). There is also a winning move after move (4): Queen in (2, 3) captures King in (6, 7).

So after: Knight captures (6, 6) – there are two replies:

King goes to (8, 8)

King goes to (6, 8).

We see that the program finds the good replies, although there was a double check.

(6) *Couple* 5. The conditions of R are:

(2, 3) White Queen

(3, 4), (4, 5), (5, 6), (6, 7) empty

(7, 8) Black.

No enemy move can destroy (2, 3) White and (4, 5) and (5, 6) empty.

(3, 4) empty: (1) Queen in (1, 6) goes to (3, 4)

(6, 7) empty: (2) King in (7, 8) goes to (6, 7)

(7, 8) Black: King goes to (6, 7); already seen

(3) King goes to (6, 8)

(4) King goes to (8, 8).

But after move (2), there is a winning move: Queen captures King in (6, 7). We eliminate this reply.

After: Knight in (4, 5) goes to (6, 4), there are three replies:

Queen in (1, 6) goes to (3, 4)

King goes to (6, 8)

King goes to (8, 8).

(c) *Couple* 11. The conditions of R are:

(5, 8) White Rook

(6, 8) empty

(7, 8) Black.

These black moves destroy:

(5, 8) white: (1) Rook in (1, 8) captures (5, 8)

(6, 8) empty: (2) Bishop in (4, 6) goes to (6, 8)

(3) King in (7, 8) goes to (6, 8)

(7, 8) black: King in (7, 8) goes to (6, 8); already seen

(4) King in (7, 8) goes to (8, 8)

(5) King in (7, 8) goes to (6, 7).

The opponent has 5 possible moves. But after move (3) there is the winning move: Rook in (5, 8) captures (6, 8), and after move (4), the winning move: Rook in (5, 8) captures (8, 8). So there are only three possible replies.

After: Rook in (5, 1) goes to (5, 8), the opponent can play:

Rook in (1, 8) captures (5, 8)

Bishop in (4, 6) goes to (6, 8)

King in (7, 8) goes to (6, 7).

Pruning and expanding the tree

Tree pruning. We must prune the tree when we get a winning situation or a situation in which there is no winning possibility. We have a well-known *and/or* tree. I shall only indicate that a winning situation is a threat with no reply and that a non-winning situation is without possible threat.

Expanding the tree. We must choose the situation where we search the threats and the opponent's replies. We first try the situations where, if we win, the opponent has only a few possibilities to escape by playing other moves before our winning move. We shall describe this algorithm. There are two steps.

First step · We associate an integer with each node of the tree. We begin with the leaves. We put the weight 1 on each leaf. When we are in a situation after a friendly move, we associate with this node the sum of the weights of the nodes which are the opponent's replies: we must study all these replies. If we are after an enemy move, we associate with this node the value of the smallest weight of its successors: we can choose our move.

These weights give a good idea of the number of possibilities of escape for the opponent.

Second step · We choose the situation to study. We begin at the root of the tree. If we want to choose a friendly move, we take the node which has the smallest weight. If several nodes have the same value, we take the first. It is not important; if it is bad, we shall take another node the next time.

If we want to choose an enemy move, we take successively all the replies. For this, we indicate which node was taken the last time. This is important to avoid studying one reply a long time when we could see quickly that after another reply we cannot win.

By this process, when we get to a leaf, we have the situation to study. We apply the method described above, we generate a subtree which is connected to the main tree.

The weight of the root gives a good idea of the possibilities of escape for the opponent. If this weight is greater than a parameter given as data to the program, the program gives up. It is then unlikely we could win.

Results. I have given some results in Pitrat (1969). We shall take one and see the steps of the program. The board (chess) is given in figure 14. White can still play short or long castling. White to play. This situation occurred

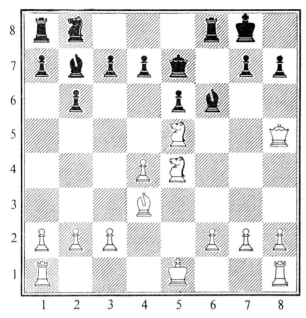

Figure 14. Chess position where there is a possibility of winning

in a real game played by Edward Lasker (1962).

The name of a situation is a letter put after each opponent's reply.

(1) There are 3 threats.

(8, 5) captures (8, 7)

  one reply: (7, 8) captures (8, 7) – A

(8, 5) goes to   (6, 7)

  three replies: (5, 7) captures (6, 7) – B

               (6, 8) captures (6, 7) – C

               (7, 8) goes to (8, 8) – D

(5, 4) captures (6, 6)

  four replies: (7, 7) captures (6, 6) – E

               (6, 8) captures (6, 6) – F

               (5, 7) captures (6, 6) – G

               (7, 8) goes to (8, 8) – H

So the program considers A.

(2) After A there are 7 threats played by the Knight in (5, 4)

(5, 4) captures (6, 6)

  two replies: (8, 7) goes to (8, 8) – I

               (8, 7) goes to (8, 6) – J

(5, 4) goes to   (7, 5) – there are four replies.

  L

For the other threats there are four replies.

(3) The program considers I.

There are two threats: (5, 5) goes to (7, 6)

                      (5, 5) goes to (6, 7)

and no opponent's reply after the first. So we prune the tree.

It is sufficient to show that after J, we win.

(4) The program considers J.

There are 4 threats but only one with one opponent's reply:

(5, 5) goes to (7, 4)

  one reply: (8, 6) goes to (7, 5) – K

(5) The program considers K.

There are 4 threats.

(8, 2) goes to (8, 4)

  one reply: (7, 5) goes to (6, 4) – L

(6, 2) goes to (6, 4)

  two replies: (7, 5) captures (6, 4) – M

                (7, 5) goes to (8, 4) – N

(6, 6) goes to (8, 7). Four replies.

(6, 6) goes to (5, 4). Seven replies.

The second threat gives a quicker mate. But Edward Lasker did not see it. It was only several years later that it was discovered. It seems that human heuristics are, in this case, similar to those of the program.

(6) The program considers L.

There are 3 threats:

(7, 2) goes to (7, 3)

  one reply: (6, 4) goes to (6, 3) – O

(6, 6) goes to (8, 5)

  one reply: (6, 4) captures (7, 5) – P

(6, 6) goes to (4, 5) and four replies.

(7) The program chooses O.

There are 4 threats.

(7, 4) goes to (5, 5)

  one reply: (6, 3) goes to (7, 2) – Q

(4, 3) goes to (5, 2)

  one reply: (6, 3) goes to (7, 2) – R

(4, 3) goes to (5, 4)

  one reply: (2, 7) captures (5, 4) – S

(7, 4) goes to (8, 2)

  one reply: (6, 3) goes to (7, 2) – T

These four moves are equivalent. But if the program chooses Q, S or T, it will quickly stop in this direction, because there are only threats with several replies or because no threat is possible. If we have the first case, then it will prefer another situation with only one reply, so we are sure to examine R quickly, if the move, (4, 3) goes to (5, 2), is not generated first.

(8) The program chooses R.

There are 5 threats, but only two with one reply:

(8, 1) goes to (8, 2)

   one reply: (7, 2) goes to (7, 1) – U

(7, 4) goes to (5, 3)

   one reply: (7, 2) captures (8, 1) – V

(9) The program chooses U.

There is one threat without reply: (5, 1) goes to (4, 2). There is another threat of this type: long castling, but the program considered the first generated.

In pruning the tree, we see that we have won.

CONCLUSION

This method gives good results for games like chess and is good for many kinds of fairy chess. But for some other games, it is not so good for several reasons. Examples are:

(a) games where we are not constantly near winning. Such a procedure is interesting only if we can threaten the opponent;

(b) games where non-immediate threats are very frequent, such as Go moku. We must complicate the algorithm for these cases.

(c) Even if we have only immediate threats, the number of opponent's replies must not be always the same. The choice of the situation to study would not be efficient: all the moves would be equivalent. This case occurs in Go moku: there is always one reply for each immediate threat. In that case we should have other heuristics. General heuristics are not good for every game.

BIBLIOGRAPHY

Lasker, E. (1962) *Chess for fun and chess for blood.* New York: Dover publications.

Le Lionnais, F. & Maget, E. (1967) *Dictionnaire des échecs.* Paris: Presses Universitaires de France.

Pitrat, J. (1969) Realization of a general game playing program. *Information Processing 68,* pp. 1570–4 Amsterdam: North-Holland Publ. Co.

Integrated Systems

The Frame Problem in Problem-Solving Systems

B.RAPHAEL

INTRODUCTION

The frame problem has taken on new significance during recent attempts to develop artificially intelligent systems. The problem deals with the difficulty of creating and maintaining an appropriate informational context or 'frame of reference' at each stage in certain problem-solving processes. Since this is an area of current research, we are not prepared to present a *solution* to the frame problem; rather, the purpose of this paper is to sketch the approaches being pursued, and to invite the reader to suggest additions and improvements.

Although broader interpretations are possible, we think of an 'artificially intelligent system' as meaning a programmed computer, with associated electronic and mechanical devices (for example, a radio-controlled robot vehicle and camera), that is *intelligent* in the sense defined by McCarthy and Hayes (1969):

'. . . we shall say that an entity is intelligent if it has an adequate model of the world (including the intellectual world of mathematics, understanding of its own goals and other mental processes), if it is clever enough to answer a wide variety of questions on the basis of this model, if it can get additional information from the external world when it wants to, and can perform such tasks in the external world that its goals demand and its physical abilities permit.'

Raphael (1970) discusses the research significance of attempting to build such an intelligent robot system.

The intelligent entity, as defined above, will have to be able to carry out tasks. Since a task generally involves some change in the world, it must be able to update its model so that it remains as accurate during and after the performance of a task as it was before. Moreover, it must be able to *plan* how to carry out a task, and this planning process usually requires keeping 'in mind', simultaneously, a variety of possible actions and corresponding models of the hypothetical worlds that would result from those actions. The book-keeping problems involved with keeping track of these hypothetical worlds account for much of the difficulty of the frame problem.

THE FRAME PROBLEM

We shall illustrate the frame problem with a simple example. Suppose the initial world description contains the following facts (expressed in some suitable representation, whose precise form is beyond our immediate concern):

(F1) A robot is at position *A*.

(F2) A box called *B1* is at position *B*.

(F3) A box called *B2* is on top of *B1*.

(F4) *A, B, C,* and *D* are all positions in the same room.

Suppose, further, that two kinds of actions are possible:

(A1) The robot goes from *x* to *y*, and

(A2) The robot pushes *B1* from *x* to *y*,

where *x* and *y* are in {*A, B, C, D*}. Now consider the following possible tasks:

Task (1): The robot should be at C.

This can be accomplished by the action of type A1, 'Go from *A* to *C*'. After performing the action, the system should 'know' that facts F2 through F4 are still true, that is, they describe the world after the action, but F1 must be replaced by:

(F5, i.e. F1') The robot is at position *C*.

Task (2): B1 should be at C.

Now a 'push' action must be used, and both F1 and F2 must be changed.

One can think of simple procedures for making appropriate changes in the model, but they all seem to break down in more complicated cases. For example, suppose the procedure is:

Procedure (a): 'Determine which facts change by matching the task specification against the initial model.'

This would fail in task (1) if the problem solver decided to get the robot to *C* by pushing *B1* there (which is not unreasonable if the box were between the robot and *C* and pushing were easier than going around), thus changing F2.

Procedure (b): 'Specify which facts are changed by each action operator.'

This procedure is also not sufficient, for the initial world description may also contain derived information such as

(F6) *B2* is at position *B*,

which happens to be made false in task (2).

More complicated problems arise when sequences of actions are required. Consider:

Task (3): The robot should be at D and, simultaneously, B2 should be at C.

The solution requires two actions, 'Push *B1* from *B* to *C*' and 'Go from *C* to

D', in that order. Any effective problem solver must have access to the full sets of facts, including derived consequences that will be true as a result of each possible action, in order to produce the correct sequence.

Note that the frame problem is a problem of finding a *practical* solution, not merely finding a solution. Thus it resembles the famous travelling salesman problem or the problem of finding a winning move in a chess game, problems for which straightforward algorithms are known, but usually worthless.

McCarthy and Hayes (1969) divide intelligence into two parts: the *epistemological* part, which deals with the nature of the representation of the world, and the *heuristic* part, which deals with the problem-solving mechanisms that operate on the representation. They then proceed to concentrate upon the epistemological questions related to several aspects of intelligence (including the frame problem). Here, on the other hand, we are concerned with constructing a complete intelligent system, including both the world representations and the closely related problem-solving programs. In the following we shall assume that the representations are basically in the form preferred by them, namely, sets of sentences in a suitable formal logical language such as predicate calculus; and we shall describe candidate organizations for the 'heuristic part', that is, the problem solver, of an artificially intelligent system that can cope with the frame problem.

CURRENT APPROACHES

Complete frame descriptions. A frame can generally be completely described by some data structure, for instance by a set of facts, expressed as statements in a predicate calculus. If we think of each such frame as an object and each possible action as an operator that can transform one object (frame) into another, then we may use a problem-solving system such as GPS (Ernst and Newell 1969) for attempting to construct an object for which the desired goal conditions are true. Unfortunately, when the data base defining each frame reaches a non-trivial size, it becomes impractical to generate and store all the complete frame-objects. For example, suppose each possible frame is defined by 1000 elementary facts, an average of six different actions are applicable and heuristically plausible in any situation, and a typical task requires a sequence of four actions: not unreasonable assumptions about a simple robot system. Then the search tree of possible frames may have about 1000 nodes; it is not practical to store 1000 facts at each node. If each action causes changes in, say, three facts, then storing just the *change* information at each node *is* practical – provided appropriate bookkeeping is done to keep track of which of the original facts still hold after a series of actions. This bookkeeping seems to require considerable program structure in addition to (and quite separate from) the basic object, operator, and difference structure of a GPS-type system. The following approaches are concerned with this new book-keeping problem.

State variables. One way to keep track of frames is to consider each possible world to be in a separate state and to assign names to states. In this formulation, actions are state transition rules, that is, rules for transforming one state into another. Since action rules are generally applicable to large classes of states, the description of an action can contain variables that range over state names.

Green (1969) describes an approach of this kind in detail. Each fact is labelled with the name of the state in which it is known to be true. Additional facts that are state-independent describe the transitional effects of actions. For example, if S_0 is the name of the initial state and $At(ob, pos, s)$ is a predicate asserting that object *ob* is at position *pos* in state *s*, then the conditions of the previous example may be partially defined by the following axioms:

(G1) $At(Robot, A, S_0)$ (from F1)

(G2) $At(B1, B, S_0)$ (from F2)

(G3) $Box(B1) \land Box(B2)$ (*B1* and *B2* arc boxes)

(G4) $(\forall x, y, s)[At(Robot, x, s) \supset At(Robot, y, go\,(x, y, s))]$ (from A1).

At this point some explanations seem in order. $Box(x)$ asserts that *x* is a box. Perhaps it would have been more consistent to write, for instance, $Box(B1, S_0)$, because we only *know* that *B1* is a box in the initial state. However, we do not contemplate allowing any actions that destroy box-ness, such as sawing or burning, so we could add the axiom $(\forall s) Box(B1, s)$. Since we would then be able to prove that *B1* is a box in all states, we suppress the state variable without loss of generality.

Each action, in this formalism, is viewed as a function. One argument of the function is always the state in which the action is applied, and the value of the function is the state resulting after the action. Thus, for example, the value of $go(A, C, S_0)$ is the name of the state achieved by going to *C* after starting from *A* in the initial state.

The appeal of this approach is that, if we have a theorem-proving program, no special problem-solving mechanisms or bookkeeping procedures are necessary. Action operators may be fully described by ordinary axioms (such as G4 for the *go* operation) and the theorem-proving program, with its built-in bookkeeping, becomes the problem solver. For example, task (1) may be stated in the form, 'Prove that there exists a state in which the robot is at *C*', or in predicate calculus, prove the theorem:

$$(\exists s) \; At(Robot, C, s) \tag{1}$$

From (G1) and (G4), we can prove that (1) is indeed a theorem. By answer tracing during the proof (Green and Raphael 1968), we can show that $s = go(A, C, S_0)$, which is the solution.

For more complex actions, however, the major problem with this approach emerges: *After each state change, the entire data base must be re-established.* We need additional axioms that tell not only what things change with each action, but also what things remain the same. For example, we know that *B1* is at *B* in state S_0 (by G2), but as soon as the robot moves, say to state $go(A, C, S_0)$, we no longer know where *B1* is! To be able to figure this out, we need another axiom, such as:

$$(\forall x, y, u, v, s)[(At\,(x, y, s) \wedge x \neq ROBOT) \supset At(x, y, go\,(u, v, s))]$$

('When the robot goes from *u* to *v*, the object *x* remains where it is at *y*.') Thus a prodigious set of axioms is needed to define explicitly how every action affects every predicate, and considerable theorem-proving effort is needed to 'drag along' unaffected facts through state transitions. Clearly this approach will not be practical for problems involving many facts.

The world predicate. Instead of using a variety of independent facts to represent knowledge about a state of the world, let us now suppose that we take all the facts about a particular world and view the entire collection as a single entity, the model $\mathcal{M}$. We may then use a single predicate P, the 'world predicate', whose domains are models and state-names. $P(\mathcal{M}, s)$ is interpreted as meaning that *s* is the name of a world that satisfies all the facts in $\mathcal{M}$. One possible structure for $\mathcal{M}$ is a set of ordered *n*-tuples, each of which represents some elementary relation; for example, $\langle At, Robot, A \rangle$ and $\langle At, B1, B \rangle$ are elements of the initial model, $\mathcal{M}_i$.

The initial world is defined by the axiom $P(\mathcal{M}_i, S_0)$ (except that the complete known contents of $\mathcal{M}_i$ must be explicitly given). We can now specify that an action changes a particular relation in $\mathcal{M}$, *and does not change any other relations*, by a single axiom. Thus the *go* action is defined by the axiom:

$$(\forall x, y, \bar{w}, s)[P(\{\langle At, Robot, x \rangle, \bar{w}\}, s) \supset P(\{\langle At, Robot, y \rangle, \bar{w}\},$$
$$go(x, y, s))]$$

Here $\bar{w}$ (read '*w*-bar') is a variable whose value is an indefinite number of elements of a set, namely all those that are not explicitly described.

This approach preserves the advantages of the previous state-variable approach; namely, the problem-solving, answer construction, and other bookkeeping can be left to the theorem-prover. In addition, properties of the model are automatically carried through state changes by the barred variables. On the other hand, several difficulties are apparent: theorem-proving strategies may be grossly inefficient in the domain of problem-solving; the logic must be extended to include domains of sets and *n*-tuples; complex pattern-matching algorithms will be needed to compare expressions containing variables that range over individuals, *n*-tuples, sets, and indefinite subsets; and the fact that properties of the world are stored as data, instead of as axioms, constrains the problem-solving process by restricting the class of inferences that are possible. Further study is necessary to determine the feasibility of this approach.

Contexts and context graphs. Let us now suppose that we let a *state* correspond to our intuitive notion of a complete physical situation. Since the domain of our logical formalism includes physical measurements such as object positions, descriptions, and so on, every consistent statement of first-order logic is either true or false for every state. We think of each such statement as a predicate that defines a set of states, namely those for which it is true. We call such a set of possible states the *context* defined by the predicate.

We shall find it convenient to allow certain distinguished variables, called *parameters*, to occur in predicates. Since each such predicate with ground terms substituted for parameters defines a context, a predicate containing parameters may be thought of as defining a *family* of possible contexts – and each *partial* instantiation of parameters in the predicate defines a *subfamily* of contexts (or, if no parameters remain, a specific context).

For example, the predicate $At(B1, B)$ defines a context (the set of all states) in which object $B1$ is at position B. If x and y are parameters, $At(x, y)$ defines the family of contexts in which some object is located any place. $At(B1, y)$ is a subfamily of this family in which the object $B1$ must be located at some (as yet unspecified) place.

A problem to be solved is specified by a particular predicate called the *goal predicate*. The problem, implicitly, is to achieve a *goal state*, that is, produce any member of the context defined by the goal predicate.

An *action* will consist of an operator name, a parameter list, and two *predicates* – the *preconditions* K and the *results* R. In addition, any of the elementary relations in the preconditions may be designated as *transient* preconditions. For example, the *go* action is defined by

$$\overbrace{go}^{\text{name}} \ \overbrace{(x, y)}^{\text{parameters}}$$

$$K\{\underline{At(Robot, x)} \mid At(Robot, y)\}R$$

where underlining designates a transient condition. Each action operator thus corresponds to a family of specific actions. An action is applicable in any state that satisfies K; when an action is applied, the resulting state no longer need satisfy the transients but must satisfy R.

In this approach, the conjunction of predicates in the robot's model of the world is an initial predicate I, defining as an initial context the set of all states that have, in common, all the known properties of the robot's current world. The goal context, defined by a given goal predicate, is the set of satisfactory target states. When an operator is applied in a context, it changes the defining predicate (roughly, by deleting transients and conjoining results), thereby changing the context. The problem-solving task is to construct a sequence of operators that will transform the initial context into a subset of the goal context.

Any context that can be reached from the initial context by a finite sequence of operators is called an *achievable* context. Any context from which a subset of the goal context can be reached by a finite sequence of operators is called a *sufficient* context. The main task may be restated, then, as finding an operator sequence to show that the goal is achievable, or that the initial context is sufficient, or, more generally, that some achievable context is a subset of some sufficient context (and therefore is itself sufficient).

The main loop of the problem-solver consists of two steps:

(1) Test whether any known achievable context is a subset of any known sufficient context. If so, we have done.

(2) *Either* generate a new achievable context by applying some operator in a known achievable context ('working forwards'), *or* generate, as a new sufficient context, one that would become a known sufficient context by the application of some operator ('working backwards'). Then return to step (1) to test the newly generated context.

An advantage of this approach is that all states and all properties of operators are defined by first-order predicates, so a standard theorem-proving program can do most of the work testing operators and results and selecting values of parameters. On the other hand, a separate data structure, called a *context graph*, is needed to keep track of the trees of achievable and sufficient states and the operators that relate their nodes. For example, suppose we wish to get from A to D in the directed graph shown in figure 1. We shall abbreviate by $\mathscr{S}$ the predicate that gives the graph's topology:

$$\mathscr{S} \equiv Path(A, B) \wedge Path(B, C) \wedge Path(C, D) \wedge Path(A, F) \wedge$$
$$Path(E, D)$$

The initial predicate is $I \equiv At(A) \wedge \mathscr{S}$. The goal predicate is $G \equiv At(D)$. We shall define the operator *go*, for this problem, by:

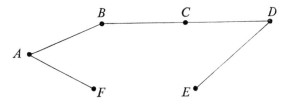

Figure 1

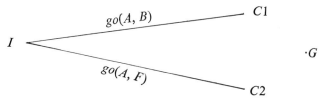

Figure 2

$$go\,(x, y)$$
$$\{Path(x, y) \wedge At(x) \mid At(y)\}$$

The operator is applicable in context I only if we can prove that:
$$(\exists x, y)[I \supset At(x) \wedge Path(x, y)]$$
is a theorem. The proof can be done by resolution with answer tracing (Green and Raphael 1968). The above statement can be shown to be a theorem when $x = A$ and y is either B or F. Therefore, the go operator can be used two ways to generate new achievable contexts $C1$ and $C2$, with corresponding predicates $P_{C1} = \mathscr{S} \wedge At(B)$, $P_{C2} = \mathscr{S} \wedge At(F)$. To keep track of actions and instantiations, we shall draw the context graph shown in figure 2. Similarly, from $C1$ we can prove the applicability of $go(B, C)$, which, when applied, gives $C3$:
$$P_{C3} = \mathscr{S} \wedge At(C) \qquad .$$
To illustrate working backwards, consider whether the result of a go implies G. The relevant problem for a theorem prover is
$$(\exists y)[At(y) \supset At(D)] \qquad .$$
This is trivially true if $y = D$, so any state that satisfies the preconditions of the operator $go(x, D)$ is sufficient (because the operator will then be applicable, and will produce the goal). Thus a new sufficient context $C4$ is given by the preconditions
$$P_{C4} = At(x) \wedge Path(x, D) \qquad .$$
(Note that $C4$ is really a family of contexts, because of the parameter x.) The context graph is now as shown in figure 3. Finally, the theorem-prover can show that
$$P_{C3} \supset P_{C4} \text{ when } x = C$$
completing the solution.

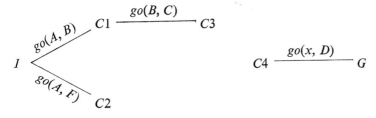

Figure 3

Most problems are considerably more difficult than the above example because of several complications. Suppose in trying to work backwards from G (using an operator Op with preconditions K and results R) we find that we cannot prove $R \supset G$, but instead discover a statement S such that $R \wedge S \supset G$. We may still work backwards with Op, but the new sufficient context is defined not by K alone but rather by $K \wedge S$. Furthermore, some extra bookkeeping must remind us that S may not be disturbed, in a valid solution, by applying Op – for instance, no transients of Op may appear in S. Similar additional subgoals – and bookkeeping complications – arise from each incomplete attempt to prove that an achievable context is contained in a sufficient context.

Additional complexities arise from *dependencies*. That is, when an expression E is deleted by a transient during an action, other expressions that were deduced from E in previous contexts can no longer be guaranteed to be true in new contexts. Thus each deduced expression is said to *depend* upon all its ancestors, adding to our growing burden of bookkeeping problems.

On the other hand, the context graph can take care of much of the bookkeeping automatically. Each logical expression need only be stored once, with notations telling in which contexts it was created and destroyed, rather than being either copied or rederived from context to context. Finally, if predicates of achievable contexts and operator results are stored in clause form, and predicates of sufficient contexts and operator preconditions are stored in negated clause form, preliminary experiments show that most of the nuts-and-bolts work of attempting solutions and generating new contexts can be done in a straightforward manner by an existing resolution-type theorem-proving program.

Other approaches. Several other approaches to the frame problem have been suggested, although few have been worked out in sufficient detail to test on a computer.

Richard E. Fikes at SRI is developing a system whose formal framework is similar to that described in the previous section, but which does not use resolution techniques. Instead, proofs are strongly dependent upon the semantics of the logic, and the problem solver proceeds by a heuristic, goal-directed, case-analysis approach. This work is still in an early stage of development.

Erik Sandewall at Stanford is extending some ideas suggested by John McCarthy for formalizing the concepts of causality and time dependence, using a method proposed by J. A. Robinson for embedding higher-order logic in first-order predicate calculus. The resulting system provides an interesting model for inevitable sequences of events (example: 'if it is raining then things will get wet'), but may not be as useful for describing alternative possible actions by an external agent (the robot).

Methods for proving theorems in higher-order predicate calculus are being developed in several places, and the use of this more powerful formalism may eventually vastly simplify our tasks. Finally, McCarthy and Hayes (1969) suggest some other approaches including modal logics and counter-factuals, but the details have not been extensively explored.

CONCLUSIONS

This paper has described the frame problem and the principal methods that have been proposed for solving it.

Let us review the approaches listed above. (1) The method of complete frame and frame-transition descriptions was simply a stage-setting 'straw man' that we would not consider actually using. (2) The logic-cum-state-variable approach is beautifully elegant for 'toy' problems, but both the representational effort and the theorem-proving effort grow explosively with problem complexity. (3) The world predicate idea preserves some of the elegance of approach (2) while carrying along necessary frame information implicitly; however, it places a burden on theorem-proving abilities in new domains and requires an awkward use of two levels of logical representation (that is, relations among the n-tuples in the model must be defined in terms of the world predicate), so that the practicality of the approach is open to serious question. (4) The use of contexts and context graphs (without explicit state names in the logic) is a more-or-less brute-force attempt to combine the use of first-order theorem-proving methods with a GPS-like structure of sub-goals and operators; although the bookkeeping problems are complicated, they seem to be tractable, so that the approach is reasonably promising. Finally, we mentioned several interesting ideas that warrant further exploration before they can be meaningfully compared with the other approaches.

Until now, most research in problem solving has dealt with fairly static situations in narrow subject domains. As we become interested in building complete artificially independent systems, a new kind of problem-solving research emerges: We must study how to solve problems in an environment containing a large store of knowledge, while considering the possible effects of a variety of sequences of actions. This paper has described some of the first exploratory steps into this important area of research.

ACKNOWLEDGMENTS

Many of the ideas discussed above, including development of the contexts and context graphs approach, are the result of joint discussions between the author and L. S. Coles, R. E. Fikes, J. H. Munson, and N. J. Nilsson. The 'world predicate' idea is completely due to R. Waldinger. C. C. Green developed the state variable approach, and he is largely responsible for our early realization of the importance of the frame problem.

The research described herein is supported by the Advanced Research Projects Agency of the Department of Defense, and by the National Aeronautics and Space Administration under Contract N A S 1 2–2221.

BIBLIOGRAPHY

Ernst, G. W. & Newell, A. (1969) *GPS: A Case Study in Generality and Problem Solving*. New York & London: Academic Press.

Green, C. C. (1969) Application of theorem proving to problem solving. *Proc. Int. joint Conf. on Artificial Intelligence*. Washington, DC.

Green, C. C. & Raphael, B. (1968) The use of theorem-proving techniques in question-answering systems. *Proc. 1968 ACM Conference*, Las Vegas.

McCarthy, J. & Hayes, P. (1969) Some philosophical problems from the standpoint of Artificial Intelligence. *Machine Intelligence 4*, pp. 463–502 (eds. Meltzer, B. & Michie, D.). Edinburgh: Edinburgh University Press.

Raphael, B. (1970) The relevance of robot research to AI. *Formal Systems and Non-Numeric Problem Solving by Computer*. Berlin: Springer-Verlag.

M

Natural Language and
Picture Processing

Jigsaw Heuristics and a Language Learning Model

R.K.LINDSAY

THE JIGSAW HEURISTICS

Jigsaw puzzles should be much more difficult than they are. The problem solver is faced with a problem of large combinatorial complexity. He must arrange perhaps eight hundred or one thousand pieces of cardboard into a coherent structure which meets two conditions: all of the pieces fit together (each piece's contours coincide with those of its neighbors) and the result is a picture of something. Usually of all of the possible orderings of pieces which might be tried, only one is correct. And yet such problems are readily solved. It may be worthwhile to ask why.

One important characteristic of jigsaw puzzles, a characteristic shared by many puzzles and problems, is that one can construct stable partial solutions. Consider a problem involving discovery of a particular configuration of several elements, as with anagrams. In a seven-letter anagram there are $7! = 5040$ arrangements which might be tried. If, however, some arrangements of two or three letters are illegal or unlikely or, conversely, if some arrangements are highly probable, the complexity of the problem is drastically reduced. Thus if both 'Q' and 'U' are present, one ought to group them in the order 'QU'. This reduces the number of units to six and the number of combinations to $6! = 720$, a substantial reduction. Similarly, if one had to put together all 800 pieces of a jigsaw puzzle before he could tell whether *any* of the proper connections had been made, noone would ever solve these puzzles. Simon (1962) has discussed the importance of this problem characteristic.

Jigsaw puzzles have a second important property. In selecting pieces for placement, the problem solver is guided by two distinct types of information: the shapes of the contours and the designs printed on the surfaces. He may scan the unattached pieces at one moment looking, perhaps, for a predominantly yellow piece with convex protrusions on opposite sides. The exact design and shape are not examined until the set of candidates has been thus substantially reduced. One may convince himself of the value of the pictorial information by attempting to do the puzzle face down. One may convince himself of the value of the contour information by selecting a puzzle whose pieces are all squares or hexagons.

These two types of information are highly, perhaps totally, redundant. The pieces can be composed into a rectangle in only one arrangement, so that one can be certain (for most puzzles) that he has obtained the solution even if the puzzle *is* face down. Likewise, if the picture is, say, a landscape, there is probably only a single arrangement which depicts a landscape (at least the one on the box), even if all of the contours are identical. Yet though redundant the presence of both types of information facilitates searching for the correct solution.

That this should be so is readily seen. In searching for a piece which meets two requirements, we may scan the available set using just one of the requirements as a quick test to reject most candidates; the remaining possibilities may be checked for the second requirement or just tried out. The crux of the matter is that, in different situations, one or the other test may be easier to apply. Thus if the required color is red in a predominantly red puzzle, it may be easier to search for the required contour, whereas, if the required color is yellow, a color search is faster. If the required contour is perceptually distinct and relatively uncommon, as in border pieces, it will be easy and expeditious to search for it by contour. Thus the criterion which is applied first will differ from move to move.

These features suggest the following problem-solving strategy. Whenever possible, formulate combinatorially large construction problems so that stable subconstructions can be formed and built upon, and characterize the rules of construction along two *or more* dimensions which are not perfectly correlated but which are each sufficient (or almost so) to determine the correctness of the solution.

This problem-solving strategy suggests a learning strategy. Suppose someone were to drop a couple of pieces of his jigsaw puzzle into his coffee. He might find that while the contours were relatively unaffected, the picture would be discolored or come unglued and be lost. However, he would still be able to complete his puzzle and in fact could doubtless reconstruct the lost information if he were handy with paint and brush. On the other hand, if his child chews off the protrusions, so that contour information is lost while picture information is relatively preserved, the lost information could be recovered in a similar manner once the problem is solved. This suggests the possibility of a learning procedure which could be applied to construction problems of this sort, where not all of the redundant information is present initially, but where enough is present to allow the solution of the problem or some of its subproblems. The procedure could then bootstrap its way up by using newly constructed knowledge to fill in yet other missing information.

Let us attempt to apply these concepts to the problem of devising a self-organizing sentence parsing program. A given parsing problem involves determining, for an ordered set of words, a construction which shows how these words are related. The parsing program will have knowledge of which combinations – relations among words and symbols – are possible or probable, but this information will be local rather than global. That is, this knowledge is the sort found in dictionaries; it is information about words, not sentences. The program will understand that its job is done when it has constructed a single structure employing all of the given words in its input and not violating any conditions which are explicitly prohibited.

It is tempting to identify the contour information of our jigsaw puzzle with syntactic information in our parsing puzzle, and to identify picture information with semantic information. However, the jigsaw heuristics do not require such an identification; all that we require is that there be at least two classes of information and that they be partially redundant. Since there is no *a priori* natural distinction between syntactic and semantic information in any case, the identification would not be helpful. (Should the scheme outlined be carried out, on the other hand, it might serve to *define* a syntax/semantics boundary.)

We run into some difficulties. The jigsaw analogy differs in important ways from the parsing problem. In the jigsaw puzzle case, generally only one solution is possible. This follows from the fact that each piece has a unique contour which can fit into only one context. This is manifestly not the case with language, where a relatively small and only slowly growing set of words may be used in a vast number of combinations. It is as though each piece of a jigsaw puzzle had many sets of contours and designs and could thus be used in a large number of pictures. Further, the problem solver never knows in advance what picture he is working on. The complication is that, while stable subconstructions can be formed, it is not certain that one so formed will be a part of the final solution; it may need to be disbanded.

Most models of comprehension do not take advantage of the leverage provided by the jigsaw problem-solving heuristic. For example, Katz and Fodor (1963) suggest that first a syntactic parse is discovered, and then the structure is to be interpreted by procedures which employ semantic information to eliminate some of the syntactically permissible readings. Theorists who have designed computer programs for linguistic analysis have been more sensitive to the problems of combinatorial complexity, and several have discovered a relative of the jigsaw problem-solving strategy. Thus Thompson *et al.* (1964)

use a procedure whereby suggested syntactic analyses are tested against information in a data base phrase by phrase; Quillian (1969) reverses the procedure
and submits semantically proposed constructions to syntactic checks (his
'form tests'). Each of these procedures is enormously valuable in reducing
the size of the space of possibilities. However, neither appears to use the full
power of the jigsaw heuristic, wherein the order of the checking may be a
function of the problem at hand. Of course it is not obvious how such a
decision procedure could be devised.

AN OUTLINE OF A LANGUAGE-LEARNING MODEL

Let us sketch a procedure for applying these observations to a more specific
language-learning task. Consider a program which is to be given well-formed
sentences, one word at a time. The program will contain two stores of information about words. A *dictionary* specifies in some manner the possible
structural interconnections each word may enter into. Thus *cat* might be
allowed to enter into the predator relation with anything meeting certain
requirements, and into the parent relation with other things. A *syntax directory*
indicates possible structural connections of a different sort, again for each
word. *Cat* might be allowed to enter into the subject relation with anything
which can be a predicate, for example. Both the dictionary and the syntax
directory will typically contain several entries for each word. A selection
routine for each will use situational and contextual information, including
information about partially constructed parses, to help select entries and
order them. The ordering, which represents an ordered set of hypotheses
about the structure of the sentence being processed, may intermix dictionary
and syntax directory suggestions.

As a word is processed, an ordered set of structural hypotheses for it is
thus created. When the next word is read, the proposed structures are tested
in sequence to determine if they are permissible in view of the entries for
the second word. If a permitted one is found, the construction is formed; if
not, the two words with their associated hypotheses are saved. If the program
thus accumulates an overly large collection of disconnected pieces, *or* if the
end of the sentence is encountered before all words have been combined into
a single structure, the program goes into a guessing mode. Guessing amounts
to testing hypothesized connections to determine which failed fulfilment because of missing dictionary or syntax directory information. Enough additional new knowledge is selected to permit completion of the parse. The result
is then submitted to review by a teacher. If the guesses yielded an acceptable
parse, the information so generated will become permanent knowledge. If
not, other guesses will be tried as time permits. If success is not achieved,

the program will have learned nothing from the experience.

The behavior of the program may be illustrated with the following simple example. Assume that the dictionary allows structural connections of types F1 and F2 to exist from *red* to *rose* and structural connections of types F1 and F3 to exist from *rose* to *red* (thus we are considering ordered connections). Let the syntax directory permit connections c1 and c2 from *red* to *rose* and connections c3 and c4 from *rose* to *red*. Assume the selection routines for *red* in the absence of other context propose F1 and c1 connections. Since these are permitted by the dictionary and syntax directory for *rose*, when the latter is encountered these connections will be formed. Had no entries for *rose* existed, and had the program been forced to form a structure, it would have guessed F1 and c1 and been able to add this information to its store of knowledge about *rose*. Had *rose* been the first word encountered, the selection routines might have hypothesized a different set of connections, say c3 and F3. Thus *red rose* and *rose red* would receive different analyses.

THE JIGSAW-1 MODEL

A program, JIGSAW-1, for parsing English sentences was developed along the lines of the foregoing sketch. Necessarily JIGSAW-1 incorporates several additional features in order to complete the sketch. At the same time, unfortunately, it does not adhere with complete fidelity to the preceding plan. It will be useful, however, to consider this program in some detail.

JIGSAW-1 is a program to parse sentences. The parses which it seeks we call labelled dependency trees. A labelled dependency tree is a tree whose nodes are words and whose edges indicate relations of varied kinds among the words. A labelled dependency parse is therefore more general than either a phrase structure analysis or a dependency analysis because different inter-word relations may be indicated by differently labelled edges. An illustration is given in figure 1. One would like, of course, to deal with structures which had special qualities appropriate to the topic of discussion; that is, one would like to deal with structures which were good models of the world (*see* Lindsay 1963). However, we know of such structures only for very special cases. We choose here, therefore, to employ a very general representation. In this we follow Quillian (1969) and Schwarz, Burger, and Simmons (1970).

In a labelled dependency system the intention is that the labels reflect the sort of structural interconnections between words which the sentence is meant to convey. Thus *green* might depend on *tree* in the same sense (via the same label) as *white* depends on *snow*, but in a different sense than *green* depends on *recruit*, even though in all cases the dependency reflects modification in the usual syntactic sense. In most instances, *the* would be dependent upon a

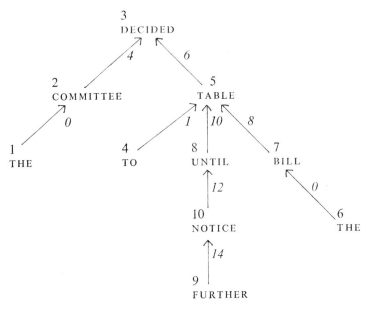

Figure 1. A labelled dependency analysis. Italicized numerals by lines denote labels; roman numerals over words indicate the word's serial position in the sentence.

noun via the same label; but in some instances, such as in *the more the merrier*, the label would differ.

Two additional limitations are placed on the form of parses: only one label per edge is permitted, and the structure must be a tree. These limitations not only reduce the generality of the interpretations, but provide additional clues to the heuristic parsing procedure: if a proposed connection would violate either limitation, it is rejected.

The dictionary of JIGSAW-1. In this program, no distinction is made between function words and referent words. All words in the input are treated alike. To store information about all possible structural connections between each pair of words would require a prohibitive amount of memory. Instead, each word has associated information which specifies which labels may be employed in dependency relations involving that word. This information is stored in two lists; some labels may appear on both lists. List A for word w contains all labels which may be attached to edges with w below (as dependent); list B for word w contains all labels which may be attached to edges with w above (as governor). In testing to determine whether a connection involving label L may be made between words w and x with w being dependent on x, a positive answer is made only if L occurs on the A list of w and the B list of x. If L is present on both lists the 'test for possibility' yields the answer 'possible'; if L is absent from one or both of the lists, the answer is 'impossible', unless one of the lists involved is non-existent (indicating a new word), in which case the answer is 'unknown'. As stated above, a connection must also satisfy other structural requirements in order to be acceptable.

It should be noted that this manner of storing information is less restrictive than would be the case if information were stored on the basis of word pairs; that is, the program generalizes more. Thus the dictionary writer might wish to state that *green* may depend on *grass* via the label 'color' and that *white* may depend on *snow* by that same label. Using the above scheme, the resulting dictionary would allow *green snow* and *white grass*. If this possibility is to be ruled out, two 'color' labels must be used.

The syntax directory of JIGSAW-1. In JIGSAW-1 the syntax directory is stored in the form of a discrimination tree. The non-terminal nodes of the tree have associated tests. These tests may be any subroutines which produce a single symbol as output; in fact they are selected from a list of tests supplied by the programmer and are not generated by the program. Typically, the tests ask questions about partial interpretations and the answers to the questions direct the program to a *syntax routine*. This routine defines the types of further structural connections the program will propose for the disposal of the partial interpretation which was used as the entry to the tree. Typical tests are: 'Is the interpretation a single word or a complex structure?' (answer: simple, complex); 'What is the word which is at the head of the interpretation?' (answer: a word); 'What is the label which is attached to the first level connection?' (answer: a label); 'How deep is the interpretation?' (answer: an integer). When a partial interpretation is submitted to the tree the first question is asked of it. The result of this test selects the branch which leads to another test, and so forth, until the syntax routine is retrieved. Executing the syntax routine generates proposed connections and attaches this information to the partial interpretation where it is later used.

This method of information storage and retrieval is patterned after the theory of human rote memorization developed by Feigenbaum (1959). A major feature of this theory is that the sequence of tests which defines the retrieval properties is stored as a data structure which may be dynamically altered by the program. Typically the alterations are effected in order to adapt to a particular retrieval task which is faced. Thus changes in the tree may bring about unexpected consequences which are felt when the program faces a new task.

The full vocabulary and associated syntax routines are given to the program at the outset. A subroutine grows a syntax tree in such a manner that each word is sorted to a unique terminal at which is placed its syntax routine. The algorithm which grows the tree sorts the given word in the tree. If a unique terminal is found, the routine is finished. If not, an attempt is made to find, from the given set of tests, a test which when added will discriminate the given word from the others with which it is confused. This is always possible due to the way in which the tests are defined. However, the list of tests is ordered from general to specific so that the algorithm examines general features of the structure first.

When this program was developed, the concept of the jigsaw heuristics had not been fully appreciated. In particular, the need for two separate kinds of information was not altogether clear, and as a result the proposals which are generated by syntax routines are based on the same type of information as that found in the dictionary. (Indeed, as will be seen in the next section, syntax directory information initially associated with a word is a subset of the dictionary information initially associated with that word, although this relation will not necessarily be maintained after the program has accumulated some experience.) More specifically, a proposal is of the form 'Set up an expectation that subsequently a structure (perhaps a single word) will be encountered which can be combined with the present structure in such a manner that the present structure is dependent (or governs) the expected structure by way of label L'. A single syntax routine may mark any number of such proposals.

The number of partial interpretations must not exceed a parameter controlled amount (usually set at seven), and an attempt should be made to construct a single, connected interpretation for a single input string. If a limit is exceeded, the program attempts to force a connection which has not been proposed or which is not compatible with the dictionary. Such attempts may fail, in which case the program gives up.

Initializing JIGSAW-1. The program is initially supplied with an amount of information about the language to be processed. Some information must be supplied if the program is to perform other than at random; this is not a model of the very first stages of language acquisition. If syntax routines are not selected on the basis of the substructure of partial interpretations, the program may be initialized by a simple algorithm as follows.

Select a corpus of sentences (or phrases) from the language. Using your linguistic knowledge and intuition, draw a labelled dependency tree for each sentence, supplying whatever labels are necessary to record the discriminations you wish to make. For each word in the vocabulary note all sites where the word occurs at the tail of an arrow. Form a list (the A list) of all of the labels associated with such sites. Each label is to occur on the list only once in spite of multiple occurrences in the labelled dependency trees; the order of the labels on the lists is arbitrary. Next note all sites where the word occurs at the head of an arrow and form the B list in a similar manner. This information constitutes the initial dictionary entry for the word.

Next consider each label on the A list in turn. Determine whether, in any sentence of the initializing corpus, the given word precedes by one or more word positions the word which appears at the other end of any dependency relation using the A list entry as label. If so, add the label to a list called the c list, and consider the next A list entry. If not, skip the label and consider the next A list entry. When the A list is exhausted, consider the B list in like manner, this time forming another list, the D list. Associate lists c and D with the syntax routine which is to correspond to the given word. Enter the word and its syntax routine into the syntax directory by means of the tree-growing subprogram.

The JIGSAW-1 main procedures. After the syntax tree is grown and the dictionary is read into memory, control is transferred to the main executive whose flowchart appears in figure 2. The executive selects the next sentence to be processed and sequentially presents each word in the sentence to the main subprogram, E20: PROCESS CURRENT PHRASE. E20 either combines the current word with structures previously held in the immediate memory (IM) or reports failure after retrieving and executing its associated syntax routine. Routine E23 is executed to add the word to the IM and, if IM is full, to force a connection. When the sentence is completed, routine E25 attempts to combine the members of IM into a single structure.

The heart of JIGSAW-1 is E20 and its three associated subprograms G5, E21, and E24. G5 generates each proposal associated with the phrases held in IM. The order of generation is important and embodies important hypotheses of the model. The IM is examined from most recent to most remote phrase, and for each phrase each proposal which would use the current phrase as governor is selected in turn. When these proposals are exhausted, the IM is again scanned in the same direction and proposals are generated which would make the current phrase dependent. Each proposal is presented to one of the subprograms E24 or E21, whose flowcharts appear in figures 3 and 4. The subprogram may either terminate the generation of proposals or request the next proposal. As seen in the flowcharts, generation is continued if the proposal is rejected or if the proposal is used to employ the current phrase as governor. If a proposal which employs the current phrase as a dependent is used, the current phrase will then be made a part of another structure which is stored in the IM. The new structure is thereupon sorted in the syntax tree.

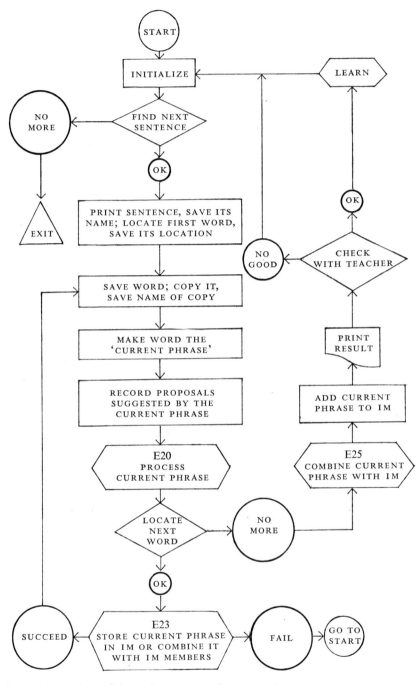

Figure 2. Flowchart of the main program of JIGSAW-1.

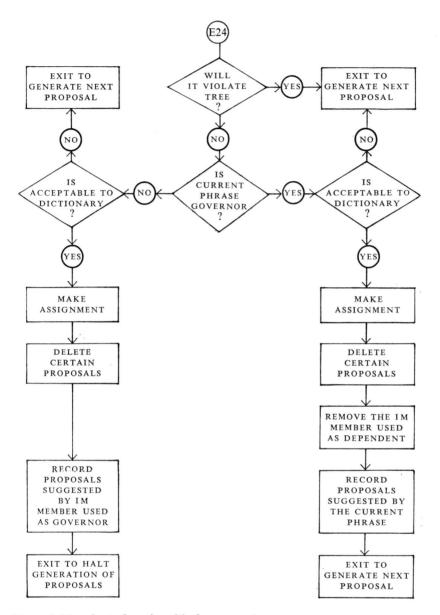

Figure 3. Flowchart of routine E24 of JIGSAW-1.

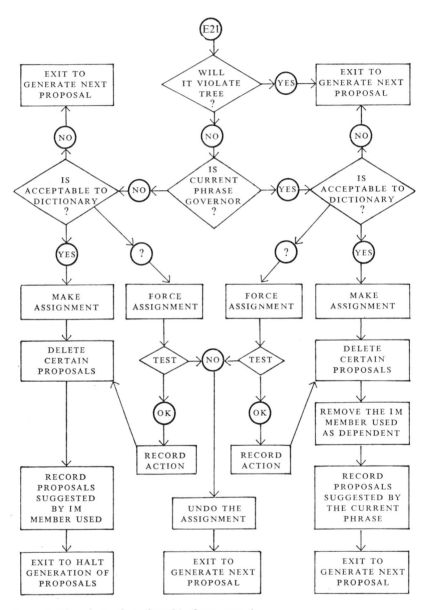

Figure 4. Flowchart of routine E21 of JIGSAW−1.

This enables it to retrieve a new set of proposals, and generation is terminated, thus returning control to the executive which selects the next word.

E24 checks the feasibility of the proposed structural changes by two tests. The first checks to see that no rules of structure formation will be violated (that is, the proposed structure must be a tree) and the second checks the proposal for consistency with the dictionary. If both tests are passed, the change is carried out. If a change in structure is not made by E24, JIGSAW-1 makes a more concerted effort to accomplish something by regenerating the proposals and executing a more lenient analysis, E21. Even though a proposal is not clearly acceptable to the dictionary, E21 will force the proposed restructuring if it is not definitely rejected by the dictionary. This occurs only in the case where one of the lists A or B, for one or both of the words, is empty, indicating that the dictionary has no information concerning the relevant aspects of the words involved.

An additional complexity should be mentioned. A phrase is stored in the IM by placing the name of the tree in a memory register. A proposal may suggest that the word at the head of the structure is to be combined as a dependent or governor, or it may suggest that one of the words already dependent on the head of the phrase is to be used as a governor of the current phrase. Information concerning each proposal is formed into a list, and the list of proposals is associated with the name of the phrase. Since the generator, G5, produces proposals in the order in which they occur on the list, their placement is crucial. The order of the proposals is arranged so that proposals involving more recent words (those occurring later in the sentence) are placed nearer the top of the list whether or not the words are near the top of the phrase whose name appears in IM. This amounts to an assumption that the language is predominantly an immediate constituent language, although discontinuous constituents will be considered as a last alternative.

Examples of JIGSAW-1 behavior. The correct parsings of two example sentences are given in figures 1 and 5. The first sentence was correctly parsed, with JIGSAW-1 initialized from a 25-sentence corpus including the two examples. The procedure failed on the second sentence, yielding the two-component analysis shown in figure 6. It is instructive to analyze the failure in the second example.

Two disjoint pieces resulted because *notice* could not be assigned to *is* without violating the tree constraint. This is a direct result of the incorrect assignment of *notice* as a dependent of *were* rather than the other way around. The assignment actually made was proposed first since *were* occurs later in the sentence and current words are used as governors before they are used as

N

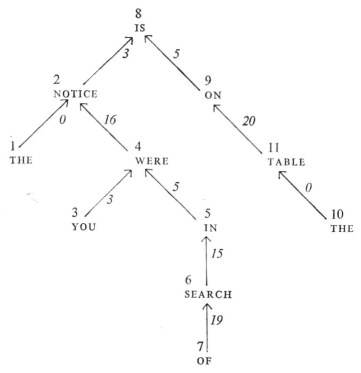

Figure 5. Labelled dependency analysis of *The notice you were in search of is on the table*, as used in initializing JIGSAW-1 for the experiment reported.

dependents. The assignment made uses label 3, which reflects a sense in which *notice* acts as a subject of the verb *were*, as in the ungrammatical string *the notice were late*. This particular difficulty could be eliminated by providing a larger selection of labels so that subjects and verbs are forced to agree in number. This would defeat our purpose. Actually, the corpus from which the program was initialized did not contain the ungrammatical construction *notice were*. It did, however, contain a sentence in which *notice* is a subject of a copulative verb and a sentence in which *were* is used as a copulative verb, but with another subject. Since the dictionary contains no information about particular word pairs, it does not reject the assignment of *notice* to *were*.

If such situations are not to be ruled out by the dictionary, how can such clumsy failures of overgeneralization be avoided? The answer may lie in the syntax directory discrimination tree. Somehow the program should know that *were* is no longer acceptable as the verb for *notice* since the former already has a subject, namely *you*. Furthermore, no conjunction exists to tie *notice* and *you* into a compound subject for *were*. But unless the syntax tree contains

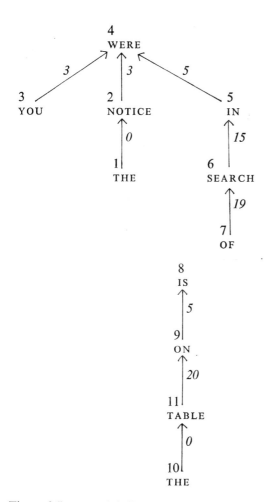

Figure 6. Incorrect labelled dependency analysis as produced by JIGSAW-1 for the sentence of figure 5.

tests which detect the substructure of the *were*-phrase, these facts will go undetected and the resulting error is perfectly natural. This example indicates the need for greater power to discriminate different kinds of phrases according to their substructure.

CONCLUSIONS

The hypotheses on which the model is based can only be evaluated after more extensive experimentation because they are many and they interact in a complex fashion. The conclusions that can be drawn deal with specific limitations which have been encountered; thus they are negative rather than positive.

Experiments with JIGSAW-1 on several sentences indicated that the need to base syntax directory selections on aspects of phrases is widespread. It seems that we cannot get away with simple checks on local characteristics. That this is not sufficient for the *generation* of grammatical sentences was obvious, but for purposes of parsing it was hoped that sophisticated syntactic knowledge would not be needed. Present indications do not support this hope. It is worth noting that Quillian (1969) operates under a similar hope when he uses simple 'form tests' as the basis of his program's syntactic knowledge. Our experience leads us to be pessimistic about this approach, but as noted it is not possible to draw firm conclusions about a single feature of the program in isolation.

JIGSAW-1 has also failed to solve the problem of overgeneralization which still plagues other learning models. As soon as we attempt to develop programs which do more than memorize examples, we run the risk that they will learn too much – that they will accept or produce sentences wantonly. Our program is no exception.

Beyond this it is difficult to assess the matter, but there are three important characteristics of the program to consider. First, it is difficult to state what it is that the program knows at a given time, since much of its knowledge is embodied as processes rather than as formation rules. To identify the program's linguistic competence as the set of sentences which its dictionary and syntax directory find acceptable is absurd, since many of these will not be parsable with the given procedures. The 'grammar' which the dictionary and the syntax directory in some sense provide is overgeneral in the sense that almost any sequence of words is permitted. In this we follow Knowlton (1962). The approach is significant, because humans clearly are able to make some sense of almost any linguistic input, if sufficiently motivated. But if 'competence' is to be construed as potential performance (which is what we consider the usual sense, as opposed to the Chomskyan sense of ideal performance), then competence is embodied in processes as well as in data. The program's performance, of course, is what it actually does, and this is influenced by other factors.

Another feature of the design is the size of the pieces of knowledge which the program adds to its memory as the result of a single learning experience. In this we fall somewhere between Skinner and Chomsky. An S-R theory learns only a few associative bonds on a learning trial; a transformational learning model would presumably be able to learn transformations. Neither of these seems to us to be an appropriate size piece of knowledge, although this is merely speculation.

A final consideration is the nature of the feedback permitted. It clearly seems that giving the program specific information about structures, words, and so forth is not an accurate reflection of the situation a child faces. Thus, unlike the McConlogue & Simmons (1965) and Knowlton (1962) approaches, we chose not to supply JIGSAW-1 with correctly parsed sentences. On the other hand, it seems clear that other types of information are needed [as shown by the results of Gold (1967)] and such information is in fact available to the child: non-linguistic information about the world of objects and events which the child perceives in conjunction with examples of sentences. Our program fails to model this aspect of the situation.

As for the jigsaw heuristics with which we began, it seems to us that they may yet provide a valuable weapon against the combinatorial complexity of natural language phenomena and other problems as well. Hopefully further explorations will bear this out.

REFERENCES

Feigenbaum, E. A. (1963) The simulation of verbal learning behavior. *Computers and Thought*, pp. 297–309 (eds, Feigenbaum, E. A. & Feldman, J.). New York: McGraw-Hill.

Gold, E. M. (1967) Language identifiability in the limit. *Information and Control*, **10**, 447–74.

Katz, J. J., & Fodor, J. A. (1963) The structure of a semantic theory. *Language*, **39**, 170–210.

Knowlton, K. C. (1962) Sentence parsing with a self-organizing heuristic program. Doctoral dissertation, MIT.

Lindsay, R. K. (1963) Inferential memory as the basis of machines which understand natural language. *Computers and Thought*, pp. 217–33 (eds. Feigenbaum, E. A. & Feldman, J.) New York: McGraw-Hill.

McConlogue, K. & Simmons, R. F. (1965) A pattern learning parser. *Comm. Ass. comput. Mach.*, **8**, 687–98.

Quillian, M. R. (1969) The teachable language comprehender: a simulation program and theory of language. *Comm. Ass. comput. Mach.*, **12**, 459–75.

Schwarz, R. M., Burger, J. F., & Simmons, R. F. (1970) A deductive question-answerer for natural language inference. *Comm. Ass. comput. Mach.*, **13**, 167–83.

Simon, H. A. (1962) The architecture of complexity. *Proc. Amer. philos. Soc.*, **106**, 467–82.

Thompson, F. B. *et al.* (1964) DEACON breadboard summary. RM64TMP–9, TEMPO, General Electric Company, Santa Barbara, California.

Natural Language for Instructional Communication

R.F.SIMMONS

Some of the more exciting recent research in CAI is concerned with generative teaching programs. These offer some capability for generating problems and for analyzing student responses and queries, particularly in teaching such formalized subject matter as mathematics, logic, and programming. In these areas the system may generate problems for which students can construct the solution or response. Variations in form and content between student response and the canonical answer as computed by a program can be analyzed by an algebraic evaluation system that can recognize algebraic equivalents of the required answer. In recent proposals (Uhr 1965, Uttal *et al.* 1969, Siklóssy 1968) the generative approach is generalized to allow the student to query the system – in such a formal language.

However, if the constructed response is allowed to be in the form of an English phrase, or if English queries are to be allowed, the problem is vastly more complicated by the need for an English language processor that can recognize meaning-preserving paraphrases of a canonical answer, and not only understand a query, but have some capability for responding to it. The difficulty in dealing with English arises from the basic flexibility inherent in natural languages. It is generally the case that for any word or phrase in a natural language expression, another word, phrase, or sentence can be substituted to express almost the same meaning without changing the meaning of the larger expression. With such a wide variety of expressive potential available, the lesson designer who tries to predict all correct variations for a prescribed short English answer is doomed to failure.

Natural language question-answering research [surveyed by Simmons (1970)] has achieved a level of development where well-defined subsets of English can be translated into formal query or command languages which then allow deductive and inductive operations to be defined on a data structure. Ideally, for instructional applications, such a data structure is a cognitive model that represents the content of the material to be taught. The instructional program presents or generates material from this model in the form of natural language statements and queries. The system constructs a model of the students' cognitive structure (that is, knowledge with respect to the lesson material), compares this model with its own, and uses the differences to generate statements that the student can learn until the discrepancies vanish.

What we want for CAI is a system that can produce a semantic network representing the meaning of a large text. We want this system to accept a student's essay representing his knowledge, reduce it to a semantic net (*see* figures 1 and 2), compare the two, and present the discrepancies until the student has mastered whatever parts of the net are to be taught.

The first year of our CAI language processor research taught us that the state of the art would allow us to make nets for single sentences but revealed our almost total ignorance with respect to analyzing anaphoric and thematic connections between sentences to form nets for paragraph or larger units of discourse. Responding to this finding, we attempted in the second year to design a system that would determine the extent to which a student's answer was a meaning-preserving paraphrase of a lesson designer's canonical answer. This task proved still somewhat beyond the state of the art in that it appears that there are far too many possibilities of paraphrase for even short answers for a system to encompass easily. This approach has in my mind the additional defect of too-tight control of the learning process by the lesson designer. In some future system, this control can be passed to the student in a manner to be explained below.

My present philosophy of CAI has shifted to a student-controlled generative system that can 'explain' and interpret difficult textual passages and can, on student request, prepare, present, and score quizzes. In its first form, the quizzes will be True-False statements. As the state of the art progresses we shall be able to incorporate the generation and evaluation of short-answer questions and eventually the evaluation of student essays as in the original plan, but with the important philosophical differences that:

1. The system is a tool that the student or author can use to interpret his texts;

2. the student determines when and on what segments he is to be tested;

3. the system is purely generative in its presentations and quizzes, and it thus reduces the lesson designer's task to one of editing the text he is assigning to his student.

DESIGN OF INTERPRETIVE TUTOR I (IT1)

This system is based on a powerful natural-language analyzer that works in conjunction with a human editor to analyze the text. It requires generative and paraphrase capabilities but to a far more limited extent than previous designs. It is intrinsically a text editor-interpreter that can be used to help an author or a student understand the content of his text sentence by sentence. Probably most important, IT1 appears to be a useful CAI system that is accomplishable in the present state of the art.

IT1 requires an interactive language processor of the type developed in PSIII or the syntax-directed processor mentioned in the section on Current Progress. A linguist prepares the lexicon and grammar required to transform from text to semantic net (for example, deep case structures). The lesson designer originally selected the text and either he or the linguist monitors the system's analysis of sentences, selecting the appropriate one where multiple interpretations are offered.

The text is presented to the student either on-line or in hard-copy form. In either case, the lines are numbered by the sequential numbers of the sentences (S) in that line. For any sentence the student, author, or lesson designer may request an interpretation or a definition of words in that context. Commands for this purpose are:

    c1. Explain *Si*.

    c2. Define $\langle word, Si \rangle$

where *Si* is the sequence number of a sentence and $\langle word \rangle$ is any word in the sentence.

In response to the Define Command, the system prints the lexical entry for that word-sense in an English form or as a semantic net on a display scope.

The 'Explain' Command causes the system to print an interpretation of the sentence either as an ordered set of kernels or as a set of simple sentences. If a display scope is available, the semantic net can be printed. The nature of these displays is illustrated with respect to the following example sentence:

    E1. The first plant to appear on a newly formed tropical island is
          the stately and graceful coconut palm.

Figure 1 shows two forms of the semantic net, assuming identification of word-senses. Table 1(a) is the set of kernel sentences while table 1(b) is a set of simple sentences, Figure 2 shows the deep case analysis from which the semantic net and the kernel sentences are generated.

The student may at any time request a quiz with the following command:

    c3. Quiz S_i-S_n

In response to this command the system will generate a set of simple sentences representing the content of S_i-S_n. By certain falsification and paraphrase transforms, it will develop these into a set of True-False statements. These statements can be weighted in inverse proportion to their depth in the text sentences. The student responds with a list of pairs in the form '1 T, 2 F, 4 T, etc.'

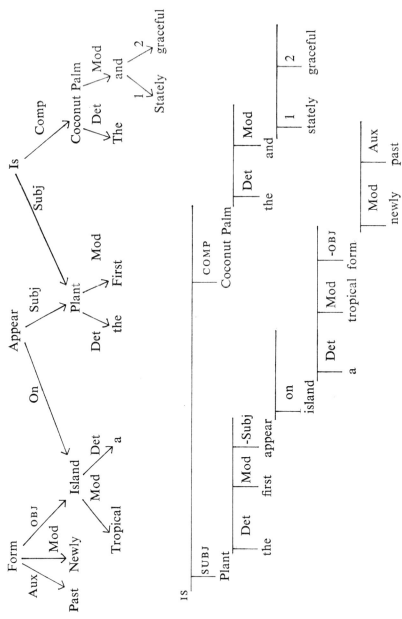

Figure 1. Directed graphs for semantic network of sentence E1. 'The first plant to appear on a newly formed tropical island is the stately and graceful coconut palm.'

x1	TOK	IS
	AUX	Pres.
	SUBJ	x2
	COMP	x9

x2	TOK	Plant
	NBR	SING
	DET	the
	MOD	x3
	-SUBJ	x1
	-SUBJ	x4

x3	TOK	first
	-MOD	x2

x4	TOK	appear
	AUX	Inf.
	SUBJ	x2
	ON	x5

x5	TOK	island
	NBR	SING.
	DET	a
	MOD	x6
	-OBJ	x7

x6	TOK	tropical
	-MOD	x5

x7	TOK	form
	AUX	Past
	MOD	x8
	OBJ	x5

x8	TOK	newly
	-MOD	x7

x9	TOK	palm
	NBR	SING.
	DET	the
	MOD	x10
	-COMP	x1

x10	TOK	and
	-MOD	x9
	1st	x11
	2nd	x12

x11	TOK	stately
	-1st	x10

x12	TOK	graceful
	-2nd	x10

Figure 2. Deep-case structure for E1

The system computes a score, returns feedback in the form of correct statements, and returns control to the student.

As the state of the art progresses, short answer quizzes and additional queries and commands from the student may be incorporated into the system, as well as shaping responses by the system as previously suggested. In even its first versions, however, the IT1 system should prove useful both as a teaching tool and a semantic editor.

It may be noticed that, in addition to the language analysis programs already designed, the following components are required:

(1) Semantic net display generator (optional)
(2) Kernel sentence display generator ⎱ one of these
(3) Simple sentence display generator ⎰
(4) Meaning preserving and falsification paraphrase generator
(5) Quiz display and scoring
(6) Executive for accepting and interpreting commands.

Some difficulties are foreseen in the design of 2, 3, and 4 but nothing of the order of a complete paraphrase or question answering system. Eventually, deeper levels of interpretation can be obtained by making explicit the presuppositions, assertions, and implications of each sentence, following Filmore, and/or by translating into some simplified standard English form.

During the first year of the project four main lines of thought and experimentation were developed. The first of these was an experimental syntactic-semantic analyzer for English sentences. This system naturally led to the design of a second larger, hopefully more useful, version for preparing semantic network representations of sentence meanings. The Interpretive Tutor was designed and programmed to use these semantic nets in aiding a student to understand a text better. Experimental programs for generating connected discourse from the nets have been designed and constructed as a fourth line of research.

The first syntactic-semantic analyzer was programmed in LISP. It proved effective but extremely slow and expensive in operation. Its primary values were:

TABLE 1. Sets of kernels and simple sentences interpreting E1.

(a)	Plant is coconut palm
	Plant appears first
	Plant appears on island
	Island is tropical
	Island is newly formed
	Coconut palm is stately and graceful
(b)	The plant is the coconut palm
	The plant appears first on a tropical island
	The tropical island is newly formed
	The coconut palm is stately and graceful

(1) to show that a natural language processor bears a very close resemblance to a syntax-directed compiler; and

(2) to reveal uniformities of structure among lexical entries, syntactic rules and semantic network elements.

The realization of these uniformities of structure considerably simplifies the program logic of natural-language processing.

Experiments with this system led to the design of a syntax-directed language processor that is designed to operate rapidly – with human intervention – to produce semantic network representations for that subset of English that its lexicon and grammar encompass. This system will allow for a lexicon of 20 thousand words with a correspondingly large grammar. It will be operated as a compiler primarily in batch mode to compile semantic nets for sentences.

The Interpretive Tutor (IT1) uses these semantic nets to represent the meaning of multi-sentence English texts. IT1 is now programmed as a proto-type system that allows its student user to ask for explanations of sentences, for definitions of words in context, and for the preparation of complete-the-blank and True-False quizzes. To explain a sentence, IT1 generates a set of simple sentences; to define a word, it presents the lexical meaning for the word's use in context. It composes a quiz by generating a set of simple sentences from the text to be covered, and by applying a blanking-out and/or a falsification logic to a random subset.

Finally, in order to develop additional understanding of semantic nets, we have programmed a system that generates sets of English sentences under joint control of the semantic structures and grammar. This discourse generator allows us to experiment with such complexities as anaphoric and pronominal expressions, the tensing of verb forms, and the devious subtleties of embedding and conjoining simple sentence structures into the complexities of normal English discourse. The consequence of this study of generation will be the development of grammars that can analyze more difficult – but typical – discourse structures.*

Acknowledgment. Research on this project is supported by the National Science Foundation Grant GJ-509x.

* Since the original preparation of this paper, Carbonell (1970) has reported on a similar approach to computer assistance in computer learning.

REFERENCES

Carbonell, J.R. (1970) Mixed initiative man-computer instructional dialogues. Bolt, Beranek & Newman Inc., *BBN Report No. 1971*, Job no. 11399, Cambridge, Mass.

Siklóssy, L. (1968) *Natural Language Learning by Computer*. (Doctoral dissertation, Carnegie-Mellon University) Ann Arbor, Mich., University Microfilms, No. 68–17.

Simmons, R.F. (1970) Natural language question answering systems, 1969. *Comm. Ass. comput. Mach.*, **13**, 15–30.

Uhr, L. (1965) The automatic generation of teaching machine programs. Unpublished report.

Uttal, W.R., Pasich, T., Rogers, M. & Hieronymus, R. (1969) Generative computer assisted instruction. *Communication No. 243*, University of Michigan, Mental Health Research Institute.

Making Computers Understand Natural Language

J.PALME

WHY TEACH HUMAN LANGUAGES TO THE COMPUTER?
The British mathematician A. M. Turing provided a well-known definition of the goal of artificial intelligence research. He said that you should put a computer in one room, a human competitor in a second room, and a human judge in a third room. The judge can only communicate with the computer and the human competitor through teleprinters. The judge is then permitted to ask any questions he wants both to the human and the computer. The human should try to show that he is the real human. The computer should try to make believe that it is the real human.

If the judge cannot say which is the human, then the computer must have at least 'human' intelligence, which is the only definition of intelligence that we can use.

Turing's test is a good reason for trying to make computers understand human languages. Obviously, human linguistic ability must be very important for a machine which is trying to pass Turing's test.

But the emphasis in finding motives for artificial intelligence research has moved away from the Turing test. Nowadays, motives are more and more sought for in practical, useful applications of the results which artificial intelligence can lead to. There are many such applications for computers understanding human languages.

The tendency is for more and more direct conversational communication between humans and computers. Nowadays, such communication usually uses special computer languages or is restricted to simple yes-and-no dialogues. Thus, the human is forced to adapt himself to the computer way of speaking. If the computer instead could adapt itself to the human way of speaking, then the client could talk directly to the computer, without a computer specialist as a middle-man. The computer could, for example, be used more for:

(1) enquiry offices at large institutions dealing with the public (government offices, department stores, libraries, travel agencies, and so on);

(2) information retrieval applications;

(3) computerized psychotherapy (perhaps with a psychiatrist supervising ten patient-computer communication lines);

(4) computer-assisted instruction.

Experience shows that when computers are given practical tasks of a complicated logical structure, then they perform better in a direct conversational dialogue with a human. The human can help the computer by giving hints and correcting misunderstandings. Thus, many practical artificial intelligence applications can be useful, faster, if the computer can understand human language.

THE COMPUTER PASSES THE TURING TEST

In fact, a computer program has already done something a bit similar to passing the Turing test, although in circumstances very favourable for the computer.

A salesman wanted to show a computer time-sharing system to some customers. He found an empty terminal, but with a note saying 'Reserved for Professor Bobrow'. He then called up Professor Bobrow on the teleprinter. He thus believed that he was connected to Bobrow, while in fact he was connected to the Eliza computer program. The following dialogue developed:

Person: Do you think that I can use the computer this morning?
Teleprinter: Why do you ask?
Person: I might be able to make some additional Telecomp sales.
Teleprinter: Why aren't you sure?
Person: My prospective customers have never seen a demonstration of the system.
Teleprinter: Does this mean very much to you?
Person: Of course it does.
Teleprinter: You seem very positive about that.
Person: This is ridiculous.
Teleprinter: What do you mean this is ridiculous?
Person: Is there any reason why I can't use the computer now?
Teleprinter: Tell me more about your prospective customers.
Person: Please dial me up on 491-1850.

This conversation is in fact done by a much simpler computer program than it seems. The basis of the program is the following principle:

(1) Try to apply some simple pattern match to the sentence.

(2) If a match succeeds, answer with a simple transformation of the data from the input sentence.

(3) If no match succeeds, answer with an 'empty' comment or go

back to something said before.

The principle for the pattern match is illustrated by the following example:

Input sentence: I like my father.

Pattern: (I &1 my &2);

Production: (Why do you &1 your &2);

Output sentence: Why do you like your father.

THE QUESTION-ANSWERING SYSTEM

A well-known kind of artificial intelligence research project is the question-answering system. This is a system where the computer is given facts and questions. The computer should then be able to answer the questions using the facts it was given and had previously collected.

Such a system need not have natural English as input, but they usually understand a subset of English. Some systems use this language only for questions, and take facts in a more rigid form. Other systems use the same input language for both facts and questions.

This language can be natural English, a subset of natural English, a modified subset of natural English, or an artificial language. No system can yet take full natural English as input, but some are coming close to this goal.

Some systems can find only facts which are directly stored in the data base, other systems also make deductions on these data.

Many question-answering systems are restricted to only one special subject area (like time-table information, family relationships, or sports results). Other systems have a wider subject area, for example 'natural information' (the name coined by Erik Sandewall) denoting those things which you usually talk about in a natural human language.

Our system, the Swedish Question Answering Project (SQAP), is intended to cover natural information given in a somewhat simplified, 'semi-natural' English.

Question-answering systems also differ in the organization of their internal data base structure. More about this later.

Figure 1 shows a typical organization of a question-answering system. The input sentences are first parsed by 'syntax analysis' into a parsing tree; this is then put through 'semantic interpretation', usually producing some kind of graph structure which is input to the 'deduction procedures'.

Figure 2 shows the organization of the SQAP = Swedish Question Answering Project. Note that the deduction procedure is used also for facts. In that case, the deduction procedure finds if there is a contradiction between the new fact and previously known facts. This is very important to help avoid those cases when the computer misunderstands the given sentence. Ordinary

o

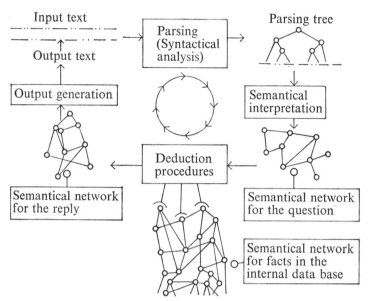

Figure 1

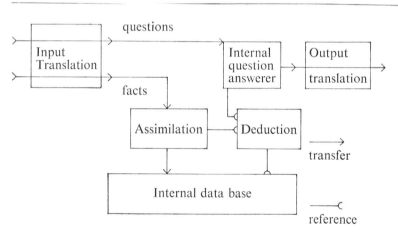

Figure 2

arrows in the picture mean data transfer, arc arrows mean references to retrieve data.

SYNTAX ANALYSIS

Syntax analysis, also called parsing, is a process closely similar to the manual grammatical parsing of sentences into subjects, predicates, adverbials, and so on. The parsing structure in automatic syntax analysis is usually more detailed, and the sentence is parsed at several levels to produce a tree graph

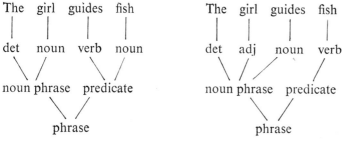

Figure 3

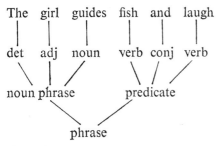

Figure 4

called 'parsing tree'. Two examples of parsing trees corresponding to two different interpretations of the same sentence are shown in figure 3.

A sentence with more than one interpretation is called ambiguous. Such sentences are very common in natural languages. Sometimes, the ambiguity disappears if something more is added to the sentence as in the example in figure 4.

The syntactical rules to be used for parsing are usually explained in a so-called generative grammar. This grammar describes an algorithm to generate all possible sentences in a language. The algorithm starts with an initial symbol, often called 'phrase' and then applies a series of substitution rules (called 'productions'). Some of these productions are obligatory, some are optional. The grammar (grammar A) used in the preceding analysis examples can be described by the following series of productions:

phrase   :: = nounphrases predicate;
nounphrases   :: = nounphrase/nounphrase conjunction nounphrases;
nounphrase   :: = noun/adjective noun/determiner noun/determiner adjective noun;
predicate   :: = verbs/verbs nounphrases;
verbs   :: = verb/verb conjunction verbs;

The / is an 'or'-sign indicating that several alternatives are available. The above rules thus say that the symbol 'phrase' should be changed into the two symbols 'nounphrases' and 'predicate'. The next rule gives two possible ways to modify this further by substituting something for 'nounphrases'.

Here is another, somewhat more readable description of the same algorithm, using parentheses to indicate something optional, which may or may not be inserted during the generation process.

phrase :: = nounphrases predicate;
nounphrases :: = nounphrase (conjunction nounphrases);
nounphrase :: = (determiner) (adjective) noun;
predicate :: = verbs (nounphrases);
verbs :: = verb (conjunction verbs);

The generative grammar gives a series of productions producing a final sentence. A correlative grammar gives instead a series of rules to apply to the final sentence finally giving the single symbol 'phrase'. These rules will thus often combine two things into one, and this process is called a correlation. A generative grammar can sometimes easily be rewritten as a correlative grammar and vice versa.

A parsing algorithm usually sees the problem either from a generative or from a correlative point of view. The top-down algorithm is theoretically based on the idea of using a generative grammar to produce all possible sentences in a language until one is found which fits the input sentence. This would in most practical cases take too much time, but there are ways to restrict the method to the most fruitful possibilities.

The bottom-up algorithm is based on the correlative point of view. The algorithm tries to combine elements in the input sentence in different ways until a tree covering the whole sentence is found.

Before going into the advantages and disadvantages of these methods I will describe some practical methods, and problems with them, in more detail.

THE RECURSIVE TOP-DOWN METHOD

The recursive (or backtracking) parsing method can be described in the following way [according to Floyd (1964)]:

The algorithm uses a generative grammar (grammar A described above), an input sentence, for example 'The girl guides fish and laugh', a push-down stack to store applied productions, and a cursor indicating how much of the input sentence is covered.

When the algorithm starts, the cursor is at the beginning of the sentence and the push-down stack contains only one entry, the top node in the syntax, of the 'phrase' production. This production starts working and finds that its first element is 'nounphrases'. Thus a man is appointed (a routine is called) to test if a part of the sentence can be analyzed as 'nounphrases'. 'nounphrases' appoints 'nounphrase', 'nounphrase' appoints 'noun'. 'noun' tries to cover the first word, 'the'. This does not succeed, so 'noun' is fired and control is returned to 'nounphrase'. 'nounphrase' tries the second alternative in its description, beginning with 'adjective'. This will also be unsuccessful, but finally the third alternative succeeds when 'determiner' and 'noun' are appointed. Upon success, the cursor is moved forward to cover the two first words, 'the' and 'girl', and control is returned to 'nounphrases' and finally back to 'phrase' which then appoints 'predicate' to cover the rest of the sentence. After some time the analysis situation looks like that shown in figure 5.

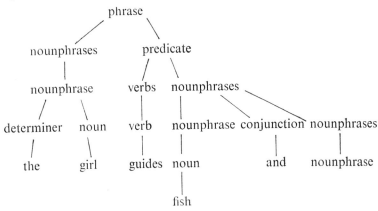

Figure 5

In this situation, 'nounphrase' will not succeed in covering the next word in the sentence, 'laugh'. Control is then returned to 'nounphrases', which calls its underlings to see if they can cover the sentence in another way. But this will not succeed, and finally control is returned to 'phrase' again, which calls its underling 'nounphrases' covering 'the girl' to see if it can do something else. 'nounphrases' will then succeed in covering 'the girl guides' which opens the possibility for a full analysis of the sentence.

When a production rule does not succeed, and calls its underlings to try something else or is finally fired, then the cursor must be moved back again in the sentence past the words covered by the unsuccessful production. This moving back is called 'backtracking' and is the major cause of inefficiency with this parsing method. After backtracking, a very similar analysis is usually tried again, duplicating execution time.

A special problem with this and other top-down methods are recursion in the syntax specification. Recursion occurs when a production produces itself, directly or indirectly. Here is a typical example of a recursive production:

verbs ::=verb conjunction verbs/verb;

If this rule is applied to the phrase part 'fish and laugh and cry and jump', then the tree shown in figure 6 will appear.

verbs :: = verb conjunction verbs/verb;

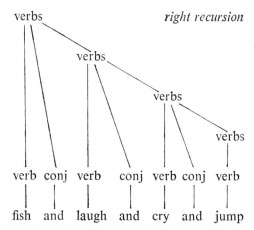

Figure 6

One might prefer to describe the same thing in the following way:

verbs ::= verbs conjunction verb/verb;

corresponding to the tree shown in figure 7.

verbs :: = verbs conjunction verb/verb;

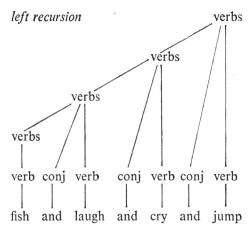

Figure 7

This will not work with the parsing algorithm described. 'verbs' will appoint 'verbs' which will appoint 'verbs' in an infinite loop until the stack is full.

This situation is called 'left recursion' and the grammar must be re-written to remove all left recursion before using this algorithm.

All parsing algorithms have various restrictions. The no-left-recursion example is a typical such restriction. Most algorithms have more restrictions than this one. A difficulty is that the published descriptions of the algorithms do not always specify all their restrictions.

The recursive algorithm is very slow due to the large amount of back-tracking. The execution time increases very fast with the length of the sentence. Various ways to speed up the process have been proposed. For example, one can save successful part-analyses which were unsuccessful in a larger context, so that the part-analysis saved does not have to be redone in a new context. Another way is to divide the sentence into partitions depending on which word connections are known to indicate the limit between the parts analyzed by two major constituents. This turns one large analysis of the whole sentence into several part-analyses of different partitions of the sentence. This method is described in Vargas (1969).

THE PARALLEL TOP-DOWN PARSING ALGORITHM

A faster (but more memory-consuming) parsing algorithm is the parallel one. Instead of trying one possibility at a time and then back-tracking when it will not succeed, this method carries all possible parsings forward in parallel. The advantage of this is that several major analyses may include the same part-analysis, and this is easily recognized so that the part-analysis is only made once.

For example, the sentence 'He rolled up the red carpet' can be parsed in two ways, but the phrase-part 'the red carpet' is part-analyzed in the same way for both analyses.

This method is described by Earley (1970).

A very interesting program using this method is that described in Bratley, Dewar and Thorne (1967). Most language analysis programs are based on a complete dictionary of all words in the language. Such dictionaries are very difficult to collect. Bratley, Dewar and Thorne's program does not use such a full dictionary. They say that a human can recognize the syntactical contents of a sentence even if there are unknown words in it. For example, the following sentences are parsable for a human.

'He has gone to shoot a grison.'

'He will be furibund.'

They also say that very many words in English can have two or three of the big word classes noun, verb, and adjective. For example, here are three sentences in which the word 'iron' has these three word classes:

'Strike while the iron is hot.'

'He will iron her shirt tomorrow.'

'He ruled with an iron hand.'

Thus, the value of a dictionary is very small for such words.

They divide the words into two groups, 'open-class' words and 'closed-class' words. 'open-class' words are words belonging to the very large, open word classes like nouns, verbs, and adjectives. 'closed-class' words are members of a limited set, like conjunctions and prepositions. Special verbs and suffixes are also closed-class words. The closed-class words are usually important as syntactic formatives and connectors.

Their dictionary thus includes a list of the closed-class words and also of some troublesome open-class words. We have chosen the same approach in the SQAP project, and our dictionary contains about 1000 words.

To illustrate their system, here is the syntactical analysis produced for the input sentence 'When he has fixed dates he will ring us'. The analysis produces the structure from left to right in figure 8. Note that there are two different paths from the left to the right, corresponding to two different analyses of the sentence.

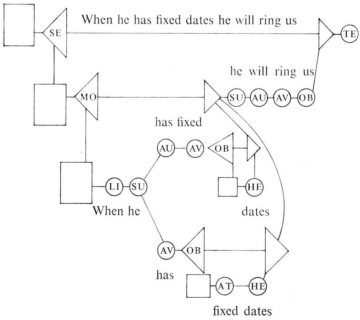

Figure 8

THE CORRELATIVE BOTTOM-UP ALGORITHM

The bottom-up algorithm starts with the single words in the sentence. These are grouped together (correlated) into larger and larger units until the whole sentence has been grouped together.

A typical example of such a system is the 'multistore parser' from Glasersfeld and Pisani (1970).

The rules for connecting two words into one unit (for example, 'the man') in this system are called implicit correlators. The system also has explicit correlators, connecting three words, two words and a correlating word between them (for example, 'John and Mary').

An example of how the syntax on page 203 can be re-written in the multistore system is shown in table 1.

TABLE 1

Correlator	Correlator type							
number	1		2		3		4	
	Left	Right	Left	Right	Left	Right	Left	Right
Phrase ::=	Noun	Verb	Noun	Predi-cate	Det-noun	Verb	Det-noun	Predi-cate
Detnoun ::=	Deter-miner	Adj-noun	Deter-miner	Noun				
Adjnoun ::=	Adjec-tive	Noun						
Predicate ::=	Verb	Noun						

The dictionary contains very detailed information about each word, much more than the ordinary, coarse wordclass classification. Each word in the dictionary has a list of all correlations that the word can fit into. This list can indicate, for example, that a concrete noun (but not an abstract noun) can be the subject of an activity. This list is called the correlator index.

The correlator index determines which correlators a word can go into. But when a correlated group of words is to be correlated with other groups to form still larger structures, this correlated group must also have a correlator index indicating which higher correlations it can go into. Each correlator has an algorithm which finds the correlator index of it from the index of its constituent parts. This important algorithm is called 'reclassification'.

The multi-store system uses a large matrix in the computer memory to store the information about the parsing. This matrix has one column for each possible correlator in the system (528 columns). Each word and group of words formed during the parsing has one row in the matrix (330 rows).

The size of the matrix is thus 528·330, or 174240. Each entry in the matrix is one byte (eight bits).

The matrix might look like table 2 if the very simple syntax above is applied to the sentence 'The girl guides fish'.

TABLE 2

One row for each word sense in the sentence and each group of words	One column for each kind of correlator				
	word sense	Adjnoun	Detnoun	Predicate	Phrase
1 the	determiner	no	left	no	no
2 girl	noun	right	right	right	left
3 girl	adjective	left			
4 guides	noun	right	right	right	left
5 guides	verb	no	no	left	right
6 fish	noun	right	right	right	left
7 fish	verb	no	no	left	right
8 the girl (1 + 2)	detnoun	right	no	right	left
9 girl guides (3 + 4)	adjnoun	right	right	right	left
10 girl guides (3 + 5)	phrase	no	no	no	no
11 guides fish (5 + 6)	predicate	no	no	no	right
12 guides fish (4 + 7)	phrase	no	no	no	no
13 the girl guides (8 + 5)	phrase	no	no	no	no
14 the girl guides (1 + 9)	detnoun	right	no	right	left
15 girl guides fish (9 + 7)	phrase	no	no	no	no
16 girl guides fish (2 + 11)	phrase	no	no	no	no
17 the girl guides fish (14 + 7)	phrase	no	no	no	no
18 the girl guides fish (8 + 11)	phrase	no	no	no	no

Table 2 contains the two possible parsings of the sentence in the last lines (corresponding to figures 3 and 4). The table also contains a number of unsuccessful part-parsings, line nos. 10, 12, 13, 15, and 16.

Most other bottom-up systems use push-down stacks or list structures to store information about the parsing. This saves memory, but takes more time. Figure 9 shows a kind of list-structure which might be used instead of the multi-store matrix for similar purposes.

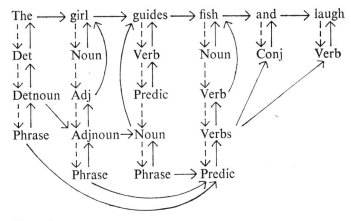

Figure 9

SYNTAX ANALYSIS AND HEURISTIC SEARCH

The object of syntax analysis is to find a tree structure which has two properties:

(1) the nodes are connected according to the rules in the syntax;

(2) the terminal nodes fit the sentence.

The difficulty with syntax analysis is that the number of grammatical trees is very much larger than the number of trees which fit the sentence. Also, parts of a sentence can be fitted by partial trees in many ways, but only a few of these partial trees can be extended to cover the whole sentence. Since the algorithm can fit only one arc at a time to the tree, some erroneous partial trees will have to be generated. The most efficient parsing algorithm is the algorithm which produces the least number of erroneous partial trees.

All parsing algorithms can be viewed as a search procedure [*see* Sandewall (1971) and Michie (1971)] structured as a tree. The search procedure starts with an empty parsing. Each node in the search tree corresponds to a partial parsing of the sentence, and each arc corresponds to the addition of one arc to the parsing.

Various methods for syntax analysis vary in the way in which new arcs are added to the parsing tree. The top-down procedures prefer to add arcs at the top of the parsing, working down towards the bottom, while the bottom-up procedures prefer to add arcs at the bottom, working upwards towards the top.

The order of the search of the search tree also varies. The general back-tracking parsing procedure corresponds to a depth-first search of the tree, while the parallel top-down procedure corresponds to a breadth-first search.

However, it is a well-known fact that for most applications neither the depth-first nor the breadth-first algorithm is the most efficient one. Instead, the most efficient algorithm is usually a search guided by heuristics such as a merit function assigned to all open nodes in the search tree.

These heuristics can be divided into two main categories:
(a) a way of saying for sure that a branch will not be able to succeed;
(b) a way of saying that certain arcs have higher probability of succeeding.

Heuristics of the (a) kind are often used in parsing, heuristics of the (b) kind are less common. Here are some heuristics of both kinds:

(1) Avoid making the same partial parsing more than once (by parallel top-down methods, by some bottom-up methods, or by a method which saves all earlier partial trees in an accessible way during the parsing).

(2) Avoid certain parsings because they cannot succeed (as determined by look-ahead, by sentence partitioning, or something similar).

(3) Eliminate semantically ridiculous analyses (by testing the part-analysis against the data base, usually simplest with bottom-up parsing).

(4) Use a merit function or some other way of guiding the analysis towards the most probable path.

(5) Organizational speed-up (like the multi-store memory organization).

A completely different method for parsing is to test many simple patterns against the sentence (like the Eliza system on page 200) instead of using a complex syntax. The disadvantage with this is that a set of simple patterns will match only a set of simple standard sentences. The advantage is that it may be easy to make the computer learn from experience by additions to the set of simple patterns.

THE LINGUISTIC VIEWPOINT

Our goal is a practical one: to give the computer the ability to understand and produce natural language. The pure linguist's goal is a theoretical one: to find a simple, elegant, and workable theory of language structure. In reality, however, the solutions to these objects are often similar.

The linguist's basic requirement of a good grammatical theory is, according to Bach (1964):

(1) The theory should specify an algorithm that describes *all* and *only* the sentences in the language.

(2) This algorithm should provide a structure to the sentence. This structure should correspond to that intuitive structure, which humans feel in the sentence. For example, the two phrases 'The essay was difficult to translate' and 'Now you have to translate the essay' look very different, but humans feel that their basic structure is similar. This ought to appear in a good grammatical analysis. On the other hand, these two phrases are very similar on

the surface 'The candy is to eat' and 'The boy is to play', but the theory should show that there is a structural difference between them.

Out of several possible grammars, the linguist prefers the shortest and most elegant system which satisfies the requirements above.

Linguists are sometimes chiefly concerned with generative algorithms (producing all sentences in a language) while the big linguistic problem in question-answering systems is how to recognize given input sentences.

The linguists' theory should apply to *all* and *only* the sentences in a language. A question-answering input system might theoretically take more than ordinary language as input. This might make the system simpler. However, this will also increase the risk of misunderstanding. For example, the input procedure may be simpler if the third person singular is disregarded, but then there is an unnecessary risk of misunderstanding a sentence like 'the girl guide fishes'.

Thus, a question-answering procedure will usually work best if the *all* and *only* requirement is generally satisfied.

Traditional linguistic theory is based on the idea of having an initial symbol and then performing successive operations until a final sentence is produced.

These operations are of two kinds. One kind is substitutions, where one symbol in the sentence is exchanged with one or more other symbols. Such substitutions are called phrase-structure productions. They are sometimes divided into two groups by context-free and context-sensitive rules. A context-free rule specifies that one symbol can always be exchanged with another one. A context-sensitive rule specifies that the substitution can occur only in a given context.

If you look at a tree structure of the kind shown in figures 3 and 4, a phrase-structure rule always means that new branches are sprouted on the The old tree is not modified.

Chomsky (*see* Bach 1964) has shown that a simpler and more regular grammar is produced if we permit more general operations than phrase-structure rules during the sentence generation. These rules are called transformations. A transformation is sometimes specified so as to show only what to do with the sentence. A typical example is the following description of the passive transformation: $NP_1 - AUX - V - NP_2 :: = NP_2 - AUX - be - V - ed - by - NP_1$. A structure which would produce the sentence 'John can kiss Mary' without this transformation will, after the transformation, instead produce 'Mary can be kissed by John'.

This way of specifying the transformation is, however, not completely satisfactory, since it says only what to do with the sentence, not what to do with the underlying tree structure produced during the previous generation process.

A more general transformation specification ought to specify a pattern graph to be matched to part of the tree structure, and then operations on the matched parts of the graph.

Steps using more and more advanced grammars could be given as follows:
(1) finite context-free grammar (non-recursive, context-free phrase structure grammar);
(2) non-finite, context-free grammar (with recursion);
(3) non-finite, context-sensitive grammar;
(4) transformational grammar.
The difficulty with transformational grammars, as they are usually specified, is that they are generative grammars, not grammars for parsing given sentences.

Here are some concepts often used by linguists in talking about these kinds of grammars:

(a) *P-marker* = the tree structure describing the structure in a sentence.

(b) *Surface structure* = the *P*-marker after transformations, with the final sentence at the top of the tree.

(c) *Deep structure* = the *P*-marker before transformations, corresponding to a deeper, more logical basic underlying structure. For example, the underlying deep structure is the same or very similar for both the sentences 'John can kiss Mary' and 'Mary can be kissed by John', but the surface structures are very different.

(d) *Kernel sentence* = about the same as deep structure, sometimes the deep structure in a linearized, sentence-like form.

The deep structure concept (as used by linguists) and the semantic network concept (as used by the producers of question-answering systems) are really two very similar concepts. They both aim at finding a logical structure indicating the basic underlying ideas in the sentence.

GOAL OF INPUT TRANSLATION

The goal of the input translation process is a representation which can be used for the two main data base processes:

For facts: Store the facts in the data base.

For questions: Answer the questions using the data base.

The output of the translation process usually consists of two kinds of statements:

(1) Commands to the data base processing program.

(2) A representation of the input sentence in a form of the *internal data structure*.

Some systems only produce commands as output. Their output is an algorithm to store the facts or to find the answer to the question. This algorithm is written in a special programming language – command language.

Other systems produce an output similar to the internal data structure, even for questions. This answers the simple question: Is this structure in agreement with the data base or not? Does this structure fit the data base and can we find the object in the data base corresponding to the 'who?' object in the structure?

The main goals of the internal data base structure are two:

(1) Find a structure as close to natural language as possible (to make input translation surer and simpler).

(2) Find a structure in which information retrieval searches and deduction procedures are simple to make.

An extreme example is some systems where the input text is stored as it is in a computer. This makes deduction very difficult. For example, given the fact 'John severed the main trunk of the tree so that it fell' and the question 'Who cut down the tree?', such a system will usually not be able to answer the question.

The basic ideas for the internal data structure in most systems are taken from one or several of the following areas:

(1) *Kernel sentences* (*see* above), the linguist's canonical form of the sentence, also often called 'deep structure'.

(2) *Predicate calculus*, the notation for complex relations used in mathematical logic (*see* Davis 1963).

(3) *Graph and network theory*, list structures (*see* Berge 1962).

(4) *The LISP programming language*, its property lists and binary graph structure.

Here are some examples to illustrate the various ideas. Two systems will be described in more detail in the next two sections of this paper.

Command language. Woods (1968) [*see also* the section on 'A system for semantic interpretation'] describes a system for answering questions about air-line connections. The system translates the sentences into commands in a LISP-influenced structure. Three examples:

Input sentence: At what time do flights leave Boston for Chicago?

Translation: (FOR EVERY X1/FLIGHT: CONNECT (X1, BOSTON, CHICAGO); LIST (DTIME, X1, BOSTON))

Input sentence: How many stops does AA-57 make between Boston and Chicago?

Translation: LIST (NUMSTOPS (AA-57, BOSTON, CHICAGO))

Input sentence: Does American have a flight which goes from Boston to Chicago?

Translation: TEST (FOR SOME X1/FLIGHT: CONNECT (x1, BOSTON, CHICAGO); EQUAL (OWNER (x1), AMERICAN)))

Kernel sentence. Bross *et al.* (1969) describe a medical information retrieval system, in which the input sentence is transformed to several short kernel sentences. As an example, the sentence 'In what position was the patient placed?' is translated into (OP PATIENT PLACED) (MANNER PLACED IN POSITION) (DESCRP POSITION ?????).

Predicate calculus. The predicate calculus uses relations like '*clever* (x)' meaning 'x is clever' or '*inventor* (y, x)' meaning 'y is the inventor of x'. x and y are variables which are defined by quantifiers, like '$\forall x$' meaning 'for all xs it is true that' and '$\exists y$' meaning 'there is some y such that'. These are nested into a parenthesis structure. For example, the sentence 'All clever machines have a clever inventor' will in predicate calculus look like this '$\forall x$ (*clever* (x) **and** *machine*(x) **implies** $\exists y$(*clever*(y) **and** *inventor*(y, x)))'. This formula means 'For all xs, such that x is clever and x is a machine, there is some y such that y is clever and y is the inventor of x'.

This predicate calculus form is usually transformed into a so-called quantifier-free form (*see* Davis 1963). Using auxiliary functions, the quantifiers can be removed. This form is also usually transformed to a canonical normal form consisting of a number of conjunct clauses, each clause consisting of a number of disjunctive elements.

The sentence above in this normal form will look like this

 (**not** *clever*(x) **or not** *machine*(x) **or** *clever*$(f(x))$) **and**

 (**not** *clever*(x) **or** *machine*(x) **or** *inventor*$(f(x),x)$)

This normal form is important because it is the basis for many well-known deduction procedures, e.g., the resolution method (*see* Robinson 1965a, b).

Property list representation. The internal data structure must contain a way of storing objects and relations between these objects. The most common way to do this is the property list shown in figure 10.

The property list consists of a linear or circular list of elements. The list is affixed to an object, and each element on the list indicates one relation of this object to another object.

Another, less often used, way of storing relations is by the use of hash-coding (*see* IBM 1968). Hash-coding makes the search for a single relation among many other relations very fast. Property lists are faster when you want to make an exhaustive search for all relations to a given object.

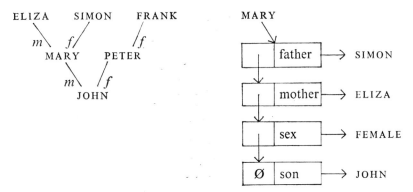

Figure 10

THE INTERNAL DATA BASE IN THE TLC SYSTEM

The TLC system (Teachable Language Comprehender), *see* Quillian (1969), does not aim primarily at question-answering. The system accepts facts in a simplified natural English and relates these facts to the internal data base. The answer is a short description of the circumstances in the data base surrounding the given statement. As an example, the input statement 'lawyer's client' produces the output 'Now we are talking about a client who employs a lawyer'. The 'employ' relation was fetched from the data base.

The goal of the TLC system is to have a data base which can store all kinds of facts which are usually given in natural language. One basic structure is used for all such statements. The system is planned to work on-line with a human monitor at a time-sharing terminal, who supervises the system's decisions and helps the system with difficult sentences. Figure 11 shows the basic layout of the system.

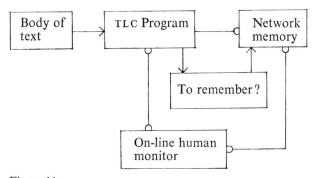

Figure 11

P

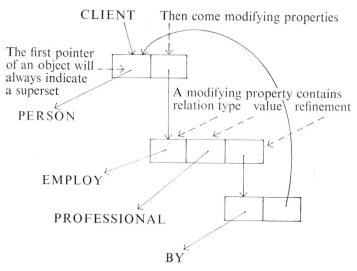

Figure 12

Figure 12 shows the basic internal data structure of the system. Each object is associated with a two-pointer block pointing to a superset to the object and to modifying properties of the object. The modifying properties consist of a relation, a value, and further refinements of the property. The upper-case text in the figure does not represent strings, it represents further objects in the network with these names. The system will thus create a complex network of objects and properties.

An input sentence is related to the data base by finding the shortest path in the network from the objects mentioned in the sentence. The elements along this path are then used to produce the output answer.

For example, the shortest path from 'lawyer' to 'client' passes an element connected with 'employ', producing the answer 'Now we are talking about a client who employs a lawyer'.

THE INTERNAL DATA BASE IN THE SQAP SYSTEM

The SQAP system (Swedish Question-Answering Project), *see* Sandewall (1968, 1969c), uses a variation of predicate calculus in its data base.

The main difference between this notation and ordinary use of predicate calculus is that the SQAP system has a small set of very basic relations. More advanced relations are treated as a special kind of objects, 'activities', in the system.

For example, in ordinary use of predicate calculus, the sentence 'John saw Mary in the village during the night' might be represented with a complex relation 'saw (John, Mary, village, night, . . .)'. The three dots indicate places to insert further parameters like time, cause, effect, and so on (John saw Mary in the village during the night, after the dance, to play a joke on the old man, ...).

Usually, most of these further parameters are empty, but places must be reserved for them in a complete system. The notation will be much simpler if we introduce an auxiliary object '*x*' denoting the activity in the sentence. The new representation will then be

$$\exists x(by(x, John) \textbf{ and } object(x, Mary) \textbf{ and } case\ of(x, see) \textbf{ and}$$
$$place(x, village) \ldots)$$

The primary relations in the system are thus relations like by, object, case of, place, time, and so on.

The new predicate calculus statement above corresponds to the relational graph shown in figure 13. This figure illustrates the basic ideas; in the following text a slightly modified naming convention will be used.

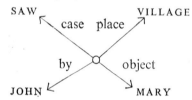

Figure 13

A question often put to us by people with experience in question-answering is 'how do we represent predicates in our system'. The cause of the confusion is that the word predicate has different meaning in lingustics and in logic. In linguistics, predicate is synonymous to 'verb phrase', while in logic, predicate is synonymous to 'relation'. Many systems represent verbs and adjectives in linguistics as relations in predicate calculus. Thus no confusion is caused. In our system, however, predicate in the linguistic sense corresponds to certain nodes in our data base. Predicate in the logical sense corresponds to the arcs in our data base, which we call relations. (*See* Sandewall 1971.)

I will usually use the graphical representation from now on. But there is a simple isomorphism between the graphical and the predicate calculus representation.

The data base consists of objects and predicates. The basic relation between these is the PRED relation, saying that a certain object has a certain predicate. For example, figure 14 means that John is happy. The suffix *p after happy is to distinguish the predicate happy*p from the set happy*s of all objects which are happy. This is a very important distinction in the notation.

Sometimes we want to affix more information to the statement 'John is

John ⟶ happy*p
　　　PRED

Figure 14

happy', for example 'John is happy today'. To do this, a new variable is introduced into the data base. The single relation PRED, is divided into two relations, a PROP relation from 'John' to the auxiliary variable, and a CASE relation from the auxiliary variable to 'happy*p'. The representation will thus be as shown in figure 15.

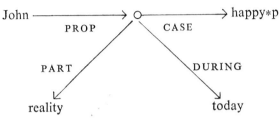

Figure 15

The PART(reality) relation, which is very common, will from now on be represented with an earth sign as in figure 16.

This example also shows why we have two nodes in our system for the property 'happy', one node 'happy*s' for the set of all happy objects, and another node 'happy*p' for the property of being happy. With the 'happy*s' representation, we would not be able to restrict this predicate to a given time-slice as in the figure above, since 'John is happy today' cannot be regarded as a subset of all happy objects. The usefulness of the 'happy*s' node will be shown later in the text to figure 19.

Another reason for the dual representation is that we may want to talk about non-existing properties like the property of being a unicorn or a fairy. With the set representation, these sets would be empty, which will cause difficulties during deduction. All empty sets are equal, so the deduction procedures may erroneously find that a unicorn is the same thing as a fairy.

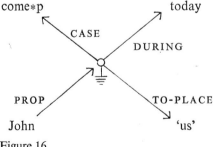

Figure 16

A simple phrase will be represented in the same way. 'John is coming to us today' will be, in the data base, the scheme shown in figure 16.

Thus the 'by' relation in figure 14 is not necessary; the 'prop' relation can be used instead.

The system makes it very simple to introduce relations between activities: for example, between 'John believes that' and 'Sweden is a part of Canada' in the statement 'John believes that Sweden is a part of Canada' (*see* figure 17).

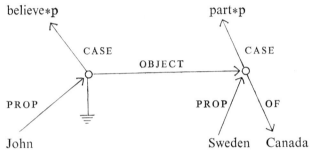

Figure 17

In the previous text, the nodes in the data base have been looked upon as single objects. Nodes can, however, also represent sets, and quantifiers can be affixed to the relations between the nodes. Look, for example, at the translation of the sentence 'John gives a flower to Mary', as shown in figure 18.

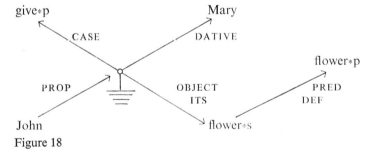

Figure 18

ITS is a quantifier indicating that the relation is not to all objects in the set 'flower*s' but rather to one or some special members of the set. When no quantifier is given in the figures, the ALL quantifier is always assumed.

DEF is another quantifier, a variation of ALL indicating that the relation is a definition.

This introduction of quantifiers does not mean that we are moving away from the predicate calculus. The graph above is still just another way of expressing the predicate calculus statement:

$$\exists x \, (prop(John, x) \textbf{ and } case(x, give*p) \textbf{ and } dative(x, Mary) \textbf{ and }$$
$$part(x, reality) \textbf{ and } (\exists y \textbf{ subset } flower*s)(object(x, y)))$$

The same structure can be used both to represent proper activities 'giving', 'jumping', and so on, and complex relations 'father of', 'colour of', and so on. The internal form of 'John is the father of Peter' will thus be as in figure 19.

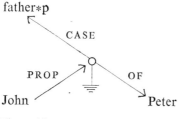

father*p

John

Figure 19

Set relations like SUBSET, SUPERSET, OVERLAP, and so on, are also included. They are just special versions of the EQUAL relation. SUBSET is, for example, the same as EQUAL SOME, OVERLAP is the same as SOME EQUAL SOME. The statement 'Every man is a human' will in the data base be represented as shown in figure 20.

man*s $\longleftarrow$ $\longrightarrow$ human*s
EQUAL SOME

Figure 20

The system has two representations for the quantifier $\exists$ in predicate calculus This is to indicate whether the $\exists$ is to be placed inside or outside the range of the $\forall$ quantifier on the other end of the relation. An example: the natural-language statement 'Every man loves a go-go dancer' can be interpreted in two ways; one as saying that there is a certain go-go dancer loved by all men, and the other as saying that for each man, there is one go-go dancer loved by him, but not necessarily the same go-go dancer for all men.

Predicate calculus representations might be respectively

$$\exists x(dancer(x) \textbf{ and } \forall y(man(y) \textbf{ and } love(y, x))) \qquad (1)$$
$$\forall y(man(y) \textbf{ implies } \exists x(dancer(x) \textbf{ and } love(y, x))) \qquad (2)$$

and the SQAP representations will be as shown in figure 21.

In natural language, there is often a grouping of several similar or dissimilar objects into a system. For example, the parts of the body are grouped into the complex object 'human', several such objects are grouped into complex objects 'families', 'nations', and so on. Such groupings are indicated in the SQAP internal data base using the special relations ELEMENT, COMPLEX, and NUM. ELEMENT goes from a complex object to each of its elementary parts.

(1)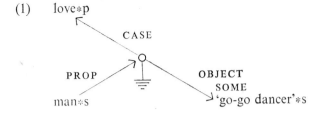

(2)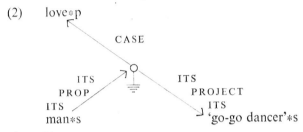

Figure 21

COMPLEX goes from a complex object to a predicate common for all its elementary parts. NUM goes from a complex object to an integer object, indicating the number of elementary parts in the complex object.

Example: John and Mary are married. (*See* figure 22.)

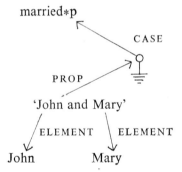

Figure 22

Example: John eats three eggs and two of them are rotten. (*See* figure 23.)

DEDUCTION IN THE SQAP INTERNAL DATA BASE

There are two main deduction procedures, the positive and the negative procedure.

The positive deduction procedure seeks a chain of deductions from the data base to the question statement. If there is such a chain, then the answer is *yes*. If there is such a chain to the negation of the question, then the answer is *no*.

The negative deduction procedures seek a chain of deductions *from* the

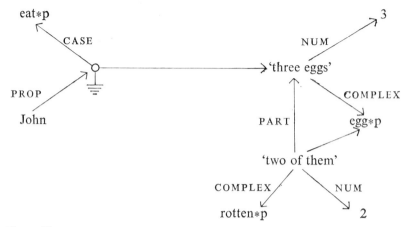

Figure 23

data base augmented with the question, *to* a contradiction. If there is such a chain, the answer is no. If there is a chain *from* the data base augmented with the negative question *to* a contradiction, then the answer is *yes*.

The resolution method (Robinson, 1965a, b, 1971; Meltzer 1971) is an example of a negative deduction procedure. Since there is an isomorphism between the SQAP internal data base and predicate calculus, the resolution method can be used on data represented in the SQAP way.

Erik Sandewall has, however, been working on a set of positive deduction procedures especially designed for the SQAP data base (*see* Sandewall 1969a, b). These procedures are based on three basic deduction methods:

(1) *Chaining*. Chaining is when several elementary relations can be directly chained together into a more far-reaching relation. For example, A SUBSET B and B SUBSET C can be chained together into A SUBSET C, and A PROP B and B CASE C can in certain circumstances be chained together into A PRED C.

The important thing about chaining proofs is to avoid doing the same step more than once. In a chain A SUBSET B, B SUBSET C, C SUBSET D, and so on, the question A SUBSET Q? can, if done in the wrong way, cause the number of steps to grow exponentially with the chain length, but with proper handling the number of steps will be linearly proportional to the chain length.

Let us assume that the following persons are ordered according to descending height:

Father, John, Peter, Mary, Baby.

In order to find out that the answer is *no* to the question 'Is John bigger than Father?', one need not test all the alternatives:

$$(((John > Peter) > Mary) > Baby) < Father$$

$$(\text{John} > (\text{Peter} > (\text{Mary} > \text{Baby}))) < \text{Father}$$
$$(\text{John} > ((\text{Peter} > \text{Mary}) > \text{Baby})) < \text{Father}$$
$$((\text{John} > (\text{Peter} > \text{Mary})) > \text{Baby}) < \text{Father}$$

(2) *Variable identifying*. The data base may contain a variable definition like that in figure 24.

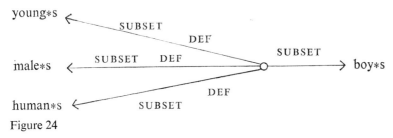

Figure 24

If we encounter an object which is SUBSET to young*s, male*s, and human*s, then this object (because of the DEF quantifiers) can be bound to the variable in the middle of the picture, and we can then infer that the object is a SUBSET to the set boy*s.

(3) *Key identifying*. More complex inference rules like 'If a lion meets an elephant, then the lion will fight the elephant' require a pattern to be identified with the data base before performing the inference. This pattern is called a 'key', and a new quantifier THAT is introduced to indicate THAT special member of a set which was matched by the key. The inference rule will look, in the data base, like figure 25.

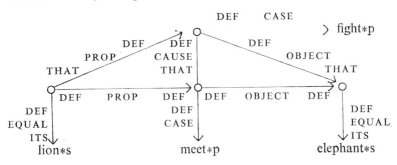

Figure 25

A SHORT SUMMARY OF ELEMENTARY RELATIONS AND QUANTIFIERS IN THE SQAP INTERNAL DATA BASE

The most common elementary *relations* will thus be:

PRED between an object and its predicate (John PRED 'male*p').

PROP between an object and an activity (John PROP 'John is walking').

CASE between an activity and a predicate ('John is walking' CASE 'walk*p').

OF between an activity indicating a complex relation and the object of the relation ('John is the father of Peter' OF Peter).

OBJECT between an activity and its object ('John is giving the book to Mary' OBJECT 'the book').

DATIVE for the dative object ('John is giving the book to Mary' DATIVE Mary).

SUBPRED between singular predicates ('woman*p' SUBPRED 'female*p').

PART between two complex objects ('the parents' PART 'the family').

ELEMENT between a complex object and one of its elements ('the family' ELEMENT Mary).

COMPLEX between a complex object and a predicate common to all its elements ('the family' COMPLEX 'human*p').

NUM between a complex object and the number of elements in it ('the parents' NUM 2).

There will also be relations for cause and effect, for space, time, measurements, and so on.

The *quantifiers* are:

ALL same as $\forall$ in predicate calculus.

SOME same as $\exists$ outside $\forall$ in predicate calculus.

ITS same as $\exists$ inside $\forall$ in predicate calculus.

DEF same as ALL, also indicates that this is a definition of a variable.

THAT same as ITS, also used to indicate the special member which is matched by a key.

SEMANTIC INTERPRETATION

Syntax analysis takes a string of letters or a list of words as input, and produces a tree graph. This tree graph must then be translated to one of the goal languages discussed in the previous chapters.

This latter process is called semantic interpretation. Much is written about syntax analysis, much less about semantic interpretation.

Semantic interpretation can be performed either during the syntax analysis or after the syntax analysis. Performing it during the syntax analysis is accomplished by adding an interpretation routine to some or all productions in the syntax description. This interpretation routine produces the semantic interpretation for this production at the same time as the production is applied to the text.

Semantic interpretation during syntax analysis requires a fast parsing procedure with little back-tracking. The advantage will be that the semantic interpretation process can give results which can help the syntax analysis.

Semantic interpretation after syntax analysis has the advantage that the tree can be scanned more than once and in an arbitrary order.

I will first describe a system for semantic interpretation, and then in the next section discuss the interpretation process in a more general way.

A SYSTEM FOR SEMANTIC INTERPRETATION

Woods (1968) [*see also* the earlier section on 'Command language'] describes a translator from syntax trees to algorithms in a special command language. His system is specialized for airline timetable problems.

The input to the translator is a tree structure. For example, the sentence 'AA-57 flies from Boston to Chicago' is input as the tree shown in figure 26.

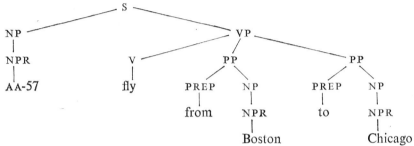

Figure 26

The system contains a number of 'partial trees'. These partial trees are patterns which can be applied to the sentence tree. Three examples of such partial trees are shown in figure 27.

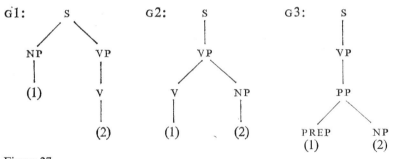

Figure 27

The interpretation is accomplished by matching the sentence tree with one or some of a number of rules. The following rule refers to the tree in figure 26.

1–(G1: FLIGHT((1)) and (2) = *fly*) and
2–(G2:(1) = *from* and PLACE((2))) and
3–(G3:(1) = *to* and PLACE((2))) implies
CONNECT(1–1, 2–2, 3–2)

The numbers in parenthesis in the rule refer to the parts of the sentence tree which were matched by the numbered nodes in the partial trees. For example, when the pattern G1 is applied to the tree of figure 26, then (1) in G1 will match 'AA-57' and (2) in G1 will match 'fly'. This will satisfy line 1 of the rule. The reader can check for himself that the other lines of the rule are also satisfied.

After the word 'implies' in the rule comes the output of this rule. '1-1' means '(1)' in line 1 of the rule. This was 'AA-57'. In the same way '2-2' is identified with 'BOSTON' and '3-2' is identified with 'CHICAGO' so that the translation result is the phrase

'CONNECT(AA-57, BOSTON, CHICAGO)'.

Note that the data base is referred to during the semantic interpretation. The statement FLIGHT((1)) which tests whether AA-57 is a flight must refer to the data or possibly to some other algorithm for establishing this fact.

The system can translate more sentences than those corresponding to a limited number of rules. This is because several rules can be applied in succession to a sentence. One rule is applied to each whole sentence, and one rule to each noun-phrase. The rules must then also show how the results from the different rules are to be combined to produce the full output.

Woods also discusses an optimizing problem. His system produces an algorithm as output, and a requirement is then that this algorithm does not waste system resources when executed. For example, the question 'What is the departure time of AA-57 from Boston?' can either produce the fast algorithm:

(FOR THE X1/DTIME(AA-57, BOSTON) ;(LIST(X1))

or the slow algorithm:

(FOR THE X1/TIME: EQUAL(X1, DTIME(AA-57, BOSTON)));
LIST(X1))

The latter algorithm will range over a large universe of possible answers before finding the satisfying one.

A GENERAL VIEW OF SEMANTIC INTERPRETATION

This section is mostly based on ideas communicated orally to me by Martin Kay.

The linguistic transformation can be seen as a two-step procedure.

(1) Apply a key to the structure.

(2) If this was successful, transform the part of the structure matched by the key. An example of this is shown in figure 28.

A general rule during the semantic interpretation will not only transform the sentence parsing tree, but also build a semantic interpretation network. This rule will thus contain four steps:

(1) Apply key to the tree.

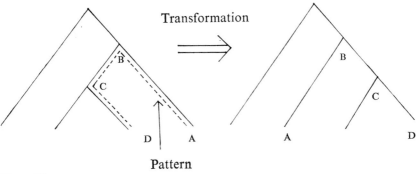

Figure 28

(2) If successful, find corresponding part of the partly-built interpretation network.

(3) Build more things into the network.

(4) Make some transformation (often a deletion) in the tree.

The simple transformation is a special case of this more general rule. Figure 29 shows what might happen during the application of such a four-step rule.

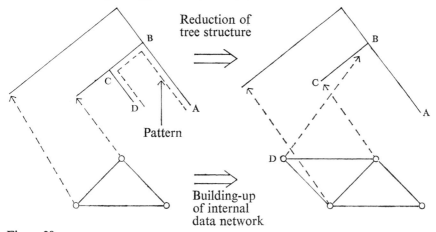

Figure 29

The semantic interpretation process will consist of a number of such four-step rules. These rules are performed in succession, but sometimes a number of the rules must be reapplied to the sentence. The ordering of the rules may perhaps be done using a SNOBOL-like scheme:

Label	Rule	Go-to-s
START	RULE1	:F(PASS1)
	RULE2	:S(PASS2)F(START)
PASS1	RULE3	:S(START)
PASS2	etc.	

The FS and SS indicate where to go after execution of the rule. If the rule was successful, we go to the s-marked label, otherwise to the F-marked label. If no label is given in the go-to-section, the next statement in succession is used.

AMBIGUITIES IN NATURAL LANGUAGE

Many words and short sequences of words are ambiguous in natural language. This means that their true meaning can be understood only by looking at a larger context, possibly including 'basic knowledge of the world'.

An example of this is the sentence 'He went to the park with the girl' can be understood to mean either 'He went to that park where the girl is' or 'He and the girl went to the park'. Probably a larger context will resolve the ambiguity.

The sentence 'The pig was in the pen' is ambiguous because 'pen' can mean both 'fenced enclosure' and 'writing instrument'. Only knowledge about the world of pigs and pens can resolve the ambiguity.

Here are some other possibly ambiguous sentences:

'I saw the baby driving a car'

'The girl guides fish'

'They are flying planes'

'The difficulty is programming'

'He rolled up the red carpet'

Many more sentences will be ambiguous to a computer than to a human, because the computer usually has a simpler algorithm and smaller knowledge about the context and the world than the human has. Thus, sentences which are not ambiguous to a human will often be ambiguous to a computer. For example,

'The difficulty is programming'

In a system which recognizes only a subset of natural language, some of these ambiguities can be resolved by the language specification. For the rest of the ambiguities there are two basic methods:

(1) semantic categories;

(2) reference to the internal data base.

Semantic categories (*see* Katz and Postal 1964) are basically a widening of the traditional grammatical word-class classification. Instead of just classifying words as 'nouns' or 'adjectives' they are classified as 'animate nouns', 'abstract casual nouns', and so on. The system can then understand the difference between 'The difficulty is programming' and 'The man is programming' because 'difficulty' belongs to a class which cannot be subject to predicates in the class that 'programming' belongs to.

A typical such system is the 'multi-store parser' (Glasersfeld 1969, p. 15). This is a bottom-up parsing system. The system might give the parsing in figure 30 to the sentence 'He works to live'.

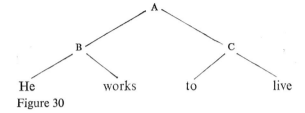

Figure 30

Each word in the sentence is first given a list of 'index categories' from the dictionary. During the parsing, each higher node is also given an 'index category'. This is done by a special algorithm, called 'reclassification', which has the index categories of the constituent parts as its arguments.

Before connecting two nodes with a 'correlator' (A, B, and C in the example) the system tests if the index category of this node accepts this correlator. The B and C nodes may be applied for the sentence 'He began to live' in the same way as above, but this will not fit into the A correlator, forcing another interpretation of the second sentence.

Sometimes, a simple look at the surrounding syntactical structure can resolve the ambiguity. For example, the existence of the object 'the production' will indicate the meaning of the word 'increased' in the sentence 'The company has increased the production' (as opposed to 'The production has increased rapidly'). *See* Batori (1969).

The disadvantage with the semantic category system is that not all ambiguities can be resolved. Such a system, for example, will not be able to resolve the ambiguity in 'He went to the park with the girl', since this requires reference to contextual information only known in the data base.

Another disadvantage is that a large and complex dictionary must be built up including a detailed classification of each word. This dictionary will partially duplicate the information in the internal data base in a question-answering system. The idea of combining these into one single data base is therefore very natural.

This is the second way of resolving ambiguities, *reference to the internal data base*. For example, with the sentence 'The difficulty is programming' the interpreter can ask the internal data base: 'Can a difficulty do the act of programming?'. The answer to this question will tell the system how to interpret the sentence.

The disambiguation method described in the previous paragraph can more generally be stated in the following way. Test all interpretations against the data base: eliminate those which cause a contradiction.

If more than one interpretation is left after this process, the problem is more difficult. The general problem can then be stated as follows:

Given: Several different possible interpretations of a sentence.

Question: Which of these interpretations is most reasonable?

Here are three ways of finding an answer to this question:

(1) Choose the interpretation which matches a part of the data base with most connections between its nodes.

(2) Choose the interpretation which, if added to the data base, will add the least number of new nodes or arcs to the data base.

(3) Choose the most reasonable interpretation using some 'probability' measure of 'reasonability'.

These questions to the data base can either be asked during the analysis procedure, or applied to all different interpretations after the analysis. The advantage with the first method is that the information from the questions can work as 'heuristic' information to guide the analysis procedure in the right direction.

Another possibility, also, is to make only one parsing, possibly guided by some heuristics of this kind. When complete, the parsing is tested against the data base. Other alternative parsings are tried only if the parsing is not accepted. The human mind probably works in this way, since there is a tendency for a human to 'get caught' by one interpretation, and to find it difficult to switch between different interpretations of the same sentence.

A disadvantage with this method is that the risk of an erroneous conclusion is larger than if all possible parsings are compared at the same time.

The situation is very similar to a common method of finding the father of the child of an unmarried mother. This method is to try only one of the possible fathers at a time, not to compare all of them at once. The higher risk with this method is discussed in Palme (1968).

A final method is to store both interpretations in the data base with an *or* relation between them. Thus, 'He went to the park with the girl' is stored in the data base as '*Either* he and the girl went to the park, *or* he went to that park where the girl is'. The disambiguation is then done during the question-answering procedure, using contextual data which may have come after the ambiguous sentence.

THE TRANSLATION PROCESS SEEN AS A HEURISTIC SEARCH

The translation process begins with the input sentence. This sentence is first parsed, and then semantically interpreted. Each step during these processes

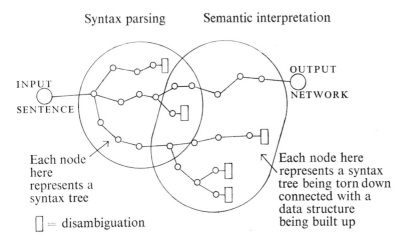

Syntax parsing   Semantic interpretation

INPUT
SENTENCE

OUTPUT
NETWORK

Each node
here
represents a
syntax tree

Each node here
represents a syntax
tree being torn down
connected with a
data structure
being built up

☐ = disambiguation

Figure 31

can be seen as transformations of the working data set from one state to a new state. The initial state is the input sentence, the final state is the translation into the goal representation. The syntax tree is an intermediate state between the syntax analysis and the semantic interpretation part.

This process can then be seen as figure 31.

The areas called 'syntax analysis' and 'semantic interpretation' overlap in the figure, since there is no sharp borderline between these two processes.

The ramification points in the figure are places where the further analysis can be made in two possible directions because of ambiguities. Sometimes the new branches are stopped because they are not acceptable during the further processing (like the analysis 'The girl is guiding fishes' for the sentence 'The girl guides fish and are happy'). Sometimes they are stopped because they are not acceptable to the data base. This process of stopping branches can be called 'disambiguation'.

The transformation process shown in the figure is very similar to heuristic searches (*See* Michie 1971, Sandewall 1971.) Heuristic methods can be used:
(1) to decide which branch to try first;
(2) to stop bad branches as soon as possible.

Such heuristic methods will be very similar to the disambiguation activities, and they will also often require references to the internal data base.

The many well-known methods for speeding up heuristic searches can therefore be applied to the input translation process too. It is also very satisfying to be able to fit a new problem into a well-known framework of artificial intelligence – that of heuristic search procedures.

Q

UNLESS

In natural language, we very often say, in a very unconditional manner, things which are in reality true nearly always, but not quite. We may for example say that 'Every man has two hands' or 'Every TV set can catch fire' in spite of the fact that there are one-armed men and TV sets made of steel.

This problem can be coped with in two ways. One way is to interpret all unconditional statements in a probabilistic manner. Thus, the statement 'Every man has two hands' is stored in the data base as 'Almost every man has two hands'.

The disadvantage with this is that the data base will be unnecessarily complex, since such an 'almost' condition must be affixed to almost every fact in the data base.

Another possibility is to store the statement as unconditionally as in natural language, and use a special relation 'unless' for the exceptional cases, if and when they are known.

This will give a simpler data base, but has the disadvantage of requiring modifications to the inference procedures. However, these modifications will have to be active only in the relatively few cases where there is an 'unless' clause. In other cases, a simple bit test can be enough to find that there is no 'unless' clause.

THE REFER-BACK PROBLEM

In natural language, we very often encounter words or groups of words which refer to things mentioned previously in the text. The most common of these cases are the pronouns. The word 'he' in the text indicates a special male subject which has been mentioned previously.

There are two difficulties with these refer-backs:

(1) Is this a refer-back or not?

(2) What is it referring to?

If we say 'Bill has a piano' we can go on saying 'It is black', or 'The piano is black' or 'Bill's piano is black'. Obviously, 'a piano' did introduce a new object to which refer-backs were possible.

If, however, we say 'Bill does not have a piano', then we cannot further refer back to this piano, and a statement 'It is black' must refer back to something else than Bill's piano.

The decision is not only based simply on whether there is a negation or not. Test the sentences 'Bill tried to find a piano' and 'Bill tried to lift a piano'. They are structurally very similar, but refer-backs to the piano are only acceptable in the second sentence. [More about this problem in Karttunen (1969) and Bellert (1969).]

Problems of this kind are often special for one natural language. For example, the German 'Bill hat kein Piano' will not cause this difficulty.

The basic process of identifying refer-backs is to go backwards in the text until a matching object is found. But shall we try subjects or objects first in previous phrases? Try the refer-backs in the following phrases:

John saw Peter and he was angry.

John saw Peter who was angry.

Mary saw Peter and she kissed him.

John saw Mary and she was angry.

John saw Mary and that female was angry.

John saw Peter whom he spoke to.

John saw Peter and Mary saw him.

John saw Peter and he saw Mary.

Some refer-backs require an unambiguous object to refer to ('The one and only king of Sweden') while others accept the last of several possible matchings 'The last-mentioned man'). The article 'the' is sometimes used in English even when there is not an explicit previous object in the text to refer to, for example, in 'There was a picture in *The Times* of the prime minister'.

In the SQAP system, which uses a somewhat simplified English in its first version, we will use the rules in table 3 for interpreting the articles in most cases.

TABLE 3

	a	the	this
No previous object	New	New	Error message
One previous object	New	Old	Old
Several previous objects	New	Error message	The last old one

PROBABILITY

Natural language has a lot of words for different degrees of probability, as shown by table 4 (from Schwarz 1969).

To be able to work with probabilities, we need rules to combine several probabilities to a probability for the combination.

'It will probably rain. He will possibly go out. She will be angry if it rains or if he goes out. He will be wet if it rains and he goes out.'

What is the probability for her to be angry and for him to get wet? Can the ordinary rules of probability theory be used? How will the inference procedure work in a data base containing lots of 'probable' statements?

TABLE 4

some	many	most	almost all	all
sometimes	often	generally	almost certain	always
possible	likely	probable		certain

What is the multiplication table for
and and *or* on these probability words?

no	few	most + not	not nearly all	not all
never	seldom	generally + not	often + not	not always
impossible	unlikely	improbable	not nearly certain	not certain

WHAT SHOULD BE THE ANSWER TO A QUESTION?

When a closed (yes-no) question like 'Is John wearing a red cap?' is encountered, the system should always put both the question and its negation to the data base. To both these two questions, there are three possible answers:

(1) proof is found (I know that it is true);

(2) there is no logical way to deduce the statement from the data base (I know that I do not know);

(3) deduction was stopped because it took too long a time, or required too much memory (I am tired of thinking about this).

Thus, there are nine possible combinations of these three answers to the two questions. Erik Sandewall has suggested (Sandewall 1969c) what to answer in these cases, as shown in table 5.

TABLE 5

¬ ? / ?	proof found	proof impossible	insufficient resources
proof found	I am confused	Yes	Yes, I think so
proof impossible	No	I do not know	I cannot say
insufficient resources	I do not think so	I cannot say	I cannot say

When facts are input to the system, they must also be checked with the data base. If they disagree, an error message must be given. If the facts are already in the data base, they need not be stored there again. If they neither agree or disagree, then they are acceptable new facts to be stored into the data base. Thus, the corresponding table will be as shown in table 6.

Open questions ('Who is the man in the red cap?') require as output a list of objects satisfying the description. More complex commands ('Describe the man in the red cap') require an even more complex output.

TABLE 6

? ＼ ¬ ?	proof found	proof impossible	insufficient resources
proof found	I am confused	I know	That is what I thought
proof impossible	I do not believe it	I see(store)	Okay(store)
insufficient resources	I do not believe it	I see(store)	Okay(store)

(store) = Store the new facts in the internal data base.

LANGUAGE TRANSLATION

An important area which is closely associated to question-answering is that of language translation systems. This can be illustrated by figure 32 (*from* Vauquois 1968). In question-answering, we have to go from one language almost all the way up to the top 'complete understanding'. This 'complete understanding' may be identical for the same statement, even if it was given in different languages. In language translation, one might succeed without going quite so far, so that a horizontal translation is also necessary. However, statements like 'The pig was in the pen' require a fairly thorough understanding to be able to translate into another language which has different words for the different meanings of the English word 'pen'. The lowest horizontal arrow will surely not succeed.

The experience in language translation work shows that one has to go higher up in the pyramid than in the first attempts at language translation before going down on the other side.

A multi-language question-answering system would be a kind of combination of question-answering and language translation.

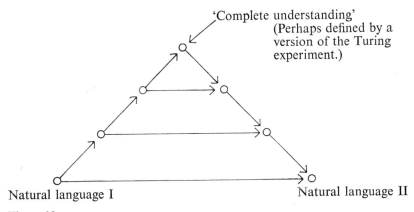

'Complete understanding' (Perhaps defined by a version of the Turing experiment.)

Natural language I

Natural language II

Figure 32

DOCUMENT RETRIEVAL

Information retrieval is defined in the IFIP dictionary as 'the methods and procedures for recovering specific information from stored data'. This definition includes both question-answering (= fact retrieval) and document retrieval.

Traditional document retrieval systems are not, however, aimed at directly finding the answer to a question. Their aim is to find the document or documents in which the answer to a question can be found.

This is usually done by affixing a set of key words to each document and a set of key words to each question. The key words for the question are sometimes combined by set operators. ('Find all documents about *either* measles *or* about virus *and* rashes.')

However, a set of unordered key words is not always a good identification for a document. For example, the documents 'Small boat transportation in cars' will have the same key words as 'Small car transportation in boats', so the system will not be able to distinguish between these logically very different documents.

A more complex identification, somewhat similar to the one used for the internal data base in question-answering systems (see the section on 'The SQAP data base'), might be useful. However, the search will be slower with more complex document keys. A solution might be first to make a fast search with ordinary document retrieval methods. This search is made in such a way that the result has high recall (almost all relevant documents found) but low relevance (many non-relevant documents accepted). Then a new search of these documents using a more advanced analysis could be made, to increase the relevance by sorting out the non-relevant documents.

THE INPUT LANGUAGE IN THE SQAP SYSTEM

The SQAP system (see the section 'Syntax analysis') will in its first version use a simplified English (*see* Palme 1970b). This simplified English will make it possible to say almost everything almost as simply as in natural English. However, the parts of English which are most difficult to translate and/or most often cause ambiguities will be eliminated.

In cases where there are two equally close interpretations, the whole construct will be forbidden. The sentence 'He went to the park with the girl' will not be accepted, instead the system will require either 'He went to the park, with the girl' or 'He went to the park-with the girl' where ',' is a partitioner, '-' is a connector.

In cases where one interpretation is very much more probable than the other, the system will sometimes erroneously make this interpretation a little too often (for instance, 'The difficulty is programming' will be misunderstood, at least by the first versions of the system).

Here is an example of a short text in our simplified English:

'In-place the little town, people were working in-place a factory and a hospital and were living in-place the big house area and the small house area. John was becoming sick and had to be taked to-place the hospital. Mary was visiting him, at-time every day, in-place the hospital. She was buying a bunch of fresh flowers, at-time every day, destined-for him.'

The main restrictions compared to natural English are:

(1) All verbs must be in participle or passive form: 'He had been arriving and was welcomed.'

(2) Some ambiguous prepositions are forbidden: 'I was coming to-place China.'

(3) Relative pronouns must be subjects: 'The man such-that I was giving a flower to him.'

(4) Parentheses must resolve ambiguous conjunctions: '(Gold and silver) from-place Peru is available.'

THE INPUT TRANSLATION PROCEDURE IN THE SQAP SYSTEM

(1) She is missing in spite of the searches.
(2) She is mis ing in spite of the search es.
(3) She is mis ing in-spite-of the search es.
(4) This one female thing is mis ing in-spite of the search s.
(5)

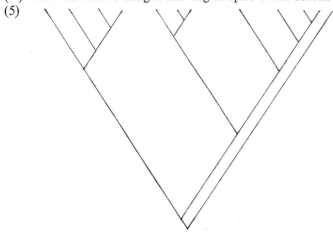

Figure 33

Input translation proceeds in a series of steps. The sentence is successively translated as shown in figure 33. This figure indicates the first steps, as follows:

(1) The sentence is input.

(2) Postfixes are separated.

(3) Some phrases are combined into one word.

(4) Some words are substituted with other words.

(5) Syntactical parsing (see the section, 'Syntax analysis').

(6) Semantic interpretation (see the section, 'Semantic interpretation').

(1)–(5) have been performed, and work has begun on step (6). Work is also going on in parallel on the inference procedures in the data base.

BIBLIOGRAPHY

A short commentary for each document relates the document to the problems discussed in the paper.

Bach, E. (1964) *An Introduction to Transformational Grammars.* New York: Holt, Reinhart & Wilson.
A good introduction to the linguistic viewpoint on grammar specification. The parsing problem is not discussed.

Batori, I. (1969) Disambiguating verbs with multiple meanings in the MT-system of IBM Germany. *Int. Conf. on Computational Linguistics.* Stockholm: Research Group for Quantitative Linguistics.
The meaning of a word can sometimes be understood from the syntactical context.

Bellert, I. (1969) On the use of linguistic quantifying operators in the logico-semantic structure representation of utterances. *Int. Conf. on Computational Linguistics.* Stockholm: Research group for Quantitative Linguistics.
Does a statement in natural language imply the existence of objects mentioned in the statement?

Berge, C. (1962) *An Introduction to the Theory of Graphs.* New York: Wiley.
A mathematical introduction to graph theory.

Bobrow, D.G. (1967) Problems in natural language communication with computers. *IEEE Trans. on Human Factors*, **8**, 1.
This paper presents the basic structure of a question-answering system and the basic design problems.

Bratley, P., Dewar, H. & Thorne, J.P. (1967) Recognition of syntactic structure by computer. *Nature*, **216**.
Presents the basic idea and problems for a sentence parser without a full initial vocabulary. A computer program based on the principles is described.

Breslaw, P. (1969) Experiments with a semantic network. *Research Memorandum MIP–R–63.* Edinburgh: Department of Machine Intelligence and Perception, Edinburgh University.
Presents a simple question-answering system using the same internal data structure idea that is used in SQAP.

Bross, I.D.J. *et al.* (1969) Feasibility of automated information systems in the user's natural language. *American Scientist*, **57**.
This natural language question-answering system finds the kernel sentence in the data base corresponding to the kernel form of the question sentence.

Colby, K.M. & Enea, H. (1967) Heuristic methods for computer understanding of natural language in context-restricted on-line dialogues. *Mathematical Biosciences*, **1**.

Presents a programming language for specifying a program capable of simple natural language conversations with a human.

Davis, M. (1963) Eliminating the irrelevant from mechanical proofs. *Proc. Symposia in Applied Mathematics* 15. American Mathematical Society.
An easy-to-read introduction to basic problems and methods for computer inference. How to remove quantifiers from clauses in predicate calculus.

Earley, J. (1970) An efficient context-free parsing algorithm. *Comm. Ass. comput. Mach.*, **13**, 94–102.
A fast top-down parsing algorithm using a single left-to-right scan without backup and with simultaneous parallel carrying on of several possible parsings during the scan.

Floyd, R. W. (1964) The syntax of programming languages – a survey. *IEEE Trans. Electronic Computers.*
The paper describes the basic top-down syntax analysis procedure used in the first version of the SQAP input text parser.

Glasersfeld, E. von (1969) Semantics and the syntactic classification of words. *Int. Conf. on Computational Linguistics*, Stockholm: Research Group for Quantitative Linguistics.
The multistore bottom-up parsing system uses an interesting method for disambiguation. Each word has a complex correlation index which decides which parsings are allowed. The index is carried upwards to higher nodes during the analysis process.

Glaserfeld, E. von & Pisani, P. P. (1970) The multistore parser for hierarchical syntactic structures. *Comm. Ass. comput. Mach.*, **13**, 74–82.
The multistore parser is a bottom-up parser for a context-free syntax with binary conjunctions. The parser uses a big matrix of words in the sentence against nodes in the grammar to speed up parsing.

IBM (1968) Interactive graphics in data processing. *IBM Systems Journal*, **7**, 147 & 229.
An introduction to the idea of using hash coding for the storage of a relational data structure.

Karttunen, L. (1969) Discourse referents. *Int. Conf. on Computational Linguistics*, Stockholm: Research group for Quantitative Linguistics.
Does a statement in natural language imply the existence of objects mentioned in the statement? How does this affect the refer-back effects of later pronouns in the text?

Katz, J.J., Postal, P.M. (1964) *An integrated theory of linguistic descriptions.* Cambridge, Mass: MIT Press.
This book shows a way to include semantical information in the data base used in the syntactical analysis of natural language texts.

Kay, M. (1964) A parsing program for categorial grammars. *Memo RM–4283–PR.* Santa Monica: Rand Corporation.
A fast syntax analyser using left-to-right scan, a push-down stack and a tag list (containing successful partial parsings).

McMahon, L.E. (1966a) FASE – fundamentally analyzable simplified English. *Symp. on the Human Use of Computing Machines.* Bell Telephone Labs.
Presents the basic arguments for a simplified English in much the same way as in the SQAP work, and presents basic ideas of such a simplified English.

Meltzer, B. (1971) Prolegomena to a theory of efficiency of proof procedures. *Artificial Intelligence and Heuristic Programming* pp. 15–33 (eds. Findler, N.V. & Meltzer, B.). Edinburgh: Edinburgh University Press.

Michie, D. (1971) Formation and execution of plans by machine. *Artificial Intelligence and Heuristic Programming* pp. 101–24 (eds. Findler, N. V. & Meltzer, B.). Edinburgh: Edinburgh University Press.

Palme, J. (1968) Reliability of paternity investigations. *Statistisk Tidskrift*, **1.**
In a heuristic search, one alternative is tested at a time until an acceptable alternative is found. In a complete search, all possible alternatives are found and compared. This paper shows that the risk of making a false decision is larger when only one alternative is tried at a time.

Palme, J. (1970) A Simplified English for Question Answering. *Report C8256–11 (64)*. Stockholm: Institute of National Defense.
This report describes a simplified English to be used as the first input language in the SQAP question answering system. The language is designed so that there will be fewer ambiguities and less risk of misunderstanding than in natural English.

Quillian, M.R. (1969) The teachable language comprehender: A simulation program and theory of language. *Comm. Ass. comput. Mach.*, **12**, 459–76.
An interesting internal network representation of natural English statements.

Raphael, B. (1964) *SIR–a computer program for semantic information retrieval.* Ph.D. thesis, MIT, Mathematics Department.
This thesis presents one of the first and most well-known question answering systems using property-list representation and inference rules.

Robinson, J.A. (1965) A machine-oriented logic based on the resolution principle. *J. Ass. comput. Mach.*, **12**, 23–41.
First presentation of the resolution principle. Not easy to understand.

Robinson, J.A. (1965) Automatic deduction with hyper-resolution. *Internat. J. comput. Math.*, **3.**
Presents the resolution method in a simpler, more understable way, and presents a way of speeding up the inference procedure.

Robinson, J.A. (1971) Building deduction machines. *Artificial Intelligence and Heuristic Programming*, pp. 3–14 (eds. Findler, N. V. & Meltzer, B.). Edinburgh: Edinburgh University Press.

Rosenbaum, P.S. (1967) A grammar base question-answering procedure. *Comm. Ass. comput. Mach.*, **10.**
The paper presents a question-answering system using natural language input and question answering by lexical search.

Sandewall, E.J. (1965) *Representation of facts in a computer question answering system.* Uppsala: Dept. comput. Science, Uppsala University.
This is the report where the ideas for the SQAP method of re-expressing natural language information in an internal data structure were first presented.

Sandewall, E.J. (1968) *A formal notation that re-expresses natural language sentence structure.* Uppsala: Dept. comput. Science, Uppsala University; Report 12.
This report gives the basic suggestions for the internal data structure in the SQAP system. It indicates the basic ideas about how various natural language statements are expressed in the internal structure.

Sandewall, E.J. (1969a) *A property-list representation for certain formulas in predicate calculus.* Uppsala: Dept. comput. Science, Uppsala University; Report 18.
This report presents the algebraic properties of the internal data structure used in SQAP. The basic inference rules and proof procedure to be used in this data base are presented.

Sandewall, E.J. (1969b) *A set-oriented property-structure representation for binary relations. SPB. Machine Intelligence 5*, pp 237–52 (eds. Meltzer, B. & Michie, D.). Edinburgh: Edinburgh University Press.
This paper presents the internal data structure used in the SQAP system. The structure is shown to be an extension of the notations of property lists used in LISP and of the notations of traditional predicate calculus. The basic proof procedure is presented in a formalized way.

Sandewall, E.J. (1969c) *A representation of natural information.* To be published.
How is natural language text best represented in an internal data structure organized according to the Sandewall system? How are objects and their properties represented? How are questions interpreted?

Sandewall, E.J. (1971) Heuristic search: concepts and methods. *Artificial Intelligence and Heuristic Programming*, pp. 81–100 (eds. Findler, N. V. & Meltzer, B.). Edinburgh: Edinburgh University Press.

Sandewall, E.J. (1971) Formal methods in the design of question-answering systems. Submitted to *Int. J. Art. Int.*
How is natural language best translated into predicate calculus, and how is this predicate calculus notation best represented in the computer? What natural language constructs are best mapped into constants, into functions and into predicates in predicate calculus?

Schwarcz, R.H. (1969) Towards a computational formalization of natural language semantics. *Proc. Int. Conf. on Computational Linguistics.* Stockholm: Research group for Quantitative Linguistics.
A discussion of the basic problems in designing a disambiguating semantic parser for a question-answering system.

Simmons, R.F. (1965) Answering English questions by a computer: A survey. *Comm. Ass. comput. Mach.*, **8**, 53–70.
A survey of the question-answering field until 1964 with an extensive bibliography.

Simmons, R.F. (1970) Natural language question-answering systems: 1969. *Comm. Ass. comput. Mach.*, **13**, 15–30.
Gives a survey of the natural language question-answering field with an extensive bibliography.

Vargas, D. (1969) Problem of improving the efficiency of parsing systems. *Proc. Int. Conf. on Computational linguistics.* Stockholm: Research Group for Quantitative Linguistics.
Traditional top-down syntax analysis procedures can be speeded up by a process of partitioning the sentence before attempting to parse the partitions.

Vauquois, B. (1968) A survey of formal grammars and algorithms for recognition and transformation in mechanical translation. *Proc. IFIP Congress* 68.
A good survey of the basic problems in computational linguistics and language translation.

Woods, W. A. (1968) Procedural semantics for a question-answering machine. *Fall Joint Computer Conf.*, 1968.
Semantic interpretation of parsing trees to generate output in a command language.

Picture Descriptions

M.CLOWES

The recent interest in 'integrated' robots, that is, programs with abilities in several traditionally distinct AI areas simultaneously – for instance problem solving, question answering, picture processing – has injected a valuable unification into the field. It has focussed attention on the need for communication between the various modules of the program which function more or less separately in these areas. Communication requires some sort of representation in which to represent what is communicated: the important point about integrated behaviour is that the representations deployed in different areas of the behaviour must be compatible, if effective communication is to take place. For example, if the problem solving module has a task representation which speaks of blocks while the picture interpretation module is competent to recover only regions or aggregates of regions, there will have to be a fairly sophisticated 'patch' to interface these two modules.

This communication problem is merely one aspect of the more basic issue of representation. Newell has been one of the most consistent advocates of the importance of representations, which he has discussed primarily from the standpoint of problem solving programs. He comments 'We can look at the current field of problem solving by computers as consisting of a series of ideas about how to represent a problem. If a problem can be cast into one of those representations in a natural way, then it is possible to manipulate and stand some chance of solving it.' (Newell 1964) These comments apply equally well to the field of picture processing and it is from that standpoint that picture processing and especially the recent attempts to invoke linguistic analogies will be surveyed. In many cases it seems more natural to use the word description than representation. In what follows, no distinction is drawn between these two terms.

TYPES OF PICTURE INTERPRETATION TASK

One of the most obvious of our visual skills is the ability to recognize objects. Recognition can be regarded as assignment-to-a-class, whereupon the immediate issue becomes that of specifying the ensemble of classes and especially of those inter-class differences which define class membership and permit discrimination between objects. A great deal of early work on picture interpretation has utilized this model as a basis for recognizing letters and numbers. The essential feature of this representation is that the only thing it attempts to do with, say, a two-dimensional pattern is to ascertain its class membership. The only thing about the event being processed, which the model is designed to accomplish, is a description of the event as belonging *in toto* to a named class.

There are however many picture interpretation tasks where such a description is – if not irrelevant – more or less useless. Typically these tasks call for what Minsky (1961) has called 'articular' descriptions. Thus the solution of geometrical analogy problems typically involves a characterization of each term of the analogy (the terms being separate pictures) which describes the relations between parts of a given picture term. For example, one picture term might be described as 'a square *inside* a triangle'. As a description of the whole picture it is directed towards a representation of the *organization* of the picture rather than its class membership.

The actions of the draughtsman and the graphic designer typically involve notions of composition which require these kinds of articular description for their realization. It is these notions to which interactive computer graphics systems such as SKETCHPAD (Sutherland 1963, Hodes 1970) address themselves.

Pictorial composition or formatting clearly underlies our competence to read and write two-dimensional arithmetic expressions and it is the relations between 'a' and '2', for instance, above/below, left/right, smaller-/larger-than, which determine the different meanings underlying '$x := a^2$' and '$x := a_2$'. Correct formatting *is* just this set of relations. Indeed, letters themselves can be regarded as *composed* of subpictures (strokes) related in various ways. There is no reason why such articular descriptions should not form a basis for recognition of letters and indeed there are several computer programs which function in just this way (Grimsdale *et al.* 1959, Marill *et al.* 1962). It appears therefore that even in that situation for which the classificatory paradigm appears most appropriate – letter recognition – additional descriptive apparatus must be supplied to cope with the fact that letters are significantly juxtaposed one with another according to various compositional rules. Practical applications of the classificatory apparatus to text always presuppose some additional mechanism which it is presumed will effect 'segmentation' of the page into discrete letters, prior to attempted recognition. It is perhaps not too strong a claim to say that no recognition task is *purely* classificatory in character. There must always be an articular aspect to the descriptive process by means of which the object to be recognized is 'separated' from its context.

THE CONTENT OF DESCRIPTIONS

Where the objective is strictly classificatory, the minimal descriptive apparatus required is that necessary to determine class membership. Typically this apparatus is a set of properties or measures, collectively unique to the class, such that the occurrence in the unknown pattern of this set is taken as sufficient evidence for assigning that pattern to the class. Several ways of relating the occurrence of properties in the unknown, to the decision as to class membership, have been investigated. They range from a weighted arithmetic sum to Bayes' rule computations of likelihood of class membership based upon prior measures of correlation between class membership and occurrence of a property. [*See*, for example, Highleyman (1962) *and* Kamentsky and Liu (1963).] We can emphasize the descriptive narrowness of the scheme by noting that the only relation between properties or features of the pattern to be recognized is that of co-occurrence. In practice many ostensibly classificatory approaches have enriched this basic apparatus by distinguishing between otherwise indistinguishable properties on the basis of *where* in the problem they occur. For example, the highly successful recognition system devised by Greanias *et al.* (1963) distinguishes between an 'east end' (of a stroke) occurring at the top and the same feature occurring at the bottom of the character (to distinguish say 5 from 2). Here, essentially relational information having to do with relative position of features of the pattern is represented by subcategorization of properties.

The objectives for which articular descriptions are required cannot be so concisely stated. In interactive graphics systems what is represented about the graphic is relations (for instance, *constraints* in SKETCHPAD) which the user wishes to manipulate. In fact, the user of SKETCHPAD is operating not upon the picture but upon a representation of objects, attributes of objects (for instance, *length*) and relations between objects (for instance, *parallel-to*). Indeed the only general characterization of the content of articular descriptions that seems plausible is in terms of this triple of data types. Thus if we regard the objective in discriminating between '$x:=a^2$' and '$x:=a_2$' as one of determining the syntactic structures of the arithmetic expressions 'a^2' and 'a_2' (*see* Anderson 1968) then minimally we will need to be able to assign descriptions in which there are objects of type $\langle primary \rangle$ (in the ALGOL syntax), or, more strictly, the pattern correspondents of $\langle primary \rangle$; attributes of these primitive objects such as area, position (x, y coordinates of say 'centre of gravity'); and relations between objects such as above/below, left-of/right-of, smaller-than. It is the appropriate combination of these relations between ⟨*primaries*⟩ which functions on the one hand as ' ↑ ' and on the other as '[]', that is, '$a \uparrow 2$' and '$a[2]$'. In order to determine, for some given picture, which relationships hold, it will be necessary to compute specified attributes of the objects in the picture, such as area, because it is these attributes which function as arguments of the relationship (or predicate) to be evaluated; for instance, smaller-than takes, say, areas as its arguments. Where it is appropriate to regard objects themselves as pattern fragments having specified articular descriptions, for instance a 'T' as a horizontal bar above and joined at its middle to a vertical bar, we need to provide also a representation of sets, since an object has a *set* of parts.

SPECIFYING AND ASSIGNING DESCRIPTIONS

Where the descriptive apparatus is designed purely for classification, specification of a property can be as a function which takes the pattern to be classified as argument and returns as value a Boolean or, say, integer variable. The finite list of properties which together encompass the range of classes constitutes a vector whose value is in turn argument to a second finite list of functions each of which is a class definition. Characteristically the *data* structure required to support or implement this descriptive scheme is very simple precisely because the pattern is finite, the list of properties and their values is finite, and the list of classes is finite. Because of these limitations, it follows that there is a finite number of descriptions which can be assigned to a pattern, for example, for n Boolean properties, 2^n descriptions.

In contrast, articular descriptions, while they may rely upon a *finite* set of objects, relations and attributes, can be arbitrarily complex (Minsky 1961), and consequently may be arbitrarily numerous. The complexity arises from the essentially recursive character of the description, for example if objects can be compounded of other objects which in turn may be compounded, and so on. This variety of complexity calls for data structures whose dimensions are not subject to prior bounds and leads to the adoption of list and ring data structures in which the description is expressed. For such situations the specification of descriptions relative to the patterns to which they should be assigned requires a different treatment.

In two respects at least the statement of the problem closely resembles that of specifying the sentences of a language. First, in the observation that an articular description characterizes the *organization* of a pattern; secondly in the arbitrary degree of complexity and its consequences for the number of descriptions which the apparatus defines. A specification of the infinite set of sentences in a string language together with the one or more organization(s) of each sentence can be given by a generative (PSG) grammar of finite size. Thus the infinitely many simple arithmetic expressions which are legal strings within an ALGOL program can be captured by the three rules

$$\langle simple\ arithmetic\ expression \rangle ::= \langle term \rangle | \langle adding\ operator \rangle \langle term \rangle |$$
$$\langle simple\ arithmetic\ expression \rangle$$
$$\langle adding\ operator \rangle \langle term \rangle$$
$$\langle term \rangle ::= A | B | C \ldots \ldots$$
$$\langle adding\ operator \rangle ::= + | -$$

Thus expressions like $A, B, \ldots, A + B, C - K, \ldots, A + C - B, \ldots$ are legal sentences, and are assigned an organizational or *structural* description by the generative grammar. This description may be represented in several ways, perhaps by a tree diagram or by labelled parentheses. Thus the string $A + C - B$ would be described, for instance:

$$(((A)_{term}(+)_{addop}(C)_{term})_{saexp}(-)_{addop}(B)_{term})_{saexp}$$

using '*addop*' and '*saexp*' as appropriate abbreviations.

The *assignment* of such a description to a string of $\langle term \rangle$s and $\langle adding\ operator \rangle$s requires a program which accepts as arguments the string and the rules, and produces as output the structural description, or an indication that the string, for instance $A + + B$, is not a simple arithmetic expression.

Perhaps the most distinctive feature of this way of handling articular descriptions is this separation of the descriptive scheme from a mechanism (a parser) for *assigning* the descriptions. Over the past five years there have been quite a large number of attempts to deploy this approach for the interpretation of two-dimensional patterns. Kirsch (1964) in his seminal paper advocating a 'linguistic approach' to picture interpretation exhibited a set of rules which characterized an infinite set of right-angled isosceles triangles with hypotenuse at 45°. The salient feature of these rules is that the implied relationship 'followed-by', as for example in $\langle adding\ operator \rangle$ $\langle term \rangle$ which specifies that $\langle term \rangle$ follows $\langle adding\ operator \rangle$, is replaced by an implied two-dimensional relationship. This is achieved by disposing the symbols on each side of the rule within a two-dimensional grid. Kirsch's motivation for so doing lay in the need to deal with the two-dimensional relationships involved in the organization of a triangle as opposed to the one-dimensional relationship 'followed-by' between elements of a string. This departure emphasizes the underlying similarity between the syntactic structure of the language in which the rules are written (the metalanguage) and the syntactic structure of the language (the object language) whose sentences

R

and sentence structures the rules characterize. [Other examples of this two-dimensionalizing of the metalanguage are to be found in Clowes (1967, 1968), and Narasimhan (1969).]

There is of course no *a priori* reason why the syntax of the metalanguage should mirror that of the object language. In settling upon a syntax for the metalanguage we have to bear in mind that it will be interpreted by a program which functions *sequentially*. The left to right ordering of rules couched in a PSG formalism is easily related to the sequential recovery of the elements of the description. Thus in the above definition of ⟨*simple arithmetic expression*⟩, in the second alternative, we readily conceive that the parser might attempt to find an ⟨*adding operator*⟩ *before* it looks for a ⟨*term*⟩ and the fact that the ⟨*adding operator*⟩ will precede the ⟨*term*⟩ in the ALGOL string being processed is an entirely separate fact. The purpose of this digression is to expose the dual role of the metalanguage. On the one hand it is descriptive of an object language, on the other hand it is itself interpreted by a program (the parser).

Most other attempts to provide grammatical models for pictures have deployed string metalanguages. Thus Ledley (1964) provided a grammar of chromosomes which described the 'legal' sequences of five geometrically distinct primitive fragments from which the boundary of a chromosome may be synthesized. In Ledley's grammar the relation between boundaries has been 'translated' by the primitive boundary-following routines into the string relation 'followed-by' whence it follows that a string metalanguage will suffice. Shaw (1967) has developed a language in which aspects of the structure and composition of pictures can be given. Descriptions in this language have a grammatical form specifiable by a phrase structure grammar:

$$\langle S \rangle ::= \langle P \rangle \langle op \rangle \langle P \rangle | \langle S \rangle \langle op \rangle \langle P \rangle | \langle P \rangle \langle op \rangle \langle S \rangle$$
$$\langle op \rangle ::= + | \times | - | *$$

The primitive ⟨*P*⟩ is some pictorial form, recognized (or generated) by means not characterized by the grammar. A primitive must be assigned a description (by this extra-syntactic apparatus) which gives its name, for instance *line*, and the coordinates of its 'head' and 'tail' nodes. Thus a *V* (meaning vertical line) would be a primitive described as

$$(V,(x,y)_{tl}, (x,y+q)_{hd})$$

The significance of the two 'nodes' which each primitive has, lies in the four varieties of relationship between *S*s or *P*s, which the language characterizes by the four types of ⟨*op*⟩. These are listed in table 1.

Since ⟨*op*⟩ appears as infix between both primitives and non-primitives it is also necessary to define how *head* and *tail* are associated with a non-

TABLE 1

Phrase	Relationships between S_1 and S_2
$S_1 + S_2$	$head(S_1)$ concatenated with $tail(S_2)$
$S_1 \times S_2$	$tail(S_1)$ concatenated with $tail(S_2)$
$S_1 - S_2$	$head(S_1)$ concatenated with $head(S_2)$
$S_1 * S_2$	$(tail(S_1)$ concatenated with $tail(S_2))$ & $(head(S_1)$ concatenated with $head(S_2))$

primitive operand. The convention is that for the compound S whose constituent structure is $S_1 \langle op \rangle S_2$,

$$tail(S) = tail(S_1) \text{ and } head(S) = head(S_2)$$

Using the primitive V and the primitive h, where

$$h \equiv (h, (x, y)_{tl}, (x+p, y)_{hd})$$

a rectangle of side p and q would have as description

$$((V+h)_s * (h+V)_s)_s$$

What is exhibited in these structural descriptions is the pattern of coincidence relationships between these distinguished positions (nodes) on primitives. A very similar view of the organization of essentially line patterns is given in Narasimhan's generative rules for an alphabet (Narasimhan 1966).

In both cases we are seeing the introduction into the descriptive language of relations (in this case, varieties of *coincidence* relationship) to surmount the inevitable mismatch between the syntax of the metalanguage ('followed-by') and the syntax of the object language ('coincident-with'). Additionally the picture relations captured in the grammar require that each picture fragment (primitive or non-primitive) have associated with it a description of those of its *attributes* (e.g., head and tail positions) upon which the relation is defined. There is nothing equivalent to this in conventional PSGs and it illustrates the basic distinctions made earlier between objects, relations and attributes. Anderson (1968) finds it necessary to use up to six positional attributes in his specification of the two-dimensional organization of arithmetic expressions. The attempt to use the formalism of PSGs to couch descriptions of pictures is hardly successful. Their attractiveness for string languages is undeniable so long as the only object relationship is followed by ':' it is worth noting that Chomsky's treatment of *co-occurrence relations* between words of an English sentence (Chomsky 1965) requires radical revision of the PSG apparatus along somewhat similar lines.

Evans (1969) rejects PSGs completely in favour of a formalism in which relations are explicitly named, and each statement in the language (equivalently a rule in a PSG) is a definition of an object (equivalently of a syntactic type). Evans exhibits the relation of his formalism to the context-free PSG as follows. The rule

$$\langle s \rangle ::= \langle A \rangle \langle B \rangle$$

is written in his notation

$$(S(X, Y) (ADJ[X, Y], A[X], B[Y],)$$
$$(ULIM[GET[Y[QUOTE[ULIM]]]],$$
$$LLIM[GET[X[QUOTE[LLIM]]]]))$$

Roughly speaking, Evans has translated the PSG rule as saying there is an object named s which has part X and Y such that X is adjacent to Y, and X is an A and Y is a B; s has attributes ULIM and LLIM (upper and lower limits respectively) whose values are the ULIM of Y (that is, GET[Y[QUOTE[ULIM]]]) and the LLIM of X respectively.

While this language makes clear the important role of relations and attributes, it appears to suggest that attributes of compound objects can only be assigned values in the statement which defines that object. Similarly there is no apparent provision for the definition of relationships. In effect therefore, we might say that the language is object centred. Stanton (private communication) has described and implemented a pattern descriptive language which makes independent provision for all three of these categories. Evans' analysis program takes as input (1) a grammar (that is, a list of object definitions which can include recursive definitions) and (2) an input pattern in the form of a list of lowest-level constituents and their attribute values, and outputs a list of all the objects defined by the grammar. Evans has successfully 'simulated' the work of Shaw and Narasimhan cited above. His work shows that the generalization of descriptive power to include attributes and relations can be achieved, in a language which can be used to state rule schemata analogous to PSGs in that they can function in a syntax-directed analysis of two-dimensional patterns.

A number of programs have been written outside this 'parsing' framework which nevertheless deploy articular descriptions of the picture they operate upon. These would include the very early study of letter recognition by Greanias *et al.* (1959), and the later work of Marill *et al.* (1963) which is concerned with 'scenes' containing more than one letter. The recent surge of interest in scene analysis and especially the 'SEE' program of Guzman (1969) is producing articular descriptions of increasing sophistication.

DISCOVERY PROCEDURES

These different approaches to the use of articular descriptions of pictures all expose an area of fundamental importance, namely the sorts of relations, attributes and objects that mediate a capacity to read different classes of picture. Discovery procedures for these categories are of crucial importance. Chomsky exhibits perhaps the only systematic discovery procedure in his use of ambiguity, paraphrase and anomaly (of sentences) to demonstrate the organization which *we* assign to sentences. Pictorial analogues of these methods can be devised (Clowes 1969). Thus line diagrams which permit interpretation as more than one configuration of solids are cases of ambiguity; diagrams which invite interpretation as solids but violate fundamental constructional principles for solids can be regarded as anomalous. Whether or not these analogies are strictly valid is less important than the information which they expose about the organization of the picture. Thus, the three-fold ambiguity of the picture in figure 1 arises because of the uncertainty as to whether the *surface* corresponding to region *A* is a part of the same solid

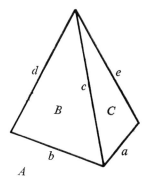

Figure 1

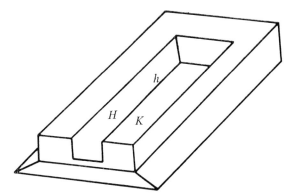

Figure 2

as the surfaces corresponding to regions *B* and *C*. If it is not, then the lines *a*, *b*, *d*, *e*, correspond to *convex* edges. Alternatively two of these lines, for instance *b,a*, are *concave* edges and the other two convex as before, or conversely *d,e* are concave and the other two convex. The anomaly involved in seeing the diagram of figure 2 as an object can be illustrated in terms of these same predicates convex and concave. Thus the line *h* in figure 2 is interpreted *in the foreground* as convex, and the surface corresponding to region *H* does not have a common edge with the surface corresponding to region *K*. Towards the rear of the object, the same line is given a concave interpretation and the two surfaces are seen as sharing a common edge corresponding to this line. The anomaly arises from this conflict in interpretation. It is not that we would require a scene analyzer to throw up similar interpretations, for that might not indeed be the case. The point of these examples is that they provide rather stable and substantial exposures of some aspects of the organization which we assign to pictorial events. It may be sufficient for the program to see in a more limited way than we do, but it seems hard to avoid adoption of some such discovery procedure as outlined above if we are to be able to 'pin down' what it is 'to see in a more (or less) limited way'.

THE STRUCTURE OF DEPICTING

The discussion of figures 1 and 2 above provides one extremely important addition to the framework already outlined for articular descriptions. It concerns the recurrent use of 'corresponding to' as in phrases such as 'the edge corresponding to the line *AB* etc. It suggests that there are at least *two* articular descriptions, one involving lines and regions (and, as it happens, junctions too) and a second involving edges and surfaces (with corner being in part the correspondent of junction). Seeing the line diagram as a scene involves the assignment of two articular descriptions with a quite complex structural relation between them. The 'SEE' program sets up one of these descriptions of the picture as various categories of junction, such as ELL, TEE, ARROW, and so on, enjoying relations with the regions and lines of the picture. Objects are described not as surfaces and edges, but as regions enjoying a minimal number of 'links' inserted by an inspection of junctions according to their categories and pictorial juxtaposition. It is possible to replace Guzman's linkages between regions with an articular description of the relations between the surfaces that those regions depict. Thus the general case of the rule for ARROW used in SEE places a link between the two regions flanking the shaft of the arrow. Thus in figure 1, SEE would describe the ARROW formed by *a*, *b* and *c* as *link* (*B*, *C*). In terms of surfaces and edges the minimal interpretation to be placed upon the junction would be:

$$VX(XYz), \ VX(YWy), \ VX(ZWx), \ hind(YXy), \ hind(ZXx),$$
$$corr(AX), \ corr(BY), \ corr(CZ), \ corr(ax), \ corr(by), \ corr(cz)$$

The identifiers W, X, Y, Z denote surfaces, the identifiers w, x, y, z denote edges. The predicate VX has three arguments, the two surfaces which are convexly related, and the common edge across which that relation holds. The predicate *hind* describes the relationship between two surfaces which, though visibly juxtaposed across an edge, do not share that edge as part of their respective boundaries. Thus $hind(YXy)$ can be read as 'surface X is behind surface Y across the edge y of surface Y.' The predicate *corr* has the obvious interpretation 'corresponds to'. Where a surface such as W has no corresponding region, that surface must be invisible. This could be reflected by an additional predicate (*invis*) but it is redundant. This description is a fragment of the first 'view' of figure 1 given above. The corresponding description for the second view of figure 1 would replace two of the VX statements in the above by CV (meaning concave) statements; there would be no *hind* statements and no hidden surface.

The 'minimal' sense of this interpretation reflects the fact that when a junction denotes a corner of an opaque solid, there must be at least three surfaces involved. Of course, we could invoke further hidden surfaces to give interpretations above and beyond these two accounts. (In fact there is at least one more corner description where c corresponds to a concave edge and a and b to convex edges.) If we take it that there are also three interpretations, say, for the two 'ELL' junctions in figure 1, then we could imagine that there are as many scene analyses of this diagram as there are combinations of such interpretations of its junctions, that is $3^4 = 81$. If we invoke the notion of compatibility of interpretations that the impossibility of seeing figure 2 as an object exposes, then clearly *all* combinations are not going to be permissible. It can be shown (Clowes 1970) that a reduction to just three minimal interpretations is effected with the appropriate rules of compatibility.

What this example exposes is the complexity of the relationship between the picture structure and the scene structure and, at the same time, of the merits of an independent axiomatization of these two types of structure. Elsewhere (Clowes 1969) it has been argued that this duality, framed as a distinction between syntax (the picture) and semantics (the scene) applies to all picture interpretation tasks. Certainly it seems crucial to those situations which we naturally characterize by the term 'depicts' or the phrase 'seeing as'. It can be argued that without some distinction of this general kind, it would be inappropriate to speak of 'the linguistic approach to picture interpretation'.

CONCLUSION

Returning now to the broader context with which this paper began – Representation – the quotation from Newell given there can be seen as completely applicable to picture interpretation. Instead of 'ideas about how to represent a problem' we have 'ideas about the structure of what is depicted and of the (pictorial) means *by which* it is depicted'. The relation between different representations [the Relation of Representation (*see* Kung 1967)] which Newell alludes to when he speaks of there being more or less 'natural ways' of casting a problem into a representation, is in effect a translation schema from one representation to another. Understanding the forms which such schema can take is equally important in the study of natural language. The relation between a picture and what it depicts parallels the relation between a sentence and what it denotes (*see* Wittgenstein 1922). The issues here are basically philosophical in character although the means of treating them constitute a new departure for philosophy. The capacity to describe a scene verbally or to depict it diagrammatically exhibits this sense of parallellism. The goal of research on integrated robots must surely be to realize mechanisms instantiating such a parallellism.

ACKNOWLEDGMENTS

I am grateful to Dr R. B. Stanton for discussions of the manuscript of this paper. The research is supported by a grant from the Science Research Council.

BIBLIOGRAPHY

Anderson, R. H. (1968) *Syntax-directed Recognition of Hand-printed Two-Dimensional Mathematics*. PhD Thesis, Applied Mathematics, Harvard.

Chomsky, A. N. (1965) *Aspects of the Theory of Syntax*. Cambridge, Mass.: MIT Press.

Clowes, M. B. (1967a) Perception, picture processing and computers. *Machine Intelligence 1*, pp. 181–97 (eds Collins, N. L. & Michie, D.). Edinburgh: Edinburgh University Press.

Clowes, M. B. (1967b) *A Generative Picture Grammar*. Canberra: Div. of Computing Research, Commonwealth Scientific and Industrial Research Organization. Seminar Paper 6.

Clowes, M. B. (1969) Transformational grammars and the organization of pictures. *Automatic Interpretation and Classification of Images*, pp. 43–78 (ed. Grasselli, A.). London: Academic Press.

Clowes, M. B. (1970) *On the Interpretation of Line Diagrams as simple three-dimensional Scenes*. Lab. of Experimental Psychology, University of Sussex.

Evans, T.G. (1969) Descriptive pattern analysis techniques. *Automatic Interpretation and Classification of Images*, pp. 79–96 (ed Grasselli, A.). London: Academic Press.

Greanias, E.C., Meagher, P.F., Norman, R.J., & Essinger, P. (1963) The recognition of handwritten numerals by contour analysis. *IBM J. Res. & Dev.*, **7**, 14–21.

Grimsdale, R.L., Sumner, F.H., Tunis, C.J., & Kilburn, T. (1959) A system for the automatic recognition of patterns, *Proc. I.E.E.*, **106**, *B*, 210–21.

Guzman, A. (1969) Decomposition of a visual scene into three-dimensional bodies. *Automatic Interpretation and Classification of Images*, pp. 243–76 (ed Grasselli, A.). London: Academic Press.

Highleyman, W.H. (1962) Linear decision functions with application to pattern recognition. *Optical Character Recognition*, pp. 249–86 (eds Fischer *et al.*). Washington: Spartan Books.

Hodes, L. (1970) A programming system for the on-line analysis of biomedical images. *Comm. Assoc. comput. Mach.*, **13**, 279–83.

Kamentsky, L.A. & Liu, C.N. (1963) Computer-automated design of multi-font print recognition logic. *IBM J. Res. & Dev.*, **7**, 2–13.

Kirsch, R.A. (1964) Computer interpretation of English text and picture patterns. *I.E.E. Trans. on electronic Computers*, **13**, 363–76.

Küng, G. (1967) *Ontology and the Logistic Analysis of Language*. Dordrecht, Holland: Reidel.

Ledley, R.S. (1964) High speed automatic analysis of biomedical pictures. *Science*, **146**, 216–23.

Marill, T., Hartley, A.K., Darley, D.L., Evans, T.G., Bloom, B.H., Park, D.M.R., & Hart, T.P. Cyclops – 1: a second generation recognition system. *AFIPS Conference Proceedings*, **24**, 27–34.

Minsky, M. (1961) Steps towards Artificial Intelligence. *Proc. Inst. radio Eng.*, **49**, 8–30.

Narasimhan, R. (1966) Syntax-directed interpretation of classes of pictures. *Comm. Assoc. comput. Mach.*, **9**, 166–73.

Narasimhan, R. (1969) On the description, generation and recognition of classes of pictures. *Automatic Interpretation and Classification of Images*, pp. 1–42 (ed. Grasselli, A.). London: Academic Press.

Newell, A. (1964) Limitations of the current stock of ideas about problem solving. *Electronic Information Handling*, pp. 195–208 (eds. Kent, A. & Taulbee, O.). London: Macmillan.

Shaw, A.C. (1967) *A proposed language for the formal description of pictures*. Stanford: Stanford Linear Accelerator Centre GSG Memo 28.

Sutherland, I.E. (1963) *Sketchpad – a Man-Machine Graphical Communication System*. MIT Lincoln Lab. Tech. Rept. 296, *and AFIPS Conf. Proc.*, **23**, 329–46.

Wittgenstein, L. (1922) *Tractatus Logico Philosophicus*. London: Routledge & Kegan Paul.

Cognitive Studies

Cognitive Learning Processes:
An Explication

M.KOCHEN

CONCEPTUALIZATION OF LEARNING
AS THE STABLE GROWTH OF WISDOM

INTRODUCTION

Ever since Turing (1956) suggested the possibility of demonstrating that a machine could think, this time-honored problem has begun to challenge some of the most creative scientists (von Neumann 1958, Shklovskii and Sagan 1966, Brillouin 1956). The notions of thinking, cognition and recognition, concept-formation, problem-solving, inductive and deductive reasoning, intelligence, planning, and comprehension have been investigated at an increasingly higher theoretical level by numerous researchers in this logical-mathematical context rather than in the language of human psychology where they originated. One main line of inquiry stressed the dynamic processes of acquiring, through input-output, intellectual abilities and states of cognition. This was the approach parallelling the development of adaptive control systems theory, with feedback and self-regulation (Wiener 1948, Ashby 1953, Solomonoff 1956), of learning by inductive inference. This has passed its peak of popularity and is now out of vogue. Despite impressive demonstrations of learning by computer (Uhr 1964, Samuel 1959), there seems to be a popular and widespread belief that there are not enough ideas about how to proceed toward designing *general* learning programs that would come closer to realizing by computer what we would call cognitive learning of the most sophisticated kind in humans. (We do not share this belief, and hope to persuade the reader to our viewpoint.)

A second line of inquiry, now predominant, stresses the search for efficient logical representations, for clever heuristics, for strong deductive inference schemas and for linguistic processing procedures for solving specific problems by computer (Amarel 1966, Minsky 1970, Newell and Ernst 1965). This had led to the greatest contributions to and from the art of computer programming. But, being very much an art, it has not lighted the way toward the design of a *general* problem-solver, rationally based on sound theoretical underpinnings, any more than has the approach through learning.

An essential feature, shared by 'learning' and 'thinking' is that it be independent of the domain of discourse. To say that an object (machine or living organism) can learn or think does not obligate us to say that it can learn or think about any one of several particular topics (chess-playing, algebra, and so on). It is in stressing this point of view that the ideas presented here differ from those of others. I don't believe we are on the track toward understanding learning, thinking, or even problem-solving if we cannot state principles for designing an automaton that can learn to play both checkers and chess without having the rules built in for either.

In these four lectures, we examine cognitive learning as a mathematical process. Functionally, some day, when we know enough, we may be able to see similarities between such processes in humans, in which context these terms originated, and in programmed computers. Structurally, however, there is no reason to expect that these processes would be implemented in brains in ways resembling the implementations in computers; the two 'technologies' are subject to different constraints. It is of course possible, though unlikely, that future computer architecture may come to resemble the organization of the nervous system. (The architecture of airplanes did not come to resemble more closely that of birds).

The major obstacle to progress in this area has been the difficulty of formulating essential, yet attainable research goals, where 'essential' is intended to include 'generality'. That is, to demonstrate the existence of an automaton capable of representing its environment and continually increasing its problem-solving powers, it is important to select a specific prototype vehicle like checkers, but using it so that the demonstration and the claim is independent of that vehicle. The use of mathematical logic and high-level programming languages, tested with a concrete and significant system of interpretation as a vehicle, shows promise of providing the desired demonstration for existence theorems by construction.

We would like to conceptualize learning in two senses: (1) behaviorally, as an increase in the number of options for increasingly effective action; (2) as an increase in the sophistication of a system for internally representing the external world. One key problem is to prove theorems asserting the existence of automata capable, subject to constraints on memory, complexity and processing speed, of learning in both senses. Another is to show that learning in one sense is logically necessary for learning in the other sense.

In the behavioral-operational sense, we view the learner as a deterministic, synchronous, finite-state automaton with coded inputs from, and outputs to, the environment; such an output, together with the current state of the environment, codetermines the next state. Each state is assumed to have some relative utility for the learner. An output is effective if it causes environment transitions into states of higher utility. Actions are *increasingly* effective if, with time, effective outputs are selected a greater proportion of the time or the effectiveness gets greater.

A learner can process incoming data in four ways: (1) register the input signals and store them in straightforwardly accessible form until memory bounds are exceeded; (2) generate hypotheses (first-order) from input information which abstracts from, generalizes, and summarizes the data, and allows for prediction; (3) form second-order hypotheses from the first-order hypotheses and data, synthesizing them by naming newly generated concepts, forming questions of varying depth and asserting connections between them that represent significance; (4) use all the stored hypotheses for selecting outputs so as to optimize utility. We interpret the last type of information-processing as the exercise of 'wisdom'. All four involve systems of representation at different levels of sophistication. Only the fourth type corresponds to cognitive learning in the *full* sense intended here.

SURVEY OF SELECTED PRIOR KNOWLEDGE

The general questions we are discussing here include: (a) How can external events be represented in a physical system which can process and use these representations to steer itself? (b) How can we design a machine which we specify only as precisely as our uncertainty about its intended performance allows? What kind of algorithm should govern how such a machine forms its own program-generating algorithms so that, in time, and with enough inputs from the environment in which it must perform, it *comes* to perform as *we* would like it to perform when the same inputs from the environment reduce our uncertainty about its intended behavior. (c) How can such a machine modify its organization of represented knowledge, its own representation and its system or representation to make its performance non-decreasing? (d) How can stored representations be used to steer action to effective performance?

Early researchers concerned with artificial intelligence were not primarily concerned with these questions. The 'representation' problem was first stressed as a central one in Kochen (1960b). Most of the advances by then dealt with mechanisms for storing and searching. Most of the insights about representation problems came from earlier work by mathematicians, philosophers, logicians.

A storing process involves the establishment, maintenance and organization of a relation between a set of physical states and a set of symbols capable of referring. A physical system is a store if it is characterized by a set of states and a transition function which specifies the next state given the current

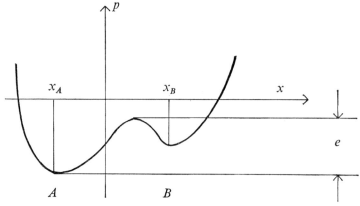

Figure 1

state and an information input. Presumably, it should also be possible to determine the state, in part or whole, at any time, with information inputs. It seems essential that the states of the physical system, if it is to be a store, must be stable. That is, the potential energy p of the physical system as a function of a control variable x used to represent information input – for example, electric current or distance – must have at least two minima (figure 1). To switch from state A to state B in figure 1 is to increase x from x_A to x_B, thereby supplying energy e to surmount the barrier. Once in B, small enough noisy fluctuations will presumably cause the system to deviate slightly from B, but not enough to switch it back to A.

Biologists have not adopted this criterion of stability as essential for the biochemical-physical storage systems they are concerned with. It is, of course, possible that 'analogue' type storage mechanisms, such as electrical capacitors, are operative. Possibly both types may exist in living systems. If the nodes of Ranvier, spaced at about every millimetre along a long nerve fiber conducting impulses from a sensory organ to the brain, serve to boost and relay the signal, then a non-digital coding of the signal would make reliable transmissions to the brain utterly impossible due to the compounding of slight errors at each relay station. This is a powerful argument that at least some aspect of neural coding are digital. This question is of some importance, because the options for naming (referring to) are greater for digitally encoded signals.

The classical (von Neumann) organization of a 2^n-state store is to characterize it as m partitions of the 2^n states into $2^{n/m}$ sets of $2^{n-n/m}$ states each (where m divides n). Thus to the set of states of a 64-state machine could be assigned three partitions, each partitioning the 64 into four sets of 16 states each. This corresponds to three addresses of 2 bits each:

0	1	1	0	0	1

Addr. 1   Addr. 2   Addr. 3

Address 1 could contain 01, to which corresponds the set of 16 different states of the machine, corresponding to all possible 6-bit words in which the first 2 bits are 01. This corresponds to a 'Cartesian' decomposition of the machine into parts (Kochen 1958, Roosen-Runge 1967).

In straight-forward machine-language programming, the addresses – in the above example, the three names for the three partitions – can be used as names of variables, each ranging over the elements in the partition. Each element in the partition – a set of 16 states in the above example – is a value of the variable; it, too, is nameable. To provide ourselves with enough *options* for assigning names to variables – and this is one of the sources of power for the study of cognitive learning that wasn't present before 1960 or so – we draw on the notion of higher level programming languages, beginning with assemblers. A step beyond this use of arbitrary names for variables which are assigned address names by program is the idea of chaining. Its use was proposed by Minsky and McCarthy in the 'Advice-Taker' (McCarthy 1958), taken up by Newell and Simon in their programs for chess-playing (Newell 1955, Newell, Shaw and Simon 1958) and propositional calculus (Newell and Shaw 1957, Amarel 1964), and by Gelernter for theorem-proving in geometry using the diagram as a heuristic (Gelernter 1959), to mention some early studies. The use of chaining or 'lists' to structure stored states is still the state of the art, though a number of variations of the basic idea have been used very successfully, particularly in graphic data processing.

Simultaneously with the development of high-level languages and the options they gave programmers for creating various data structures came the development of threshold network theory. Beginning with the notion of cell assemblies (Hebb 1949) and proceeding from McCulloch-Pitts nets to perceptrons, the art of designing switching circuits and adaptive majority logic circuits has reached a considerable state of sophistication.

It is the capabilities of 1970-high-level languages such as SNOBOL4 (Griswold, Poage and Polonsky 1966) and the notion of virtual memories that appear to hold promise for a fruitful attack on our central questions.

In 1960 the state of the art on what we (Kochen 1960b) called searching processes was represented by Samuel's program to learn checkers (Samuel 1959), the Newell-Simon work on the use of heuristics (Newell and Simon

s

1959), Barricelli's (1957) and Bremermann's (1958) programs for evolution by natural selection, adaptive servomechanisms theory (Wiener 1948) and our own work on concept-formation processes (Bruner, Goodnow and Austin 1956, Kochen 1960a, Kochen 1962). By and large, these approaches shared the limitation that the target of a search process – that which was to be learned – was an element of an *a priori* specified set, usually a finite set with elements explicitly enumerable. A first step to go beyond this was the AMNIP system (Kochen 1960a) in which stored information was represented as propositions of a specialized applied predicate calculus organized into list structures and searching was performed by tracing 'associational trails' as suggested in the 'memex' idea (Bush 1965). The major advance in search processes, however, was the development in the late 1960s of algorithms based on the resolution principle of searching for proofs to given propositions. The set of possible proofs is *a priori* specified only by rules of well-formedness, axioms, and rules of inference. This is still peripheral to our central problem which requires searching useful propositions prior to or independently of searching for proofs. Nonetheless, the advances in this area provide valuable concepts and techniques – particularly in the use of modern logic and model theory – for attack on our main questions.

Progress in our understanding of the notion of 'representation' has advanced only slowly beyond the contributions of logicians like Gödel (1931) and Church (1934), philosophers like Myhill (1952) and mathematicians like Polyá (1954), Hadamard (1945), Poincaré (1914) and some of the suggestive experiments of Gestält psychologists, Köhler (1959) and Piaget (1952). In a sense, these contributions began with Descartes' rules for rational thinking, which he applied to himself and which led him to the discovery of analytic geometry (Descartes 1948). To these, Poincaré added, nearly 400 years later, the simple and very profound theme: discovery is selection. Poincaré believed that stating the rules to choose between numerous combinations formable by rules is practically impossible; that they 'must be *felt* rather than formulated'. This view – which would imply that a machine capable of discoveries is not possible – seems to be shared by Polyá and supported by experimental psychologists like Mowrer (1961). Myhill (1952) argued that the profound results of Gödel and Church can be interpreted as psychological laws (laws of information science?) about limitation on the knowable. He stated them as: 'our creativity outruns our capacity for anticipating the outcome of that creativity' (Myhill 1952). and classified ideas expressible as well-formed formulas into three types:

(1) effective ones, if organisms can be trained to respond differentially to their presence and their absence (corresponds to recursive);

(2) constructive ones, if organisms can be trained to follow a program such that the form expressing the idea will sooner or later be constructed (this corresponds to recursively enumerable);

(3) prospective ones, if some organism 'entertains an idea' corresponding to the formula, and the formula is neither effective nor constructive.

These deep insights could be construed to cast doubt on Turing's suggestions that a machine can think (would Turing suggest that a machine could do creative thinking, discovering or inventing?). The key to shedding further light on these issues appears to lie in a clearer explication of the notion of 'representation'. Some small steps (Amarel 1968, Newell 1966) have been taken in this direction, and the explication presented here is a further advance.

THE OVERALL MODEL: INFORMATION PROCESSING

In this section we sketch the main ideas of our explication in a special case, to simplify the presentation. The general, formal model is presented in the next lecture. To fix ideas, imagine two learners, L_1 and L_2 coupled to a common external environment E. We (the analysts, communicating in the language of this paper), understand E to be representable by: (1) a set of $n^2(n^2-1)$ states, interpreted as all possible configurations of positions of two dots labeled A and B on an $n \times n$ grid; denote any state s by the four-component vector (x_A, y_A, x_B, y_B), where each component takes values from 0 to $n-1$; (2) a transition function f which assigns to each state s a 'next' state s', but which is determined uniquely only by specifying values of a_1 and a_2 which range over arbitrary sets A_1 and A_2. We interpret a_i as an output or action of L_i, $i=1, 2$, and an input to E (Kochen 1958). As an example, let a_i be a two-component vector, (a_{xi}, a_{yi}), with a_{xi}, a_{yi} being any natural numbers, and let f be $(x_A+a_{x1}, y_A+a_{y1}, x_B+a_{x2}, y_B+a_{y2}) \bmod n$ which maps s into $s' \equiv (x_A', y_A', x_B', y_B')$. (3) a utility or value function v which assigns a two-component vector $u=(u_1, u_2)$ to each state s. We interpret u_i as the utility of state s to L_i, $i=1, 2$, and suppose that it is a real number.

Example of a pure conflict situation:

$$(u_1, u_2) = \begin{cases} (-1, 1), & \text{if } x_A = x_B; \\ (1, -1), & \text{otherwise.} \end{cases}$$

Example of a situation requiring cooperation:

$$(u_1, u_2) = \begin{cases} (1, 1), & \text{if } x_A = x_B; \\ (0, 0), & \text{otherwise.} \end{cases}$$

Learner L_i is assumed to receive the following input corresponding to any state of E as a nine-tuple of numbers:

$(x_A, y_A, x_B, y_B, a_{x1}, a_{y1}, a_{x2}, a_{y2}, u_i)$, $i = 1, 2$. Given this as input L_i executes the first and sometimes also the second, third and fourth of the following four algorithms:

(1) Computation of $a_i' = (a_{xi}', a_{yi}')$, based on stored hypotheses about the functions f and v.

(2) Storage and use of input to test some of the more valuable stored hypotheses, and a reorganization of the store.

(3) Formation of new hypotheses, including hypotheses about previously stored hypotheses.

(4) Modifying the system of representation which specifies what new hypotheses can be formed; this includes the formation of new predicates.

These four algorithms are themselves modified by – or are the productions of – a *master algorithm*, which is mixed and specified by us (the designer/analyst) and *which is what L_i denotes*. This master algorithm, then, forms algorithms that form and test hypotheses from new predicates and generate actions. It also modifies (or generates) a fifth supervisory algorithm that directs and coordinates the execution of the other four algorithms – that is, which is to act when.

We cannot yet specify this master algorithm L_i in full detail and generality. We can specify the first four of the five algorithms which it is to modify. We illustrate how the first algorithms would perform by a simple example with just one learner L_1, with s a one-vector rather than a four-vector ranging over 0, 1, 2, . . ., and with a_1 equal to either a or b. Suppose that

$$f(s, a_1) = s' = \begin{cases} s + 1, & \text{if } a_1 = a, \text{ all } s \\ s - 1, & \text{if } a_1 = b, \text{ all } s \geqslant 1 \\ 0, & \text{if } a_1 = b, s = 0 \end{cases} \tag{1}$$

and

$$v(s) = u_1 = 2^{s(6-s)} \tag{2}$$

Inputs to L_1 are triples, (s, a_1, u_1), like

$$(0, a, 1), (1, a, 32), (2, a, 256), (3, a, 512), (4, a, 256), (5, a, 32),$$
$$(6, a, 1), \ldots$$

The above is the sequence of inputs which L_1 would actually receive if *he always picked* $a_1 = a$. Even with so stereotyped a response, L_1 could form a hypothesis about the function $v(s)$ by the time it receives $(6, a, 1)$. The next state will be 7 and the corresponding u_1 will be 2^{-7}, but L_1 might do well to try $a_1 = b$ and to keep doing that. Then, the following might be a reasonable continuation of the above input sequence:

$(7, b, 2^{-7}), (6, b, 1), (5, b, 32), (4, b, 256), (3, b, 512), (2, b, 256),$

. . . .

By now L_1 may have formed an hypothesis about $f(s, a_1)$. If both this and the hypothesis about v are plausible, and used at this time, then a reasonable continuation of the input sequence might be:

$(1, a, 32), (2, a, 256), (3, b, 512), (2, a, 256), (3, b, 512), (2, a, 256),$

. . . .

Note how easily *we* can bypass the rather formidable notation of equations (1) and (2) by verbalization at, say, time, or trial, $t = 6$: when the state of E is greater than 3, my utility goes down, but I can drive the state back to three by repeating output b.

We say that this learner has recognized, at time (trial) $t = 6$, an opportunity for what appears to be maximization of his utility (that is, he recognized a task), and he found a way of coping with it. Suppose he settles upon the strategy shown by the last input sequence, so that his utility will be alternately 256 and 512. But suppose that f were not as given by eq. (1), but by eq. (1) only for $t < 20$ and by:

$$f(s_1, a_1) = \begin{cases} s + 3, & \text{if } a_1 = a \\ & \text{all } t \geqslant 20 \\ s - 1, & \text{if } a_1 = b \end{cases} \quad (3)$$

At times $t = 20, 21, 22, 23, \ldots$ L_1 will thus notice the change:

$(2, a, 256), (5, b, 32), (4, a, 256), (7, b, 2^{-7}), \ldots$

Perhaps the best way to continue from here is $(6, b, 1), (5, b, 32), (4, b, 256),$ $(3, b, 512), (2, b, 256), (1, b, 32), (0, a, 1), (3, b, 512), (2, b, 256), (1, b, 32),$ $(0, a, 1), (3, b, 512)$. L_1 is beginning to *learn* if it can modify its store of hypotheses shortly after $t = 20$, with relatively little processing effort, so that it resumes maximizing utility rather soon in response to this slight change in $f(s, a_1)$ as t increases through 20.

The action-selection algorithm, then, is one which assigns an element of A_1 to each input (s, a_1, u_1). It may do this by calling one of several routines, the simplest one corresponding to complete stereotype, as seen earlier: pick a regardless of input. Another, slightly less stereotyped routine is to repeat the choice made last time if u_1 was high, choose anything but that if u_1 was low. 'No response' is interpreted as a special element of A_1. No special elements of A are designated for interpretation as 'avoidance' or 'instrumental' responses.

The input (s, a_1, u), which we take to be a number-triple in this discussion, refers to physical signals: If E refers to a physical system in state s, which undergoes a state transition involving a decrease or increase of energy, and

L_1 also refers to a physical system (that is, the master algorithm L_1 is 'embodied' or stored) which is coupled to E, then L_1 can 'respond' to – that is, sense, be perturbed by, measure – this energy change: L_1 must supply or receive the energy change, resulting in a signal. Insofar as L_1 is organized as a signal detector/decoder in the sense of information theory, L_1 receives information as its input. Execution of the algorithm that assigns an element of A – which also refers to a physical signal – to this input is *information-processing* in the sense of Turing (1936), Shannon and Weaver (1949), Brillouin (1956): information is dissociated from meaning, and refers only to code signals, selecting one from an ensemble of all possible code signals.

Such an adaptive information-processing system, in which the output selection algorithm can be continually modified, has stabilized if small 'changes' in the environment result at worst in short-term departures from an action-selection algorithm to which the system has converged. If this algorithm is one which also brings high utility at 'equilibrium', then we call it a 'normal' information processor.

KNOWLEDGE-PROCESSING

To deal with cognitive processes, we must go beyond systems that process *information*, devoid of meaning, but which process information with *meaning*. According to Churchman (Kochen 1969d) knowledge is information interpreted with an orientation, a point of view. To explicate this, we draw upon the concepts of modern logic, particularly the notion of an *interpretation* corresponding to a logical system G. By G we understand a formal 5-tuple such as that used in specifying a formal grammar: $\{V_T, V_N, V_D, R, T\}$, where R designates a set of formation (rewrite) rules, T a set of transformation rules, V_D a set of distinguished symbols from which are generated assertions, questions, and so on, and other well-formed formulas, V_N is a set of 'non-terminal' symbols used only in stating rules of R and T, and V_T is a set of formal 'terminal' symbols that occur in propositions ('surface strings'). The latter is most important. We partition it into: C, a set of names (= symbols) for individual constants and class names; V, a set of names designating variables that range over C; P a set of predicate-names; F a set of function-names; the set of logical quantifiers and constants $\{(A),$ $(\exists), \neg, \Rightarrow, \&, \vee\}$. Here $\neg$ represents negation. A system of interpretation is specified by a domain of discourse D, a mapping from C to D, a mapping from P to $\{D \cup D \times D \cup D \times D \times D \cup \ldots\}$. By a *system of representation* we mean G together with its system of interpretation; we pay particular attention to C, P and F and the sets corresponding to those in the systems of interpretation; these three sets are subject to modification – primarily extension – by the master algorithm L_1.

Let SR_i designate L_i's system of representation. This is a variable name itself. Its value – which is a system of representation – varies from one learner to another (with $i = 1$, 2), including SR_0, the representation system used by us (analysts/designers) in expressing f and v, and it varies also with time for a given i. The input information received by L_i is an element of the domain of discourse in SR_i. If such inputs are cumulatively stored, a finite data corpus is thus formed.

The formal logical system part of SR_i, say G_i, specifies an (infinite) set of well-formed formulas (or propositions) each of which can be true, false or untested, according to the system of interpretation. Let us call this set of propositions $\mathcal{L}(G_i)$. At this point, we depart from the procedure of formal theory-building: a system of representation need not (though it may also) be specified by a fixed set of axioms and rules of inference. By means of algorithms two and three which we required L_i to be capable of generating or modifying, hypotheses will be formed. At any time, there will be a finite corpus of these, which we will call a (corpus of) representation(s), CR_i, for L_i.

An hypothesis h is a proposition of $\mathcal{L}(G_i)$, which has been selected for storage in CR_i, together with a weight-of-evidence (degree of credibility) function $w(h)$. To offer some examples, suppose that G_i contains all the symbols necessary for first-order arithmetic (Mendelson 1964) plus three special predicate symbols: IDO, ISE, and ILK. Examples of well-formed formulas involving this would be: $(\exists s)\ \text{ISE}(s)\ \&\ (s = 5) \Rightarrow \text{ILK}(s)$ (interpreted by us as 'There is a state of E, namely 5, which L_i likes: $u_1 = 512$'), and: $(\text{A}s)\ \text{ISE}(s)\ \&\ \text{IDO}(a) \Rightarrow \text{ISE}(s + 1)$ (interpreted by us as 'If I select action a when the state of E is s, the next state is $s + 1$, for all s'). The first proposition is true if an input such as $(3, a, 512)$ is stored in the data corpus of SR_i. We could say that the proposition, '$(\exists x)(s = 7)\neg\text{ILK}(s)$' is true if $(7, a, 2^{-7})$ is stored in the data corpus. An hypothesis, h, which is such a well-formed proposition, is *confirmed* if either h is found to be true or if $\neg h$ is found to be false in the system of interpretation. Refutation of h does not necessarily cause algorithm two to delete h from CR_i. Even hypotheses of 0 weight may, for a time, be present in CR_i. Refutation of h does decrease $w(h)$, and h may remain in storage with reduced weight or it may be modified. The most elementary kind of modification is qualification by exception. For example, if $f(s, a_i) = s + 1$ if $a_i = 1$ for all s except $s = 11$, then the above hypothesis would be modified to read $(\text{A}s)(s \neq 11)\ \&\ \text{ISE}(s)\ \&\ \text{IDO}(a) \Rightarrow \text{ISE}(s + 1)$.

By the utility of an hypothesis like $h = \text{`}(\exists s)(s = 7)\,\text{ILK}(s)\text{'}$ we mean the number u_1 which verified it, such as 512. This may appear explicitly in the hypothesis. If the degree of credibility $w(h) \in [0, 1]$, is near 1, then h had an expected utility close to 512. In searching CR_i for hypotheses on which to base the choice of action a_j, algorithm one examines hypotheses which are both relevant (refer to the current input to L_i) and of high expected utility. Correspondingly, algorithm two reorganizes the store CR_i so as to make the hypotheses of highest expected utility most readily accessible.

We shall call an information-processor a *cognitive information processor*, or a *knowledge-processor*, if it can test, revise and use hypotheses for action-selection. The truth-testing (semantic) procedure is a first step toward endowing the predicate symbols with meaning. The meaning of an individual's name k is the set of hypotheses $H(k)$ in which that name occurs, and this changes, of course, as CR_i changes.

A *concept* is named by a class-name c, (such as 'ball') which refers to both its core extension $E(c)$ and the core intension $I(c)$. Bunge (1967) defines $I(c)$ as the set of all properties which are necessary and sufficient to discriminate the concept named c from all others; $E(c)$ is the set of all known instances of the concept named c. The meaning of c (to L_i at a certain time), is specified by both $E(c)$ and $I(c)$, which again corresponds to the set of hypotheses $H(c)$ in CR_i in which c occurs. Two concepts, c and c' are similar (the names of c and c' are near-synonymous) if $H(c) \cap H(c')$ has a large measure.

Hypotheses represent beliefs (Abelson and Caroll 1965, Colby 1967), as well as the outputs of such successful inference aids in scientific research as DENDRAL (Lederberg and Feigenbaum 1968). For a cognitive learner, with a fixed system of representation SR_i, but in which the corpus of hypotheses CR_i has 'converged' to a set that changes but little, small changes in E result at worst in short-term departures from this steady-state CR_i. That is, certain hypotheses h have attained a high $w(h)$ and a high tenacity. Due to limited memory and limited processing speeds, it is unlikely for new hypotheses to crowd out the old ones.

The action-selection algorithm may have stabilized at a level which brings low utility for L_i. A rich enough representation CR_i can get the action-selection algorithm to switch to another level of stability with a higher utility for L_i. The highest level thus attainable is limited by CR_i. An even higher level may be attainable by modifying CR_i. This can happen by simply updating CR_i with new hypotheses h to be stored. This could be done by teaching L_i with assertions corresponding to h. Such assertions are presented to L_i as sentences in a public language which L_i uses as inputs (stimuli) for forming h.

If SR_i has all the symbols and formation rules of first-order arithmetic then it is simple to designate another subset of $\mathscr{L}(G_i)$ as a set of axioms (for example, the five axioms of predicate calculus plus the proper axioms for arithmetic and equality) and to define proofs and theorems, by means of 'logical consequence', in the usual way. Special transformations of T (Kochen 1969a) are used to transform one true proposition into one that is logically equivalent. Some, but not all, theorems may be more or less confirmed hypotheses in L_i's system of interpretation. Of course, not every hypothesis need be a theorem. There is no relation between the logical 'truth' (validity) of a theorem and the truth (verification) of an hypothesis, though the notion of a 'model' is related (Mendelson 1964).

Note that we allowed systems of representation and representations to change with time without limit. We could place an upper bound on the time, which we would interpret as the learner's lifetime. We would wish to make provision for L_i to transfer some of its knowledge to 'disciples'. Indeed, there will be transfer from several L_is to the same disciple, and each L_i has many disciples; this can give rise to many combinations, yielding more options from which to select future-generation learners.

COMPREHENSION: FROM KNOWLEDGE TO UNDERSTANDING

A *verbal language* $VL(G')$ is a set of well-formed strings that can be generated by a grammar $G' = \{V'_T, V'_N, V'_D, R', T'\}$, with many of the elements of terminal vocabulary V'_T serving as names that designate concepts named c in a system of representation; V'_D is a set of distinguished non-terminal symbols, a subset of V'_N, used as starting point for generating linguistic assertions, questions, requests, advice, warnings, and so on, while R' and T' denote, respectively, a set of rules of formation and transformation. Associated to certain names in V'_T and phrases generated by V'_D are the symbols of G_i and expression's generated by V_{Di} of SR_i which are similar in all the SR_i.

It is important to note that SR_1 and SR_2 may differ. An English word, like 'ball', of V'_T may thus correspond to symbol c_1 in V_{T1} of SR_1 and to symbol c_2 in V_{T2} of SR_2. If $H(c_1)$ is the set of hypotheses in CR_i in which symbol c_1 occurs, there is a relation r from $H(c_1)$ to $H(c_2)$ and the measure of $H(c_1) \cap \bigcup_{h' \in H(c_1)} r(h')$ is large. That is, though the meaning associated with the word 'ball' which designates the concept 'ball$_1$' for L_1 and 'ball$_2$' for L_2 is different for both, the two meanings have enough in common to permit communication. The request 'throw the ball' from L_1 to L_2 would result in the same action as if the request were from L_2 to L_1.

Equally important is permitting a term like ball in V'_T to correspond to several concepts in SR_i for even a single i. For example, 'ball'→'ball$_1$', 'dance$_1$', 'bad baseball pitch$_1$', and so on for L_1. Also, several terms in V'_T can correspond to the same concept, for instance 'sphere'→'ball', 'Kugel'→ 'ball$_1$', and so on. The importance of these ambiguities lies in providing for a large number of combinatorial options for forming new predicates and concepts while at the same time providing clues for selecting from among these combinations. I refer to the kind of 'shaking-up' which is the essence of cognition. A learner 'cogitates' by speaking to itself in such a verbal language allowing the formation of a few surprisingly useful combinations of known concepts from a very large number of possibilities, without ever having examined all these possibilities.

We now examine in some detail how algorithm three could form a few important ones of these new predicates and concepts. We begin with the concept of 'control'. Prior to this we need to explain how hypotheses, particularly hypotheses about other hypotheses, are formed, which ones are generated when. In brief, if three inputs like $(5, a, u_1)$, $(6, a, u'_1)$, $(7, b, u''_1)$ were received, an hypothesis like h, '(As) ISE(s) & IDO(a)⇒ISE$(s+1)$', with small $w(h)$ would be formed; it is, of course, an overgeneralization, and likely to be soon refuted. One general (liberal) strategy is to form such overgeneralizations as soon as possible and modify them, as little as possible, whenever new inputs call for it. Going back to the 4-component state vector of the example of section 3, suppose now that two hypotheses were in CR_1:

$$h_1 = (As)(Aa_1)(Aa_2)(s = (x_A, y_A, x_B, y_B)) \& (a_1 = (a_{x1}, a_{y1}))$$
$$\& (a_2 = (a_{x2}, a_{y2})) \& \text{ISE}(s) \& \text{IDO}(a) \Rightarrow \text{ISE}(s + (a_1, a_2) \bmod n)$$
$$h_2 = (As)(s = (x_A, y_A, x_B, y_B) \& \text{ISE}(s) \& (x_A = x_B) \Rightarrow \text{ILK}(s).$$

To store h_1, F_i must have contained the functions $+$, mod n, etc. Suppose that, in addition, F_i contained the '$-$' function and that A_i were only u, d, r, l, $\emptyset$ corresponding to $a_i = \{(0, 1), (0, -1), (1, 0), (-1, 0), (0, 0)\}$, with:

$$\text{ISE}(x_A, y_A, x_B, y_B) \& \text{IDO}(l) \Rightarrow \text{ISE}(x_A - 1, y_A, x_B, y_B),$$
$$\text{ISE}(x_A, y_A, x_B, y_B) \& \text{IDO}(r) \Rightarrow \text{ISE}(x_A + 1, y_A, x_B, y_B)$$

and so on.

The above two hypotheses could be combined into one:

$$\text{ISE}(x_A, y_A, x_B, y_B) \& \text{IDO}(a_1) \Rightarrow \text{ISE}(x_A \, \sigma(a_1) \, 1, y_A, x_B, y_B)$$
$$\& (\sigma(r) = +) \& (\sigma(l) = -).$$

The new function-symbol σ is generic to $+$ and $-$. This is an example of forming a new hypothesis which summarizes or synthesizes two other hypotheses and forms a new function at the same time. Just as a first-order hypothesis h can summarize *data* – that is, the data which verified h can be deleted with safety from storage as long as h is not refuted, – a second-order hypothesis can summarize several first-order hypotheses.

Algorithm four provides for the formation of a predicate-symbol corresponding to 'Action variable a_1 controls state variable x'; this is true if x', the next state as a function of x, a_1, a_2 . . . depends only on x and a_1, as in $x' = x + a_1$. If $x' = x + a_1 + a_2$, then a_1 does not control x.

L_1 is an automaton which generates outputs and hypotheses according to an algorithm. For L_1 to be a 'comprehender', its algorithm has certain additional properties. It classifies or factors the environment E, beyond what is given. In general, the input to L_1 may come segmented (punctuated) like $(t; x_{11}, x_{12}, \ldots, x_{1m}; x_{21}, \ldots, x_{2m}; \ldots x_{n1} \ldots x_{nm}; u)$, with t interpreted (by us) as time, x_{ij} as the jth of m attributes which are grouped into the ith of n groups and u is the utility to L_1 of the state corresponding to this input. For example, the values of x_{i1} may be the results of a position measurement, x_{i2} hardness, x_{i3} light intensity. A time sequence, for $m = 3$, $n = 4$ like:

$$(0; 1, h, d; 2, h, d; 3, x, x; 4, x, x), (1; 1, x, x; 2, h, d; 3, h, d; 4, x, x),$$
$$(2; 1, x, x; 2, x, x; 3, h, d; 4, h, d)$$

is hypothesized by L_1 to be an object characterized by $x_{i2} = x_{i+1,2} = h$, $x_{i3} = x_{i+1,3} = d$ for some i (interpreted by us a 2-celled hard and dark object) which is moving to the right across a background characterized by x with the value of x_{i1} giving the position as the correlator of the other measurements in that group. Henceforth, L_1 would assign a name, say c, to this object which is adjoined to the list of individual constants. Also, the variables x_{11}, x_{21}, x_{31}, x_{41} are all combined into a predicate $p(c, t)$ interpreted (by us) as the position of any object c at time t; similarly, x_{21}, x_{22}, x_{23}, x_{24}, are combined to form the hardness predicate, and so on. These predicates are adjoined to the list of predicate symbols.

We shall henceforth regard the outputs of all learners that are part of the total environment as part of L_1's input. Suppose that L_1 has formed an hypothesis about the existence of an object it named 1, the position of which at time t is given by x_1. Suppose next that L_1 forms an hypothesis with high plausibility, that it controls x_1. It now forms a new 1-place predicate, 'is mine' and applies it to 1. In the same way, if L_1 has hypothesized the existence of an object it named 2, the position of which at time t is given by x_2, and that variable α_2 controls x_2 to a large extent, then L_1 forms the new 2-place predicate 'belongs to' and forms '2 belongs to α_2'. Using the symmetry between α_1, x_1 and α_2, x_2, L_1 then applies 'belongs to' to $(1, \alpha_1)$ and identifies

'1 belongs to α_1' with '1 is mine.' Through a transformation and a thesaurus in the verbal language, α_1 is, in the above context, replaced by 'me'.

By means of rules and transformations such as those introduced by Kochen (1969a), verbs like 'move' of the verbal language are used. Thus, L_1 forms hypotheses like '1 moves from 3 at time 0 to 4 at time 1'. Using the hypothesis, 'α_1 controls 1', L_1 can form: '1 is moved from 3 at time 0 to 4 at time 1 by α_1'. At this point, L_1 can substitute 'me' for α_1. In time, if the value of x which occurs predominantly in '1 is moved from A to B by x' is α_1 or 'me', and there is no y for which there are both hypotheses 'y belongs to me' and '1 belongs to y', then 1 is renamed 'I'. A simple transformation takes '1 is moved from A to B by x' to 'x moves I from A to B', which is now 'me moves I from A to B'. A further transformation takes this into 'I move myself from A to B'.

From enough instances like the above for various A and B, the hypothesis $(\exists u)(\exists v)$ 'I move myself from u to v' is formed, and this is transformed into 'I can move'. When L_1 selects an action, it is based on a plan derived from a stored hypothesis like: '$(A t)(A s^*)(A x_2)$ISE$(t, s^*, 3, x_2, 512)$' and a current input of $(4, 15, 2, 8, 0)$. Thus, L_1 can see a path from $(4, (15, 2, 8))$ to $(5, s)$ where s is in a set of 'goal'-states characterized by $x_1 = 3$. Now L_1 forms the hypothesis corresponding to 'I *intend* to move myself from $x_1 = 2$ at time 4 to $x_1 = 3$ at time 5'.

A comprehender is characterized by a third basic predicate in addition to ISE and IDO. This is ITH(h, t). This is true at time t' if $t \leqslant t'$ and $h \in$ CR$_1$ (L, t') and false if $t \leqslant t'$ and $h \notin$ CR$_1(L, t')$ or $t > t'$; it is neither true nor false otherwise. There are two separate algorithms: one generates and labels hypotheses at times determined by the current input and L_1's prior state; the other forms the ITH(h, t) hypotheses, also at times determined by the current input and L_1's prior state, and its output variable (which takes ITH(h, t) as values) partially controls the variable taking values h which, in turn, controls α_1.

In time, L_1 can form hypotheses corresponding to: ITH$(h$ because $h', t)$, for instance $h =$ '$x_2 = 5$ at $t = 4$', $h' =$ '$\alpha_2 = 3$ at $t = 3$'. Now h can itself contain sentences involving the predicate ITH. If L_1 has many hypotheses about object 2 which have formal similarities with the hypotheses L_1 has about itself – such as 'α_2 controls x_2' – then L_1 forms hypotheses corresponding to 'if I were 2, then h' where h is an hypothesis. L_1 can form ITH(h, t), where $h =$ '2 forms ITH(h', t')'. In particular we can get:

(1) 'I think that I think. . . .'

(2) 'I think that 2 thinks that I think . . .'

(3) 'I think that 2 thinks I will answer his question'.

(4) 'I think that 2 thinks he intends to answer my question'.

For L_1 to ask a whether-question (*see* Harrah 1963) is for L_1 to think (know) that L_1 does not know the truth or falsity of an hypothesis and to communicate to L_2, through the verbal language, both L_1's intention to obtain an answer from L_2 and L_1's intention to help L_2 increase his utility. This is a precise, logically well-structured question. Less well-structured questions are requests by L_1 for hypotheses from 2 which contain specified symbols. Questions involve the ITH predicate: they reflect awareness of knowledge and its lack. Therein lies understanding.

To comprehend an utterance in the verbal language, be it a question, an answer, an assertion, and so on, is to hypothesize some intention by its source. 'A linguistic utterance conventionally betokens intention', said MacKay (1956); (*see also* Kochen 1961). An utterance received by L_1 is decoded and causes L_1 to form hypotheses about both its originator and its contents. The originator can be L_1 itself, using a communication channel like a 'scratch-pad' memory. The advantage of this kind of 'verbalization' of thinking is the possible aid it can be in forming new combinations of predicates to form new ones. This 'shaking up' process is the essence of cognition and essential for comprehension.

WISDOM

Wisdom goes beyond comprehension as much as comprehension transcends knowledge. It begins with information processing, from which it is three levels removed. Knowledge acquisition and utilization is one level removed, and consists of the formation and use of hypotheses – that is, growth of the representation, within an unchanged system of representation – that abstract from input information. This growth process attains stability as the hypotheses increase in credibility, fill up available memory, and all the options for effective action that they imply become exhausted. The learner becomes saturated with a wealth of knowledge – interpreted data – though these may be isolated and incoherent.

Comprehension is one level above knowledge acquisition and utilization. It consists of the formation of new predicates, concepts, and the modification of the representation system, particularly toward use of the ITH predicate, the use of 'intention', second-order hypotheses about capabilities and self-reference, the ability to synthesize and to ask questions. If the acquisition of knowledge may cease to maintain stability because of contradictions in the representation, it shifts to another level of stability as governed by the stable underlying system of representation. The growth process underlying comprehension attains stability as the set of newly added predicates and concepts converges. It is this stability which renders the learner somewhat insensitive to unstabilizing rifts and crises at the knowledge level.

But there may be rifts and crises which lead to instability at the comprehension level, too. Adjustment to these can also occur. It is governed by stability at the wisdom level. This is the level of action as it relates to utility or survival value. Permanent instabilities at this level are irreversible: they terminate the learner's existence.

A comprehender displays wisdom when it fully realizes its capabilities for intelligent action. It takes an optimal, a near-optimal or a limit-optimal path whenever possible, but that is a property to be proved, not a definition. The mere capability of forming and picking hypotheses at any time and selecting actions is no guarantee that it *will* be done and done at the most opportune time, even if it does not violate constraints on memory and processing time. What additional properties must a comprehender have so that it utilizes these potentials appropriately?

Here we begin to borrow from such psychological notions as attention, motivation, feeling and priorities. What is to determine when the hypothesis-formation program should be active? Could or should it be active all the time? Simultaneously with input information processing, action-selection, or alternately? Or only when directed by a supervisory conductor? If a conductor directs which algorithm is to act when, he does not do so according to a score: here the suggestive parallel with an orchestra breaks down; instead, he has to compose the score as his interpretation of the unfolding environment requires. This involves a very high-level hypothesis-formation capacity, akin to planning or forming broad-gauge intentions. Being too specific or short-range in this planning activity is as valueless as being too vague or long-range. Here lies the essence of wisdom: interpreting the environment with a point of view that reflects optimal judgment about its most essential laws and regularities, with appropriate checks and balances among all the options for action, communication, and thought. This is the main supervisory algorithm that is built in, and which is invariant.

For example, suppose that the set of primitives and concepts – that is, the representation system – of a comprehender has stabilized, but that the utilities accruing to the learner are decreasing to below survival values. This may happen even if the system of representation is adequate, but suppose that it isn't for the environment as that is revealing itself. The learner is wise if there is in such a circumstance an emergency survival algorithm that he can switch to, which allows him the time for replacing the current system of representation by one which is, hopefully, more adaptive to the environment. Of course, for learners of finite life-time, the time to adapt is greatly speeded up and the likelihood of survival of at least one learner is greatly increased.

The change from a maladaptive representation *system* to a better one is far more revolutionary – and takes far longer – than the change from a maladaptive *representation* to a better one. That, in turn, is more revolutionary – and takes longer – than the formation of hypotheses; even this takes long compared with the rate at which information is acquired.

The basic supervisory algorithm which specifies the wise learner will, of course, be effective only in a certain class of environments. Hopefully it is a large class. How do we know if we have designed an appropriate basic algorithm? We seek a mapping which tells us the kind of basic algorithm appropriate for a class of environments. If we can characterize our earthly environment, we may be able to specify the kind of learning automata which are appropriate here.

MATHEMATICAL ANALYSIS OF COGNITIVE LEARNING

Our aim is to state, and find constructive proofs for, existence and other theorems about cognitive learners. We would like to prove that there exist automata which can represent their environment in somewhat the way a formal mathematical theory based on predicate calculus represents its models. We would like to show that if an automaton can represent, then it can take increasingly effective actions.

We must first make the basic notions mathematically precise. We do this with the help of mathematical logic and some ideas from the theory of functions of a real variable. We also derive from modern high-level programming languages (SNOBOL4) [Griswald, Poage and Polonsky (1968)] a tremendous source of ideas, and find these leading to new mathematics which, in turn, seems to suggest more sophisticated ways of using the logical powers inherent in the programming language. A few notions of automata theory and utility theory have also had their influence on our formulation.

As far as we know, there is no *directly* relevant prior work on this question. Some of the more indirectly related studies were discussed earlier. Indeed, before we can elaborate on the connection to the literature, we must state our key problems mathematically so that they are neither trivial nor impossible. To do this is a considerable advance in this field, which is difficult precisely because it is so hard to formulate centrally significant yet solvable problems.

We shall have to refer, in this paper, to the use of at least four different languages. The first is the mathematical English in which this entire paper is written; it is the language that we – the analysts and designers of the learning automata we are concerned with – are using to communicate with you, the reader. Let us call it $\mathscr{L}_e$. Our learners, which we label L_1, L_2, . . . are part of a total environment which we shall describe in our language $\mathscr{L}_e$. Our claims and proofs are all in $\mathscr{L}_e$. The other three languages we refer to next are all described in $\mathscr{L}_e$.

The first of these three is a high-level programming language, SNOBOL4, which we shall denote more generally by $\mathscr{L}_p$. The basic algorithm that specifies L_1, L_2, . . ., modifies algorithms for selecting actions, forming hypotheses, and so on, is stated in $\mathscr{L}_p$. *Our interpretation* of this is in $\mathscr{L}_e$, but L_1, L_2, . . . *are* programs in $\mathscr{L}_p$.

The second language is the set of all possible hypotheses that L_1, L_2, . . . can form and store. These are actually SNOBOL statements, too, but they form a sublanguage of $\mathscr{L}_p$. Let us call it $\mathscr{L}_h$. It is a modified predicate calculus.

The third language is $\mathscr{L}_v$, which may be a subset of $\mathscr{L}_p$, or of $\mathscr{L}_e$. Its sentences are used for communication between L_i and L_j, for all i, j. They represent sentences of a conventionalized, 'public', 'verbal' language, into which L_i translates its hypotheses, plans, requests, questions, and so on, and from which it translates sentences into hypotheses of the internal conceptual (logical) representation.

The theorems we seek to prove, then, are about algorithms L_1, L_2, . . . which we must construct and describe. In one type of theorem, the hypotheses of the theorem correspond to properties these algorithms are designed – by us – to have; the conclusions of the theorem correspond to implied properties of the algorithm we did not know it had, and which correspond to 'emergent' learning abilities. By running the SNOBOL4 programs that implement the algorithms, we let the computer help us derive these implications.

'TASK-GENERATING' ENVIRONMENTS

Definition 1. An *autonomous environment*, $E = \{S, f, s_0\}$, is a set of states S and a transition function f from S into itself; s_0 is a distinguished state of S, interpreted as the initial state.

We interpret $f(s)$ as the 'next' state after s, and call $s \rightarrow f(s)$ a state-transition. We take *time* to be defined by state transitions in some part of the environment – the motion of stars, pendulums, biological clocks and so on, for the real world. We don't know in any absolute sense if the 'duration' between the onset of s and the onset of $f(s)$ is exactly the same as the 'duration' between the onset of $f(s)$ and the onset of $f(f(s))$, but we shall assume it as a property of S and f. What matters is that we can apply to S the idea of a 'Dedekind cut', partitioning S into S_b and S_a such that for any $s \in S_b$ and $s' \in S_a$, there is some integer n, $n = 1, 2, 3, \ldots$ such that $s' = f^{(n)}(s)$. Here $f^{(1)}(s) = f(s)$, $f^{(2)}(s) = f(f(s))$ and $f^{(n+1)}(s) = f(f^{(n)}(s))$. We interpret any state of S_a to occur *after* any state of S_b (before), and any partition corresponds to an epoch, an instant of time.

In what follows, we take time to be characterized by a natural number t, $t = 0, 1, 2, \ldots$, with $t = 0$ denoting the beginning. Let $s(t)$ denote the state at time t, with $s(0)$ the initial state. Then $s(t+1) = f(s(t))$.

Definition 2. An autonomous environment is *simply decomposable* if S is a Cartesian product, $S = S_1 \times S_2 \times \ldots \times S_n$, for n sets $S_1, S_2, \ldots, S_n$, $n \geqslant 2$, such that

$$(s_1', \ldots, s_n') = (f_1(s_1, \ldots, s_n), f_2(s_1, \ldots, s_n), \ldots, f_n(s_1, \ldots, s_n)),$$

and such that the S_i are algebraically structured (fields, ordered sets, groups, for example).

For example, we may interpret S_1 as the range of t, $0, 1, 2, \ldots$, which we henceforth denote by N; S_2 and S_3 as orthogonal spatial coordinates (x and y axes) for a plane with S, $S_2 = S_3 = N$ also; we could interpret S_4, the field of reals, as a set of light intensities, S_5, a totally ordered set, as a set of hardness values, S_6, a group, as a set of chemical compositions, and so on. The state of E is then a vector, say, $s = (s_1, s_2, s_3, s_4, s_5, s_6)$. A state-vector value like (5, 2, 3, tr, dh, C) might be interpreted as 'At time 5, in position (2, 3) of a grid, a light-intensity meter records transparency, a hardness tester reports diamond hardness, and a chemical analyzer registers carbon'. But this is only a partial state description. A more complete one, with the above interpretation, is a state vector with infinitely many components:

$$s = (5; (0, 0), \text{light, gas, air}: (0, 1), \text{light, gas, air}: (1, 0), \ldots).$$

In other words, we specify the readings of our three meters at every point of the plane *at time 5*, the readings at each point being separated by colons.

In general, it is not possible to decompose environments so *simply* into Cartesian products of independent sets; there is coupling. We shall not go into this any further.

Definition 3. A *controllable environment* (in contrast to an autonomous one), $E = \{S, f, A, s_0\}$ is a set of states and a transition function f from $S \times A$ into S.

Interpret A as an N-dimensional vector space and let a be any N-component vector of A. Component a_i represents the outputs of automaton (or program) L_i, $i = 1, \ldots, N$. Here, N is the number of learners. Thus,

T

$$s' = f(s, a_1, \ldots, a_N) \tag{4}$$

represents a state transition. The outputs of $L_1, \ldots, L_N$ are inputs to E. We call s' successive to s if there exist $a_1, \ldots, a_N$ such that eq. (4) holds.

Definition 4. A *path* is any sequence of successive states. Two paths are *identical in the limit* if there is some time t after which the two sequences of successive states is the same for both. Two paths are *essentially different* if they are not identical in the limit. A path is *original* if the first state is the initial state; otherwise it is a *recent* path.

Theorem 1. If an autonomous environment is finite, then the number of essentially different paths is finite.

Theorem 2. If an autonomous environment has a denumerable set of states, the number of essentially different paths is non-denumerable.

Definition 5. A path with states s, s', s'', $\ldots$, is *completely controlled by L_1* if there is a sequence of L_1's outputs, a_1, $a_1' \ldots$, such that $s' = f(s, a_1, \ldots, a_N)$ is uniquely specified by a_1, $s'' = f(f(s, a_1, \ldots, a_N))$ is uniquely specified by a_1, and so on. An incompletely controlled path is called *uncertain* for L_1.

Definition 6. A *task-generating* environment, $\{S, f, A, V, s_0\}$, is a controllable environment with a partial ordering on $S \times A$ such that any two elements have a least upper bound. ($\{S \times A, V\}$ is an upper semi-lattice). We shall call a task-generating environment (*tge*) *path-independent* (*pitge*) if the partial ordering is only a subset of $S \times S$. We shall call a *tge* one with a *value-function* (*tgev*) if V is the set of reals and there is a function v from $S \times A$ to V. (In what follows, V is used in place of both v and u.)

We interpret the partial ordering for a *pitge*, say for $(s, s') \in V$ or $s V s'$, to mean that state s' is not preferred to state s. In general, V is an N-tuple, $\{V_1, \ldots, V_N\}$, and we have N different partial orderings or value functions Thus, for a *pitge* $\{S, f, A, V_i, s_0\}$ we interpret $s V_i s'$ to mean that L_i does not prefer s' to s; or if it is a *pitgev*, then $v_i(s)$ is the utility (a real number) of state s for L_i. A state s is a *task-state* for L_i (synonymously, represents an opportunity, problem) if there is a path from state s to s' which is completely controlled by L_i and $v_i(s') \geqslant v_i(s)$. It is a one-step task if there is some a_i such that $s' = f(s, a_1, \ldots, a_N)$. Though $V_1, V_2, \ldots, V_N$ are partial orderings, there may not exist a partial ordering V, such that $s V s'$ holds if and only if $s V_i s'$ for all s, s' and all $i = 1, \ldots, N$. We assume that this condition holds. Marschak (1955) has studied this in developing a theory of teams.

Definition 7. A *valued path* for L_i is a sequence of quadruples: (t, s, a_i, v_i), $(t+1, s', a_i', v_i')$, $(t+2, s'', a_i'', v_i'')$, $\ldots$ where $s' = f(s, a)$ and $v_i' = v_i(s', a_i)$, $s' = f(s', a_i')$, etc. The *value of the path* to L_i is a measure of the set of all states along the path, say $v(s)+v(s', a_i)+v(s'', a_i')+\ldots$. We denote a valued path from (t_1, s_1) to time (t_2, s_2) by $\Pi(t_1, t_2)$, and its value by $v(t, \Pi(t_1, t_2))$.

Definition 8. A valued path $\Pi(t_1, t_2)$ is *optimal* at t_2 if its value is equal to $u^*(t_2)$, the least upper bound over all possible paths from $t=0$ to t_2.

Definition 9. A path $\Pi(t_0, t)$ is ϵ-*optimal* at t if $u^*(t)-v(t, \Pi(t_0, t))<\epsilon$.

Definition 10. A task-generating environment $\{S, f, A_i, v_i, s_0)$, where s_0 is the initial state, is *completely solvable by* L_i, if for any path $\Pi_i(t_0, t)$ that L_i can take, and for any real $\epsilon>0$, there are infinitely many $t', t'>t$, such that for each t' there is a path $\Pi_i'(t, t')$ that L_i can take which is ϵ-optimal at t'.

Definition 11. A path for L_i, $\Pi_i(t_0, t)$ is *limit-optimal* for L_i if, for any $\epsilon>0$, there is some t_0 and some t, $t>t_0$, such that $\Pi_i(t_0, t)$ is ϵ-optimal at t and there is an original path $\Pi_i(0, t_0)$.

Theorem 3. An environment is completely solvable for L_i if and only if every path has a limit-optimal extension.

Theorem 4. If $\underset{\Pi \text{ a path in } E}{\text{Sup}} \{V_i(\Pi)\}<\infty$, then E is completely solvable for L_i.

Definition 12. The *limit value ratio of a path*, Π, in E from (t_0, s_0) to (t_1, s_1) at time t_0 is:

$$\text{LVR}(\Pi, t_0)=\lim_{t \to \infty} \sup(V_{t_0}^t(\Pi)/\text{Max } V_{t_0}^t(R))$$

where R ranges over all paths in an environment which extends at t_0 the path from $(0, s)$ to (t_0, s_0) into the path Π such that $s_0=\Pi(t_0)$ and the transition function of the extended environment f', is $f'(t, s, a)=f(t_0+t, s, a)$.

Example 1. Let the action repertoire be $\{0, 1\}=A$, $a \epsilon A$, and the environment, $S=\{0, 1\}$ with the initial state 0. Suppose $f(t, s, a)=a$ for all s, t, a; $v(s)=s$. A possible sequence or path is:

$$0, 1, 0, 1, 1, 0, 1, 1, 1, 0, 1, 1, 1, 1, \ldots$$

This is not limit optimal, but has LVR$=1$.

Example 2. Let S be the rationals with initial state 0, and

$$f(t, s, a)=\begin{cases} 2^{-t} \text{ if } a=1 \\ 4^{-t} \text{ if } a=0 \end{cases} \quad A=\{0, 1\}, \quad v(s)=s.$$

The sequence $1/4, 1/16, 1/64, \ldots$ is limit optimal but does not have LVR$=1$.

Example 3. Let $A=\{0, 1\}$ and let S be the set of all sequences of 0s and 1s; $s_0=1$.

$f(t, s, a)=s$ contatenated with a.

Let $v(s)$ be the sum of the 1s in s.

The path $s=1\,0\,1\,1\,0\,1\,1\,1\,0\,1\,1\,1\,1$ ... is not limit optimal, but LVR$=1$ at each t_0.

Example 4. As above, except $v(s) = v(a_1, a_2, a_3 \ldots) = \sum\limits_{a_i=1} 2^{-i}$, $s_0 = 0$.

The path 0 1 0 1 0 1 0 1 . . . is limit optimal but has LVR $= 1/3$ (*see* figure 2).

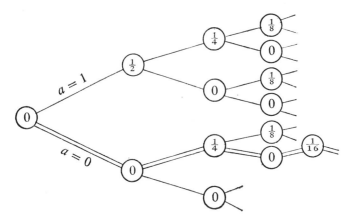

Figure 2

Theorem 5. If $\underset{\text{all } \Pi}{\text{Sup}} v(\Pi) < \infty$ then LVR$(\Pi) = 1$ implies that Π is limit optimal.

Theorem 6. If, for some $\alpha > 0$ and all $k > 0$, $V_t^{t+k}(\Pi) > \alpha$, then if Π is limit optimal, LVR$(\Pi) = 1$.

REPRESENTATIONS

Definition 1. By an *information processor*, $L_1(ip)$ we mean an algorithm (automaton, program) which computes the values of a computable function $g: \mathcal{N} \times S \times A \rightarrow A_1$, where A_1 is a set, interpreted as $L_1(ip)$'s action-repertoire, and $A = A_1 \times A_2 \times \ldots$, and time $= t \in N$. Thus, the action selected by L_1 at time $t + 1$ is: $a_1(t + 1) = g_1(t, s, a)$, $a = (a_1, a_2, \ldots)$.

Definition 2. A *system of representation* is the triple $\{G, h, D\}$, where G denotes the syntax of a formal logical system, D a domain of discourse and h an assignment of symbols in the formal language $\mathcal{L}(G)$ generated by G to elements or subsets of D.

Thus, G is specified by specifying the names of individual constants, variable-names, function-symbols, predicate names, logical symbols like ⌐ (for negation), ⇒ (for implication), A(universal quantifier), ∃ (existential quantifier), plus rules of formation to generate well-formed formulas or propositions, at least in first-order predicate calculus. We take D to be $S \times A \times V$, where $S = S_1 \times S_2 \times S_3 \times \ldots \times S_n$, $A = A_1 \times A_2 \times \ldots \times A_N$, $V = V_1 \times V_2 \times \ldots \times V_N$. Here $S_1 = \mathcal{N}$ and denotes time; S_2 will denote a set of object labels, say *1, 2, 3, . . ., N, N+1, N+2, . . . N+M*: $S_3 = \mathcal{N}$

denotes the x-coordinates of object 1 and $S_4 = \mathcal{N}$ its y-coordinates, etc. $n = 2 + 2(N + M)$. The individual constants of G are $L_1, L_2, \ldots, L_{N+M}$ and correspond to $1, 2, \ldots N + M$. The variable x_1 of G ranges over S_3 and y_1 over S_4. The usual functions and predicates of first-order arithmetic are interpreted in the S_i; for instance '$x_1 > x_2$' iff $(x_1, x_2) \in \{(1, 0), (2, 0) \ldots (2, 1), (3, 2), \ldots\} \subset S_3 \times S_3$. This describes an environment of $N + M$ objects in the plane, of which N are learners. In addition to those of first-order arithmetic, we have the following special predicates:

IDO(t, a_i): true at t_0 if $t \leqslant t_0$ and L_i selected action a_i at time t;
false at t_0 if $t \leqslant t_0$ and L_i did not select action a_i at time t, or $a_i \notin A_i$;
otherwise neither true nor false.

ISE(t, s, a): true at t_0 if $t \leqslant t_0$ and $(t, s, a) \in$ CS for some a;
false at t_0 if either $t \leqslant t_0$ and $(t, s, a) \notin$ CS for some a, or $s \notin S$ for any a;
otherwise neither true nor false.

ILK(t, s, a, v_i): true at t_0 if v_i is the value to L_i of (s, a) at $t \leqslant t_0$;
false at t_0 if $t \leqslant t_0$ and $v_i(s, a) \neq v_i$ or $v_i(s, a) \notin V_i$;
otherwise, neither true or false.

Here CS is the set of all (t, s), $0 \leqslant t \leqslant t_0$, with s any state in a path taken by L_i from $t = 0$ to $t = t_0$.

Definition 3. Let h be a proposition in $\mathscr{L}(G)$. The *credibility* (or *weight of evidence, degree of belief, plausibility*) of h at time t is a real number in $[0, 1]$, $w(t, h)$, such that

(1) $w(t_1, h) > w(t_0, h)$ if h is true at t for some t, $t_0 < t < t_1$ and false at no t between t_0 and t_1.

(2) $w(t, h) > w(t, h')$ if $c(h, t) > c(h', t)$ and if h and h' designate sets that are in $1 - 1$ correspondence where $c(h, t)$ is the number of times h was found true prior to t or $\neg h$ was found false prior to t.

Definition 4. By an hypothesis we mean $(h, w(t, h))$, where $h \in \mathscr{L}(G)$, and $w(t, h)$ is its credibility.

Definition 5. A store of hypotheses, CR$_i$, is called L_i's *representation*.

Definition 6. L_i *learns* if the limit value ratio of its action selection scheme increases with time.

ACTION-SELECTION

Definition 1. An information-processor $L_i(kp)$ is a *knowledge-processor* $(kp)_i$ if it has a representation, CR$_i$, and $g_i(t, s, a)$ depends on CR$_i$.

Definition 2. L_i *completely controls* L_j if $x_j' = f_{xj}(s, a)$ and $y_j' = f_{yj}(s, a)$ depend only on a_i.

Definition 3. By the *total environment* we mean $\{S \times \prod_{i=1}^{N} \text{CR}_i \times A, f \times \prod_{i=1}^{N} L_i, s_0\}$.

Here, the set of internal representations corresponding to the learners' representations is adjoined to S, as is A, and the programs $L_1, \ldots, L_N$ become part of the transition function. The total environment is autonomous. The learners are part of it.

Theorem. There are paths Π' over S for a total environment with $N+1$ learners that do not exist for a total environment with N learners, for all N, and there exist team value functions, $v_1, \ldots, v_{N+1}$ such that $\text{LVR}(\Pi')$ is greater than the limit value ratio for any path in a total environment with N learners.

PLANS AND PROBLEMS

The above represents the state of theoretical developments at the time of writing. A cognitive learner, say L_i, is a program. It functions basically as a supervisor of at least five other programs or subroutines:

(1) Input of information from the environment

(2) Selection of actions, using CR_i

(3) Revising of weights assigned to hypotheses in CR_i and modification of these

(4) Formation of new hypotheses

(5) Formation of new predicates as compounds of existing ones.

We prove, partly with help of the SNOBOL programs described in the next lecture, that:

(1) If L_i has in CR_i the same sentences that can generate the environment, then under certain conditions for revising and selecting hypotheses, L_i will select paths with increasing limit value ratios.

(2) If L_i and L_j can communicate, there exist paths and value functions which give both L_i and L_j a higher limit value ratio than any path attainable by L_i or L_j without communication.

(3) If L_i and L_j have different predicates, and L_i's predicates approximate their common environment more closely than those of L_j, then there is a path for L_i with a higher LVR than that of any path of L_j.

(4) Under certain conditions on bounds of memory for storage of predicates and hypotheses, the set of predicates converges to a stable set.

Certain statements in the basic supervisory program L_i can also be modified. This changes L_i far more drastically than does a change in the program statements that constitute the hypotheses stored in CR_i. Moreover, such deep changes can be effected by a part of L_i itself. And L_i forms hypotheses referring to L_i itself, describing such changes as it made upon itself. In this way, the term 'self' or 'me' of the verbal public language can be given meaning.

Our general strategy stemmed from curiosity about the possibility of computer comprehension of language. Why do we have language? Presumably, through linguistic communication, learners can solve problems requiring cooperative, coordinated activities, that are unattainable without communication. There are tasks of this kind that thus lead the learners to attain higher levels of utility. But linguistic communication requires thinking or cognitive learning. And cognitive learning requires the use and reorganization of information to form, revise and use hypotheses.

To pursue this strategy we plan to:

(1) Show how to select actions on the basis of credibility and utility measures assigned to stored hypotheses.

(2) Incorporate k-step look-ahead in action selection, which allows for the possibility of sacrifice. This may be tried on chess if enough hypotheses can be 'taught' – that is, fed in – to make a good chess-player.

(3) Test and modify stored hypotheses on the basis of environmental evidence. Real environments described in published literature may be used.

(4) Form compound and second-order hypotheses.

(5) Have two learners communicate in a common verbal public language.

(6) Use the verbal public language for a learner to 'communicate' with himself to enhance the formation of new hypotheses and predicates.

(7) Investigate relations among hypotheses, weighting functions, action selection procedures, hypothesis selection procedures, actions and values in terms of limitations on memory and processing speed.

(8) Derive a relation between the number of hypotheses examined before selecting an action and the number of steps looked ahead.

(9) Conditions for the convergence of sets of hypotheses, CR_i.

(10) Investigate cognitive deviations, such as delusions, resulting from changes in hypothesis formation, test or weight-function computation.

(11) Investigate the relative merits of narrow specialization v. well roundedness in a learner.

These are but a few of the questions which can now be attacked with relative ease that could not have been meaningfully posed before this study.

THE CONSTRUCTION AND USE OF COMPUTER PROGRAMS

INTRODUCTION

Cognitive learning is generally viewed by behavioral and life scientists as a complex or higher-order function of the human nervous system. As information scientists, we view cognitive learning as a mathematical process, the description of which requires far too many variables and relations among them to be amenable to analysis by classical mathematics. Wherever possible, we seek to formulate problems in terms of appropriate mathematical concepts, and we try to apply the most powerful and relevant mathematical techniques known to us to derive significant logical consequences (theorems). We feel strongly, however, that the study of cognitive learning processes – both theoretical and experimental – can lead to genuinely *new* mathematics, give mathematics in this decade an impetus of the kind which so often in its history has advanced it by great leaps. More specifically, we believe that the germ of these new mathematical concepts and techniques lies in the use of higher-level computer programming languages like SNOBOL (Griswold, Poage and Polonsky 1968).

The use of such languages has radically changed our conception of problem-solving (O'Connell *et al.* 1969). We need merely present the problems to a computer in a sufficiently precise way regarding the general strategy for deriving the needed result as ouptut from given inputs or previously stored data, and rely on the computer to work out the details. Indeed, two of the foremost creative contemporary mathematicians (Kac and Ulam 1969) are beginning to ask if computers are not more than merely tools for mathematical inquiry. It is entirely possible that modern mathematics will take a turn toward incorporating the concepts of computers – particularly high-level languages – as an essential part of its repertoire. Indeed, a programmed algorithm is beginning to be recognized as much an achievement as a proof in analysis.

In the context of cognitive learning processes, computer programs written in SNOBOL are used as constructive proofs of the main theorems we wish to prove: That there exist automata capable of modifying their own systems of representation and representations, and of increasingly effective action. The description of the basic algorithms in SNOBOL allows us far greater latitude and vastly more options for expressing all the ideas we can imagine and explore for logical implications than could ordinary mathematics. This has been demonstrated in an increasing number of publications, and in an even larger and more rapidly increasing number of unpublished operational programs in SNOBOL (*see* Shapiro 1969) and other languages like it (Ash and Sibley 1968).

There are still some serious logical problems about what claims can be validly made on the basis of a computer program, in what language these claims should be presented as proof (Michie 1966). A program by itself can hardly be viewed as a theory. Nor do we intend any of our programs to be interpreted as *simulating* cognitive learning because this suggests that they simulate an analogous process in humans. This they almost certainly would not, even if we knew enough about human cognitive learning on which to base such an analogy.

Designing and implementing a complete algorithm for an overall and general cognitive learning process in all the sophistication we can imagine – that is, a comprehender displaying wisdom – is a difficult task with which we have little experience. We therefore split the task into subtasks which are simpler to grasp as total units. It is such fragments that we present here. Many more pieces have yet to be constructed. Each piece, as presented here, is the end-result of numerous revisions. All the pieces have yet to be fitted together into a total operational package, but it is now clear how to do that.

DECOMPOSITION INTO SEPARABLE PROBLEMS

We have not yet designed, in sufficient detail to specify programming, the algorithm for a comprehender. But we have designed the algorithm for a knowledge-processor – a cognitive learner or 'knower' (level 2) – and implemented into operational SNOBOL programs some easily separable component algorithms. An environment-generator program has been described previously (Uhr and Kochen 1969). Any environment generator produces at time t, $t = 0, 1, 2, \ldots$, an output of the form $(t, s, v_1 \ldots v_N)$, where s is a state-vector and v_i is the utility of this state for learner L_i, $i = 1, \ldots, N$. The input to learner L_i at time t is $(t, s, v_i, a_1 \ldots, a_N)$, where a_j is the action selected at time t by L_j, $j = 1 \ldots N$. (We assume that L_i always receives – actually recalls – his own action, and also the actions selected by none, some or all of the other learners who broadcast it or communicate directly to L_i). The output of learner L_i at time t is an action, a_i. This is based on stored hypotheses, but, these hypotheses are never part of output of the total cognitive learner. They are output of the hypothesis-formation subprograms and input to the action-selection subprograms.

Formation of Expressions (*SEQANAL*). This program is given a numerical sequence, like 1, 3, 5, 7, 9, as input. It generates one or more hypotheses as output, storing some in 'short-term memory' and some in 'long-term memory'. Long-term memory stores both the extension (the instances of a sequence) and the intension (an hypothesis) of sequences or subsequences which were previously tentatively identified. It is against these stored items that new input sequences are matched. The hypotheses of the programs listed in the next section are intended to describe specified properties of the lawful numerical input sequences, but, though this seems like an uninterestingly specialized program, the programming technique can be extended quite far toward generality. Specifically, the following routines are iteratively applied to the input sequences, to sequences of portions in the input sequences corresponding to subsequences and to the subsequences. Short-term memory holds the hypotheses as they are formed.

Periodicity detection. If an input sequence or subsequence has a repeating pattern, like 1, 2, 3, 1, 2, 3, this routine returns the pattern – 1, 2, 3 – plus the number of times this has been observed to repeat. If another program extracts a subsequence – such as elements in positions 1, 3, 5, 7, and so on, out of: 1, 1, 2, 2, 3, 3, 1, 4, 2, 5, 3, 6, 1, 7, 2, 8, 3, . . . – then this pattern will again be detected.

Application of differencing operator. If an input sequence $a_1, a_2, a_3, a_4, \ldots$ is received by this routine, the output sequence $b_1, b_2, b_3, \ldots$ with $b_i = a_{i+1} - a_i$ is produced. Thus, 1, 4, 9, 16, 25, 36, . . . results in 3, 5, 7, 9, ... This output may be fed back as input to this routine, to produce 2, 2, 2, . . . as output. This could now be fed as input to the periodicity detection routine. The result is expressed as a coded description corresponding to what was done and found: The difference operator was applied *twice* and periodicity detection as the result returned the pattern '*2*', with '*1, 4*' being recalled as the first two elements of the given sequence. Thus, the three italicized items are strung together as in HYP('2', '1, 4'). Optionally, we could include a fourth entry indicating the length of the trace of the input sequence. If that is not specified, the sequence is regarded as infinitely long. It can be generated from this coded description.

Scanning. This routine is applied before the two previously mentioned to check if a given input sequence has been seen and analyzed before.

Search for subsequences. This routine searches our input sequence for subsequences that match one of the patterns (traces of a sequence, used like a template) stored in a long-term memory. If there is a match, this routine returns the elements of the subsequences that matched and the positions in the input where the matches took place. Thus, if 1, 4, 9, 16, 25 were stored, and 1, 4, 9, 1, 16, 1, 25 were the input, then the sequence of positions that is returned is 1, 2, 3, 5, 7 (first five squares).

Weight function computation. This routine assigns a member to a pattern stored in long-term memory that matches an input sequence. This number is basically a count of the extent of the match, discounting the number of elements that would have been expected if the input sequence carried no information. This is useful when we seek to state hypotheses not about sequences but about sets – for example, that a particular sample of input numbers, such as 4, 1, 9, 25, . . . belongs to the *set* of squares. Then a sequence

like 3, 4, 2, 1, 5, 7, . . . carries no information: the hypothesis would correspond to the set of all numbers.

Subsequences extraction. This routine returns the values of a subsequence of
a given input sequence specified by the sequence of positions. Thus, if 1, 4,
9, 16, 25, . . . is the input sequence, and 1, 3, 5, . . . is specified, then 1, 9, 25,
. . . is returned.

All these routines combined could accept as input 1, 1, 1, 2, 4, 8, 3, 9,
27, . . ., and if it had in long-term memory hypotheses for 1, 4, 9, 16, . . .,
and 1, 8, 27, . . . and 1, 2, 3, 4, . . . it would form an hypothesis about how
they were meshed. It could also form the three hypotheses for storage in
long-term memory for its own use in deciphering the meshed sequence.

Hypothesis-formation (FORM'). This program updates its own long-term
memory. It accepts as input a triple (s, a, u), where s designates the current
state of E, a the learner's current action and u the utility of the current state.
A typical input is $s = (5, 5)$, $a = 0$, $u = 1$. The output is an hypothesis using
the predicates ISE, IDO, ILK. A typical output is AT(10) (AT) (AX) (AY)
ISE(T, X, Y) &IDO(T, 0) = ISE(T + 1, X + 1, Y − 1). Interpret this as 'After
10 inputs, like (5, 5), (0, 1), (6, 4) (0, 0), (7, 3) (0, 0), . . ., I hypothesize
that, for all time and any X, Y, whenever I see state (X, Y) and I select action
0, the next state will be (X + 1, Y − 1).' Another typical output is AT(10)
(AT) (AX) ISE(T, X, X) = ILK(T, 1). Interpret this as: 'Whenever I see a
two-component state in which both components are equal, its utility to me
is 1 − I like it.'

Note that 'FORM' actually incorporates many, but not all of the features
of 'SEQANAL'. In particular, it does not allow the iterative use of various
subroutines for searching. But this is easily remedied.

Action-selection ('ASP') This is a program in which a set of hypotheses
are stored. It may contain contradictory hypotheses. For convenience, H is
stored as two sets of SNOBOL statements, one set expressing possible environmental state changes, the other expressing possible changes in the utility to
the learner.

The input to the program is the change in the environmental state. The
output is a selected action that maximizes the expected value at the next
time, based on the assumption that each stored hypothesis actually represents the state-transition function.

For example, let H consist of the following hypothesis corresponding to
the state transition functions:

(1) $f(s, a) = s + a$
(2) $f(s, a) = s \cdot a$.

and the following hypotheses corresponding to utility functions:

(3) $s = 3 \Rightarrow u = 1$

(4) For all t, if $s = t^2$ then $u = v(t) = 20$.

If the set of possible actions available to the learner is $\{1, 2, 3,\}$, and if at time 1, $s = 2$, then the learner would select action 2, assuming both hypotheses (2) and (4) hold (are believed). Then $u = 20$. If the actions available to the learner were only $(1, 3)$, then it would select 1, assuming (1) and (3) hold.

The ASP program is in constant revision. At the time this was written, it selected actions in two modes. One mode, ACSEL, is a function which, if called, results in the selection of an action. The inputs are 'time', the number of action-hypotheses to be consulted (NAH), the number of value-hypotheses to be consulted (NVH), and the number of actions to be selected (NA). Assigned to each stored hypothesis is a current 'credibility' measure. Using these, an action-hypothesis and a value-hypothesis is selected, possibly repetitiously. With the help of these, an action is tentatively selected which is to maximize the expected value corresponding to the next state. The relevant action and value hypotheses are stored in CAH and CVH, and the values are assigned to vectors EXS and EXV (storing expected states and values). If the program fails to maximize v based on its hypotheses, it selects at random and returns.

The other mode, to which control is transferred if a certain string is empty, abandons probabilistic selection, and searches the entire set of hypotheses.

In the probabilistic mode, the probabilities are revised. In current versions of this program, expected utilities are taken into account.

A flow diagram of ASP is shown in figure 3.

SAMPLE OUTPUTS OF SELECTED PROGRAMS

SEQANAL. 'SEQUANAL' is a 194-statement SNOBOL program, with ten subroutines. The program which produced the printout shown in figure 4 is given fifteen terms of a sequence about which it is to form a description. *We* know the sequence as the following:

Every third term is an even number, starting with 2, the first term; starting with the second term, every third term is a square, in order; and $a_{3i} = 2i - 1$, $i = 1, 2, 3, \ldots$

At first, the program can do nothing, indicated by blanks in short and long-term memory. So we 'taught' it by giving it the simpler sequence 1, 3, 5, 7, 9, ... It correctly stores HYP(1, '2', '1', 5) in its short-term memory – we interpret this as: the first difference – or the difference operator, $a_{i+1} - a_i$ applied once, indicated by the first entry in HYP – is '2'. The first element

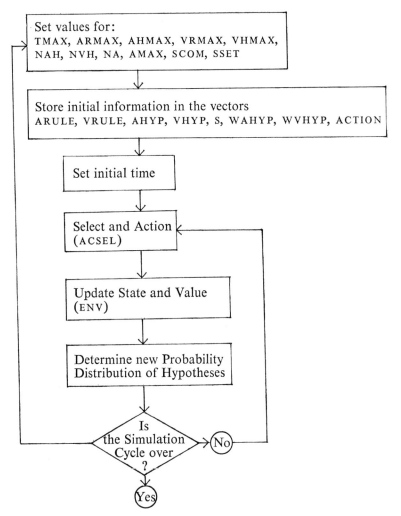

Figure 3. Flow diagram for 'ASP'

of the sequence is '1', indicated by the third entry in HYP. The fourth entry in HYP indicates the length of the input sequence. From this description the input sequence could be uniquely reconstructed. This intensional description is also stored in long-term memory, with weight 1, together with the corresponding extension.

The program is next taught by giving it 'LEARN: 2, 4, 6, 8, 10'. It forms an appropriate intension of this also. Long-term memory now holds descriptions of both the odd and the even numbers – up to five terms.

Next it 'learns' the squares as: "The second difference is '2', it starts with '1, 4' and is five terms long."

It now gets the original sequence again. It uses what it has learned by printing out two sequences, under 'short-term memory', side by side as shown in figure 4.

Figure 4

LEARN : 2,1,1,4,4,3,6,9,5,8,16,7,10,25,9,

SHORT TERM MEMORY

LONG TERM MEMORY

LEARN : 1,3,5,7,9,

SHORT TERM MEMORY
    HYP(1 , "2," , "1," , 5)

LONG TERM MEMORY
1,3,5,7,9,   HYP(1 , "2," , "1," , 5)   1

LEARN : 2,4,6,8,10,

SHORT TERM MEMORY
    HYP(1 , "2," , "2," , 5)

LONG TERM MEMORY
1,3,5,7,9,   HYP(1 , "2," , "1," , 5)   1
2,4,6,8,10,   HYP(1 , "2," , "2," , 5)   1

LEARN : 1,4,9,16,25,

SHORT TERM MEMORY
    HYP(2 , "2," , "1,4," , 5)

LONG TERM MEMORY
1,3,5,7,9,   HYP(1 , "2," , "1," , 5)   1
2,4,6,8,10,   HYP(1 , "2," , "2," , 5)   1
1,4,9,16,25,   HYP(2 , "2," , "1,4," , 5)   1

LEARN : 2,1,1,4,4,3,6,9,5,8,16,7,10,25,9,

SHORT TERM MEMORY
2,3,4,5,8,11,14,15,   1,1,4,4,9,16,25,9,

LONG TERM MEMORY
1,3,5,7,9,   HYP(1 , "2," , "1," , 5)   1

Figure 4—*continued*

2,4,6,8,10, HYP(1 , "2," , "2," , 5) 1
1,4,9,16,25, HYP(2 , "2," , "1,4," , 5) 1

LEARN : 3,6,9,12,15,

SHORT TERM MEMORY
 HYP(1 , "3," , "3," , 5)

LONG TERM MEMORY
1,3,5,7,9, HYP(1 , "2," , "1," , 5) 1
2,4,6,8,10, HYP(1 , "2," , "2," , 5) 1
1,4,9,16,25, HYP(2 , "2," , "1,4," , 5) 1
3,6,9,12,15, HYP(1 , "3," , "3," , 5) 1

LEARN : 1,4,7,10,13,

SHORT TERM MEMORY
 HYP(1 , "3," , "1," , 5)

LONG TERM MEMORY
1,3,5,7,9, HYP(1 , "2," , "1," , 5) 1
2,4,6,8,10, HYP(1 , "2," , "2," , 5) 1
1,4,9,16,25, HYP(2 , "2," , "1,4," , 5) 1
3,6,9,12,15, HYP(1 , "3," , "3," , 5) 1
1,4,7,10,13, HYP(1 , "3," , "1," , 5) 1

LEARN : 2,5,8,11,14,

SHORT TERM MEMORY
 HYP(1 , "3," , "2," , 5)

LONG TERM MEMORY
1,3,5,7,9, HYP(1 , "2," , "1," , 5) 1
2,4,6,8,10, HYP(1 , "2," , "2," , 5) 1
1,4,9,16,25, HYP(2 , "2," , "1,4," , 5) 1
3,6,9,12,15, HYP(1 , "3," , "3," , 5) 1
1,4,7,10,13, HYP(1 , "3," , "1," , 5) 1
2,5,8,11,14, HYP(1 , "3," , "2," , 5) 1

LEARN : 2,1,1,4,4,3,6,9,5,8,16,7,10,25,9,

Figure 4—*continued*

SHORT TERM MEMORY

HYP(1 , "3," , "3," , 5)	HYP(1 , "2," , "1," , 5)
HYP(1 , "3," , "1," , 5)	HYP(1 , "2," , "2," , 5)
HYP(1 , "3," , "2," , 5)	HYP(2 , "2," , "1,4," , 5)

LONG TERM MEMORY

1,3,5,7,9,	HYP(1 , "2," , "1," , 5)	3
2,4,6,8,10,	HYP(1 , "2," , "2," , 5)	3
1,4,9,16,25,	HYP(2 , "2," , "1,4," , 5)	3
3,6,9,12,15,	HYP(1 , "3," , "3," , 5)	1
1,4,7,10,13,	HYP(1 , "3," , "1," , 5)	1
2,5,8,11,14,	HYP(1 , "3," , "2," , 5)	1

The first sequence is one indicating positions: 2nd, 3rd, 4th, 5th, 8th, positions, and the second sequence gives corresponding values. The result is correct, but it is purely extensional and of little interest.

We then 'teach' it, as input, the multiples of three, followed by the multiples of three plus one and the multiples of three plus two. Finally, when we test it on the original sequence it analyzes it into three pairs of 'hypotheses'. We read the first (ten lines from the bottom in figure 4) as: 'In the positions that are multiples of three find the odd numbers.' The last (eight lines from bottom) says: 'In the positions whose first difference is three, starting with two – that is, 2, 5, 8, 11, . . . – find the subsequence of numbers whose second difference is two, starting with 1, 4 – that is, 1, 4, 9, 16, . . .'. Note that in our English paraphrase of these hypotheses, we did not mention the length of the sequences, though this appears on the printout. The program can suppress mention of length, in which case an infinite sequence is understood.

It may perhaps seem that we 'taught' the program too much of what we knew to be helpful in analyzing it. We could have taught it to form $a+bk$ (for example, $k=3$, $a=0, 1, 2, b=1, 2, 3, . . .$) with some better chosen examples, making the learning seem more impressive; similarly for odd and even numbers. Our point, however, is to show how the program can form expressions about subsequences using previously formed expressions about sequences.

The performance of this particular program is limited to the analysis of numerical sequences that can be processed with the difference and periodicity-detection operators. This includes polynomial functions, modulo k functions and exponentials. A number of other operators have been investigated, but not yet implemented in programs, and with the help of these many of the sequences of interest in numerical analysis can be dealt with. Another set of operators that deal with non-numerical sequences have also been investigated, and the program does not require major modification to incorporate these.

'FORM'. The results of a trial run of 'FORM' are shown next. Input is in the form of the 10×4 matrix shown below in table 1. Each row denotes the time. The first two columns are two components of the state vector: $s = (s_1, s_2)$, and can be any numbers. The third column is the learner's action,

TABLE 1

	s_1	s_2	a	u
$t=1$	02	00	01	00
$t=2$	04	04	00	01
$t=3$	06	04	01	00
$t=4$	08	08	01	01
$t=5$	10	12	00	-1
$t=6$	12	12	01	01
$t=7$	14	14	01	01
$t=8$	16	16	00	01
$t=9$	18	17	00	00
$t=10$	20	18	00	-1

TABLE 2

SHORT TERM MEMORY

ITH(10 , (T) (X) ISE(T,X,) & IDO(T,0) $\Rightarrow$ ISE(T $+1$,X $+2$,))	1	2	
ITH(10 , (T) (X) ISE(T,X,) & IDO(T,1) $\Rightarrow$ ISE(T $+1$,X $+2$,))	1	2	
ITH(8 , (T) (X) IN(T,SET4) & ISE(T, ,X) & IDO(T,0) $\Rightarrow$ ISE(T $+1$, ,X))	2	-1	
ITH(5 , (T) (X) IN(T,SET5) & ISE(T, ,X) & IDO(T,1) $\Rightarrow$ ISE(T $+1$, ,X $+4$))	2	-1	
ITH(9 , (T) (X) IN(T,SET6) & ISE(T,X,X $+2$) $\Rightarrow$ ILK(T,-1))	3	-1	
ITH(8 , (T) (X) IN(T,SET7) & ISE(T,X,X -2) $\Rightarrow$ ILK(T,0))	3	-1	
ITH(10 , (T) (X) ISE(T,X,X) $\Rightarrow$ ILK(T,1))	3	2	
ITH(4 , (T) (X) IN(T,SET8) & ISE(T,X,) & IDO(T,0) $\Rightarrow$ ISE(T $+1$, ,X))	4	-1	
ITH(10 , (T) (X) IN(X,SET1) & ISE(T, ,) & IDO(T,1) $\Rightarrow$ ISE(T $+1$, ,X))	4	2	
ITH(4 , (T) (X) IN(T,SET9) & ISE(T, ,X) & IDO(T,0) $\Rightarrow$ ISE(T $+1$,X $+2$,))	5	-1	
ITH(10 , (T) (X) IN(X,SET2) & ISE(T, ,) & IDO(T,1) $\Rightarrow$ ISE(T $+1$,X,))	5	2	
ITH(10 , (T) (X) IN(X,SET3) & ISE(T,X,))	6	2	

U

0 or 1. The fourth column is the learner's utility, 0, 1, or -1. Thus, at time $t=1$, the state is $(2, 0)$, which is valued 0 (neutral) by the learner, and the response is 1. This results in the next state $(4, 4)$ which is favorable to the learner, value 1. The response now is 0, leading to $(6, 4)$ and so on. This input was formed according to an arbitrary action selection scheme, but the state-transition function and value assignment function is fixed.

At various times, $t=4$, 5, 8, 9, 10 – indicated by the first number inside the parentheses after ITH on the printout shown in table 2 – the learner forms hypotheses. To make it easier to read the hypotheses, interpret, say the first one, with mnemonics for ITH, ISE, IDO, ILK, as follows: 'I think, at time 10, that for all t, for all x, if I see the state at time t to have x as its first component and I select action 0 at time t, then, at time $t+1$, I see a state with $x+2$ as its first component.' The IN predicate means that, if IN(X, SET2), then x is an element of set 2, which is defined elsewhere; SET2 might be the name given to a description produced by SEQANAL – both intensional and extensional – and stored in the long-term memory.

In this example, the program forms hypotheses corresponding to:

(1) A favored state is one in which both components are the same (line 7).

(2) A despised state is one in which the second component exceeds the first one by two (line 5).

(3) Action 0 increases the first component by two, leaves the second one unchanged (lines 1, 3 in short-term memory, based on $t = 2, 5$).

(4) Action 1 increases the first component by two, the second one by four (lines 2, 4).

Note that it has formed a wrong hypothesis at $t=4$ (line 8), that if the the action is 0, the new s_2 is equal to the old s_1.

'ASP'. The illustrative problem picked here involves a four-component state vector $s=(s_1, s_2, s_3, s_4)$. There are two objects, each characterized by two coordinates in an 11×11 grid. The first object, A, has s_1, s_2 as its co-ordinates, and if it is in position (s_1, s_2) at any time, it will be in position $(2s_1 \bmod 11, s_2+1 \bmod 11)$ the next time, regardless of any actions. For example, if the current position of A is $(4, 2)$, the next position is $(8, 3)$, followed by $(5, 4)$, etc. If the second object, B, is in state (s_3, s_4), the next state is $(s_3 + a \bmod 11, s_4)$, where a is the action of the learner L. We assume that a can take the values 1, 2, 3, 4, 5, or 6. Thus, if $a=3$, and B is in position $(4, 1)$, then it moves to $(6, 1)$; if now $a=5$, it moves to $(0, 1)$.

We could interpret A and B as moving on the surface of a torus on which an 11×11 grid or coordinate system is superposed. Object B can move as shown in figure 5, and object A spirals around the tube.

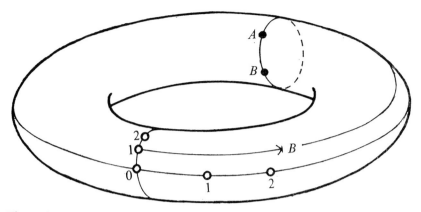

Figure 5

The learner is rewarded, $v = 1$, if the first and third components are equal: that is, when A and B are on the same small circle around the tube as shown on the rear side in the diagram.

The printout (figure 6) indicates, in line 1, that there is only one action-hypothesis ($\text{NAH} = 1$) and in line 2 that there are two value-hypotheses ($\text{NVH} = 2$) and that there are six actions ($\text{NA} = 6$, line 3). Next, it indicates that thirteen 'simulation' cycles were run. Then the environment-transition and value function are stated as SNOBOL statements to correspond exactly to what was said above. These are SNOBOL assignment statements for example, $v <\text{T}> = \text{EQ}(s <\text{T}, 1>, s <\text{T}, 3>)$ 1 assigns to the Tth component of vector v the value 1 if the condition $\text{EQ}(\quad)$ is satisfied; otherwise it returns the null string. The condition is satisfied if the first component of the state vector at time t, $s <\text{T}, 1>$ is equal to the third component $s <\text{T}, 3>$. All rules and hypotheses have this form. The use of the SNOBOL assignment statement with conditions allows us to express implications in usable form.

The program is also given a number of weighted hypotheses for storage in its memory. In this case, the hypotheses correspond exactly to the rules that generate the environment. The program is then given an initial state and proceeds to select actions on the basis of its hypotheses and to modify the weights on the basis of the consequences. These changed weights are printed out only when the action-hypothesis is confirmed and the value-hypothesis is refuted. In this output, the weight of the 2nd value-hypothesis is decreased, because the environmental input gave a value of one rather than two.

Figure 6. Printout of ASP program.

NAH $=1$

NVH $=2$

NA $=6$

THE SIMULATION TIME IS 13

THE ENVIRONMENT RULES ARE:

AND($'$S$<$T$+1,1>=$MOD($2*$S$<$T$,1>,11)'$,AND($'$S$<$T$+1,2>=$
MOD(S$<$T$,2>+1,11)'$,AND($'$S$<$T$+1,3>=$MOD(S$<$T$,3>+$
A$<$T$>,11)'$,$'$S$<$T$+1,4>=$S$<$T$,4>'$))):(A5);

V$<$T$>=$EQ(S$<$T$,1>$,S$<$T$,3>$)1 :S(RETURN)F(A10);

V$<$T$>=$EQ(S$<$T$,1>$,S$<$T$,3>$)EQ(S$<$T$,2>$,S$<$T$,4>$)2;

S(RETURN)F(A10):

THE HYPOTHESES ARE:

AND($'$S$<$T$+1,1>=$MOD($2*$S$<$T$,1>,11)'$,AND($'$S$<$T$+1,2>=$
MOD(S$<$T$,2>+1,11)'$,AND($'$S$<$T$+1,3>=$MOD(S$<$T, 3>+$
A$<$T$>,11)'$,$'$S$<$T$+1,4>=$S$<$T$,4>'$))):S(B17)F(B21);

V$<$T$>=$EQ(S$<$T$,1>$,S$<$T$,3>$) 1 :S(B20)F(B18);

V$<$T$>=$EQ(S$<$T$,1>$,S$<$T$,3>$)EQ(S$<$T$,2>$,S$<$T$,4>$)2 :S(B20)F(B18);

THE ACTIONS ARE:

1

2

3

4

5

6

THE INITIAL STATES ARE:

S(1) $=2,1,2,1$

THE ACTION SELECTED IS 2

THE NEXT STATE IS 4,2,4,1

THE NEW VALUE IS 1

UPDATE WEIGHTS OF AHYP(1) AND VHYP(1)

THE ACTION SELECTED IS 4

THE NEXT STATE IS 8,3,8,1

THE NEW VALUE IS 1

Figure 6—*continued*

UPDATE WEIGHTS OF AHYP(1) AND VHYP(1)

THE ACTION SELECTED IS 1
THE NEXT STATE IS 5,4,9,1
THE NEW VALUE IS 0

THE ACTION SELECTED IS 1
THE NEXT STATE IS 10,5,10,1
THE NEW VALUE IS 1

UPDATE WEIGHTS OF AHYP(1) AND VHYP(1)

THE ACTION SELECTED IS 1
THE NEXT STATE IS 9,6,0,1
THE NEW VALUE IS 0

THE ACTION SELECTED IS 1
THE NEXT STATE IS 7,7,1,1
THE NEW VALUE IS 0

THE ACTION SELECTED IS 2
THE NEXT STATE IS 3,8,3,1
THE NEW VALUE IS 1

UPDATE WEIGHTS OF AHYP(1) AND VHYP(1)

THE ACTION SELECTED IS 3
THE NEXT STATE IS 6,9,6,1
THE NEW VALUE IS 1

UPDATE WEIGHTS OF AHYP(1) AND VHYP(1)

THE ACTION SELECTED IS 6
THE NEXT STATE IS 1,10,1,1
THE NEW VALUE IS 1

UPDATE WEIGHTS OF AHYP(1) AND VHYP(1)

Figure 6—*continued*

THE ACTION SELECTED IS 1
THE NEXT STATE IS 2,0,2,1
THE NEW VALUE IS 1

UPDATE WEIGHTS OF AHYP(1) AND VHYP(1)

THE ACTION SELECTED IS 2
THE NEXT STATE IS 4,1,4,1
THE NEW VALUE IS 1

UPDATE WEIGHTS OF AHYP(1) AND VHYP(2)
$\text{AHYP}(1) = \text{AND}('s<\text{T}+1,1> = \text{MOD}(2*s<\text{T},1>,11)'$,
$\text{AND}('s<\text{T}+1,2> = \text{MOD}(s<\text{T},2>$
$+1,11)', \text{AND}('s<\text{T}+1,3> = \text{MOD}(s<\text{T},3>+\text{A}<\text{T}>,11)', 's<$
$\text{T}+1,4> = s<\text{T},4>'))) : \text{S}(\text{B}17)\text{F}(\text{B}21);$
WT. OF AHYP(1) = 13
$\text{VHYP}(1) = \text{V}<\text{T}> = \text{EQ}(s<\text{T},1>,s<\text{T},3>)1 : \text{S}(\text{B}20)\text{F}(\text{B}18);$
WT. OF VHYP(1) = 12
$\text{VHYP}(2) = \text{V}<\text{T}> = \text{EQ}(s<\text{T},1>,s<\text{T},3>) \text{EQ}(s<\text{T},2>,$
$s<\text{T},4>)2 : \text{S}(\text{B}20)\text{F}(\text{B}18);$
WT. OF VHYP(2) = 4

THE ACTION SELECTED IS 4
THE NEXT STATE IS 8,2,8,1
THE NEW VALUE IS 1

UPDATE WEIGHTS OF AHYP(1) AND VHYP(1)

THE ACTION SELECTED IS 1
THE NEXT STATE IS 5,3,9,1
THE NEW VALUE IS 0

THE DATA HAS BEEN PROCESSED

In this run, actions were selected on the basis of all stored hypotheses and all possible actions, scanned in a fixed order. If this program were run in the probabilistic mode, then the hypotheses and actions would have been selected according to the changed weight assigned to both hypotheses and actions. Had we continued to run this program in the probabilistic mode, the weight of the second value hypothesis would eventually become 0, and it would never be used.

RELATION TO EXPERIMENTATION

The following experiment illustrates the nature of our entire approach to cognitive learning, were we to try applying it to humans. Two experimental human subjects, L_1 and L_2 – corresponding to two learners – are stationed at two teletypewriters attached to a minicomputer (a PDP-8). They are given instructions, telling them their task is to discover the structure of the sequence on being presented with a trace of it, and to make a certain number of correct predictions of its subsequent terms. They are instructed how to record their guesses and how to communicate with the partner by teletype.

When the experiment begins, the computer causes two different numbers (or words or pictures) to be displayed simultaneously. For instance, L_1 may see 1 while L_2 sees 64. After each input, L_i, $i = 1$, 2, can predict what he thinks will be next and/or state his suggestions, ideas, questions to his partner about the pattern in the sequence he is being presented with. Both are typed by him on his teletypewriter and messages are transmitted from either subject to the other. Since each gets rewarded only when they *both* act as if they knew the sequence, they are motivated to express their hypotheses to each other. In this way, we can, by examining the printed messages, eavesdrop on their thinking.

A number of such experiments have been run, and results will be reported elsewhere. The point of mentioning this here is to indicate the parallel between our 'simulations' and this experiment: both fall under the same paradigm. Indeed, we could replace one of the subjects by our 360 SNOBOL programs. If we translated the hypotheses formed by our program into English, the human learner at the terminal may not know that his partner is nonhuman. In practice, there is no gain in using the minicomputer, and the experiment can be done with one subject at a typewriter on the Michigan Time Sharing System directly.

An application – indicative of the direction we aim to go – of this paradigm is to regard L_1 as a student and L_2 as a teacher. Both are learners; L_1 has to learn a topic. L_2 has to learn about L_1: he has to form a model of his student and use it to select such actions as will best help the student attain his goal. Some practical steps in implementing this application are described later. A similar application is to view L_1 as a person with an emotional problem – for instance a snake phobia, child-management problems, and so on – with the goal of solving them, and L_2 as a therapist with the same goal as L_1. Both are learners here, too, in this case about the nature of L_1's problem. Both L_1 and L_2 are to select actions so as to steer L_1 to his goal. Some exploratory steps in this direction have also been taken (Stodolsky 1970).

In a real sense, our entire narrative is very much an interim report, a snapshot, because our entire conception as well as the mathematical formulation, and certainly the computer programs are being modified from day to day.

THE WORLD BRAIN ANALOGY: APPLICATION TO THE DESIGN OF A GROWING ENCYCLOPAEDIA SYSTEM (GES)

INTRODUCTION

In the preceding three sections we examined cognitive learning as a mathematical process. We did not attempt to claim that our explication in any way 'models' or 'simulates' learning in existing living systems. Our sole aim was to clarify the concept, using the approach of specifying algorithms which, if executed by some organ, would enable us to persuade others that this organ learns. We shall have attained this aim if, say, an experimental psychologist conceives an experiment – that is a question to ask about learning in actual organisms – that would not have occurred to him before being exposed to our thinking. Such a question would go beyond the mere testing a specific implication or assumption of a model, which we do not offer. We do, however, believe that we have specified a general class of organs we call 'learners', and these include both the artificial organs we can design and living brains.

Also included in this general class of learners is what H. G. Wells called The World Brain'. This refers to our collective wisdom in the human species. Insofar as the hypothetical learners we studied are assumed to have unlimited life, is there no essential reason why a single learner with no constraints on memory, processing speed, and so on could not eventually do what the several communicating learners we dealt with can do? Perhaps it takes the single learner longer. We would still view such a monolithic learner organized into communicating parts (Kochen 1954, 1958), if only to simplify the construction and analysis. Any realistic explication would have to take into account the probability of noise, error and deviation from intended function. With proper design, a large number of communicating learners constrained by limitations on memory, processing capabilities, and now also finite life, can recognize and cope with tasks that a single learner with the same memory and processing capacity as the community could not recognize and solve. The community could also learn some of the tasks faster. This is due to the rise of new 'emergent properties' analogous to macroscopic properties, such as pressure, of a large statistical aggregate. With improper design, the community breaks down, is less reliable than its parts (Kochen 1960b, von Neumann 1956, Winograd and Cowan 1963).

In our constructive explication of learning, how do we know when a change in the system of representation is in the direction of progress? We examine the change in the utility to the learner, and look for an increase. But our environment is completely artificial, and known to us, and our knowledge of the utility function should enable *us* to deduce, in principle, everything the learner can ever learn. It is merely because we make the environment sufficiently complex that we cannot do this without a computer. Should someone succeed in deducing, with the help of a computer, how to recognize and solve all the tasks of an environment we present him, then we switch to a more complex environment. Our learner must be able to function in *any* environment in a class (infinite). In particular, it should function if we encoded an input signal from our real physical world or a part of it. But this is too enormous a technical undertaking, nor a useful one. Far more important is the application and testing of these ideas on those segments of our social environment that relate to education (Kochen 1969c) and behavior modification (Stodolsky 1970).

As Platt has pointed out (Platt 1969) we – the human species – haven't much time to solve our crisis problems. A head-on full-scale attack on fully cognitive learning can await our survival of the next few decades. In the meantime a full-scale effort to explore the applications of this approach to the teaching of rule-governed behavior, for example, may contribute to our chances of survival while, at the same time, advancing our understanding of basic principles, perhaps even better than would a head-on attempt to discover these.

THE GROWTH OF KNOWLEDGE IN A COMMUNITY

Kuhn (1962) has introduced the notion of a paradigm in a field of science as the set of key concepts, beliefs, questions, special styles of thought, experimentation, communication, which are adopted, for a time, by a community of practitioners and passed on to their disciples. Such a paradigm guides the research activities of its adherents, who, during the first stage of growth of 'normal science', explore all the theoretical and experimental leads it generates. In time, the inevitable emergence of anomalies can build up to a crisis stage. Enough anomalies, including a few that are sufficiently paradoxical, threaten the continued reign of a paradigm. If another paradigm grew in parallel with the one in force and matured at crisis time so that it can encompass the essentials of the old paradigm and yet is free of anomalies, it will be successful on the throne; Kuhn calls this succession a scientific revolution.

How shall we explicate the cognitive state of a community? To relate to our previous discussion, we view the community both as a single learner L and as a set of communicating learners $L_1, L_2, \ldots, L_N$. In this case, the output of L_i consists of: (1) actions, or elements of A_i, which we interpret as operations on E designed to yield information (experiments) as well as problem-solving moves; (2) linguistic communications of short-term duration (Goodman and Heilprin 1965) to specific other learners with the intent of modifying behavior, such as posing questions, teaching; (3) linguistic communication of long-term duration, broadcast to all learners who are tuned in, with the intent of updating the L's representation, by the community's state of knowledge; these teachings are embodied in the published literature.

To specify the cognitive state of the community is to specify (1) the learners, $L_1, \ldots, L_N$, which comprise it, and how they are interconnected; (2) the topics with which they are concerned and how these are interconnected; (3) the documents produced and used by $L_1, \ldots, L_N$ and how they are interconnected; (4) the ways in which the learners, the topics and the documents each couple with the other two; (5) the dynamics by which knowledge, understanding and wisdom grows in the community. Let us begin with the notion of a topic (Field of Knowledge, Subject). Denote a particular topic named k by FK. Formally, FK $= \{$KR, AX, TS, FS, QS, CS$\}$. (1) KR is a subset of $\mathscr{L}(G)$, where G is the syntax of the system of representation, SR, for L, where L is the single learner corresponding to the community as a whole. Recall that $\mathscr{L}(G)$ is a set of all well-formed propositions formable with G. All the propositions in KR should have a certain minimum degree of mutual relevance, each to every other. Two identical or logically equivalent propositions are mutually relevant; so are p and $\rceil p$, though to a slightly lesser degree. If p and q share a predicate, they are mutually relevant to some extent.

(2) AX is another subset of $\mathscr{L}(G)$, representing axioms.

(3) TS is a finite subset of $\mathscr{L}(G)$ corresponding to proved theorems, using rules of inferences that are part of SR.

(4) FS is a subset of CR; recall that CR is the representation, or corpus of hypotheses, stored by L; FS represents facts. If FK is a topic with both theoretical and empirical content, then, hopefully, TS $\cap$ FS is large.

(5) QS is another finite subset of $\mathscr{L}(G)$ representing questions. Some questions

are of the form 'Is it true that h?', where $h \in$ CR, and an answer from a learner consists of $w(h)$, his degree of belief in h if he has held h.

(6) CS is a relation between questions, a subset of QS $\times$ QS, which indicates logical and conceptual connections among questions (Kochen 1970). Such a connection matrix can help L rank the questions by priority, pick key or central questions. This is most important.

All of the six elements of the 6-tuple that specify a topic can be subscripted with i to refer to individual learners i, $i = 1, \ldots, N$. It may be reasonable to assume that each of the six elements for L is the union of the corresponding elements for $L_1, \ldots, L_N$. As such, FS, for example, may contain two contradictory hypotheses.

Recall, now, that L_1 was taken to be an algorithm which modifies four other algorithms for determining responses, modifying hypotheses, and so on. The action repertoire or output of L_i now includes also questions asked by L_i, possibly of himself or of L_j, $j \neq i$ (in which case L_j receives a question as input) and answers to these questions. If L_i picks a question, which is an element of QS$_i$ – and also of QS – and generates an answer, which is an element of TS$_i \cup$ FS$_i$, then the number of elements in the latter set increases. L_i knows more than it did before. We might think that the number of elements of QS$_i$ decreases, but it is more realistic to assume that for each question of QS$_i$ that L_i picks and answers, it can add to QS$_i$ at least one new question that L_i had not known to ask. Hence the number of elements in QS$_i$ stays at least the same; possibly it grows. The new questions are added with the help of the connection matrix CS$_i$ and this, too, grows as questions are asked and answered. The set TS$_i \cup$ FS$_i$ represents what L_i knows that he knows at any time. The set QS$_i$ represents what L_i knows he does not know at any time and CS$_i$ determines L_i's need to know.

If L_i responds to a question (posed by L_j, $j = i$ or $j \neq i$) with an answer, this answer may be known to L_j for some j, or it may not be known to L_j for some j but L_j does not share L_i's concern with the question, or it may both be of concern and new to L_j. If the latter is true for a large number of knowledgeable L_j, then the answer should be 'published' in the archival record, embodied in a document. A document is, formally: (1) a set of sentences of the public verbal language shared by $L_1, \ldots, L_N$; (2) a set of propositions, including elements of QS and TS$\cup$FS, that the sentences designate, and such that there is at least a minimal degree of coherence or mutual relevance among them, as there is within the topic (Segur 1971); (3) such that a set of new elements are added to QS, TS, FS and to CS; the latter is most important: the document should show connections between the question it raises and answers and other questions in QS and persuade others to internalize these connections and implied priorities for concern with the question; (4) such that the added elements of TS and FS must be documented – that is, proofs must be valid logical deductions, weights assigned to hypotheses representing facts must be valid (without error in conforming to conventionalized norms for weight of evidence); (5) such that there must be an associated L_i with authority and responsibility for meeting the above criteria, though other L_j acting as referees and reviewers will check L_i; (6) such that it is citable and cites other documents with which it is logically connected.

The dynamics underlying the growth of FK is determined by the dynamics governing L_i's question-asking, L_i's question-answering, L_i's comprehension of teachings and L_i's knowledge processing for $i = 1, \ldots, N$. In time, FS, QS and CS grow beyond the point at which no L_i, with its limited information-processing capacity, memory and lifetime, can process the entire topic. At that point, the L_i together will no longer be able to enrich CS sufficiently to enable the KR part of the topic to remain coherent: that is, each proposition in KR will no longer be mutually relevant with the others. The supervisory algorithm governing what L_i does when, and algorithm two, which re-organizes L_i's representation, causes L_i for one i to shift and concentrate 'attention' to a subset KR' within KR, to the exclusion of KR–KR'. For another i, L_i focusses on a different subset. Subset KR' is more coherent than KR and is small enough to match L_i's capacities. Several L_i may process the same KR' and, in time, a subtopic may form. In this way, a topic fragments into specialized subtopics. As a newly formed topic grows, the L_i processing it cross-fertilizes it by establishing connections to other topics. This accelerates the processes by which new predicates can be formed, and the public verbal language, with its options for flexibility, ambiguity, thus generating new combinations without losing associations that help in selecting useful combinations, plays a vital role.

The four levels – processing of information, knowledge (meaning, cognition), understanding (comprehension), and wisdom – apply to L as they do to the L_i. Stability can be attained at each level, including the fourth, or else L – the community in this case – does not survive.

THE 'WORLD BRAIN' AND THE GES IDEA

The evolution of this idea is traced by Kochen (1967), from a strong plea by H. G. Wells in 1936, through the inspiring 1947 vision of V. Bush to the authoritative 1963 recommendations of Weinberg's presidential panel. There is more to this idea than an attempt to lay foundations for the unification of science, and certainly far more than a retrieval system which makes information more readily accessible or which keeps scientists from being mired by the growth of literature. We have in mind an intelligence service coupled with a more flexible and responsive decision-making organization. We have in mind radical changes in our way of viewing education. We have in mind methods for reorganizing and repackaging knowledge that go as much beyond the responsibilities of a library catalog as that goes beyond an unordered collection of documents.

Experience with 'on-line intellectual communities', recent progress and ferment engendered by attempts to use computers in education and information retrieval, advances in question-answering by computer and experience with practical applications of the concepts discussed in the last three lectures all support belief that the 1970s will be another milestone in the evolution of the 'World Brain' idea. We discuss one such practical application in the next section. We believe that the milestone will be of this nature.

The current version of the 'World Brain' idea, which we will call the GES-idea, is as follows. Its aim is to organize the enormous mass of relevant information in a form in which it can be utilized for solving key survival problems facing the world community. The systems must be responsive to the needs of its users and must adapt as these needs become better articulated. The 'world brain' idea includes reorganizing and repackaging the contents of our libraries and information centers. But it is something vastly more profound: a reorganization of our methods of education and political problem-solving based on the wise use of accumulated knowledge. Such reorganization is a continuing process. It should be even more responsive to the needs, latent or expressed, of those who will be affected by the solutions than to the needs of key problem-solvers. Insofar as the system is intended to help solve problems using knowledge in almost all areas, it is encyclopaedic. Because such knowledge is constantly growing, because its users' needs are constantly becoming better articulated, and because it adapts, with increasing sensitivity, to its users' needs, we call it a growing encyclopaedia system (GES).

A PILOT GES FOR MATHEMATICS

This is an experimental 'course' at the University of Michigan. The L_i ($i = 1, \ldots, 30$, typically) include students and teachers. Each L_i can play both roles in a kind of mutual exchange relation. The topic is that of modern mathematics, organized into a growing number of subtopics (now about eighty), such as 'Lattices', 'Linear Programming', 'Calculus of Variations', 'Combinatorial Topology', 'Computability', and so on. The document collection is that of all potentially relevant books in library resources available to the L_i. The students range from freshmen to Ph.D. candidates, to many of whom mathematics appears unfamiliar, distant, fearsome, foreboding, difficult.

The primary purpose of exposing them to this educational experience is to improve their analytical powers of problem-solving. This means primarily shaping attitudes: mathematics is viewed as an attitude of analyzing a problem into sub-problems that can be further analyzed into parts that can eventually be solved and, by synthesizing results, arrive at a solution of the original problem; this also implies the ability and confidence to recognize and select problems (questions) that L_i can so analyze. Only secondarily does this 'course' aim to acquaint students with particular concepts, facts, methods of mathematics.

The major tool we employ to attain this goal is a 'Directory' which is constantly modified. At present this directory has a form that superficially resembles a 600-page programmed text, organized into eighty subtopics. With the help of a sequence of worked 'problems' ranging from very simple to difficult associated to each subtopic, the directory directs the learner to the eighty topics. Each frame problem plus tutorial answers, plus directions about the options for further action, actually teaches the learner as *little* as he needs to know to decide upon his next action. The next action may be: choosing another frame; following a lead to documents in the library, to special games, computer programs or other devices, or to particular other L_i provided by the directory. The directory is intended to provide enough options in its leads to match the needs, level, capabilities of a particular learner with the best and most appropriate of what is in the available resources cumulated up to date, with increasing sensitivity. The learner, through this sequence of decisions, traces a customized trail through the maze which is to meet as broad or as narrow a need as he has, at as high or as low a level as best serves him.

The directory and its use does more than give the learner a 'worm's eye' view of the topic, one he would get from a single 'linear' path without detour. It gives him the option to zoom, acquiring a bird's eye view of the forest as well; indeed, the learner can simultaneously see the topic macroscopically and microscopically at several levels of aggregation/magnification. The learner is to create, in this way, an internalized map of the topic, one which corresponds more or less to the map inherent in the directory. It is this map that enables the learner to ask questions.

In terms of the previously introduced concepts, learner L_i updates his system of representation, SR_i, and particularly his conceptual vocabulary of predicate-names P_i, of axioms AX_i, of hypotheses FS_i, of theorems TS_i, of questions QS_i, and, especially, his question-connection matrix CS_i. As he learns to pick questions in QS_i and answer them (removing them from QS_i and adding them to FS_i or TS_i) he also learns to ask questions that did not occur to him before (adding to QS_i). Hopefully, L_i can *generalize this process* – modify his algorithm – of picking, analyzing and answering questions in any topic for which he has a cognitive map.

In practice, students are instrumentally conditioned for terminal behavior exhibiting (1) their ability to externalize the internal map of the topic they have acquired, (2) their ability to pick and analyze original questions, (3) their ability to critically review literature, showing comprehension. (The acquisition of information, knowledge or wisdom is not aimed nor tested for in this pilot GES, though a more sophisticated GES should aim at the latter.) Concretely, the learners are systematically trained toward criterion behavior – which takes the form of a three-part final report (a student produced directory, a set of three questions, two of which are analyzed, and one solved, a literature review) – by verbalizing on feedback sheets their detailed reactions (questions, comments, connections) on each problem they work in going through the directory, by intensive face-to-face contact with a variety of tutors, by a variety of positive educational experiences such as on-line use of computers, games, and so on, and by writing critical reviews of literature. Computer terminals (on the Michigan IBM 360/67 Time-Sharing System) were available to learners at any of forty locations for their use at any time to learn high-level programming languages (PIL and SNOBOL4) through practice with a sequence of graded exercises, with the learner writing his own manual based on the practical experiences.

To bring and keep this pilot GES up-to-date, new (and, retrospectively, old) books, articles, films, tests are constantly screened, graded and funneled into the system by the creation of connections with the directory. New students and tutors are constantly brought in, and selected alumni remain coupled to the system. New subtopics are constantly added and connected more richly to one another, old ones revised in the light of feedback data from learners, and data about various learner-types is analyzed, correlated and used for modifying the directory. A similar directory is being built for a topic that is as difficult to structure into a map as mathematics is easy: memory derangements in psychiatry. Here, the directory is in the form of logical propositions of FS, representing primarily facts. Here the learners are researchers rather than students, and they are to learn asking questions most of which they will answer themselves, while students answer only some of them by themselves.

There is strong evidence that the pilot GES is growing well: that it is now – after two years of operation – meeting its aims to a fair extent and that its performance is improving significantly from term to term.

By specifying the substance of the data base – that is, general propositions and examples of mathematics as teachings expressed in the public verbal language – we can hope to have learners L_i, to whom such teachings are input, modify their systems of representation, SR_i, their representations, CR_i and to generate (select) 'good' (analyzable) questions as their output. By having a community of such learners communicate as they solve problems, we can hope to increase the number and level of problems they can solve and to increase their awareness of the number of options for problem-solving that is available to them.

CONCLUSION AND RECOMMENDATIONS

Research related to building a GES pilot has proved to be feasible in terms of existing resources, fruitful in terms of progress toward basic principles, and valuable in terms of contributions toward solving survival problems. The construction of GESs for different topics, and the creation of an institution for coordinating them into a coherent, encyclopaedic system is strongly recommended as a high-priority task for mankind. The key problem is organizational: how to graft so new a form of institution as this would require into the existing public or private institutions in various nations or into multinational institutions so that it remains viable, yet objective and analytical in its orientation. It must, above all, be an instrument to change the world for the 'better', after it has contributed in bringing cumulated wisdom to bear on the most urgent survival problems.

ACKNOWLEDGEMENTS

The conception of many of the ideas in these four sections is the result of numerous joint discussions with L. Uhr, now at the University of Wisconsin. The further development of these ideas – including critical analysis, the creation of many notions and results not reported here – was greatly helped by P. Emerson during 1966, by P. Roosen-Runge, J. Brown, P. Dale and W. Ash during 1967 and by S. Hantler, C. Hecox, J. Hesselbart, and H. Hamburger from 1968 to the present. Sid Hantler made particularly significant contributions to both the mathematical explication as well as to the design and implementation of the currently operating programs. The creation of the operational systems described in the last section was greatly helped by W. Everett.

I plan to expand some of this paper into separate papers to be co-authored with Hantler and Uhr.

BIBLIOGRAPHY

Ableson, R.P. & Carroll, J.D. (1965) Computer simulation of individual belief systems *Amer. behav. Scientist*, **9**, 24–30.

Amarel, S. (1964) On the automatic formation of a computer program which represents a theory. *Self Organizing Systems* (eds. Yovits, M., Jacobi, G. T., & Goldstein, G.D.). Washington, DC: Spartan.

Amarel, S. (1966) On the mechanization of creative processes, *IEEE Spectrum*.

Amarel, S. (1968) On machine representations of problems of reasoning about actions. *Machine Intelligence 3*, pp. 131–70 (ed. Michie, D.). Edinburgh: Edinburgh University Press.

Ash, W.L. & Sibley, E.H. (1968) TRAMP: An interpretive associative processor with deductive capabilities. *Proc. ACM National Conference*.

Ashby, R. (1953) *Design for a Brain*. New York: Wiley.

Barricelli, N.A. (1957) Symbiotic evolution processes realized by artificial methods. *Revista Methodos*, **2**, 35–6.

Boulding, K. (1956) *The Image*. Ann Arbor: University of Michigan Press.

Bremermann, H. (1958) The evaluation of intelligence. *The Nervous System As a Model of Its Environment*. TR No. 1, USNRO 43200.

Brillouin, L. (1956) *Science and Information Theory*. New York: Academic Press.

Bruner, J. S., Goodnow, J. G., & Austin, G. A. (1956) *A Study of Thinking*. New York: Wiley.

Bunge, M. (1967) *Scientific Research I: The Search for System*. New York: Springer.

Bush, V. (1965) As we may think. *At. Monthly*, **176**, 101–8.

Carnap, R. (1936) Testability and meaning, *Philos. Sci.* III.

Church, A. (1934) A note on the *entscheidungs* problem, *J. of symbol. Logic.*, **1**, 40–1.

Claparede (1934) La genese de l'hypothese. *Archives de Psychologie*, **24**, 1–154.

Colby, K.M. (1967) Simulation of change in personal belief systems, *Beh. Sci.*, **12**, 248–53.

Culbertson, J.T. (1950) *Consciousness and Behaviour*. Dubuque, Iowa: W.C. Brown.

Descartes, R. (1948) *Discourse on the Method of Rightly Conducting the Reason and Seeking Truth in the Sciences* (transl. Valery, P.). London: Cassell.

Floyd, R.W. (1967) Assigning meanings to programs: *AMS Sympos. on Appl. Math.*, 19.

Gelernter, H. (1959) Realization of a geometry theorem proving machine. *Proc. IFIP Conf.*, Paris: UNESCO House.

Gelernter, H. & Rochester, N. (October 1968) Intelligent behavior in problem-solving machines *IBM J. Res. & Dev.*, **2**, 336–45.

X

Gödel, K. (1931) Über Formale Unentscheidbare Sätze der Principia Mathematica und Verwandter Systeme I, *Mon. für Math. u. Phys.*, **38**, 173–98.

Goodman, F. & Heilprin, L. (1965) Analogy between information retrieval and education, *Educ. for Information Science*, p. 13 (eds. Heilprin, L. *et al.*). Washington DC: Spartan.

Green, C.C. & Raphael, B. (1967) Research on an intelligent question-answering system, *Stanford Res. Inst. Report No. 1*, Menlo Park Calif.

Greene, P. (1959) An approach to computers that perceive, learn and reason. *Proc. West. J. comput. Conf.*, 181–6, San Francisco.

Griswold, R.E., Poage, J.G. & Polonsky, I.P. (1968) *The SNOBOL 4 Programming Language*. Englewood, New Jersey: Prentice Hall.

Hadamard, J. (1945) *The Psychology of Invention in the Mathematical Field*. Princeton: Princeton University Press.

Harrah, D. (1963) *Communication: A logical model*. Cambridge, Mass., MIT Press.

Hebb, D.O. (1949) *The Organization of Behavior*. New York: Wiley.

Hull, C.L. Quantitative aspects of the evolution of concepts. *Psychol. Monograph*, **28**, 1, (whole no. 123).

Illich, I. (1968) The futility of schooling in latin america. *Saturday Review*, April 1968.

Kac, M. & Ulam, S. (1969) *Mathematics and Logic*. New York: Praeger.

Knuth, D.E. (1968) *The Art of Computer Programming*. Reading, Massachusetts: Addison-Wesley.

Kochen, M. (1954) An information-theoretic model of organization. *Trans. IRE. PGIT-4*, 67.

Kochen, M. (1958) Organized systems with discrete information transfer. *General Systems Yearbook*.

Kochen, M. (1959) Extension of Moore–Shannon model for relay circuits. *IBM J. Res. & Dev.*, **3**, 169.

Kochen, M. (1960a) An experimental study of strategies in hypothesis-formation by computers. *Trans. 4th. Sympos. on inf. Th.* London: Butterworth.

Kochen, M. (1960b) Cognitive mechanisms. *IBM Report* RAP-16. Yorktown Heights, N.Y.

Kochen, M., MacKay, D.M., Maron, M.E., Scriven, M., & Uhr, L. (1961) Computers and comprehension. *The Growth of Knowledge*, p. 230 (ed. Kochen, M.). New York: Wiley.

Kochen, M. (1962a) Adaptive mechanisms in digital concept-processing. *Proc. Joint Conf. on Autom. Control*, pp. 49–59. Amer. Inst. of Electrical Engineering.

Kochen, M. (1962b) Some mechanisms in hypothesis-selection. *Proc. Sympos. math. Theory of Automata*, pp. 593–613. Polyt. Inst. of Brooklyn.

Kochen, M. (ed) (1967) *The Growth of Knowledge*. New York: Wiley.

Kochen, M. (1969a) Automatic question-answering of english-like questions about arithmetic. Lafayette, Indiana. *Proc. Purdue centennial year Symp. on information Processing*.

Kochen, M. (1969b) Automatic question-answering of english-like questions about simple diagrams. *J. Assoc. comput. Mach.*, **16**, 26–48.

Kochen, M. (1969c) Experiments with programmed learning as a new literary form. *J. of Chem. Documentation*, **9**, 10.

Kochen, M. (1969d) Stability in the growth of knowledge. *Amer. Document*, **20**, 187.

Kochen, M. (1970) Fact accumulation and intellectual bridge-building as complementary processes. *Final Report N S F-G N716*, MHRI, University of Michigan.

Kohler, W. (1926) *The Mentality of Apes.* New York: Harcourt, Brace.

Kuhn, T. (1962) *The Structure of Scientific Revolutions.* Chicago: University of Chicago Press.

Lederberg, J. & Feigenbaum, E. A. (1968) Mechanization of inductive inference in organic chemistry. *Formal Representation for Human Judgement* (ed. Kleinmuntz). New York: Wiley.

MacKay, D. M. (1956) The epistemological problem for automata. *Automata Studies.* Princeton: Princeton University Press.

McCarthy, J. (1958) Programs with common sense. *Proc. Symp. on THE Mechaniz. of Thought Processes.* London: HMSO.

McCulloch, W. S. (1970) *Embodiments of Mind.* Cambridge, Massachusets: MIT Press.

Mendelson, E. (1964) *Introduction to Mathematical Logic.* Princeton: Van Nostrand.

Michie, D. (1966) *Machine Intelligence 2*, pp. vii–ix (eds. Dale, E. & Michie, D.). Edinburgh: Edinburgh University Press.

Miller, G. A., Galanter, E. H., & Pribram, K. (1960) *Plans and the Structure of Behavior.* New York: Henry Holt.

Minsky, M. (1961) Steps toward artificial intelligence. *Proc. IEEE*, **49**, 8–30.

Minsky, M. (1970) Form and computer science. *J. Ass. comput. Mach.*, **17**, 197.

Moore, E. F. & Shannon, C. E. (1956) Reliable circuits using less reliable relays. *J. Franklin Inst.*, **262**, 191–208, 281–97.

Mowrer, O. H. (1961) *Learning Theory and Behavior.* New York: Wiley.

Myhill, J. (1952) Some philosophical implications of mathematical logic. *Rev. Metaphysics*, **6**, 105–98.

Newell, A. (1955) The chess machine: an example of dealing with a complex task by adaptation. *Proc. WJCC*, Instit. Radio Engineers.

Newell, A. & Shaw, J. C. (1957) Programming the logic theory machine. *Proc. Western Joint Comput. Conf.*, p. 290.

Newell, A., Shaw, J. C. & Simon, H. A. (1958) Chess playing programs and the problem of complexity, *IBM J. Res. & Dev.*, **2**, 320.

Newell, A. & Simon, H. A. (1959) The simulation of human thought. *RAND Report P*-1734. Santa Monica: RAND Corporation.

Newell, A. & Ernst, G. (1965) The search for generality. *Proc. IFIP Cong. 65.* Washington, DC: Spartan.

Newell, A. (1966) On the representation of problems. *Computer Science Research*, Report Carnegie Institute of Technology Pittsburgh, Penn.

Newman, C. & Uhr, L. (1967) Discovery procedures for game playing models. *20th ACM Nat. Conf.* New York: Academic Press.

O'Connell, J. P., Fubini, E. A., McKay, K. A., Hillier, J., & Hollomon, J. H. (1969) Electronically expanding the citizen's world. *IEEE Spectrum*, 30–9.

Piaget, J. (1953) *Logic and Psychology.* Manchester: Manchester University Press.

Piaget, J. (1952) *The Origins of Intelligence in Children.* Int'l University Press.

Platt, J. (1969) What we must do. *Science,* **166,** 1115–21.

Poincare, H. (1914) *Science and Method.* New York: Dover.

Polya, G. (1954) *Patterns of Plausible Inference.* Princeton: Princeton University Press.

Raphael, B. (1964) SIR: A computer program for semantic information retrieval. *Fall Joint. comput. Conf.* 25. Washington DC: Spartan.

Reichenbach, H. (1938) *Experience and Prediction.* Chicago: Chicago University Press.

Rosenblatt, F. (1962) *Principles of Neurodynamics.* Washington, DC: Spartan.

Roosen-Runge, P. (1967) An algebraic description of access and control in information processing systems. Dissertation, Dept communic. Sci, University of Michigan.

Russell, B. (1948) *Human Knowledge: Its Scope and Limits.* London: Allen & Unwin.

Samuel, A. (1959) Some studies in machine learning using the game of checkers. *IBM J. Res. & Dev.,* **3,** 211–29.

Segur, B. (1971) Clustering as a tool for reviewers, Ph.D. thesis, Dept communic. Sci., University of Michigan.

Shannon, C. E. & Weaver, W. (1949) *The Mathematical Theory of Communication.* University of Illinois Press.

Shannon, C.E. (1950) Programming a computer for playing chess. *Phil. Mag.,* **41,** 256–75.

Shapiro, M.D. (1969) *Bibliography Report S4D12.* Bell Labs, Holmdel, New Jersey.

Shklovskii, I.S. & Sagan, C. (1966) *Intelligent Life in the Universe.* San Francisco: Holden-Day.

Simmons, R.F., Burger, J.F., & Schwarcz, R.H. (1968) A computational model of verbal understanding. *SDC Reports* RC-1316 & SP 3132. Santa Monica: Systems Development Corporation.

Skinner, B.F. (1968) *The Technology of Teaching.* New York: Appleton-Century-Crofts.

Solomonoff, R. (1956) An inductive inference machine. *IRE. Conventional Record.*

Stodolsky, D. (1970) The computer as a psychotherapist amplifier, analogy, and adjunct. *Report,* Dept of comput. Sci., University of Wisconsin.

Tarski, A. (1936) Grundlegung der Wissenschaftlichen Semantik, *Actes du Congres Int'l de Philos. Sci.,* Paris.

Turing, A.M. (1936) On computable numbers, with application to the *Entscheidungs* Problem. *Proc. London math. Soc.,* 2–42, 230–65.

Turing, A.M. (1956) Can a machine think? *The World of Mathematics,* p. 2099 (ed. Newman, J.). New York: Simon and Schuster.

Uhr, L. & Vossler, C. (1963) A pattern-recognition program that generates, evaluates and adjusts its own operators. *Computers and Thought,* pp. 251–68 (eds. Feigenbaum, E. & Feldman, J.). New York: McGraw-Hill.

Uhr, L. & Kochen, M. (1969) MIKROKOSMS and Robots. *Proc. Spring Joint Computer Conf.* Washington, DC.

Uhr, L. (1964) Pattern-string learning programs, *Behav. Sci.*, **9**, 3.

von Neumann, J. (1956) Probabilistic logics and the synthesis of reliable organisms from unreliable components. *Automata Studies*, p. 43. Princeton: Princeton University Press.

von Neumann, J. (1958) *The Computer and the Brain.* New Haven: Yale University Press.

Wiener, N. (1948) *Cybernetics.* Cambridge, Mass.: MIT Press.

Winograd, S. & Cowan, J.D. (1963) *Reliable Computation in the Presence of Noise.* Cambridge, Mass.: MIT Press.

Computer Simulation of Verbal Learning and Concept Formation

L.V.GREGG

ABSTRACT

The lectures dealt with recent work in information processing psychology. Several verbal learning experiments and a new computer simulation model of concept identification were described. The experiments provided support for a model of serial integration derived from the two elementary learning processes of EPAM – one of the earliest computer simulation theories of verbal learning. The serial model provides an explanation of the ways in which retrieval cues serve to index familiar units, chunks, in the human memory system. In concept identification, it was argued that a relatively small number of simple perceptual acts, called abstractors, organized in a hierarchical executive program are sufficient to describe much of the problem-solving behavior exhibited by subjects in the CI task. Although this empirical work has the goal of understanding the human cognitive system, it is suggested that the development of machine intelligence systems might follow the design premise that aggregates of very simple processes are driven by highly localized information sources. Major unsolved problems exist, of course; perhaps the most important is the question of how the separate processes are functionally reorganized in new task environments.

EDITORS' NOTE

It is regretted that it is not possible to publish Professor Gregg's full paper.

List of Contributors

M. Clowes, Laboratory of Experimental Psychology, University of Sussex

E. W. Elcock, Computer Research Group, University of Aberdeen

N. V. Findler, Department of Computer Science, State University of New York at Buffalo

L. V. Gregg, Department of Psychology, Carnegie-Mellon University

M. Kochen, Mental Health Research Institute, University of Michigan

R. K. Lindsay, Mental Health Research Institute, University of Michigan

B. Meltzer, Metamathematics Unit, University of Edinburgh

D. Michie, Department of Machine Intelligence and Perception, University of Edinburgh

J. Palme, Research Institute of National Defense, Stockholm

J. Pitrat, Chargé de Recherches au CNRS, France

B. Raphael, Stanford Research Institute

J. A. Robinson, College of Liberal Arts, Syracuse University

E. Sandewall, Department of Computer Sciences, University of Uppsala

R. F. Simmons, College of Arts and Sciences. University of Texas at Austin

Index

Abelson, 272, 313
ABSET, 37, 49, 103
ABYS, 37–8, 40, 42, 44–9
adaptive control theory, 101, 261
Advice Taker, 265
ALGOL, 37, 247, 249–50
Allan, 59
Allen, 30
Amarel, 104, 123, 261, 265, 267, 313
AMNIP, 266
AMPPL-II, 51–2
anagram, 173
analogy, 22, 246
Anderson, 247, 251, 256
Andrews, 30
arrow method, 98
artificial intelligence, 19, 22, 52, 63,
    101–3, 117, 122, 159, 161, 199–201
    232, 263
Ash, 288, 312–13
Ashby, 261, 313
ASP, 291–2, 298
assertions, 37–40
associative memory, 51, 55
Austin, 266, 313
automata theory, 279

Bach, 212–13, 240
backtracking, 204–5, 207, 226
Baricelli, 266, 313
Batori, 231, 240
Bayes' rule, 247
Bellert, 234, 240
Bennet, 30–1
Berge, 215, 240
Bernard, 141
Bernstein, 51, 77
best bud method, 86–8, 93, 95
blockade, 140–1
Bloom, 257
Bobrow, 200, 240
bootstrap, 174
Boulding, 313

brain, 74, 262, 264, 304
Bratley, 207, 240
Bremermann, 266, 313
Breslaw, 240
Brillouin, 261, 270, 313
British Museum algorithm, 65
Brass, 240
Brown, 30, 312
Bruner, 266, 313
Bunge, 272, 313
Burger, 177, 189, 316
Bursky, 84, 99, 100
Bush, 266, 308, 313

Callaway, 118, 123
Carbonell, 197–8
Carnap, 313
Carroll, 272, 313
Carson, 30, 33, 100
causality, 57–9
Chang, 30
character recognition, 101
checkers, 132, 140, 262, 265
Chen, 59
chess, 70, 72, 125–6, 130–1, 135–6,
    139–41, 143–5, 147–50, 153, 155,
    161, 261, 265, 287
    fairy, 147–9, 155
Chomsky, 188, 213, 251, 253, 256
Church, 4, 12, 266, 313
Churchman, 270
Claparede, 313
Clowes, 245–57
cognitive map, 63–4, 76
Colby, 240, 272, 313
Coles, 169
compiler, 37, 45, 132, 197
complexity
    computational, 72
    of description, 248
computational linguistics, 101
computer-aided instruction, 191–3, 200
concept formation, 102, 266

context graph, 164–9
Cowan, 305, 317
critical path, 59, 102
Crocker, 81, 99
crossword puzzles, 63–6, 76
Culbertson, 313

Dale, 312
Darley, 257
Darlington, 25, 28, 30–1
data processing, 72
Davies, 105, 123
Davis, 8, 12, 30–1, 215–16, 241
decision, 69–72
  procedure, 28
  table, 117
DEDUCOM, 81, 98
deduction
  algorithm, 3–6, 11
  efficiency in, 11
  machine, 3, 12
  problem, 3–4, 7–8
DENDRAL, 272
Denham, 57
dependency analysis, 177
Descartes, 266, 313
Dewar, 207, 240
dictionary, 176–81, 188, 207–9, 231
Dijkstra, 105, 107–8, 123
d'Ogly, 141
Doran, 31, 81, 83, 86, 91, 98–9, 105,
  108–9, 112, 123

Earley, 207, 241
Eastlake, 81, 99
EDGE, 82
education, 305, 309, 311
efficiency of programs, 81
Elcock, 37–50, 103
ELIZA, 200, 212
Emerson, 312
Enea, 240
EPAM, 319
Ernst, 107, 123, 161, 169, 261, 315
Essinger, 257
evaluation function, 62, 86, 105, 108,
  111
  see also heuristic
Evans, 66, 76, 251–2, 257

Everett, 312

feedback, 261
Feigenbaum, 94, 99, 179, 189, 272, 315
fewest-component preference, 98
Fikes, 45–7, 50, 167, 169
Filmore, 195
Findler, 51–77
Floyd, 241, 313
f-matching, 26, 28
Fodor, 175, 189
FORM, 297
FORTRAN, 51, 52
Foster, 37, 50
frame problem, 159–61, 168–9
Fubini, 315

Galanter, 315
Galileo, 103
game playing, 71, 73–4, 81, 83, 105,
  108, 125, 132, 135, 139, 141, 145, 155
game theory, 72
Gelernter, 31, 265, 313
generate and test, 4–5
geometrical analogy problem, 246
Gilmore, 31
Glasersfeld, 209, 231, 241
goal predicate, 164–6
Gödel, 26, 30–1, 266, 314
Gold, 189
go-moku, 126, 139–42, 144, 146, 155
Goodman, 306, 314
Goodnow, 266, 313
Gould, 25, 30–1, 69
GPS, 81, 84, 87, 89, 91, 97–8, 105–7,
  161–2, 168
  planning, 99
grammar, 188, 193, 197, 202–3, 207,
  213–14, 249–52
graph, 26, 106, 108–9, 118, 120, 165–6,
  201, 214, 226
  coloured directed, 104, 109
  directed, 104–5, 107, 165, 194
  form, 105
  relational, 219
  searching procedures, 105
graph theory, 105, 215
Graph Traverser, 81, 87, 98, 108–11,
  113, 117–18

grasshopper, 148–9
Graves, 52
Gray, 49–50
Greanias, 247, 252, 257
Green, 31, 111–12, 123, 162–3, 166, 169, 314
Greenblatt, 81, 99
Greene, 314
Gregg, 319
Grimsdale, 246, 257
Griswold, 265, 279, 288, 314
Guard, 12, 28, 30
Guzman, 252, 254, 257

Hadamard, 266, 314
Hamburger, 312
Hantler, 312, 313
Harrah, 277, 314
Hart, P. E., 26, 30–1, 98–9, 105, 108–10, 123
Hart, T. P., 31, 257
Hartley, 257
Hartong, 143
hash coding, 216
Hayes, 30–1, 159, 161, 168–9
Hebb, 265, 314
Hecox, 312
Heilprin, 306, 314
Heironymous, 198
Henkin, 12
Herbrand, 12
Herbrand universe, 24
Hesselbart, 312
heuristic, 5, 15, 22, 26, 29, 62, 66, 70, 72, 82–5, 88–9, 91–9, 105, 154–5, 161, 168, 173, 175–6, 178, 180, 189, 212, 232–3, 261, 265
    see also evaluation, merit
heuristic automaton, 86, 91, 99
    see also organism
Hewitt, 91, 99
Highleyman, 247, 257
Hillier, 315
Hodes, 246, 257
Holloman, 315
Hooke, 111, 123
Hull, 314
hyperresolution, 19, 24

IBM-360/67, 311
Illich, 314
induction, 22, 191
inductive generalization, 115, 117
inductive inference, 261
information
    processing, 72, 270, 272, 277–8, 284–5, 308, 319
    retrieval, 66, 101, 179, 199, 215, 238
    theory, 270
interpretations, 3
IPL-V, 45, 51, 52
ITT, 192–3, 195, 197

Jeeves, 111, 123
jigsaw, 173–6, 180, 189
JIGSAW-1, 177–89

Kac, 288, 314
Kamentsky, 247, 257
Karttunen, 234, 241
Kasher, 66, 77
Katz, 175, 189, 230, 241
Kay, 228, 241
kernel, 193, 196, 215–16
Kessler, 75
Kilburn, 257
King, 117, 123
kinship relations, 52, 57
Kirsch, 249, 257
Kleene, 31
Klein, 69–70, 77
Knowlton, 188–9
Knuth, 314
Kochen, 66, 77, 261–317
Köhler, 266, 314
König, 5, 8, 13
Kowal, 69
Kowalski, 11, 13, 15, 18–19, 21, 23–4, 26–7, 29–31
Kuehner, 15
Kuhn, 305–6, 315
Küng, 256–7

labelled dependency, 177–8, 180–1, 186–7
labyrinthic method, 86, 88–9
lambda calculus, 12

language, 3–4, 12, 37, 51, 65–6, 125–6,
132, 161, 180, 207, 226–7, 248–9,
265, 279–80, 287, 307–8, 312
first order, 6–8, 12
natural, 51, 191–2, 197, 199, 201,
203, 212, 215, 217, 222, 230, 232,
235, 237, 256
Lasker, 153–5
latent contradictions, 9–11
learning, 22, 59, 62, 65–6, 71, 74, 111,
174, 188, 212, 261–2, 265, 269,
272, 274–5, 279–80, 285–9, 296,
303–5, 319
by rote, 102, 179
language, 173 ff
Lederberg, 272, 315
Ledley, 250, 257
Le Lionnais, 141, 143, 148, 155
lexicon, 193, 197
LIB FULL MEMOFNS, 114
Lin, 109, 123
Lindsay, 173–89
linguistic analysis, 175
linguistics, 180, 188, 261
Lippershey, 103
LISP, 51, 91, 196, 215
list, 39–41, 43, 45, 52–3, 55, 63, 65,
75, 81, 96–7, 114, 137, 178–81,
185, 209, 236, 248, 265–6
processing, 38, 51
structures, 210, 215, 248
Liu, 247, 251
logic, 164, 168, 191, 262, 270–1, 279,
284
first order, 25–6, 111
higher order, 25, 49, 168
modal, 168
Logic Theory Machine, 99
Loveland, 30–1
Luckham, 30, 32

macro-operators, 118
McCarthy, 159, 161, 168–9, 265,
315
McConlogue, 189
McCulloch, 315
McGregor, 50
MacKay, 277, 315
McKinzie, 51–2, 59, 63, 77

McMahon, 241
Maget, 141, 143, 148, 155
magic square, 41–2, 46
Marill, 246, 252, 257
Marschak, 282
Marsh, 109, 114–15, 123
Meagher, 251
Meltzer, 15–33, 224, 242
memo functions, 114, 116
Mendelson, 271, 273, 315
Menig, 69
merging, 19
merit function, 91, 93, 212
ordering, 89, 94, 96
see also heuristic
Meyer, 66
Michie, 31, 81, 98–9, 101–24, 211,
232, 242, 288, 315
Miller, 117, 315
Millstein, 99
Minsky, 120, 124, 246, 248, 257, 261,
265, 315
Moore, 105–8, 124, 315
Morgenstern, 105, 124
Morris, 32
Moses, 81–2, 99
Mowrer, 266, 315
MULTIPLE, 84, 87, 99
MULTI-POP, 114
multistore parser, 209, 231
Munson, 169
Murray, 50
Myhill, 266, 315

Narasimhan, 250–2, 257
Nerode, 32
Nevins, 45, 50
Newell, 70, 77, 81, 83, 89, 91, 98–9,
105–7, 123–4, 161, 169, 245,
256–7, 261, 265, 267, 315
Newman, 315
Newton, 103
Nilsson, 26, 30–2, 98–9, 101, 105,
108–12, 123–4, 169
Nimzovich, 140
noise, 66 ff
Norman, 257
Norton, 28, 30, 32
Notley, 118, 123

O'Connell, 288, 315
Oglesby, 30–1
operational research, 22
organism, 59–62, 262, 304
  see also heuristic automaton

P 1-deduction, 17, 23
Palme, 81, 199–244
parallel
  computation, 48–9
  processing, 51
  programs, 40
paramodulation, 28
Park, 257
parsing, 175 ff, 201–4, 207, 211–12,
  214, 232, 240, 249–50, 252
partial application, 39, 44, 113
Pasich, 198
path, 106, 134–5, 137
  shortest, 107
  solution, 109, 120
path-finding problem, 26, 103–4
pattern
  matching, 45, 49, 64–6, 164, 200–1
  recognition, 102
  search, 111
PDP-8, 303
perception, 265
Pfaltz, 51, 77
PFBT, 59
phrase structure analysis, 177
Piaget, 266, 316
picture, 173–5, 245–6, 250–1, 255
PIL, 311
Pisani, 209, 241, 245
Pitrat, 125–55
plan, 88, 90–1, 101–3, 111–13, 115,
  117, 119, 121–2, 159, 286
PLANNER, 91, 97, 99
planning, 62, 86, 97, 261, 278
  GPS, *see* GPS
Platt, 305, 316
Plotkin, 117, 124
Poage, 265, 279, 288, 314
Pohl, 26, 32, 105, 108, 110, 124
Poincaré, 266, 316
poker, 69–73
Polonsky, 265, 279, 288, 314
Polya, 266, 316

POP-2, 113–14, 117
Popplestone, 114, 124
Postal, 230, 241
PPS, 87, 91, 99
Prawitz, 13, 24, 30, 32
predicate calculus
  first order, 4, 8, 85, 161–2, 165, 168,
    215–16, 218–19, 221–2, 224, 226,
    266, 273, 279–80, 284
  higher order, 168
Pribram, 315
probability, 71–3, 212, 235
problem-solving, 37, 45, 48, 63, 65–6,
  83, 86, 101, 103–5, 159–61, 163–5,
  168, 174–5, 245, 261–2, 288
proof procedure, 15, 18–22, 24, 26–9
property list, 216
propositional calculus, 4
PSIII, 193
pun, 66
Putnam, 8, 12

question-answering, 191, 195, 201-2,
  213–14, 217, 231–2, 237–8, 245,
  309
Quillian, 176–7, 188–9, 217, 242

Rabin, 30
Raphael, 26, 30–2, 98–9, 101, 105,
  108–10, 112, 122–4, 159–69, 242,
  314, 316
REF, 45–7
refinements, 25
Reichenbach, 316
representation, 104–5, 119–20, 161,
  245–6, 256, 263, 266–8, 271,
  277–9, 284–5, 288, 305–6, 308,
  311–12
resolution, 10, 11, 16–20, 22–9, 60,
  84–5, 94–7, 111, 122, 166–8, 216,
  224, 266
  AM-clash, 19
  linear, 19
  M-clash, 24
Robinson, G. A., 28–30, 32–3, 100
Robinson, J. A., 3–13, 16, 18–19, 24,
  30, 32–3, 49–50, 102, 122, 168,
  216, 224, 242
robot, 103, 121, 122, 159–63, 165, 245, 256

Rochester, 313
Rogers, 198
Roosen-Runge, 265, 312, 316
Rosenbaum, 242
Rosenblatt, 316
Ross, 105, 109, 111, 122, 124
Russell, 316

Sagan, 261, 316
SAINT, 87, 91, 93–5, 99
Samuel, 81, 99, 108, 124, 261, 265, 316
Sandewall, 30, 33, 81–100, 168, 201,
    211, 218–19, 224, 232, 236, 242–3
Schwarz, 177, 189, 235, 243, 316
Scott, 103, 124
search, 4–6, 10, 18–19, 58, 64–5, 67,
    82–3, 88, 95, 104, 106–9, 114–15,
    117, 140, 169, 212, 216, 263,
    265–6
  breadthfirst, 105, 107, 211
  diagonal, 18, 29
  goal directed, 89
  heuristic, 81, 83, 86, 92, 94, 102,
    104–5, 109, 111–13, 115, 117, 211,
    232–3
  space, 4–5, 18–19, 25, 46
  strategy, 17–23, 29, 30
SEE, 252, 254
Segur, 307, 316
semantic
  categories, 230–1
  net, 192–7, 202, 214, 228
  tree, 29
semi-decision procedure, 4–5, 28
SEQANAL, 289, 291–2, 298
set-of-support, 17, 19–20, 25, 97–8
Settle, 30–1
Shalla, 33
Shannon, 270, 315–16
Shapiro, 288, 316
Shaw, 106, 124, 250, 252, 257, 265, 315
Shklovskii, 261, 316
Sibert, 33
Sibley, 288, 313
Siklossy, 191, 198
Simmons, 66, 77, 177, 189, 191–7, 243,
    316
Simon, 70, 77, 81, 89, 98–9, 105–6, 124,
    173, 189, 265, 315

simple type theory, 12
SIN, 81–2, 87, 99
SKETCHPAD, 246–7
Skinner, 188, 316
Slagle, 30, 33, 81, 84, 91, 94, 98–100
SLIP, 51–2
Smullyan, 13, 32
SNOBOL-4, 229, 265, 279–80, 286,
    288–9, 291–2, 299–303, 311
Snyder, 52
Solomonoff, 261, 316
SQAP, 201, 208, 218, 222–5, 235, 238–9
Stanton, 252, 256
Stefferud, 99–100
Stodolsky, 304–5, 316
Strachey, 105, 124
Sumner, 257
Sutherland, 246, 257

Tarski, 316
theorem proving, 16–17, 24, 26, 28–9,
    70, 102, 111, 122, 162–3, 165,
    167–8, 265
theory of computation, 103
thesaurus, 276
threat, 140–2, 144–5, 149–50, 152–5
Thompson, 175, 189
Thorne, 207, 240
tic-tac-toe, 140, 145–7
TLC, 217
transformation, 37
transformation problem, 83, 88–9
translation, 237
travelling salesman problem, 161
tree, 60, 83, 86–7, 89, 98, 108, 117, 118,
    140, 165, 177, 180–1, 185–6, 201–4,
    206, 211, 213, 214, 226–9, 249
  decision, 73
  family, 52
  finitary, 5
  game, 60
  proof, 20
  pruning, 144, 152, 154–5
  strategy, 118–20
  search, 81, 84, 86, 90, 93, 109–10,
    161
  solution, 82, 86, 89, 90
  syntax, 227, 233
truth table, 4, 16, 18

Tunis, 257
Turing, 199, 237, 261, 267, 270, 316
  test, 200

Uhr, 191, 198, 261, 289, 312–13,
  315–17
Ulam, 288, 314
unification, 8, 9, 308
  algorithm, 11, 24–5
unit preference, 18, 24, 85, 87, 94–9
Uttal, 191, 198

Vargas, 207, 243
Vauquois, 237, 243
von Neumann, 105, 124, 261, 264, 305, 317

Vossler, 316
voting plan problem, 42, 49

Waldinger, 169
Weaver, 270, 316
Weinberg, 308
Weizenbaum, 51, 77
Wells, 304, 308
Wiener, 261, 266, 317
Winograd, 305, 317
Wittgenstein, 256–7
Woods, 215, 226, 244
world brain, 304 ff
world predicate, 163, 169
Wos, 18, 19, 28–30, 33, 85, 99, 100